The Israel–Palestine Conflict

Contesting the Past

The volumes in this series select some of the most controversial episodes in history and consider their divergent, even starkly incompatible representations. The aim is not merely to demonstrate that history is 'argument without end', but to show that study even of contradictory conceptions can be fruitful: that the jettisoning of one thesis or presentation leaves behind something of value.

Published

Contesting the Crusades
Norman Housley

Contesting the German Empire 1871–1918
Matthew Jefferies

Vietnam: Explaining America's Lost War
Gary R. Hess

Contesting the French Revolution
Paul Hanson

The Israel–Palestine Conflict: Contested Histories
Neil Caplan

In preparation

European Renaissance
William Caferro

Witch Hunts in the Early Modern World
Alison Rowlands

Reformations
C. Scott Dixon

The Rise of Nazism
Chris Szejnmann

Origins of the Second World War
Peter Jackson

The Enlightenment
Thomas Munck

The Israel–Palestine Conflict

Contested Histories

Neil Caplan

⊛WILEY-BLACKWELL

A John Wiley & Sons, Ltd., Publication

This edition first published 2010

© 2010 Neil Caplan

Blackwell Publishing was acquired by John Wiley & Sons in February 2007. Blackwell's publishing program has been merged with Wiley's global Scientific, Technical, and Medical business to form Wiley-Blackwell.

Registered Office
John Wiley & Sons Ltd, The Atrium, Southern Gate, Chichester, West Sussex, PO19 8SQ, United Kingdom

Editorial Offices
350 Main Street, Malden, MA 02148-5020, USA
9600 Garsington Road, Oxford, OX4 2DQ, UK
The Atrium, Southern Gate, Chichester, West Sussex, PO19 8SQ, UK

For details of our global editorial offices, for customer services, and for information about how to apply for permission to reuse the copyright material in this book please see our website at www.wiley.com/wiley-blackwell.

The right of Neil Caplan to be identified as the author of this work has been asserted in accordance with the Copyright, Designs and Patents Act 1988.

Library of Congress Cataloging-in-Publication Data

Caplan, Neil, 1945–
The Israel–Palestine conflict: contested histories / Neil Caplan.
    p. cm.
    Includes bibliographical references and index.
    ISBN 978-1-4051-7539-5 (hardcover: alk. paper) – ISBN 978-1-4051-7538-8 (pbk.: alk. paper) 1. Jewish-Arab relations. 2. Arab-Israeli conflict. 3. Israel–Foreign relations–Arab States. 4. Arab States–Foreign relations–Israel. I. Title.
DS119.7.C3195 2009
956.04–dc22
                                            2008054920

A catalogue record for this book is available from the British Library.

Set in 10/12.5pt Photina by SPi Publisher Services, Pondicherry, India
Printed in Singapore by Ho Printing Singapore Pte Ltd

1 2010

Dedicated with deep sadness to the many victims of this protracted conflict – past, present, and future

Contents

List of Maps

Preface

The June 1967 war in the Middle East marked my first awakening, as a graduate student searching for an area of doctoral research, to the complexities of the Arab–Israeli conflict. My first impulse was a problem-solving one, flowing naturally from personal experience as my own country, Canada, was celebrating its centennial and engaging in lively public debates about how the English and French nations could continue living harmoniously under a single federal régime. A year of exploratory reading and study in London unexpectedly sparked a fascination with the historical origins and development of the conflict, and totally shifted my focus from the future to the past.

Since that time I have been researching, writing, and teaching almost exclusively about the history, diplomacy, and psychology of the Arab–Israeli conflict. Digging in archives for authentic primary sources and writing articles and monographs for a scholarly audience are the activities I have enjoyed best. This, I suppose, makes me a "positivist historian." But at the same time I have also developed a deep interest in and respect for the psycho-social dimensions of this conflict.

Very little about the dispute and the attitudes of the various parties is simple and straightforward, making it especially difficult to summarize events and issues succinctly while doing justice to the complexities involved. To create this volume of the *Contesting Histories* series I have combined lecture notes from introductory courses taught at various universities with some critical reflections about how the conflict is portrayed in academic and other writing. This book situates itself among several overview histories already available, but attempts to go beyond the mere retelling of what happened by focusing on a series of core arguments that seem to deadlock protagonists and historians alike.

One of the daunting challenges in producing this book has been to choose an appropriate level of detail in setting out the history of the conflict for undergraduates. Interested readers will, I hope, benefit from my extensive use of footnote references, pointing to additional details, nuances, and contrary interpretations that could be profitably consulted but which, if included, would make this text too dense.

Finally, there is the very tricky business of perceptions and bias. One of the hazards of writing on this subject is the near certainty that there will always be someone who will react to a word or phrase as being an oversimplification or misrepresentation of an event or a protagonist's motivation. I have done my best to listen to the voices in my head requiring me to revise frequently with sensitivity to subtleties of wording and tone. Readers, I hope, will appreciate the attempts made to allow for each of the contested versions of the history of this dispute to receive a fair hearing alongside its rivals.

I feel truly blessed with a number of colleagues and friends who have generously helped me by answering queries and by critiquing earlier draft proposals and chapters. They will most likely disagree with some aspects of my presentation of the history or the historians, so I will spare them the embarrassment of naming them here and will instead convey my thanks privately. Most generous of all, my wife Mara provided much-needed emotional support and sacrifices that allowed me optimal conditions for the long days of writing.

Montréal, Québec, Canada
December 2008

Note on Sources

This book appears at a time of greatly expanding use of web-based resources. I have included pertinent references to these sources, which include newspapers and journals (e.g., *The Guardian, Ha-Aretz, Bitterlemons, MERIA*) offering online access to articles. A proper study of this subject, however, still requires heavy reliance on printed materials (books, journals, pamphlets, magazines) available on library shelves and files accessible in public archives.

Wherever they can be found, I give preference to citing *primary* sources and first-person accounts, ahead of what historians classify as "secondary" sources. The former are the original, unvarnished building blocks needed to create any historical narrative: texts of public pronouncements, official or private correspondence, memoranda of conversations, minutes of meetings, personal diaries—generally, accounts of what happened from people who were actually present when it happened. Many primary sources are conveniently available to students in documentary volumes. In the pages that follow I make extensive use of two highly recommended collections: *The Israel–Arab Reader*, edited by Walter Laqueur and Barry Rubin, and *The Israeli–Palestinian Conflict*, edited by Yehuda Lukacs.[1]

Historians and other writers use primary sources to craft their own treatments of the events. In a sense, these writers are "processing" this "raw material" in order to create their own *secondary* works (articles, books) that reflect their particular selection and organization of the materials, and their own interpretations of the events and protagonists. (More on this in Chapter 11.)

As English-speakers we are foreigners vis-à-vis the main protagonists to this conflict; their main languages of communication and publication are

Arabic and Hebrew. Despite this linguistic barrier, we are nonetheless well supplied with a good sampling of works by Arabs and Israelis in English translation. Assuming that the bulk of my readers are not able to easily access materials in Arabic or Hebrew, I have cited primarily English-language sources. But, as my colleagues in the region rightly caution, on some issues—and especially the historians' debates (see Chapter 11)—we outsiders get to see only the tip of the iceberg via translations. We miss out on detailed discussions and the rich variety of ideas that continue to circulate in Arabic and Hebrew academic literature, memoirs, fiction, and films.

[1] *The Israel–Arab Reader: A Documentary History of the Middle East Conflict*, 7th rev. ed., eds. Walter Laqueur and Barry Rubin, New York: Penguin, 2008; *The Israeli–Palestinian Conflict: A Documentary Record, 1967–1990*, ed. Yehuda Lukacs, Cambridge: Cambridge University Press, 1992.

Part I
Introduction

1
Problems in Defining the Conflict

"Palestine, for its size, is probably the most investigated country in the world."[1]
"No conflict in the world is as well documented, mapped and recorded."[2]

If ever there was a contemporary conflict that deserved to be included in a series of historical works entitled "Contesting the Past," it is surely the Arab–Israeli or Israeli–Palestinian conflict. Although open to dispute, one scholar considers it "the single most bitterly contentious communal struggle on earth today."[3] Any attempt to simply recount its main events in chronological order is bound to be contested by someone—even if that account is deliberately neutral in intent, purged of any overt editorializing, and without passing judgment on motives, causes, or effects. Of course, such bare chronologizing is of very limited use to anyone, and the study of history is a much more complicated affair.

One telling indication of just how contested the study of this conflict can be is the vast disparity in the provenance and dates of those two quoted sentences. The first was written by Dr. Chaim Weizmann, president of the World Zionist Organization, in a letter to US president Harry S. Truman in December 1945, while the second one was penned in August 2007 by French intellectual and one-time associate of Cuban revolutionary Ernesto "Che" Guevara, Régis Debray. Juxtapositions and contrasts such as these occur frequently and provide ironic relief to those engaged in researching this enduring and perplexing dispute.

Not surprisingly, there exists a wide variety of ways of understanding and representing the Israeli–Arab or Palestinian–Israeli conflict. These efforts at explanation, whether in the realm of politics, lobbying, media, academe, or the general public, are often reflections of the highly contentious conflict itself, including its bitterness and complexity. A familiar pattern is the presentation of one side's "true" account as against the other party's "lies," "myths," or "propaganda." Less simplistic are the scholars, journalists, and analysts who acknowledge and discuss the parties' competing "narratives" of the conflict.

In Part II of this book we shall outline the history of almost 130 years of Israeli–Palestinian and Arab–Israeli conflict from its early local origins to one of regional and global dimensions. Along the way we shall highlight a number of *"core arguments"* that emerged and that contribute to the unhappy fact that the conflict is still today unresolved and is very resistant to a solution. My intentions are modest, yet challenging enough: to explore this conflict with all its paradoxes and complexities, if possible to demystify some of its features, and to offer some understanding about why the histories of Palestine and Israel are so contested.

What's in a Name?

A number of problems stem from the complexities that flow from the very act of naming the conflict and its main protagonists. In naming the conflict and defining what it is about, one is immediately, if unwillingly, taking a position that will surely be disputed by someone holding a different view. The conflict analyzed in these pages has been described variously as the "Jewish–Arab" conflict, the "Zionist–Arab" conflict, the "Arab–Israeli" conflict, and the "Israeli–Palestinian" conflict.

If we choose to call it the "Jewish–Arab" conflict, we are pitting the Jewish people as a whole against the Arab people as a whole. Is this an appropriate or accurate definition? As we will see below (Chapter 2), the designations of Jews and Arabs refer to wide groups extending beyond those directly contesting the land of Palestine/Israel. Although some writers do refer to the "Arab–Jewish conflict," in these pages we avoid this designation because it is inappropriately broad and may lend itself to confusion and misleading interpretations.

What we miss from such a wide definition are the specifically *political, national,* and *territorial* aspects of the conflict that exists today. By using the term "Zionist" rather than "Jewish," we supply these missing components for one of the protagonists. Zionists believe in and support the quest by Jews to "return to Zion" (i.e., Jerusalem and the Holy Land); in the modern period, this implied also support for the creation of a Jewish state in the area. Applying this definition, it would be accurate to say that, prior to the creation of the Israeli state in 1948, we were dealing largely with a *"Zionist*–Arab" and a *"Zionist*–Palestinian" conflict.

Who, then, are the Arabs? Not really a symmetrical designation to Jews, Arabs may be defined as an ethno-national group sharing a common history, the Arabic language, and cultural roots emanating from ancient tribes in the Arabian Peninsula. The "Arab–Israeli" conflict—perhaps the most commonly used of all these various titles—is in many ways an apt name for the territorial and political dispute since 1948 between the state of Israel, on the one hand, and the twenty or so states that consider themselves to be Arab, on the other.

Still, even this preferred designation carries with it a number of drawbacks. As we have noted, it may lead to the erroneous notion that the conflict began in 1948 with the creation of Israel, ignoring at least half a century of a pre-existing Zionist–Arab and Zionist–Palestinian dispute. Also misleading is the notion that the Arab world is a single entity that displays uniform attitudes and policies vis-à-vis Jews, Zionism, and/or Israel. In effect, historical experiences, policies, and attitudes vary among individual Arab peoples and states, with the result that it is misleading to suggest that the Arabs, as a single unit, constitute one of the two antagonists in the Arab–Israeli conflict.[4]

A further potential drawback of this definition of the conflict is that the broad term "Arab" can sometimes overlook or understate the existence of the specific struggle between Zionists (pre-1948) and Israelis (since 1948), on the one hand, and the Arabs of *Palestine* (or *Palestinians*), on the other. Thus, for example, while most discussions from 1948 to 1973 accurately speak of a wider *Arab–Israeli* conflict, in the period since 1973, and more so since 1993, many people came to see the conflict as being at its core a narrower Israeli–*Palestinian* conflict for sovereignty and self-determination on the same territory—albeit one with broader Arab dimensions.

In this book we retain the latter two ways of naming the conflict, using the common and convenient *Arab–Israeli conflict* to denote and include its wider regional dimensions, while referring to the *Palestinian–Israeli conflict* when focusing on its core and its two main protagonists. This way of defining the conflict and its protagonists, it should be pointed out, is hotly challenged by some, especially right-wing Israelis and Zionists.[5]

Loaded Terminology

As with discussions of other conflicts, terminology can deliberately or unintentionally favor one side over the other, and betray the biased perspective or partisan support of the writer or speaker. These dangers can be amply illustrated for the Arab–Israeli conflict with regard to general descriptors, the naming of the protagonists, the naming of events, and the labeling of maps.

As in all accounts of conflict and war, terminology is enlisted to help separate the heroes from the villains. The commitments and feelings of the writer or observer are reflected in the choice to be made between terms with pejorative connotations (e.g., "terrorist") and those that put the actor in a more favorable light (e.g., "freedom-fighter"). With both sides claiming virtue and nobility, observers end up taking sides by choosing when to speak of acts of "aggression" and when to refer to acts of "resistance" against that aggression.

In the naming of the main protagonists, there are, for some people, automatic connotations to be adopted, or avoided. The word "Zionist," for example, can be associated with the antisemitic pamphlet *The Protocols of the Learned Elders of Zion*, a forgery that purports to provide evidence that Jews are members of a treacherous cabal plotting to take over the world. In the eyes of Palestinian-Arabs who struggled against Zionism for control over Palestine/*Eretz-Israel* (Hebrew: "land of Israel"), the term "Zionists" will understandably be viewed negatively as signifying those who took over lands and the country they claim as theirs. Indeed, the mythological powers supposedly available to world Jewry have played their part in engendering fear, or respect, among those opposed to Zionism.

Some international campaigns on behalf of Palestinian rights have resulted in further vilification of the term "Zionist" by virtue of a resolution equating Zionism with racism adopted by the United Nations General Assembly in 1975 (and rescinded in 1991).[6] While not hiding from these pejorative connotations, our use of the word in these pages will more often reflect the usage of those who, historically, have self-identified as Zionists, i.e., adherents of ideological and political movements seeking to create a national home or state for the Jewish people in Palestine/*Eretz-Israel*.

Some readers who reject the legitimacy of the Jewish state may take offense from this book's references to "Israel" and "Israelis," preferring to designate the latter as "Zionist invaders" or "occupiers" and the former as "the Zionist entity" or "Occupied Palestine." Likewise, other readers may have difficulty with my frequent references to "the Palestinians," preferring instead to refer to these people as "Arabs," consistent with their belief that there is no such thing as a separate Palestinian people who are entitled to a separate Palestinian political state.

Similar concerns exist about the naming of events and episodes in the history of Arab–Zionist relations before 1948 and Israeli–Arab relations after that date. Outbreaks of violence that occurred during the Mandate period have been given different names, with sometimes strikingly different connotations. Calling them "disturbances" seems an exercise in understatement, while the terms "riots" or "rioting" suggest primitive and criminal behavior on the part of the population, usually referring to the Arabs but sometimes also the Jews. Some Palestinian and Arab nationalists prefer to designate these events as "protest demonstrations" (that turned violent), or acts of "resistance" against British occupation and Zionist colonization of their land.

Perhaps the most famous case of differences over the naming of events is the 1948 war (more accurately, the fighting from December 1947 through January 1949). For Israelis it is their "War of Liberation" or "War of Independence" (in Hebrew, *milhemet ha-atzma'ut*) full of the joys and overtones of deliverance and redemption. For Palestinians, it is *al-nakba*, translated as "The Catastrophe" and including in its scope the destruction of their society and the expulsion and flight of some 700,000 refugees.

Subsequent Arab–Israeli wars are also subject to disputes over naming. From an Israeli viewpoint, the 1956 war between Israel and Egypt is the "Sinai Campaign" or "Operation Kadesh," from the Israel Defense Forces' [IDF] battle plan. From an Egyptian and Arab perspective, however, it is known as the "Tripartite Aggression," highlighting the collusion between the invading Israeli army and the subsequent Anglo–French military operations in the Suez Canal Zone under the pretext of protecting the Canal from the two warring parties. More neutral ways of referring to this war would be to call it the "Suez War" or the "1956 war." For some, referring to the June 1967 as the "Six Day War" highlights and glorifies the swiftness and apparent ease of the Israeli victory, thereby perhaps offending the Arabs in their loss. Similarly, to use the name "Yom Kippur War" to refer to the October 1973 attack by Egypt and Syria against Israeli forces lined up along the Suez Canal and on the Golan Heights would be to present the war as seen from an Israeli perspective that underlines the ruthlessness of the enemy for choosing Judaism's holiest day for the surprise attack. Generally, the best way to approach neutrality in such naming is to refer to wars by their calendar dates.

Finally, another contested aspect of the Arab–Israel conflict is the geographic nomenclature on maps.[7] Maps in Arabic will normally designate the entire contested territory as *Filastin* (Palestine), without reference to a country named "Israel"—a political act of non-recognition. This, in contrast to most world and regional maps published in English and European languages between 1949 and 1967, which indicated no "Palestine" (which disappeared as a distinct entity following the 1947–1949 war) but rather the new state of "Israel" within its 1949 armistice boundaries (see below, Map 6.1, Map 6.2, Chapter 6).

Many maps in Hebrew since 1967 have shown Israel without clearly demarcating the Palestinian territories captured by Israel from Jordan (the West Bank), Egypt (the Gaza Strip) and Syria (the Golan Heights) in the June war of that year. Recently some Israeli maps have started reinstating the 1949 armistice borders, also known as "the Green Line." Maps published by the right-wing or settlers' movement in Israel will indicate the captured Palestinian territories known generally and almost universally as "the West Bank" (i.e., of the Jordan River) by their biblical Hebrew names, *Yehuda ve-Shomron* (Judaea and Samaria)—emphasizing their inclusion in the Biblically promised *Eretz-Israel* (Land of Israel) and the intention that they remain part of the modern Israeli state. These latter territories, along with the Gaza Strip, have been designated variously as "administered territories" or "disputed territories" (in mainstream official Israeli publications), "liberated territories" (in publications promoting a "Greater Land of Israel" beyond the 1949 frontiers), "occupied territories" (generally and internationally), or "occupied Palestinian territories."

Mere juxtaposition and labeling of maps can also be highly politicized (not to mention distorted and inaccurate), as a way of suggesting aggressive motives or registering a claim or grievance. Thus, for example, a recent volume of collected conference papers entitled *The Future of Palestine and Israel: From Colonial Roots to Postcolonial Realities* includes in its introduction a series of maps entitled "Palestinian loss of land, 1946–1999." Each of four maps indicates the changing shape and size of "Palestinian land" and "Jewish land," with the use of the word "Stage" registering an accusatory intent on Israel's part.[8] The equivalent maps for Zionists would ignore the Palestinians and record instead the cumulative gains and accomplishments of "Jewish land acquisition" or "Jewish land purchase," without mention of anyone's losses.

This contrast can be seen even more starkly if we compare the map of "Jewish settlements in Palestine 1855–1914" in Walter Laqueur's classic *A History of Zionism*[9] with the one entitled "The First Zionist colony in Palestine, 1878" in Walid Khalidi's *Before Their Diaspora*.[10] The former shows some fifteen black dots and triangles, but no Palestinian towns or villages—all the white space implying an empty land.[11] The latter shows all Palestinian towns, villages, and mixed towns—hundreds of red dots, six large black dots, and one barely visible, small, unnamed green dot indicating the new colony of Petah Tikvah.

Similarly, maps that show the changing shapes of Israel, Palestinian areas, and the neighboring states over time can be politicized or slanted in different ways. Zionist and Israeli complaints against the British for whittling down the area supposedly promised for a Jewish national home in 1917 can be vividly illustrated by three juxtaposed maps of pre-Mandate Palestine in

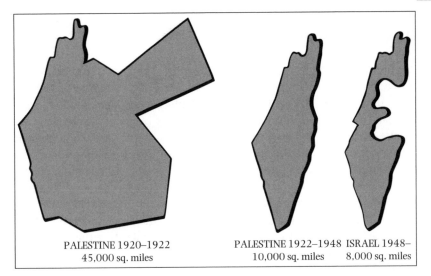

PALESTINE 1920–1922   PALESTINE 1922–1948 ISRAEL 1948–
45,000 sq. miles   10,000 sq. miles   8,000 sq. miles

Map 1.1   Palestine 1922, 1948, and Israel 1949
Source: Israel's Struggle for Peace, New York: Israel Office of Information, 1960, p. 8.

1920–1922, the official Mandated territory during 1922–1948 showing Transjordan removed, and Palestine/Israel 1948–1949 (armistice lines after the war).[12] Likewise, by framing Israel in the center of a map including all the Arab countries stretching from Morocco in the west to the Gulf States in the east and Sudan in the south, the Jewish state appears tiny and vulnerable.[13] Similarly, in Martin Gilbert's annotated historical maps, Israel's various wars from 1948 onwards are depicted in ways that clearly underscore the Jewish state's vulnerability as a country surrounded by hostile neighbors of overwhelming size, armed might, and/or aggressive intention.[14]

From the other side, however, changes over time can be portrayed to display Israel as the aggressor. For example, by placing three maps in sequence showing the growth of Israeli-assigned or -held territory from the 1947 UN partition proposal to the 1949 armistice lines to the 1967 conquered territories, readers are invited to conclude that Israel is an expansionist state.[15] Finally, those inclined to interpret the Bible as a roadmap for the present would cite references to God's promises to Moses and Joshua that the ancient Hebrews would receive the land stretching "from the wilderness and the Lebanon to the Great River [the Nile?], the River Euphrates—the whole Hittite country—and up to the Great [Mediterranean] Sea on the west." Arabs and Muslims would fear this as a master-plan for modern Israeli conquest of parts of Egypt, Syria, and Iraq, while Orthodox Jews would regard it as a deed of entitlement.[16]

Dates and Periodization

A more complex historiographical issue is one's choice of a starting date of the conflict, the selection of its major turning points, and its periodization. Some may wish to start with the Biblical antecedents of the conflict (Isaac and Ishmael, sons of Abraham, as progenitors of today's Israel and the Arabs)—reflecting a belief that we are dealing with a primordial and eternal clash, with supernatural overtones. In the pages that follow, we choose instead to begin our examination of the evolving dispute with the first modern Zionist immigrants to and settlements in Ottoman Palestine in 1882—reflecting the altogether different view that this dispute is a human product of historical and social forces that were unleashed in a particular place and at a particular time. This, indeed, is the timeframe adopted by most historians of the conflict, and Part II of this book will unfurl the events of the last 130 years of conflict.

It should be noted, however, that some critics have argued that this choice of periodization unduly sharpens our sense of the antagonism between the parties by ignoring centuries of earlier Jewish–Muslim and Arab–Jewish amity and collaboration, before the divisions and disputes brought about in the age of nationalism and colonialism.[17]

An Ongoing Conflict

Other problems arise because we are studying and attempting to understand a conflict that is ongoing, unresolved—one that is producing new victims and casualties daily, fueling and being fueled by feelings of bitterness, hatred, and revenge already many generations deep. Analyzing the historical roots and patterns of this conflict is therefore not merely of theoretical or academic interest. How we approach and analyze the past is often, consciously or unconsciously, driven by what continues to happen in Israel, Palestine, and the Middle East as the conflict either festers or rages. And how we portray the past can have implications for how we approach current questions brought up by the unresolved conflict. This case amply illustrates the dictum that "All history is contemporary history."

Tractable or Intractable?

One overriding question is: To what extent is the Arab–Israel conflict intractable—one that is inherently incapable of ever being solved?[18] Against the common wisdom that all conflicts are somehow and ultimately resolvable, some leading figures on both sides have in fact argued that they were indeed involved in an intractable conflict. While awaiting the final verdict of the 1919 Paris Peace Conference to be applied in the Middle East, David Ben-Gurion, then a labor-Zionist spokesman and future Israeli prime minister, exhorted his fellow delegates at a *yishuv* (Palestinian–Jewish community) council meeting to view the problem of their relations with the Arab population without illusions:

> Everybody [he said] sees a difficulty in the question of relations between Arabs and Jews. But not everybody sees that there is no solution to this question. No solution! There is a gulf, and nothing can fill that gulf. It is possible to resolve the conflict between Jewish and Arab interests [only] by sophistry. I do not know what Arab will agree that Palestine should belong to the Jews—even if the Jews learn Arabic [as was being recommended during those debates by an advocate of Jewish–Arab reconciliation]. And we must recognize this situation ... [and not] try to come up with "remedies" ... We, as a nation, want this country to be *ours*; the Arabs, as a nation, want this country to be *theirs*. The decision has been referred to the Peace Conference.[19]

A near mirror-image view was ventured in early 1932 by Awni Abd al-Hadi, a Palestinian lawyer, leader of the pan-Arab Istiqlal Party and former aide to Faysal Ibn Husayn (later King Faysal I of Iraq) at the Paris Peace Conference in 1919. In a private conversation with Dr. Haim Arlosoroff, head of the Jewish Agency's Political Department in Jerusalem, Awni responded negatively to feelers about the chances of an Arab–Zionist agreement, reportedly stating:

> Some time ago he had come to the definite conclusion that there was no point whatever in negotiations or attempts to reach a mutual understanding. The goal of the Jews was to rule the country, and the aim of the Arabs was to fight against this rule. He understood the Zionists quite well, and respected them, but their interests were fundamentally opposed to Arab interests, and he saw no possibility of an agreement.[20]

It is important to acknowledge and factor into our analysis such blunt and pessimistic views, especially when they are expressed by leading protagonists. One reason for doing so is to counteract the perils of wishful thinking about would-be solutions to this conflict. In our final chapter we will again grapple with the question of whether the conflict is indeed intractable.

Conflict Resolution, or Conflict Management?

The resistance of the Arab–Israeli conflict to over a century of attempts to resolve it seriously challenges the tenability and inherent optimism of the assumption that all conflicts can be resolved. As will be evident from our overview of the conflict in Part II, both Israelis and Palestinians have defined national goals and expressed beliefs which appear, even in their most minimal expression, mutually incompatible when set down side by side. To date, there have been only a few rare moments ("windows of opportunity") when all parties seemed simultaneously ready and able to concede some of what the other parties claimed they needed for the sake of agreeing to a compromise agreement. Both main parties seem, by and large, prepared to endure more bloodshed and future wars until ultimate victory—on their terms—is one day theirs.

This forces us to consider the possibility that this conflict may not be *resolved* in the commonly accepted format of an agreed international treaty, or on the pattern of a compromise formula settling, once and for all, all outstanding claims and grievances. Rather, we may have here a conflict that can only be *managed* or *contained*, at best, in the form of an unresolved low-level, or low-intensity, dispute. This notion draws directly on an elementary international relations distinction between conflict resolution and conflict management.

In the treatment that follows, readers will be asked to accept an uneasy tension or oscillation between two incompatible assumptions: (a) that the conflict can one day be *resolved* and (b) that it can be (at best) only *managed*—i.e., kept from exploding into its most violent and destructive expressions. While not clear-cut, or intellectually or emotionally satisfying, living with such an uncomfortable inconsistency is, in my view, both a reflection of reality and a necessary component to our efforts to understand the history and future of this conflict.

The "Other" Arab–Israeli Conflict

Another problem in defining this conflict is the complication caused by additional layers that are often superimposed upon the local Arab–Israeli conflict in Israel, Palestine, and the neighboring lands. Because each party has also been waging a long-term battle with a view to winning sympathizers outside the conflict and beyond the region, their quarrel has taken on its own special features in a number of spheres: international lobbying, the media, and academia—and here I borrow what one American political scientist has aptly termed, in the specific context of lobbying US presidents and congressmen, the "other" Arab–Israeli conflict.[21]

Another parallel arena in which the Arab–Israeli conflict continues to be played out is the courtroom—both metaphorical and actual. As we shall see when we examine several of the core arguments, international law and human-rights experts have engaged in "prosecuting" and "defending" one party or the other, whether in publications, lecture halls, media appearances, films, or actual courts of law. The latter activity has spawned a novel form of conflict known as "lawfare"—the using of law in battle as a substitute for other means to achieve political or other, not purely legal, objectives.[22]

By viewing the conflict through any of these external, superimposed prisms we risk developing deformed or distorted perceptions, rather than an accurate reflection, of the real conflict on the ground.

Advocacy and Censure

A final, related consideration that complicates our attempts to define the still unresolved Arab–Israeli conflict is the widespread tendency by authors and observers to allocate blame or engage in advocacy. In the course of discussing how the conflict started and why it continues, it is difficult to avoid censuring the parties one holds responsible for past errors that created or aggravated the conflict, and criticizing those parties who, by their behavior and/or policies, appear to be blocking the way to a resolution or peaceful coexistence.

It is almost impossible for analysts to focus on this conflict's events or issues in a totally neutral way, uninfluenced by their sense of justice and/ or quest for the truth. Both Palestinians and Israelis often frame their claims and grievances in terms of their concepts of justice and/or truth— and the other party's corresponding disrespect thereof. In the pages that follow, I will try to reflect the parties' own views without embracing any party's cause, and without singling out any party for special blame. I will return to the issue of advocacy again briefly at the end of Chapter 2, and more fully in Chapters 11 and 12, when we look at academics and their ways of presenting the conflict.

So, in conclusion, this book joins others that have come before in wrestling with a deceptively simple question: *What is the Arab–Israeli conflict really about?* Partly because of its longevity and complexity, the elements of this dispute "are neither easily definable nor are they static"— as Haim Shaked noted when attempting to outline the main characteristics of the conflict as he saw them in 1984.[23] Partisans of one side or the other will already have their diametrically opposing answers to this basic question. But how can a non-partisan student or observer navigate between what one party calls truth and the other side's propaganda, between the claims and counterclaims of the competing parties, between the contested narratives of Israeli Jews and Palestinian Arabs?

Such are the challenges and the difficulties. In Chapter 2 I attempt to sketch out some useful ways of defining the conflict and beginning to understand its special qualities.

Notes

1 Chaim Weizmann to Harry S. Truman, 12 December 1945, *Letters and Papers of Chaim Weizmann*, Vol. 22, ed. Joseph Heller, New Brunswick, NJ: Rutgers University / Transaction Books, 1979, p. 78.

2 Régis Debray, "Palestine: A Policy of Deliberate Blindness," *Le Monde diplomatique* (Eng. ed.), August 2007, p. 5.

3 Geoffrey Wheatcroft, "Zion Story," *The Times Literary Supplement*, 20 February 2008, accessed 15 March 2008 online at http://entertainment.timesonline.co.uk/tol/arts_and_entertainment/the_tls/article3403151.ece.

4 For a convincing treatment of this subject, see Mark Tessler, "Narratives and Myths about Arab Intransigence toward Israel," in *Israeli and Palestinian Narratives of Conflict: History's Double Helix*, ed. Robert I. Rotberg, Bloomington / Indianapolis: Indiana University Press, 2006, 174–93.

5 See, e.g., Yitzhak Shamir, "Israel's Role in a Changing Middle East," *Foreign Affairs* 60:4 (Spring 1982), 790–3; Benjamin Netanyahu, *A Durable Peace: Israel and Its Place among the Nations*, rev. ed., New York: Warner Books, 2000, ch. 3: "The Theory of Palestinian Centrality."

6 UNGA Resolution 3379, adopted 10 November 1975 by a vote of 72 to 35 (with 32 abstentions); UNGA Resolution 4686, adopted 16 December 1991, by a vote of 111 to 25 (with 13 abstentions).

7 For some firsthand discussion, see Meron Benvenisti, *Conflicts and Contradictions*, New York: Villard Books, 1986, 191–202, and *Sacred Landscape: The Buried History of the Holy Land since 1948*, transl. Maxine Kaufman-Lacusta, Berkeley / London: University of California Press, 2000.

8 Aslam Farouk-Alli, "The Poetics of Justice and the Politics of Oppression," *The Future of Palestine and Israel: From Colonial Roots to Postcolonial Realities*, ed. Aslam Farouk-Alli, Midrand, South Africa: Institute for Global Dialogue, 2007, 5, 7.

9 Walter Z. Laqueur, *A History of Zionism*, New York: Holt, Rinehart and Winston, 1972; reissued New York: Schocken Books, 1989, 41. See a similar map in Howard M. Sachar, *A History of Israel: From the Rise of Zionism to Our Time*, New York: Alfred A. Knopf, 1976, 87, available online at http://www.passia.org/palestine_facts/MAPS/Jewish_Yishuv_settlement_1881_1914.htm.

10 Walid Khalidi, *Before Their Diaspora: A Photographic History of the Palestinians, 1876–1948*, Washington, DC: Institute for Palestine Studies, 1984, 34. The latter map may be viewed online at http://www.passia.org/palestine_facts/MAPS/first_zionist_colony.htm.

11 For an extended application of this "phenomenon of the 'white patches' on the mental maps carried around in the heads of the Jews and Arabs of Palestine/*Eretz Israel*, which cover the habitat of 'the other'" (quotation from p. 1), see Benvenisti, *Sacred Landscape*.

12 See, e.g., Michael Curtis, Joseph Neyer, Chaim I. Waxman, and Allen Pollack, eds., *The Palestinians: People, History, Politics*, New Brunswick, NJ: Transaction Books [prepared under the auspices of the American Academic Association for Peace in the Middle East], 1975, 252–3.

13 See, e.g., Curtis et al., *The Palestinians*, 251; Martin Gilbert, *The Routledge Atlas of the Arab–Israeli Conflict*, 7th ed., London / New York: Routledge, 2002, 34, 60–1.

14 Gilbert, *Routledge Atlas*, 37 (Immediate response to the UN Partition plan), 38–9 (Arab attacks and the Jewish reaction), 40–2, 44 (Israel: prelude to independence), 43–4 (Battle for the Jerusalem roads), 52 (Israel's sense of insecurity, 1949–1967), 53 (Central Israel and the Jordan border, 1949–1967), 58 (Terrorist raids into Israel, 1951–1956), 60–1 (Changing balance of power in the Arab world, 1953–1973). Perhaps the most famous and most often reproduced is the map on p. 45, entitled "The Arab Invasion of the State of Israel, 15 May 1948."

15 "From the Nile to the Euphrates," *The Facts about the Palestine Problem*, Beirut: Arab Women's Information Committee, May 1968.

16 Joshua 1:3–4 (v. 3 begins: "Every spot on which your foot treads I give to you, as I promised Moses"). Translation as given in *Tanakh: A New Translation of the Holy Scriptures according to the Traditional Hebrew Text*, Philadelphia, PA: Jewish Publication Society, 1985, 337. See also Numbers 34:1–12 (ibid., 267–8).

17 E.g., Ruth Kark, in *Shared Histories*, 13–22; Edward (Edy) Kaufman and Manuel Hassassian, "Understanding Our Israeli/Palestinian Conflict and Searching for its Resolution," in *Regional and Ethnic Conflicts: Perspectives from the Front Lines*, eds. Judy Carter, George E. Irani, and Vamik D. Volkan, Upper Saddle River, NJ: Prentice Hall, 2008, 87–129. On the "golden age" of harmonious relations between Jews and Arabs (or between Jews and Muslims), see S. D. Goitein, *Jews and Arabs: Their Contacts through the Ages*, 3rd ed., New York: Schocken, 1974; Raphael Patai, *The Seed of Abraham: Jews and Arabs in Contact and Conflict*, Salt Lake City: University of Utah Press, 1986.

18 Chester A. Crocker, Fen Osler Hampson, and Pamela Aall, *Grasping the Nettle: Analyzing Cases of Intractable Conflict*, Washington, DC: United States Institute of Peace Press, 2005, 343–72 (essays by Stephen Cohen and Shibley Telhami).

19 Speech to the Vaad Zmani [Provisional Council of the Jews of Palestine/*Eretz-Israel*], 10 June 1919, Central Zionist Archives, Jerusalem [CZA], J1/8777,

my translation from the Hebrew. Cf. N. Caplan, *Futile Diplomacy*, vol. I: *Early Arab–Zionist Negotiation Attempts, 1913–1931*, London: Frank Cass, 1983, 7.

20 Moshe Shertok (later Sharett), Report of talk between Haim Arlosoroff and Awni Abd al-Hadi, 12 February 1932, CZA, S25/3051, my translation from the Hebrew. Caplan, *Futile Diplomacy* I: 7–8.

21 Steven L. Spiegel, *The Other Arab–Israeli Conflict: Making America's Middle East Policy from Truman to Reagan*, Chicago: University of Chicago Press, 1985.

22 See, e.g., Anne Herzberg, NGO *"Lawfare": Exploitation of Courts in the Arab–Israeli Conflict* (NGO Monitor, September 2008), available at http://www.ngo-monitor.org/article.php?id=2097. I am grateful to Professor Rina (Bryna) Bogoch of Bar-Ilan University for drawing this to my attention.

23 Haim Shaked, "Continuity and Change: An Overview," in *The Arab–Israeli Conflict: Perspectives*, 2nd ed., ed. Alvin Z. Rubinstein, New York: HarperCollins, 1991, 197. The first edition was published by Praeger in 1984.

2

Defining the Conflict, Nevertheless

Who Are the Conflicting Parties?

One way of framing the Israeli–Palestinian conflict is to pose two parallel, and heavily loaded, questions about the protagonists: Are the Jews a people (nation), entitled to lay claim to a national-state on the territory they call *Eretz-Israel* (the Land of Israel)—or a non-political, world religious community with no special territorial rights, claims, or aspirations? Are the Palestinians a people with distinct national and political rights and aspirations, or Arabs with no legitimate claim to separate nationhood or statehood specifically in Palestine?

Let us begin this chapter by going a bit further in attempting to define the terms Jew, Zionist, Israeli, Arab, Palestinian, and Muslim, and place them in context. While it is common practice to allow every group to define itself, others—both from within and outside the defined group—are free to, and will, disagree. In the contemporary Arab–Israel and Israeli–Palestinian disputes, each party does indeed find reasons to challenge the other's self-definition, providing an important dimension to the contested nature of their conflict.

Jews may be defined as a people comprising many ethnic, cultural, and linguistic groups, but deriving a common identity from

(a) a belief in Judaism, a monotheistic faith harking back to the Biblical land of Israel (which is generally accepted as corresponding geographically to today's state of Israel and the territories under the Palestinian Authority),

(b) biological lineage, i.e., being born to a Jewish mother, and/or

(c) a unifying sociocultural sentiment of sharing a common ancestry, traditions, customs, heritage, and future.

Given these complexities, it is no wonder that no one, not even the Israeli Knesset (Parliament), has ever been able to establish a universally accepted simple definition of who is a Jew. In 2008, there were an estimated 13.2 million Jews in the world, of whom 5.4 million lived in Israel, 5.3 million in the USA, and between 1 and 1.5 million in Europe.[1]

Beginning in the late 19th century, a growing number of Jews have chosen to define themselves as a people whose identity included *national-political* and *territorial* components, in addition to traditional and personal spiritual connections and a sense of belonging to a worldwide religious community. These Jews became adherents to, or supporters of, a movement known as Zionism. There are, of course, non-Zionist and anti-Zionist Jews who reject this collective definition and who see themselves uniquely as belonging to a religious group. But the numbers of non- and anti-Zionist Jews have declined, particularly since the rise of Adolf Hitler in the 1930s.

Muslims, Arabs, and Palestinians may well look back at centuries of harmonious interaction with Jews in their midst, and insist that these Jews have always been (and should still be seen as) mainly a religious community, i.e., without political claims or aspirations. Article 20 of the National Charter of the Palestine Liberation Organization solemnly declares that

> Claims of historical or religious ties of Jews with Palestine are incompatible with the facts of history and the true conception of what constitutes statehood. Judaism, being a religion, is not an independent nationality. Nor do Jews constitute a single nation with an identity of its own; they are citizens of the states to which they belong.[2]

But such declarations or externally imposed definitions cannot dispose of the fact—objectionable or inconvenient as it may be—that many Jews, both inside and outside of the present-day state of Israel, do indeed see themselves as part of a nation or people whose heart (if not body) is, territorially speaking, in *Eretz-Israel*, the land of Israel.

As mentioned earlier, we use the term **Zionists** to denote people (mainly, but not exclusively, Jews) who believe in and support the quest by Jews to "return to Zion" from the lands to which they were last dispersed by the Roman conquerors of Palestine. This aspiration, dormant for centuries but kept alive through religious ritual, began to find overt political expression in the mid- and late 19th century. For the next half-century, a unified Zionist movement used the organizational apparatus of the World Zionist Organization (and its offshoot, the Jewish Agency for

Palestine) to promote "the ingathering of the Exiles," i.e., the migration of Jews to Palestine/*Eretz-Israel*. This migration was part of a larger effort to establish the infrastructure of a future "national home" on that territory, which passed from Ottoman to British rule in 1917, and which was to be partitioned in accordance with a United Nations [UN] resolution in 1947. When the British left Palestine in mid-May 1948, a war erupted; at the end of the fighting, the state of Israel, the chief fulfillment of Zionism, was born and accepted as a member-state of the UN in May 1949. Citizens of this new state are called **Israelis**—not to be confused with "Israelites" or the "children of Israel" mentioned in the Bible. By late 2007 there were just over 7.2 million Israelis, 5.47 million of whom were Jews and 1.45 million Palestinian or Arab citizens of the state of Israel.

Who, then, are **Arabs**? As mentioned in Chapter 1, the Arabs may be defined as an ethno-national group with common cultural and linguistic roots emanating from ancient tribes in the Arabian Peninsula (today's Saudi Arabia, Yemen, Gulf states). There are today some 295 million Arabs living in 21 countries of the Middle East and North Africa. Of these, four—Lebanon, Syria, Jordan, and Egypt—share borders with the state of Israel and are sometimes consequently labeled the "confrontation states" in this conflict.

Apart from these independent Arab countries, there is also a **Palestinian-Arab** people not (yet) controlling an internationally recognized state—although Palestine is an accredited member of the League of Arab States. In 2006–2007 there were some 8 million Palestinians spread out in the region:

(a)   1.4 million in Gaza (of whom 1 million are registered refugees),
(b)   2.5 million in the West Bank (of whom 760,000 are registered refugees)

Together, these constitute the population of the "Palestinian National Authority," or "Palestinian Authority" [PA], in a still uncompleted transition from Israeli occupation to recognized status as an independent state. Further, there are

(c)   2.83 million refugees in 31 camps in Lebanon (422,000), Syria (461,000), Jordan (1.9 million), and also dispersed throughout the cities of the Middle East,
(d)   1.45 million citizens of the state of Israel, descendants of those Palestinians who resided in the areas that became the Jewish state in 1948.[3]

As in the case of Arab objections to Jewish national redefinition, no amount of argumentation coming from people outside the Palestinian and Arab world can alter the fact—objectionable or inconvenient as it may be to them—that, since the waning of the Ottoman Empire in the early 20th century, an increasing number of Arabic-speaking residents of the Middle East have devoted their political activity towards the eventual creation of an independent Arab state or confederation of states in the region. The fact that this vision of Arab unity has not materialized during a century of periodic attempts has been a source of great frustration to those who espoused this pan-Arab national dream.

The same applies to those who define themselves as Palestinians. As we shall see below, those Arabs living in the area designated as British Mandatory Palestine identified, at an early stage, with local leaders and formed their own nationalist organizations whose immediate aim was to resist Zionism and create an independent Arab state there. The majority of the Palestinian inhabitants of this area saw themselves as an endangered community whose rights and status were being threatened by an influx of Jewish immigrants whose numbers and growing economic infrastructure, they believed, would result in their country coming under Jewish or Zionist rule. No amount of doubt raised as to the genuineness of the Palestinians' expressed fears, or about their self-identification as a people wishing to have nothing to do with Britain's "Jewish national home" policies (see Chapter 4), can dispose of these facts.

Finally, it is important to appreciate that there are, for many people, religious dimensions to being Arab or Jewish. Since the advent of the Prophet Muhammad and the rise of the faith community (*umma*) of Islam in the 7th century CE and its subsequent spread around the globe, a majority of the world's Arabs are also practicing **Muslims**. Longstanding Christian communities exist in Lebanon, Egypt, Syria, Iraq, and Jordan, but Islamic history, culture, values, and identity have become an integral part of being Arab and living in those societies. The number of Muslims worldwide extends far beyond the Arab world and exceeds 1.2 billion.

The fact that the protagonists in this conflict also happen to be Muslims, Christians, or Jews adds a further complication to sorting out and defining the parties to the conflict. Although varying proportions of each community have become secularized, there are still significant numbers who identify strongly with their religious faith and community. In the minds of these people, what we are treating as the Arab–Israeli or Israeli–Palestinian conflict is a subset of a larger clash between religious groups and civilizations. Fundamentalist Christians, Muslims, and Jews alike tend to view the national or territorial struggle for sovereignty or supremacy over the *Holy* Land as part of a deeper and wider war between God's "chosen" people (however defined), the faithful, the believers, on the one hand, and God's "despised" people (however defined), the faithless, the unbelievers, on the other.

This religious dimension of the contest over Palestine/Israel emerges periodically when violence is perpetrated in the name of protection against perceived threats to the Holy Places, as happened in 1928–1929 (see Chapter 4). Competing mythical and religious associations with the holy city of Jerusalem also came into play as recently as 2000 to torpedo Israeli–Palestinian negotiations and helping to trigger the violent outbreak known as the "al-Aqsa *intifada*," taking its name from the holy al-Aqsa mosque. This dimension can ignite passions at any time, and most parties are aware of the dangers of exciting deeply held religious sensitivities.

But even if we do not accept this apocalyptic view of the conflict, there are other important implications of the injection of religion into what in these pages we treat essentially as a clash between two rival national movements and communities. The presence of this religious dimension aggravates and embitters an already difficult dispute by adding a layer of righteousness, accompanied by the further certainty of ultimate triumph over one's enemies. In everyday human terms, such otherworldly overtones only prolong the conflict and make it more intractable by further dehumanizing and delegitimizing the enemy, by offering hope to those who steadfastly refuse to consider any compromise with the other side, and by promising rewards to those who would commit acts of violence or revenge in response to perceived divine injunctions. Indeed, as we have seen in recent years, the fusion of nationalism and religion has produced a steady stream of idealists ready to do harm to the enemy (including those who would martyr themselves) at the behest of zealot preachers and in defiance of the many non-violent messages contained in the mainstream understanding of their faiths.[4]

What Are the Main Issues in Contention among the Parties to the Conflict?

A useful distinction can be made between tangible and intangible issues in dispute. Under the former, we include concrete, definable assets over which the parties are fighting. The intangibles are, by contrast, those psychological and existential issues that are reflected in the often contradictory historical narratives of each party.

The list of tangible issues in contention between Arabs/Palestinians and Zionists/Israelis will be brought up in historical context in Part II of this volume. For purposes of our introduction, let us summarize them under three headings: (1) Sovereignty over the land, (2) Demography, land purchase, and migration, and (3) Borders.

1   Sovereignty over the land

Both parties claim original ownership of and entitlement to inhabit and exercise sovereignty (national self-determination) over the same piece of land. The actual boundaries of the territory in dispute (see also point 3 below) are somewhat fuzzy. Several Israelite kingdoms existed in the 10th and 8th centuries BCE, but the area was for centuries under the rule of various empires.[5] There was no distinct political entity called "Palestine" between ancient times and the early 20th century. "Even as an administrative unit, it did not exist before the British arrived at the end of the First World War."[6] *Faute de mieux*, the Palestine Liberation Organization officially defines Palestine as the territory within the boundaries established under the British Mandate, from 1922.[7] Religious Zionists define the boundaries of *"Eretz-Israel"* in accordance with biblical references (above Chapter 1), while the Zionist Organization in 1919 submitted a map proposing a Jewish national home within a Palestine whose boundaries went farther north and east beyond the frontiers that the British ultimately set for the Jewish national home project.[8] Despite these ambiguities, after 1920 both Palestinian Arabs and Zionists would be aspiring to sovereignty over essentially the same territory west of the Jordan River that was to be governed under British Mandate until 1948.

Aside from ambiguities over precise boundaries, one of the most sharply contested arguments between the parties is "Whose (Promised) Land Is it?"—an argument that necessarily takes us back into ancient history. This I will propose in Chapter 3 as the first of a series of eleven *core arguments* that cumulatively shape the contested histories of Arabs, Palestinians, Jews, and Israelis. Related to this is the question "Whose Land Is It (Actually)?" Based on continuous residence and majority status dating back to ancient times, the indigenous population of Palestine was Muslim and Christian in large majority when the first waves of Zionist pioneers and settlers arrived in the 1880s. At the time, the contested territory appeared on maps as districts belonging to the Ottoman Empire.[9] Such was still the case in 1917 when the British arrived and simultaneously issued the Balfour Declaration which promised support for the creation of a "Jewish national home in Palestine." This innovation would have necessarily resulted in the granting of special privileges to a minority of the country's inhabitants, making the Declaration historic in several ways and sowing the seeds of future conflict (see Chapter 4).

When the British announced their intention of abandoning the Mandate thirty years later, the new United Nations Organization adopted the report of a Special Committee on Palestine [UNSCOP] to partition the country into an Arab and a Jewish state, with an international enclave

Map 2.1 Palestine under British Mandate, 1923

Mediterranean
Sea

SYRIA
(French Mandate)

● Beirut

● Damascus

Tyre ●

● Haifa

Jordan R.

Tel Aviv ●
Jaffa ●

● Amman

Gaza ●

Jerusalem ●

*Dead
Sea*

Rafah ●

● Beersheba

ARABIA

EGYPT

Aqaba ●

Red Sea

0   50   100
miles

Area incorporated by Great Britain in Palestine mandate
as the autonomous Amirate of Transjordan.

to include Jerusalem. Palestinian Arabs and the leaders of the Arab states rejected this plan not only because they were unhappy with the proposed boundaries of the projected Arab state, but also because they did not recognize the legitimacy of the UN to render a decision that went against the wishes of the majority of the country's inhabitants. In the fighting and warfare than ensued in 1947–1949, the independent state of Israel was created while other parts of former Mandatory Palestine were annexed to Transjordan (the West Bank) and administered by Egypt (the Gaza Strip).

In terms of two peoples claiming the right to national self-determination on the same territory, we see that, by 1949, one of these peoples (thereafter called "Israelis") had successfully established its national state. What remains in contention today is whether the other people, the Palestinians, will achieve sovereignty over designated parts (or all) of the territories they claim as their rightful homeland.

2 Demography, land purchase, and migration[10]

Demography, land purchase, and migration are inexorably linked here. Territorial sovereignty and the creation of boundaries between modern nation-states are built on the principle of respecting the majority will of national, ethnic, linguistic, and/or religious communities that inhabit a given swath of territory. In the case of the Ottoman districts that later became Palestine under the British Mandate, the territory contained a preponderant majority of Muslim Arabs for most of recent history, until 1948. (See Table 2.2 below.)

Jewish immigration, land purchase, and the creation of settlements were the essence of "practical Zionism" that sought to establish facts on the ground, a critical mass of Jewish people working the land—conditions for an eventual Jewish state in the areas defined by Jewish population density or presence. In theory, the creation of a Jewish majority through gradual but sustained immigration—known in Hebrew as *aliya*, with overtones from the verb "to rise" or "ascend"—and the purchase of lands would have resulted in the creation of radically new demographic, social, economic, and territorial facts on the ground, conditions for ultimately achieving Jewish statehood.

At first, very few Zionist or British observers foresaw insurmountable difficulties emanating from the objections of Palestinian Arabs who would, according to this plan, be made to pass from majority to minority status as the country moved towards acquiring a Jewish demographic majority.[11] As Dr. Chaim Weizmann informed the American Secretary of State at the Versailles Peace Conference in February 1919, Zionists sought the creation of an administration in Palestine "which would arise out of the

Table 2.1 *Jewish immigration to Palestine: selected years as recorded by the British Mandatory administration*

Year	Immigration	Emigration	Net migration
1922	7844	1503	6341
1924	12,856	2073	10,783
1925	33,801	2151	29,650
1927	2713	5071	−3358
1928	2178	2168	10
1929	5249	1746	3503
1932	9553	n.a.	
1933	30,327	n.a.	
1934	42,757	n.a.	
1935	61,854	396	61,458
1936	29,727	773	28,954
1937	10,536	889	9647
1939	16,405	1019	15,386
1940	4547	n.a.	
1943	8507	n.a.	
1944	14,464	n.a.	
1945	12,751	n.a.	
1946	7851*	n.a.	
1947	n.a.*	n.a.	

Source: Palestine Blue Book (London: HMSO, annual); *Survey of Palestine*, I: 185, III: 17. The above figures are for recorded *legal* immigration. British estimates of *illegal* Jewish immigration are 30,000 to 40,000 prior to April 1939 and an additional 30,000 to 35,000 between April 1939 and December 1946. *Survey of Palestine*, III: 23.
* According to various Israeli sources, the figure for 1946 should be 17,760 or 18,760, and that for 1947 21,542 or 22,098.

natural conditions of the country—always safeguarding the interests of non-Jews of the country—with the hope that by Jewish immigration Palestine would ultimately become as Jewish as England is English."[12]

The flow of Jewish immigration into Palestine was light in some years, heavier in others (see Table 2.1).

Especially after a dramatic increase in immigration from Germany in the years 1933, 1934, and 1935, Palestinians came to fear that the day would soon come when they would be outnumbered by the recently arrived Jews. While this was indeed the goal of Zionism, it is interesting to note that at about this time only a few leading Zionists cast doubt on the viability of plans for a gradual, peaceful population build-up through immigration to Palestine. One, labor-Zionist leader Dr. Haim Arlosoroff, concluded pessimistically that the goal of changing the Arab majority into a minority might never be achievable by gradualist methods and without resorting to force and violence.[13] During the 1930s a few other individuals felt forced to conclude that the Zionist dream of creating a Jewish state in the area might not be achievable after all; these people sought

Table 2.2   *Palestine population, 1930–1946*

Year	Total including nomads	Arabs(*)	Jews	Jewish immigrants	Jews as percentage of total
1930	992,559	818,135	164,796	4944	16.6%
1931	1,033,314	848,607	174,606	4075	16.9%
1932	1,073,827	871,323	192,137	9553	17.9%
1933	1,140,941	895,297	234,967	30,327	20.6%
1934	1,210,554	916,786	282,975	42,359	23.4%
1935	1,308,112	941,924	355,157	61,854	27.2%
1936	1,366,692	971,236	384,078	29,727	28.1%
1937	1,401,794	994,315	395,836	10,536	28.2%
1938	1,435,285	1,012,224	411,222	12,868	28.7%
1939	1,501,698	1,044,091	445,457	16,405	29.7%
1940	1,544,530	1,068,433	463,535	4547	30.0%
1941	1,585,500	1,098,517	474,102	3647	29.9%
1942	1,620,005	1,122,476	484,408	2194	29.9%
1943	1,676,571	1,159,996	502,912	8507	30.0%
1944	1,764,522	1,196,824	553,600	14,464	31.4%
1945	1,834,935	1,240,850	579,227	12,751	31.6%
1946	1,912,112	1,288,399	608,225	7851	31.8%

Adapted from:
Tables "Population of Palestine by Religions," and "Number of Immigrants Annually by Race," in *A Survey of Palestine*, prepared in December 1945 and January 1946 for the Information of the Anglo–American Committee of Inquiry, London: HMSO, 1946; reprinted by the Institute for Palestine Studies, 1991, vol. I: 141, 185, and revised (1944–1946) in the Supplement, vol. III: 10–11, 17.
(*) British population data record "Moslems," "Christians," and "others"—but not "Arabs." The "Arab" figures shown here represent the combined British figures for "Moslems" and "Christians."

solutions through formulae such as a bi-national state, cantons, or federal arrangements.[14]

Table 2.2 shows annual figures for recorded Jewish immigration, and its impact on the population balance between Arabs and Jews.

By 1947, there were between 600,000 and 650,000 Jews in the country, representing a ten-fold increase from the pre-World War I total. The *yishuv* now formed a critical mass, impossible to ignore. But the Arabs, whose numbers had dramatically (albeit less strikingly than the Jews) doubled to 1,300,000 during the same three decades, still constituted a two-thirds majority when the United Nations was called upon to recommend a plan for the future of the contested land. When the 1948–1949 war ended with the creation of the State of Israel, the "demographic battle" continued in new forms.

Just as immigration continued to be the main engine for increasing the Jewish population, "out-migration" during and after the war sharply reduced the proportion of Palestinians living in the contested land. A substantial number of Palestinians were displaced—some claim as a result of "ethnic cleansing" (see Chapter 6, Chapter 11)—and became refugees. Forced into exile, they claimed the right to return to, or be compensated for, the homes they had been forced to abandon during the fighting—a claim endorsed by UN General Assembly Resolution 194 passed in December 1948.[15] Over the years this population of refugees registered with the United Nations Relief and Works Agency for Palestine Refugees in the Near East [UNRWA] has grown from 760,000 in 1949 to the current number of just over 4.6 million. In addition, there may be up to 2.5 million non-registered refugees.[16]

The disposition of this refugee population and its claims—especially the questions of how many would actually return to live in Israel, how many to Palestinian territories, and how many would be compensated and resettled elsewhere—constitutes an essential element in all potential negotiations towards both an Israeli–Palestinian final accord and a comprehensive settlement between Israel and the Arab states, where most of the Palestinian refugees have lived in camps administered by UNRWA.

The continued growth of Israel's Jewish population was promoted through sustained efforts to encourage Jews to "make *aliya*," i.e., move from their diaspora homes to establish new lives in the Jewish state. A huge and sudden influx of Jews expelled or fleeing from Iraq, Yemen, and other Arab countries occurred between 1949 and 1951, contributing over 250,000 refugee-immigrants to a doubling of Israel's Jewish population from 760,000 in late 1948 to 1.4 million by late 1951.[17] Only a few of these Jews would today consider returning to their old homes, but Israeli negotiators have recently put forth compensation claims for the abandoned or confiscated assets of these Arabic-speaking Jews as a factor to be considered (as against Palestinian refugee claims vis-à-vis Israel) in any resumption of negotiations towards a comprehensive solution.[18]

Another demographic undercurrent is the continued growth, by natural increase, of the Arab-Palestinian minority within Israel's borders. By its very presence this population challenges the state's declared Jewish character and simultaneously puts to the test pledges of equality among all its citizens enshrined in the Israeli Declaration of Independence. Since 1948, the Palestinian minority has numbered between 15 percent and 20 percent of the total population, which is perceived by some nationalistic Jewish Israelis as a threat to the Zionist essence of their state. Suspicions also persist among Jewish Israelis about the loyalties of their Arab fellow-citizens, whose numbers exceeded 1.4 million out of a total 7.2 million in 2008.[19]

A final demographic consideration involves the West Bank ("Judaea and Samaria") and the Gaza Strip. With Israel's occupation of these territories during the June 1967 war, the number of Palestinian Arabs under Israeli rule skyrocketed from 350,000 to almost one million. Many decades passed without these territories, in whole or in part, being returned to Jordan or Egypt, or granted to Palestinian self-rule in the context of a peace treaty. Since 1967, hundreds of thousands of Israeli Jews—in violation of most interpretations of the Fourth Geneva Convention[20] (see Chapter 7)—have established suburbs and settlements in the lands conquered during the June 1967 war.

After 1993, portions of these territories were returned to Palestinian self-rule as Israeli forces redeployed, with the disposition of many Jewish settlements still to be decided. In spring 2002, following a serious escalation in terrorist attacks on Israeli civilians, the IDF reoccupied large portions of the West Bank. In Summer 2005, Israel evacuated all 8000 to 9000 Jewish settlers from 21 settlements in the Gaza Strip, leaving 1.4 million Palestinians to govern themselves, but still surrounded and blockaded by Israeli forces. In 2008, about 2.4 million Palestinians lived in the West Bank, along with about 125 Jewish settlements whose population reached some 280,000 (490,000 including Jewish suburbs created in the Jerusalem area since 1967).[21]

A minority of Israelis firmly believes that all lands conquered during the 1967 war should remain under Israeli jurisdiction, whether for security reasons (absence of peace, untrustworthiness of the enemy) or because of Biblical injunctions and promises. But many Israelis oppose annexation, some in order to avoid the demographic implications of becoming a Jewish minority living among a Palestinian-Arab majority population, and others to be rid of the burden of controlling and administering an unwilling and resentful occupied population.

3 Borders

Sovereignty and demographics are also inextricably linked with the question of where to draw the boundaries. In certain ways, since 1948 Israel and the Arab states, and (to a lesser extent) Palestinians and Israelis, may be seen as fighting over borders. Military encounters during the first Palestine war of 1947–1949 were terminated by means of four armistice agreements signed between Israel and Egypt (February 1949), Jordan (March 1949), Lebanon (July 1949), and Syria (July 1949). But these armistice agreements were never transformed into peace treaties, leaving supposedly temporary ceasefire lines between the combatants in place for decades rather than agreed-upon and recognized international frontiers.

This "unfinished business" of borders after the 1948 war became one of the factors contributing to the outbreaks of subsequent cross-border skirmishes and raids, culminating also in major wars in October 1956 (Israel versus Egypt), June 1967 (Israel versus Egypt, Jordan and Syria) and October 1973 (Egypt and Syria versus Israel). Although treaties signed in 1979 and 1994 have resolved border disputes among Israel, Egypt, and Jordan, there are still contested boundaries to be settled whenever Israel, Lebanon, and Syria sit down to negotiate peace treaties.

Border issues have also become part of the Israeli–Palestinian impasse since 1993, when the two sides were supposed to implement interim arrangements for Israeli withdrawal from territories occupied in 1967 and the transition to Palestinian self-government over defined territories as the nucleus of a future independent state. Borders were, under the framework of an Israeli–Palestinian framework for peace agreed at Oslo in 1993, one of the "permanent status" issues to be resolved en route to a two-state solution to the conflict. During the unconsummated 2000–2001 negotiations at Camp David and Taba, Palestinian and Israeli negotiators argued over the drawing of boundaries between Israel and the future Palestinian state.

Competing Narratives: Right versus Right, Victim versus Victim

By and large, competing claims and counterclaims of the tangible type outlined in the preceding section have the merit of being considered in terms of *interests* over which compromises are possible, in the classic dynamics of bargaining situations. Intangible issues involving psychology, myths, stereotyping, and contested narratives[22] are of a different quality. These often existential issues involve the fulfillment of demanded rights or the rectification of claimed injustices, rather than claims to concrete assets that can, theoretically at least, be settled via sharing, compensation, trade-offs, or clever formulae. And, as we shall argue further in Chapter 12, these are the issues that are the most difficult to resolve.

The distinction between negotiable *interests* and non-negotiable *rights* is well captured in the autobiography of the Palestinian academic and sometime activist, Sari Nusseibeh:

> [O]ur respective absolute rights—the historical right of the Jews to their ancestral homeland, and the Palestinian rights to the country robbed from them—[are] fundamentally in conflict, and [are] in fact mutually exclusive. ... [T]he more historical justice each side [demands], the less their real national interests [get] served. Justice and interests [fall] into conflict.[23]

Reinforcement of this point comes from historian Natasha Gill, who warns that "[i]n the marketplace of negotiation" an insistence on "rights, recognition and reconciliation" yields no results and has become a "tool of intransigence," symbolic of "the very issues that bring the peace process to its knees." Rights, she argues, "are part of an unsettled conflict over history, and they will always be called into question. Recognition will never come in the form demanded by each party." Reconciliation, she wisely notes, "will be the effect, rather than the cause, of peace"[24]—a peace necessarily built on interests and on compromise.

In order to understand the depth and longevity of the Israeli–Palestinian conflict, it is ultimately of greater importance for us to focus on myths, symbols, and stereotypes than on so-called objective facts. In Chapter 11 we shall examine the issues of bias and objectivity as they affect the ways historians treat the conflict. Here we should note how each side, with dreadful predictability, will interpret all the facts of its historical experience as reinforcing its own deep sense of grievance and victimhood at the hands of the other. As evidenced in the apt title of Benny Morris' detailed historical survey of the conflict since 1881, each side sincerely and righteously believes that it is the victim of the other side's aggression and evil intentions.[25]

In Part II, as we review the unfolding of the history of the conflict through its various stages, we will be reminded of how these parallel but mutually exclusive perceptions of victimhood express themselves. Such self-perceptions constitute perhaps the most serious obstacle to each party's ability to enter into negotiation, and also to its ability to acknowledge the legitimacy, rights, and humanity of the other side.

Ways of Visualizing the Conflict

Historians and political scientists have offered different suggestions for visualizing this conflict. A common approach among historians would be **linear**, e.g., a time-line with an agreed starting date, important turning-points (some serving as markers for periodization). Such linear presentation allows for the addition, over time, of additional players and new layers of complexity to what started out as a dispute of simpler dimensions.[26]

The conflict is also visualized by some historians and political scientists as a **cyclical** or **spiral** pattern: grievances fester, tensions build up, a spark ignites a war. Fighting ends, but only temporarily and without resolving all the war's original causes. Rekindled and new grievances then build new instability and provide the conditions that will be sparked eventually into the next outbreak of hostilities. The widening of the spiral represents the escalation of violence and inclusion of new elements, actors, or levels of complication previously absent from the conflict in its earlier forms.

Another metaphor recently proposed is the **double helix**—with the protagonists' "intertwined reckonings of the past provid[ing] fodder and direction" for their ongoing "tit-for-tat battles." Palestinians and Israelis, suggests Robert I. Rotberg, "are locked together in struggle, tightly entangled, and enveloped by a historical cocoon of growing complexity, fundamental disagreement, and overriding misperception of motives."[27]

Another aspect to consider when trying to assess the changing shape of the conflict is to view it **geographically** over time, by presenting and discussing a series of changing maps. As mentioned in Chapter 1, a key consideration before 1948 is the **demographic** change and pattern of Jewish land ownership and settlement over time, and these can be well illustrated by maps—whether as Palestinian losses or as Zionist achievements.[28] The changing borders of Palestine and Israel can also be followed through maps redrawn after the wars of 1947–1949, 1967, and 1973, and the agreements of 1979 (Israel–Egypt Treaty), 1994 (Israel–Jordan Treaty) and 1993–1998 (Palestinian–Israeli interim arrangements).

Political scientists have sometimes other graphics for visualizing the Arab–Israeli conflict, from the simple concentric circles (core / periphery) to more elaborate flow charts for decision-makers facing periodic crises.[29]

Finally, drawing on the work of experts in diplomacy and conflict resolution, we can usefully understand this conflict as **operating on multiple levels**. Itamar Rabinovich, historian, former ambassador, and former Israeli negotiator with the Syrians, suggests that "there is no single Arab–Israeli dispute" but rather "a cluster of distinct, interrelated conflicts" which he defines as:

1 the core conflict between Israel and the Palestinians—"a classic conflict between two national movements claiming title to and vying for possession of the same land";

2 a broader dispute between Israel and Arab nationalism—"a national, political, cultural, and increasingly also religious conflict" in which both sides bring with them "their historical and cultural legacies" and broad national narratives;

3 a series of bilateral disputes between Israel and the neighboring Arab states, based on conflicting geostrategic and geopolitical interests;

4 a subset of, or flashpoint for, broader international conflicts—e.g., great power rivalries, colonialism, and resistance to European hegemony.[30]

In a similar vein, Stephen P. Cohen, a Harvard-trained psychologist with decades of hands-on experience mediating between influential Israelis and Arabs in the region and in closed-door workshops, describes the conflict as operating on multiple levels. Cohen argues that successful resolution will depend not only on appreciating the existence of these layers but, more importantly, on understanding how these various levels are inter-twined.[31]

In the end, whatever methodology or visualization one chooses, I suggest that there are a minimum of two layers that we should bear in mind while trying to understand and define the essence of the Israeli–Palestinian and Arab–Israeli conflicts:

1 two peoples seeking fulfillment of their self-determination as unique national entities, competing for mastery over the same land (treated in these pages and elsewhere as the core of the conflict); and
2 this original, local conflict drawing in varying degrees of involvement of outside parties—regional actors, diaspora communities, global powers.

Indeed, the organization of this book follows these lines by focusing on the first of these layers in Chapters 3–6 (the period up to 1949), proceeds in Chapter 7 to incorporate important elements from the second layer, and then refocuses in Chapters 8–10 on the original core.

Analogies and Parables

When cold, logical analysis seems to leave important aspects of a conflict unexplained, some writers resort to fables, parables, or analogies. One of the most quoted allegories was popularized by the late Isaac Deutscher, historian of the Russian revolution and biographer of Joseph Stalin. In an interview shortly after the June 1967 war, Deutscher offered the following allegory of a falling man:

> A man once jumped from the top floor of a burning house in which many members of his family had already perished. He managed to save his life; but as he was falling he hit a person standing down below and broke that person's legs and arms. The jumping man had no choice; yet to the man with the broken limbs he was the cause of his misfortune. If both behaved rationally, they would not become enemies. The man who escaped from the blazing house, having recovered, would have tried to help and console the other sufferer; and the latter might have realized that he was the victim of circumstances over which neither of them had control.
> But look what happens when these people behave irrationally. The injured man blames the other for his misery and swears to make him pay

for it. The other, afraid of the crippled man's revenge, insults him, kicks him, and beats him up whenever they meet. The kicked man again swears revenge and is again punched and punished. The bitter enmity, so fortuitous at first, hardens and comes to overshadow the whole existence of both men and to poison their minds.[32]

At first blush this tale appears an insightful snapshot of the conflict as it looked in the aftermath of the lopsided Israeli victory in the June war. It touches raw nerves in bringing out the cruel forces of circumstance that pitted Jewish Holocaust survivors in search of a safe haven against indigenous Palestinian Arabs who suffer as a result. Yet, upon careful scrutiny, the analogy is historically flawed and each party will claim that it is being misrepresented in some way by the figures depicted (see below, Chapter 6).[33]

Other writers with a literary bent—including Amos Oz, S. Yizhar, and Sari Nusseibeh—have also offered engaging parables, such as:

- two fighting men holding each other by the throat, each afraid to be the first to let go;
- two men cast away at sea, struggling to survive by clinging to a single floating plank;
- two wrestlers, each unable to subdue the other because they are both being sucked down into quicksand.[34]

Another metaphor portrays Jews and Palestinians as having to share the same house or apartment—either benignly, as renters of separate rooms but sharing common corridors, or violently, with Zionists portrayed as home invaders kicking out the original Palestinian dwellers onto the streets. Also, Amos Oz has frequently likened the current impasse to a dysfunctional married couple in dire need of a good divorce settlement.[35]

These devices can often bring new insight, but they too are contested and contestable, reminding us of the need to handle them with care so as to avoid the pitfalls of distorted presentation and misleading conclusions.

The Conflict in Comparative Perspective

Another way to understand a conflict is to ask ourselves to what extent it is just like any other, and in what ways it is unique. Can we better explain or understand the conflict by resorting to comparisons and analogy, or by drawing on perceived similarities from international history and current events? If so, *which* other conflicts can we consider as offering valid parallels?

In efforts to help their audiences better understand the Arab–Israeli conflict, academics and propagandists alike are fond of using paradigms, or parallels with other disputes. The following four have been frequently invoked:

(a) The pre-1948 *yishuv* (and later Israel) is portrayed as a colonial-settler state, and its motive force (Zionism) as an aggressive colonialist movement, whose clear purpose was to populate what they treated as an empty frontier with foreigners, taking possession of the land by subjugating, dispossessing, and/or expelling the indigenous population.[36]

(b) Zionism is presented as a national liberation movement, rallying Jews from their vulnerable minority status in dispersion (diaspora) and facilitating their ingathering in their former homeland—but stumbling upon the obstacle of another people already inhabiting the land and seeking its own national liberation in the same territory.[37]

(c) Zionist and Israeli concern for creating and maintaining a Jewish majority in a Jewish state is seen as a variant of the racism of South African whites (Afrikaaners) who built a discriminatory apartheid régime to exclude and oppress the indigenous majority of Black Africans.[38]

(d) Zionism, whether in its original incarnation or in the post-1967 movement to populate the conquered territories with Jewish settlers, is portrayed as being akin to Ulster Protestants imposed upon Catholic Ireland and protected by England, for its own ends.[39]

Indeed, (a) and (b) are not merely contrasting ways for outsiders to represent and try to understand the conflict; they form the backbone of the very narratives of Palestinians and Israelis, respectively. They will be discussed further in Chapter 3 as one of eleven *core arguments* treated in this study.

Choosing to view the conflict through one of these lenses rather than another has important consequences for how one weighs and interprets the evidence, facts, and arguments put forth by the protagonists. As one Israeli historian has noted:

> In all the models employed to explicate the Arab/Israeli conflict, historical evidence—or its absence—are [sic] crucial. So, too, is the choice of which society in the ancient and modern worlds Palestine and Israel are to be compared with. The stakes involved in making this selection are large and deeply felt. Discriminating between conflicting appeals to histories real and imagined, and even contrived, will likely continue to challenge and aggravate the scholarly world, the public at large, and well as this participant/observer.[40]

It is not my intention to convince the reader of the correctness of one model over another. Rather, I point here to four currently used analogies or comparisons in order to show the varieties of conflicting interpretation that are possible. In the chapters that follow I will outline similar and related contested viewpoints as they arise, in historical context. Readers will be left with the task and the responsibility of making their own choices as to which seem more convincing.

Notes

1   Jewish People Policy Planning Institute, website http://www.jpppi.org.il, accessed 24 March 2009; Central Bureau of Statistics, Israel, website http://www1.cbs.gov.il/reader/, esp. Statistical Abstract of Israel 2008, tables 2.1 and 2.27, accessed 24 March 2009.

2   The Palestine National Charter: Resolutions of the Palestine National Council, 1–17 July 1968, accessed 23 March 2008 online at http://www.yale.edu/lawweb/avalon/mideast/plocov.htm#art20.

3   Palestinian Central Bureau of Statistics, website http://www.pcbs.gov.ps/DesktopDefault.aspx?tabID=3845&lang=en accessed 26 February 2008; UNWRA website http://www.un.org/unrwa/publications/pdf/uif-dec08.pdf accessed 24 March 2009.

4   Bernard Wasserstein, *Israelis and Palestinians: Why Do They Fight? Can They Stop?* 3rd ed., New Haven, CT / London: Yale University Press / London: Profile Books, 2008. 165–9.

5   See "Maps of the Changing Boundaries of 'Historic' Palestine," Jacob Lassner and S. Ilan Troen, *Jews and Muslims in the Arab World: Haunted By Pasts, Real and Imagined*, Lanham /Boulder, etc.: Rowman and Littlefield, 2007, 353–66.

6   Wasserstein, *Israelis and Palestinians*, 99.

7   Article 2, Palestinian National Charter, accessed online 9 September 2008 at http://www.yale.edu/lawweb/avalon/mideast/plocov.htm#art2. Cf. Wasserstein, *Israelis and Palestinians*, 123.

8   Zionist Plan for Palestine, February 1919, Martin Gilbert, *The Routledge Atlas of the Arab–Israeli Conflict*, 7th ed., London / New York: Routledge, 2002, 9; cf. Wasserstein, *Israelis and Palestinians*, 103–4.

9   For maps showing Ottoman administrative units, see Gilbert, *Routledge Atlas*, 4–5; Mark Tessler, *A History of the Israeli–Palestinian Conflict*, Bloomington / Indianapolis: Indiana University Press, 1994, 161.

10   For an insightful examination of the demographic aspects of the conflict, see Wasserstein, *Israelis and Palestinians*, ch. 1.

11   See, e.g., Kenneth W. Stein, *The Land Question in Palestine, 1917–1939*, Chapel Hill: University of North Carolina Press, 1984; Wasserstein, *Israelis and Palestinians*, ch. 2.

12   Chaim Weizmann, *Trial and Error: The Autobiography of Chaim Weizmann*, London: Hamish Hamilton, 1949, 305.

13 Arlosoroff to Weizmann, 30 June 1932, Weizmann Archives (Rehovot, Israel). This original letter, written in English, seems to have been translated into Hebrew and then back into English. See, e.g., *From Haven to Conquest: Readings in Zionism and the Palestine Problem until 1948*, ed. and introduced by Walid Khalidi, 2nd printing, Washington, DC: Institute for Palestine Studies, 1987, 245–54. For discussions of this remarkable letter, see Neil Caplan, "Zionist Visions in the Early 1930s," *Studies in Contemporary Jewry: An Annual* vol. IV, ed. Jonathan Frankel, Oxford: Oxford University Press, 1988, 256–9; Shlomo Avineri, "The Socialist Zionism of Chaim Arlosoroff," *Jerusalem Quarterly* 34 (Winter 1985), 84–7.

14 Caplan, "Zionist Visions"; Neil Caplan, *Futile Diplomacy*, vol. II, *Arab–Zionist Negotiations and the End of the Mandate*, London: Frank Cass 1986, ch. 1.

15 Article 11 of UNGA Resolution 194 (III), 11 December 1948, in *United Nations Resolutions on Palestine and the Arab–Israeli Conflict*, vol. I: 1947–1974, revised edition, ed. George J. Tomeh, Washington, DC: Institute for Palestine Studies, 1988, 16.

16 See PLO Negotiations Affairs Department, "Palestinian Refugees," May 2008, accessed online 5 September 2008 at http://www.nad-plo.org/facts/refugees/Palestinian%20Refugees.pdf.

17 Central Bureau of Statistics, Israel, *Statistical Abstract of Israel, 2007*, available at http://www1.cbs.gov.il/reader/cw_usr_view_Folder?ID=141. As a result, the "Ashkenazic" (or European) character of Israel's Jewish population declined, with the population balance moving from 75 percent Ashkenazic in 1948 to 55 percent by 1961, making room for an increasing element of "Sephardic" (Oriental and Mediterranean) Jews. For descriptions and a critical overview of the problems and challenges facing Jewish immigrants to Israel from Arab countries at this time, see Howard M. Sachar, *A History of Israel: From the Rise of Zionism to Our Time*, New York: Alfred A. Knopf, 1976, 395–409; Tom Segev, *1949: The First Israelis*, ed. Arlen Neal Weinstein, New York: Free Press / London: Collier Macmillan, 1986, ch. 6 ("Nameless People").

18 E.g., Justice for Jews in Arab Countries (JJAC), website accessed 3 September 2008 at http://www.justiceforjews.com. For a report on this organization's conference in London July 2008, see Nathan Jeffay, "The Other Middle East Refugees," *Jerusalem Report*, 4 August 2008, 33–4. See also Michael R. Fischbach, "Palestinian and Mizrahi Jewish Property Claims in Discourse and Diplomacy," in *Exile and Return: Predicaments of Palestinians and Jews*, eds. Ann M. Lesch and Ian S. Lustick, Philadelphia: University of Pennsylvania Press, 2005, 207–24; Yehouda Shenhav, "'Arab Jews, Population Exchange, and the Palestinian Right of Return," in Lesch and Lustick, *Exile and Return*, 225–45; Michael R. Fischbach, "Palestinian Refugee Compensation and Israeli Counterclaims for Jewish Property in Arab Countries," *Journal of Palestine Studies* 38:1 (Autumn 2008), 6–24.

19 *Statistical Abstract of Israel, 2008*.

20 Geneva Convention relative to the Protection of Civilian Persons in Time of War, 12 August 1949, available at http://www.unhchr.ch/html/menu3/b/92.htm.

21 Palestinian population figures are taken from the Palestinian Central Bureau of Statistics website http://www.pcbs.gov.ps/DesktopDefault.aspx?tabID= 3845&lang=en. Reliable and uncontested statistics on the Jewish settlers' population are hard to come by. The *Statistical Abstract of Israel, 2007* indicated 271,000 "Israelis living in Jewish localities" in "Judaea and Samaria" at the end of 2006. Generally, the most credible data can be found on the website of the Foundation for Middle East Peace, accessed 23 September 2008 at http://www.fmep.org. See also Gershom Gorenberg, *The Accidental Empire: Israel and the Birth of Settlements, 1967–1977*, New York: Times Books, 2006, 364; Idith Zertal and Akiva Eldar, *Lords of the Land: The War over Israel's Settlements in the Occupied Territories, 1967–2007*, transl. from the Hebrew by Vivian Eden, New York: Nation Books, 2007, xiii.

22 For a helpful juxtaposition of competing Israeli and Palestinian narratives, see Paul Scham's introduction to *Shared Histories: A Palestinian–Israeli Dialogue*, eds. Paul Scham, Walid Salem, and Benjamin Pogrund, Walnut Creek, CA: Left Coast Press, 2005, 1–12.

23 Sari Nusseibeh, with Anthony David, *Once upon a Country: A Palestinian Life*, New York: Farrar, Straus, and Giroux, 2007, 508.

24 Natasha Gill, "The Arab Peace Plan: Say No to Rights, Recognition," *The Forward* 6 June 2007.

25 Benny Morris, *Righteous Victims: A History of the Zionist–Arab Conflict, 1881–1999*, New York, Alfred A. Knopf, 2001.

26 For a sampling of different timelines and chronologies, see *The Arab–Israeli Conflict: Perspectives*, 2nd ed., ed. Alvin Z. Rubinstein, New York: HarperCollins, 1991, 215–22; Ian J. Bickerton and Carla L. Klausner, *A History of the Arab–Israeli Conflict*, 5th ed., Upper Saddle River, NJ: Pearson / Prentice Hall, 2007, on the first page of each chapter; Wasserstein, *Israelis and Palestinians*, 179–94; David W. Lesch, *The Arab–Israeli Conflict: A History*, New York / Oxford: Oxford University Press, 2008, 467–72; below, pages 268–79.

27 Robert I. Rotberg, "Building Legitimacy through Narrative," in *Israelis and Palestinian Narratives of Conflict: History's Double Helix*, ed. Robert I. Rotberg, Bloomington / Indianapolis: Indiana University Press, 2006, 2.

28 Among the best available maps of this type are those in Walid Khalidi, *Before Their Diaspora: A Photographic History of the Palestinians, 1876–1948*, Washington, DC: Institute for Palestine Studies, 1984, 34, 84, 237, 239; available online at http://www.passia.org/palestine_facts/MAPS. For an overview and critical discussion, see Gideon Biger, "The Boundaries of Israel–Palestine, Past, Present and Future: A Critical Geographical View," *Israel Studies* 13:1 (Spring 2008), 68–93.

29 See, e.g., the pioneering work of Michael Brecher, *The Foreign Policy System of Israel: Setting, Images, Process*, London / Toronto / Melbourne: Oxford University Press, 1972, and *Decisions in Israel's Foreign Policy*, New Haven, CT: Yale University Press, 1975.

30 Itamar Rabinovich, *Waging Peace: Israel and the Arabs, 1948–2003*, rev. and updated ed., Princeton, NJ: Princeton University Press, 2004, 3–5.

31 Stephen Cohen, "Intractability and the Israeli–Palestinian Conflict," in *Grasping the Nettle*, 348–50.

32 Isaac Deutscher, "The Israeli–Arab War, June 1967" (from an interview given to the *New Left Review*, 23 June 1967), in *The Non-Jewish Jew and Other Essays*, London: Oxford University Press, 1968, 136–7. Cf. the similar tale invented by Nusseibeh, *Once upon a Country*, 462.

33 E.g., the allegory ignores pre-Holocaust Zionism as a motive or reason for Jewish-Zionist aspirations to migrate to Palestine/*Eretz-Israel*; it does not mention pre-Holocaust objections to and fears about the newcomers on the part of the indigenous population; it says nothing about the indifference of an international community that might have opened more doors to fleeing survivors, thereby leading or allowing the jumping man to land elsewhere, without injuring the Palestinian man standing below.

34 Nusseibeh, *Once upon a Country*, 483–5. See also ibid., 486–7.

35 Amos Oz, *How to Cure a Fanatic*, Princeton, NJ: Princeton University Press, 2006, 19–20, 62.

36 Among many, see Joseph A. Massad, *The Persistence of the Palestinian Question: Essays on Zionism and the Palestinians*, London: Routledge, 2006.

37 Among many, see Jacob Tsur, *Zionism: The Saga of a National Liberation Movement*, New Brunswick, NJ: Transaction, 1977; Amos Elon, *The Israelis: Founders and Sons*, New York: Holt Rinehart Winston, 1971.

38 Among many, see Marwan Bishara, *Palestine/Israel: Peace or Apartheid: Prospects for Resolving the Conflict*, London: Zed Books / Halifax, NS: Fernwood, 2001. For an intelligent overview of the uses and misuses of Israel–South Africa analogies, see Heribert Adam and Kogila Moodley, *Seeking Mandela: Peacemaking between Israelis and Palestinians*, Philadelphia, PA: Temple University Press, 2005.

39 See, e.g., Ian Lustick, *Unsettled States, Disputed Lands: Britain and Ireland, France and Algeria, Israel and West Bank-Gaza*, Ithaca, NY: Cornell University Press, 1993; Thomas G. Mitchell, *Native vs. Settler: Ethnic Conflict in Israel/Palestine, Northern Ireland, and South Africa*, Westport, CT: Greenwood Press, 2000.

40 S. Ilan Troen, "De-Judaizing the Homeland: Academic Politics in Rewriting the History of Palestine," *Israel Affairs* 13:4 (2007), 882–3. See below, Chapter 3.

Part II
Histories in Contention

3
Background to 1917: Origins of Conflict

Ancient Ties and Historical Memories

One of the choices we made when defining the nature of the conflict was to treat it as one that took on its current form in the late 19th century, as a struggle between migrating Zionist Jews and the indigenous Arab (Muslim and Christian) population. The two communities would become rivals to exercise their self-determination over a small but strategically important and religiously sensitive area of the Ottoman Empire.

This is not to suggest, however, that ancient ties and historical memories are irrelevant. Pre-19th-century history is often invoked, and in two possible ways. On the one hand, both sides can and do call forth memories of centuries of respectful tolerance and fruitful Muslim–Jewish collaboration since the 7th century CE as a pattern to be remembered and replicated, if possible, in overcoming today's hostility. More often, however, both peoples reach back to their ancient past as tribal and religious entities to build their contemporary national identity and consciousness, and in order to lay claim to original ownership of the contested (and divinely promised) land.[1]

This leads us to discuss the first of eleven *core arguments* to be surveyed in our study: *Who was there first, and whose land was it to begin with?* Both sides evoke and reconstruct a largely mythical past, handed down through generations by written texts and oral tradition, in order to prove that their ancestors were "there" first, that their forebears and descendants controlled the territory for extended periods of time, and/or that the land in question was promised to them by God.

For some, the issue is one to be decided mainly by theological analysis and exegesis of holy texts. Proofs of the Jewish claim can be taken from Hebrew scriptures, especially those verses in the *Torah* (the Five Books of Moses, part of the Old Testament of the Christian Bible) in which, some two millennia before Christ, God is recorded as having promised defined territories as an "everlasting possession" to Abraham and his seed.[2] Abraham had two sons, Isaac and Ishmael. Despite their wanderings, dispersion, and forced expulsions over the centuries, Jews claiming descent from Abraham, through Isaac and Jacob, have maintained a continuous presence in the land, albeit for long stretches in reduced numbers as a minority community.

Muslims recognize a common ancestry and spiritual heritage in most of the Hebrew prophets, and they include Jesus in this lineage. They revere Ibrahim (Abraham) as the common ancestor of all Muslims, Arabs, and other Semitic peoples, and see their own lineage passing through Abraham's son, Ishmael. In the course of spreading the new faith of Islam in the mid-7th century CE, Arabs conquered the area known as Palestine, and lived there as part of a series of Islamic empires until the end of World War I.

Since the late 1800s the contest over the land has involved, for some, a dispute over where the boundaries of the Biblically promised land would run today, and which contemporary peoples would be classified as descendants of Abraham and heirs to that land.[3] Religious fundamentalists have no trouble accepting the higher authority and authenticity of divine promises as revealed in their respective holy scriptures. Believers in other faiths (not to mention non-believers) will, of course, not feel compelled to accept land claims based on particular holy texts.

Interestingly, a strong fascination with the Biblical Hebrews animated a number of prominent secular-socialist Zionists like David Ben-Gurion and Moshe Dayan. For them the holy book constituted a proof of the Jewish connection to the modern-day Palestine/*Eretz-Israel*, serving both as archaeological guidebook[4] and legal entitlement. During his public testimony to the Peel (Royal) Commission that investigated complaints against the British Mandate régime in 1937, Ben-Gurion explained the Jews' claim to Palestine as follows: "the Bible is our Mandate, the Bible which was written by us, in our own language, in Hebrew, in this very country. That is our Mandate. Our right is as old as the Jewish people."[5]

There are also secular, non-theological components to claims of long-standing ties to the land. Archaeology has become a tool to either sustain or discredit claims of ancestral links to earlier communities made by today's Arabs, Palestinians, and Jews in the contested territory. To establish such proofs and reinforce claims of original ownership, professional and amateur archaeologists dig up the past of the disputed land and seek to map out a chain of continuous habitation back to the ancient Canaanites, Phoenicians, Philistines, Hebrews, and other peoples. Some Palestinians, for example, claim ancestry to peoples that pre-date the Hebrews of the Biblical period; some Muslim and Arab authors interpret ancient history in ways to prove that "the Arabs had lived in Palestine from prehistoric times and had even bestowed on the Jews their religion and literature."[6] For their part, Jews focus on the Biblical period to emphasize that their national existence pre-dated the arrival of the Arabs who swept through the Fertile Crescent during the expansion of Islam beyond Arabia in the 7th century CE.

It is possible, and indeed very common, to interpret archaeological findings selectively for different ends. Palestinians are easily able to amass sufficient proofs to reinforce what they already believe about their primordial claim to the land, and have no difficulty finding evidence that would undermine Jewish claims as spurious. Similarly, Israelis are able to interpret the archaeological evidence in ways that help them feel justified in their longstanding connection to the land, while casting doubt on rival Palestinian claims. The output of published literature backing up each side in this unresolved debate is enormous, spans many decades, and shows little sign of letting up.[7]

Academic dialogue seems to do little to settle this dispute, as illustrated by a recent debate between Israeli "new historian" Benny Morris and Palestinian-American Joseph Massad. Launched in the spirit of a suggestion to establish a committee of scholars to work for "Historical Truth and Political Justice," the discussion reached a bitter dead-end on the basic question of who was there first.[8] Like most of the eleven *core arguments* that we shall encounter, this one is in many ways unwinnable.

Early Encounters: 1880s–1914

As we are focusing only on the last 130 years of the current conflict, it is more useful to examine the contexts in which two emerging national movements emerged. From the middle of the 19th century, Arabic-speaking populations of the far-flung and multicultural Muslim Ottoman Empire came to feel themselves increasingly and separately as Arabs, wishing to emphasize their "Arab-ness" or Arabism, in some cases more strongly than their identity as Muslims or as Ottoman citizens. This growing self-identification in Arab nationalist terms paralleled developments in Europe, where language and territory were also becoming defining features of new societies and states. At first, Arab nationalists constituted only a minority movement against a majority of loyal Ottoman subjects. They formed secret societies, discussed new ideas in army officers' clubs and were also able to promote Arabic language and culture in literary salons and clubs.

Three strands, or impulses, contributed to this renewed sense of pride in, and identification with, Arabism. One was the Islamic impulse. The prophet Muhammad was an Arab, the tribes of Arabia were the original founders of the Muslim *umma* (community), and the Holy Quran was written in the Arabic language. A second contributing strand was the importation of ideas from Europe, especially those promoting linguistic-cultural nationalism. These ideas were being spread through traders and missionaries (European Christians), and it was especially Christian Arabs who attempted to emphasize the new idea of the unity of all Arabic-speakers in order to cut across, or submerge, Christian–Muslim differences, rivalries, or jealousies.[9] A third impetus to the formation of distinctly Arab consciousness was the Arab reaction, following the "Young Turk" revolution in Constantinople in 1908, against attempts at the centralization of the Ottoman Empire; Arabs reacted even more strongly to the new "Turkification" of previously loose, laissez-faire, decentralized relationships between the Ottoman center and its regions and provinces. One group of nationalist Arabs formed the "Decentralist" Party, aimed at autonomy if not secession of their regions of the tottering empire.

Thus, at the beginning of the 20th century, Arab nationalist thinkers felt entitled to self-determination based on their permanent continuous majority residence in the area, albeit under a succession of Islamic empires, since the 7th century. But, at precisely this time, this assumption was challenged in the area known as Palestine by a rival movement of national awakening among the Jews of Europe. Most of the latter, known as Zionists, focused their attention not on European soil but rather on the Holy Land. Within a decade of the creation of the World Zionist Organization, an Arab nationalist writer and former Ottoman official based in Paris was able to point to the existence of

> [t]wo important phenomena, of the same nature but opposed, ... the awakening of the Arab nation, and the latent effort of the Jews to reconstitute on a very large scale the ancient kingdom of Israel. Both these movements are destined to fight continually until one of them wins. The fate of the entire world [he predicted] will depend on the final result of this struggle between these two peoples representing two contrary principles.[10]

Like Arab nationalists of the Ottoman Empire, groups of Jews in Europe also penned pamphlets and created associations to promulgate a redefinition of themselves in more secular, national terms. Following several decades of internal discussion and publications, pioneering settlers began to leave Europe and Russia in the early 1880s for the area known generally as Palestine and to the Jewish people as *Eretz-Israel*, the land of Israel. At Basle, Switzerland, in 1897 Theodor Herzl convened the first world Zionist Congress and created the organizational framework of a movement dedicated to enhancing national consciousness among Jews. Another goal of the movement was to mobilize support among the powers of the time to help acquire the territory upon which Zionist Jews hoped to rebuild their national home and future state.

Zionism was thus promoting territorial regrouping as an answer to what was known as "the Jewish question"—which can be summed up, at that time, as: what is to become of the Jews of Europe, who as individual citizens had recently enjoyed emancipation from legally defined inferiority and submission but who were finding it increasingly difficult, as a group, to fit into the new matrix of nationalities and nation-states? A number of state-inspired outbursts of violent antisemitism ("pogroms") underscored the vulnerability of the Jews and their inability to blend in with their surrounding cultures. The answer seemed to be a state of their own.

Although they were scattered among the nations, Jews were already united by common religion, customs, historical legacy, and spoken (Yiddish) and liturgical (Hebrew) languages. At first only a few thinkers dreamed of transforming their community into a single national group. Zionism sought to convince Jewish communities in various lands to reorient themselves, as it were, not only in their way of thinking, but also to mobilize them for a physical "return to Zion," the Biblical homeland of the ancient Hebrews.

This was, of course, the very same land known at the time generally as Palestine and administered as several provinces of the Ottoman Empire. Except for not being physically located on the territory needed for their national revival, the new Jewish secular-nationalists, known as "Zionists," were emulating the recent nationalist movements and nation-states created by Italians, French, and other European peoples.[11]

Much has been written about this early period in which the seeds of today's conflict were sown. In the world of international politics, the leaders of the Zionist movement sought to win the favor of the Ottoman Turks who ruled the land in question; later, high-level diplomatic efforts were directed by both Arab nationalists and Zionists towards Britain, France, the US, and other world powers. Thus began a pattern by which both contesting parties looked towards, and drew in, powerful outsiders to support their demands. This would have the complicating effect of adding external layers and actors to the core rivalry between two emerging national movements for the same territory.

During 1913 and 1914, representatives of the Zionist and Arab movements did meet several times to discuss the possibilities of an entente that might have excluded these outsiders; nothing came from these meetings.[12] On the ground, first encounters between the Zionist pioneers/settlers and the indigenous Arabic-speaking population (Muslim and Christian) contained episodes of misunderstandings, suspicion, and friction, along with examples of cooperation and good neighborly relations.[13]

An Unseen Question?

Above we quoted early evidence of Arab awareness of an emerging clash with Zionists in Palestine. During the last decades of the Ottoman period other Arab politicians, officials, and journalists in the region likewise gave expression to their fears and concern.[14]

How did the early Zionists view the indigenous population? Did they not foresee any problems in their relations with the Arabs? There is plenty of evidence that Zionists were indeed aware of the fears, suspicions, and hostility expressed by the inhabitants of the land to which they were immigrating. Noted Hebrew essayist Ahad Ha-Am produced some disturbing firsthand reports of what he saw on a tour of Zionist settlements in *Eretz-Israel* in 1891.[15] In 1899, Theodor Herzl himself felt the need to write to Yussef Zia al-Khalidi in defense of Zionism and in an attempt to allay the criticisms and fears expressed by the Mayor of Jerusalem.[16]

Other examples abound of Zionist efforts to analyze and/or dispel the opposition evinced by the inhabitants of Ottoman Palestine.[17] But none of these efforts was sustained or effective, as the successes of Zionism in Ottoman and subsequently British Palestine would be achieved on the level of high diplomacy. One can only speculate whether better attempts to win over the local population through grass-roots activity could ever have bridged the gap between what the two peoples wanted most in this contested land. We return to this question in Chapter 11 as one of the possible "missed opportunities" to avert the growth of the conflict.

Colonialism and Nationalism

It is the European origins of the reawakening Jewish national movement to "return to Zion" that bring us to consider a second *core argument* that is still today being debated by the parties in conflict and those dedicated to explaining and teaching about it. It is over the questions: *Was the Zionist solution to the Jewish question a Jewish variant of national revivals and struggles for liberation? Or was Zionism part of an aggressive colonialist expansion into the Middle East, whose raison d'être was to exploit, dispossess, or overpower the indigenous population?*

Nascent Arab nationalism and Zionism were not simply colliding in a vacuum over a piece of land; they were also operating within the broader context of a European thrust of economic, political, and cultural power over the 400-year-old Ottoman Empire, which was in a state of decline and headed for dissolution.

Within the perspective of Jewish history and emerging Zionism, Jews who moved to Palestine saw themselves as returning, while most of the Palestinian inhabitants would have viewed these foreigners as (at best) intruding or (at worst) invading. Here we have a clash of perspectives that is unlikely to be adjusted by convincing one side of the rightness of the other's view.

The way one chooses to answer the question—*Was Zionism a legitimate expression of Jewish nationalism, or part of an aggressive colonialist expansion?*—will have several sets of consequences. First, it will strongly affect how one weighs all the historical data, and how one interprets the evidence and arguments put forth by the protagonists. Secondly, and perhaps more seriously, it will amount to choosing one side over the other by endorsing the main claim of its narrative while rejecting the other. Accepting the Zionist narrative of return contradicts the Palestinian narrative of being invaded and colonized, while subscribing to the colonialist interpretation undermines the legitimacy of the Zionist case. Observers, scholars, and journalists who consider themselves open-minded, unbiased, or neutral will—immediately upon crediting one view over the other—become part of the debate itself, with the resultant approval or disapproval of the parties themselves. Even the answer that "both are true" contains a position that would be considered 50 percent incorrect by most partisans on either side.

In recent generations the colonial-settler prism has enjoyed great popularity among scholars around the world; in some academic circles it has become almost axiomatic, not even requiring demonstration or discussion.[18] Even in Israel, "post-Zionists" and many of the "new historians" (Chapter 11) consciously embrace this approach and challenge the mainstream view of heroic pioneers who brought only good and no harm to the local population. Ilan Troen, a critic of the colonial-settler view of Zionism, sees this currently fashionable approach as a deformity of arguments that, in earlier days, were convincing enough to produce widespread recognition of Jewish-Zionist national rights in Western societies and the academic world. Troen describes this as a major "paradigm shift in the scholarship concerned with Palestine" in the 20th century, and tries to convince readers of the weaknesses of this paradigm.[19]

It is to be expected that other pro-Israeli scholars and those who subscribe to the Zionism-as-Jewish-nationalism paradigm[20] will find the "Israel-as-colonialist-implant" model unconvincing. Some would also question the motives of those who promote the colonial narrative, dismissing it as propagandistic and challenging the accuracy or solidity of its underpinning scholarship. Noting the change in attitudes towards Israel in Western academe in the 1970s, Haifa University historian Yoav Gelber has characterized the situation as follows:

> The same Palestinian slogans that had made little impression on European public opinion between the two world wars and in the aftermath of 1948 now found fertile ground in Europe's newfound postcolonial guilt. The process was encouraged by Arab petrodollars and other forms of funding and spread to American universities and later even to Israel. Early signs of the change in attitude appeared in the late 1980s with the emergence of the so-called New Historians, whose principal contribution to the study of the Arab–Israeli conflict has been to deflect the focus from Israeli accomplishments to the Palestinian ordeal. Palestinians are portrayed as hapless objects of violence and Israeli oppression, Israeli–Transjordanian collusion, and treacherous British and Arab diplomacy. Some describe Israelis as intransigent, merciless, and needlessly callous usurpers who cynically exploited the Holocaust to gain world support for Jewish statehood at the expense of Palestinian rights to their country.[21]

But can the colonial paradigm be explained away as simply an artificial product of shifts in academic and international politics? Although there may be an interesting mix of noble and nefarious reasons why one paradigm becomes popular at the expense of another at any given time, it is a distortion to imagine that the "Zionism-is-colonialism" narrative was invented *post facto* in order to win contemporary debates and to undermine the Zionist narrative, or that it is simply a tool created by antisemites and Israel-haters to denounce Jews and delegitimize the Jewish claim to statehood.

What gets lost in critiques like the one quoted above is the fact that the colonial-settler model of Zionism is more than an intellectual construct: it is also an integral part of an authentic Palestinian narrative based on actual experience—just as the rival narrative of the longing for and return to Zion is a genuine reflection of Jewish diaspora experience, and not to be dismissed as mere self-serving brainwashing or propaganda. Unfortunately, scholars on both sides of this debate seldom rise above the widespread myopic tendency of the partisans and the populations they represent to believe that "Our narrative tells the facts; their narrative is propaganda."[22] We will revisit this duelling narratives concept in Chapter 11.

Contemporary academic and other treatments of Zionism as a colonial-settler phenomenon can be viewed as the continuation of claims and arguments presented by Palestinian nationalists who have been active in a struggle against Zionism since the early 1920s, if not earlier. Aside from ephemeral political protests, treatises, and pamphlets, these arguments found their first powerful expression in the 1938 publication of George Antonius' influential book, *The Arab Awakening*.[23] Major contributors to this approach in later decades have been French scholar Maxime Rodinson, whose seminal essay, "Israël: fait colonial?" was published in 1967;[24] the dean of Palestinian historians, Professor Walid Khalidi;[25] and Palestinian-American professor of literature, Edward Said.

The titles and subtitles used in Said's much-reprinted and oft-quoted 1979 book, *The Question of Palestine*, capture the essence of the anti-colonialist critique. Part Two is entitled "Zionism from the standpoint of its victims," and is subdivided into two discussions: "Zionism and the attitudes of European colonialism" and "Zionist population, Palestinian depopulation."[26] A more radical exponent of this approach is Columbia University Professor Joseph Massad, whose writings suggest that the very phrase "Israeli–Palestinian conflict" is misleading in its implied balance and symmetry between two equal and equally legitimate contestants. For him, we should rather be talking about a colonial-settler invasion, an aggression perpetrated by one supremacist, racist party (Zionists) against another (Palestinians) simply attempting to defend itself.[27]

In a debate that patently fails to persuade those who subscribe to the view that Zionism is a form of colonialism, writers like Troen, Gelber, and others advance counterarguments that either reject the colonialist analogy outright, or point to qualifications that would make Zionism not a form of pure colonialism. Troen, for example, offers evidence of the international (i.e., European) community's previous acceptance of the Jews' "reconstitution," and right to return to and rebuild their homeland, in Palestine/*Eretz-Israel*. He describes the Zionist attitude as one of building a new society (the *yishuv*) that sought to reject, rather than reproduce, European realities in the Middle East:

> Adaptation, transformation and rejection of Europe reverberated throughout the intellectual and cultural reality of the Yishuv. It was patently clear that Zionism was not engaging in mere imitation or in direct transplantation. Zionists did not see themselves as foreigners or conquerors. For centuries in the Diaspora they had been strangers. In Eretz Israel they

expended enormous creative energy to feel at home, as if they were natives. It was this rejuvenation that convinced a large portion of the world community that Jews were entitled to independence within that portion of the country they had so distinctively marked.[28]

Among the other arguments advanced against the "Zionism = colonialism" model are that:

- Zionist settlement and colonizing were nation-building activities of a people wishing to reintegrate themselves with the land, rather than create an outpost to exploit its resources for the benefit of a foreign metropolis.
- Zionists' use of force came about not as part of an original plan of aggressive conquest, but as a response to Arab violence.
- Zionists purchased, rather than conquered or stole, land.
- Zionism contained a mixture of elements of "colonial, anti-colonial and post-colonial discourse and practice."[29]

The debate over whether to view the conflict in accordance with the colonial paradigm or the rival Jewish nationalist narrative is one that, I submit, can never be won. The existence of counterarguments seems to matter little to those who hold firmly to either paradigm; counterevidence or counterargument is easily dismissed as self-serving or arrogant. An interesting recent dialogue among Palestinian and Israeli scholars, all open-minded and well-intentioned to be sure, degenerated into an inconclusive and at times heated tit-for-tat debate when the issue of Zionism/colonialism was brought up.[30] Those bent on advancing "the case for Israel" or "the case for Palestine" seem unable to go beyond treating the opponent's paradigm as a polemical thrust that needs to be discredited and debunked by skilful advocacy, as if this were merely a matter of scoring points. In our treatment of the dispute we shall treat both of these contested versions as authentic expressions of the protagonists' respective narratives.

Victims versus Victims

The perhaps unresolvable differences between viewing the Israeli–Arab conflict as being either a clash of nationalisms or as a colonial-settler invasion feed into the self-view each party has of itself as being the righteous victim of the other. As we shall illustrate elsewhere in these pages, this "victims-versus-victims" dimension is itself a large contributing factor to the intractability of this conflict. Early Zionists were imbued with a sense of mission that they were correcting the injustices and afflictions the Jews had endured for centuries as dispersed and despised victims of, at first, religious, then racial-biological, hatred and persecution. The zeal and sacrifices required by the effort they made to leave Europe for what they considered to be their ancient homeland may account in part for the blindness of Zionist pioneers to the negative impact they were having on segments of the indigenous population of Ottoman Palestine.

These Zionist idealists, even the socialists and internationalists among them, also carried with them cultural prejudices of their times about their inherent superiority as Europeans facing primitive "natives" who were in need of political stability and the social and economic progress they, as Europeans, would be bringing with them into western Asia. Zionists did indeed view the Arabs not as their equals but as an underdeveloped people not particularly attached to any particular territory, a people who respected only force and (recalling periods of repressive Turkish rule) who would bow to superior authority. Early Zionist plans for and assumptions about Palestine and Palestinians were captured in the slogan, "a land without a people for a people without a land."[31]

For their part, the indigenous population of the future Palestine/Israel saw the new Jewish arrivals as members of a mysterious people, formerly subservient and docile, but now bent on world domination, and were convinced of this (like many people of the period) by conspiracy theories of *The Protocols of the Learned Elders of Zion*.[32] This made it easy to demonize Zionism as a dangerous imperialist force with secret connections in all the world's capitals, whose sole aim was to dispossess the Palestinian and other Arabs of their homeland. Nationalist spokesmen inspired their followers with calls to resist foreign domination by these unwanted Jewish intruders.

As we'll see again during the coming decades of conflict, this sense of exclusive and righteous victimhood would become an enduring feature of each party's self-perception, not easily dislodged by soothing words of good intentions.

Notes

1 For an excellent and balanced overview of early Jewish and Arab/Muslim history, and its relevance to the current conflict, see Mark Tessler, *A History of the Israeli–Palestinian Conflict*, Bloomington/Indianapolis: Indiana University Press, 1994 (revised ed. 2009), chs. 1–2. See also Raphael Patai, *The Seed of Abraham: Jews and Arabs in Contact and Conflict*, Salt Lake City: University of Utah Press, 1986, 296–304.

2 In the standard translations of Genesis, chapter 17, verse 8, God said to Abraham, "I will give to you and to your seed after you, the land wherein you are a stranger, all the land of Canaan, for an everlasting possession; and

I will be their God." Other verses that have God promising land to the Hebrews are Genesis 12:7, 13:14, 15, 17, 16:7, 18; 26:3, 4; 28:13; 35:12; Exodus 6:4; Leviticus 20:24; Numbers 14:16; 33:53; 34:12, 13; and Joshua 1:2–4.

3   For a modern commentary on Isaac and Ishmael, see Reuven Firestone, *Children of Abraham: An Introduction to Judaism for Muslims*, Hoboken, NJ: Ktav, 2001, 10–12. For a controversial and innovative geographical interpretation, see Kamal Salibi, *The Bible Came from Arabia*, London: Jonathan Cape, 1985.

4   Moshe Dayan, *Living with the Bible*, London: Weidenfeld and Nicolson, 1978.

5   Notes of Evidence taken on Thursday, 7th January 1937, 49th Meeting, Palestine Royal Commission, *Minutes of Evidence Heard at Public Sessions (with Index)*, Colonial No. 143, London: HMSO, 1937, 288. Reproduced in *The Rise of Israel, vol. 22: The Palestine Royal Commission*, ed. with an introduction by Aaron S. Klieman, New York / London: Garland, 1987.

6   Muhammad Jamil Baihum, "Arabism and Jewry in Syria," (1957), translated in *Arab Nationalism: An Anthology*, ed. with an introduction by Sylvia G. Haim, Berkeley / Los Angeles: University of California Press, 1962, 128–46; quotation from Haim's introduction, ibid., 38.

7   Tel Aviv University historian Shlomo Sand recently challenged the established national myth of an ancient and continuous "Jewish people" culminating in Zionism and a Jewish state in his *Comment le peuple juif fut inventé* (Paris: Fayard, 2008). For a sampling from polemical, academic, and popular writing on both sides of this question, see essays by Ilene Beatty and Alfred Guillaume reproduced in *From Haven to Conquest: Readings in Zionism and the Palestine Problem until 1948*, ed. and introduced by Walid Khalidi, Beirut: 1971; 2nd printing, Washington, DC: Institute for Palestine Studies, 1987, 3–30; Amos Elon, *The Israelis: Founders and Sons*, New York: Holt, Rinehart and Winston, 1971, 280–9; G. W. Bowersock, "Palestine: Ancient History and Modern Politics," *Journal of Palestine Studies* 56 (Summer 1985), 49–57, reproduced in *Blaming the Victims: Spurious Scholarship and the Palestinian Question*, eds. Edward W. Said and Christopher Hitchens, London: Verso, 2001, 181–91; Hershel Shanks, "Archeology as Politics," *Commentary* (August 1986), 50–2; Colin Chapman, *Whose Promised Land?* Updated ed., Oxford: Lion Publishing, 1992; Albert Glock, "Archaeology as Cultural Survival: The Future of the Palestinian Past," *Journal of Palestine Studies* 23:3 (1994), 70–84 and "Cultural Bias in the Archaeology of Palestine," *Journal of Palestine Studies* 24:4 (1995), 48–59; Yael Zerubavel, *Recovered Roots: Collective Memory and the Making of Israeli National Tradition*, Chicago / London: University of Chicago Press, 1995, 22–36; Howard Marblestone, "The Great Archaeological Debate," *Israel Studies Bulletin* 16:1 (Fall 2000), 23–9; Amy Dockser Marcus, *The View from Nebo: How Archaeology is Rewriting the Bible and Reshaping the Middle East*, Boston, MA: Little, Brown, 2000; Netty C. Gross, "Demolishing David," *Jerusalem Report*, 11 September 2000, 40–6; Nadia Abu El-Haj, *Facts on the Ground: Archeological Practice and Territorial Self-Fashioning in Israeli Society*, Chicago: University of Chicago Press, 2001;

Yaacov Lozowick, *Right to Exist: A Moral Defense of Israel's Wars*, New York, etc.: Doubleday, 2003, 32–41; John Quigley, *The Case for Palestine: An International Law Perspective*, rev. and updated ed., Durham, NC / London: Duke University Press, 2005, ch. 8; Jacob Lassner and S. Ilan Troen, *Jews and Muslims in the Arab World: Haunted By Pasts, Real and Imagined*, Lanham, Boulder, etc.: Rowman and Littlefield, 2007, ch. 8; Nur Masalha, *The Bible and Zionism: Invented Traditions, Archaeology and Post-colonialism in Palestine–Israel*, London / New York: Zed Books, 2007. For the problems of recent attempts to establish lineage through DNA, see Diana Muir Appelbaum and Paul S. Appelbaum, "The Gene Wars," *Azure* 27 (Winter 2007), accessed online 21 March 2008, http://www.azure.org.il/magazine/magazine.asp?id=347.

8 "History on the Line: Joseph Massad and Benny Morris Discuss the Middle East," in Joseph A. Massad, *The Persistence of the Palestinian Question: Essays on Zionism and the Palestinians*, London: Routledge, 2006, 163–5.

9 See, e.g., Elie Kedourie, "Religion and Politics," in *The Chatham House Version and other Middle Eastern Studies*, London: Weidenfeld and Nicolson, 1970, 317–50.

10 Négib Azoury, *Le Réveil de la nation arabe dans l'Asie turque ... Partie asiatique de la question d'Orient et programme de la Ligue de la patrie arabe*, Paris: Plon, 1905, v, quoted in Neville J. Mandel, *The Arabs and Zionism before World War I*, Berkeley / Los Angeles: University of California Press, 1976, 52.

11 For a sampling of some of the basic and classic works on Zionism, see *The Zionist Idea: A Historical Analysis and Reader*, ed. and introduced by Arthur Hertzberg, Garden City, NJ: Doubleday and Herzl Press, 1959, reprinted New York: Atheneum,1969; Walter Z. Laqueur, *A History of Zionism*, New York: Holt, Rinehart and Winston, 1972; reissued New York: Schocken Books, 1989 (with a new preface by the author); Shlomo Avineri, *The Making of Modern Zionism: Intellectual Origins of the Jewish State*, New York: Basic Books, 1981; Amnon Rubinstein, *From Herzl to Rabin: the Changing Image of Zionism*, New York: Holmes and Meier, 2000. For some recent analytical interpretations, see Lozowick, *Right to Exist*, 42–9.

12 Mandel, *Arabs and Zionism*, chs. 9–10; Caplan, *Futile Diplomacy* I: ch. 1; N. J. Mandel, "Attempts at an Arab–Zionist Entente, 1914–1914," *Middle Eastern Studies* I (1964–1965), 238–67.

13 Among the rich literature on Arab–Jewish relations in the late Ottoman period, see Emile Marmorstein, "European Jews in Muslim Palestine," in *Palestine and Israel in the 19th and 20th Centuries*, eds. Elie Kedourie and Sylvia G. Haim, London: Frank Cass, 1982, 1–14; Yaacov Ro'i, "The Zionist Attitude to the Arabs, 1908–1914," in ibid. 15–59; Mandel, *Arabs and Zionism*; Gershon Shafir, *Land, Labor, and the Origins of the Israeli–Palestinian Conflict, 1882–1914*, Cambridge / New York: Cambridge University Press, 1989; updated ed., Berkeley / Los Angeles: University of California Press, 1996; Rashid Khalidi, *Palestinian Identity: The Construction of Modern National Consciousness*, New York: Columbia University Press, 1997, ch. 5.

14 Mandel, *Arabs and Zionism*, 76–92, 210–22; R. Khalidi, *Palestinian Identity*, ch. 6.

15 Ahad ha-Am (Asher Zvi Ginzberg), "Truth from Eretz-Israel," *ha-Melitz*, 19–30 June 1891, transl. in Alan M. Dowty, "Much Ado about Little: Ahad Ha'am's 'Truth from Eretz-Israel,' Zionism, and the Arabs," *Israel Studies* 5:2 (2000), 154–81.

16 Theodor Herzl to Youssuf Zia al-Khalidi, 19 March 1899, transl. and reproduced in *From Haven to Conquest*, ed. W. Khalidi, 91–3; see also the extended discussion in R. Khalidi, *Palestinian Identity*, 69–84.

17 Yaacov Ro'i, "The Zionist Attitude to the Arabs, 1908–1914" (1968), reprinted in *Palestine and Israel in the 19th and 20th Centuries*, eds. Kedourie and Haim, 15–59; Laqueur, *History of Zionism*, ch. 5; Alan Dowty, *Israel/Palestine*, 2nd ed., Malden, MA / Cambridge, UK: Polity Press, 2008, 40–4.

18 See, e.g., among hundreds of recent publications, the collection entitled *The Future of Palestine and Israel: From Colonial Roots to Postcolonial Realities*, ed. Aslam Farouk-Alli, Midrand, South Africa: Institute for Global Dialogue, 2007.

19 S. Ilan Troen, "De-Judaizing the Homeland: Academic Politics in Rewriting the History of Palestine," *Israel Affairs* 13:4 (2007), 872–84.

20 Jacob Talmon, *Israel among the Nations*, London: Weidenfeld and Nicolson, 1970; Jacob Tsur, *Zionism: The Saga of a National Liberation Movement*, New Brunswick, NJ: Transaction, 1977; Conor Cruise O'Brien, *The Siege: The Saga of Israel and Zionism*, New York: Simon and Schuster, 1986.

21 Yoav Gelber, "The History of Zionist Historiography: From Apologetics to Denial," in *Making Israel*, ed. Benny Morris, Ann Arbor: University of Michigan Press, 2007, 65.

22 E.g., Dan Bar-On and Sami Adwan, "The Psychology of Better Dialogue between Two Separate but Interdependent Narratives," in *Israelis and Palestinian Narratives of Conflict: History's Double Helix*, ed. Robert I. Rotberg, Bloomington / Indianapolis: Indiana University Press, 2006, 205–24.

23 George Antonius, *The Arab Awakening*, London: Hamish Hamilton, 1938, 386–412. For a critique, see Sylvia G. Haim, " 'The Arab Awakening,' A Source for the Historian?" *Die Welt des Islams*, new ser., 2:4 (1953), 237–50, discussed below, Chapter 11.

24 Maxime Rodinson, "Israël, fait colonial?" *Les Temps modernes* 22 (1967) 253bis, 17–88, later translated as *Israel: A Colonial Settler-State?*, transl. David Thorstad, introduced by Peter Buch, New York: Anchor Foundation, 1973.

25 *From Haven to Conquest*.

26 Edward W. Said, *The Question of Palestine*, New York: Vintage, 1980, 56–114; 2nd ed., with a new preface and epilogue, New York: Vintage, 1992. A more recent and effective presentation of Palestinian history in this light can be found in Rashid Khalidi, *The Iron Cage: The Story of the Palestinian Struggle for Statehood*, Boston, MA: Beacon, 2006.

27 Massad, *The Persistence of the Palestinian Question*, 143, 152–3, 161.

28 Troen, "De-Judaizing the Homeland," 875.

29 Derek J. Penslar, *Israel in History: The Jewish State in Comparative Perspective*, London / New York: Routledge, 2007, 91 (and ch. 5 generally); Gelber, "The History of Zionist Historiography," 64–9. See also Gershon Shafir, "Zionism and Colonialism: A Comparative Approach," in *The Israel/Palestine Question*, ed. Ilan Pappé, London / New York: Routledge, 1999, 81–96. Shafir, often identified with the "critical sociologists," tends to support the colonial paradigm, but with qualifications.

30 *Shared Histories: A Palestinian–Israeli Dialogue*, eds. Paul Scham, Walid Salem, and Benjamin Pogrund, Walnut Creek, CA: Left Coast Press, 2005, 75–91.

31 See the ironic juxtaposition of maps of (1) "The land without a people," showing Palestinian villages and towns and (2) "The people without a land," showing the first Zionist colonies in W. Khalidi, *From Haven to Conquest*, 94–5.

32 See, e.g., evidence cited in Patai, *The Seed of Abraham*, 279–96.

4
Arabs and Jews under the British Mandate: Entrenching Positions, 1917–1928

In late 1917 British forces advanced from bases in Egypt, overrunning positions of the Ottoman Army to conquer the southern half of Palestine to a line just north of Jerusalem and Jaffa. The remainder of the contested land of Palestine/*Eretz-Israel* would come under British control in a second assault within a year. For the next thirty years, what would later become the Arab–Israeli conflict simmered, festered, and became entrenched in Palestine under British rule. During the Mandate period, as it became known, a contest between two national communities would take shape and gain in intensity, building on the nascent rivalry already noted by Azoury and others during the prewar period.

The impact of the 1919 peace settlement at Versailles on the emerging Zionist–Palestinian conflict was complicated and formative. After World War I, in the place of the eastern Mediterranean provinces of the defeated 400-year-old Ottoman Empire, a number of sovereign countries and semi-autonomous territories would emerge, administered as territories mandated by the newly created League of Nations to several Christian European powers. A new map of the Middle East would show a French mandate for Syria and Lebanon, and British mandates for Iraq and Palestine.

In this chapter we examine the impact of the post-war settlement and British rule on the conflict and its protagonists. In setting out the evolving conflict during this period, we will also examine three more core arguments that contribute to its increasing complexity and intractability over time, namely:

3   Did the British create or aggravate the conflict between Palestinian Arabs and Zionist Jews by unduly favoring one party over the other?
4   Were the protests and demands of Palestinian leaders legitimate expressions of an authentic Palestinian national feeling?
5   Did Zionism bring harm or benefit to the indigenous population of Palestine and the region?

Wartime Commitments: Palestine as the "Much Too Promised Land"?

To deal properly with the period of the British Mandate, it is necessary to backtrack briefly to consider wartime commitments and promises made by Britain that would affect the competing claims of Arabs, Palestinians, and Zionists for decades to come. With the Ottoman Empire allied with Germany during World War I, Britain, France, and Russia accompanied their war efforts by the preparation of diplomatic alliances with a view to extending their respective interests and zones of influence into the Middle East. Great Britain was the prime mover in the creation of three main sets of commitments for what should happen once the guns fell silent. Much has been written about the "Eastern Question" or the "Arab Question" and the motives and maneuvers of all the players; what follows is, of necessity, a simplification of some very complicated issues.

Chronologically, the first of these commitments emerged from correspondence exchanged between the Sharif Husayn of Mecca (in the Hejaz, later to become Saudi Arabia) and Sir Henry McMahon, the British High Commissioner in Cairo. From July 1915 through March 1916, a dozen notes and letters were exchanged between the two, setting the stage for an Arab anti-Turkish revolt that began in July 1916 under Husayn and his sons Abdullah and Faysal. In exchange, they expected British support for Arab independence following the defeat of the Ottoman Turks.[1]

Meanwhile, representatives of Britain, France, and Czarist Russia were preparing among themselves a division of the region into spheres of direct and indirect rule. The plans were to include "an independent Arab State or Confederation of Arab States" under divided British and French spheres of influence, or protectorates. Under the terms of the top-secret May 1916 agreement named after Sir Mark Sykes and François Georges-Picot, Palestine was to be under "an international administration."[2]

The third wartime commitment, and the one most directly relevant for our subject, was the Balfour Declaration issued on 2 November 1917, pledging British support for a "Jewish national home" in Palestine. It illustrates the important role of powerful outsiders in this conflict and became one of the seminal, most discussed, and most disputed documents to shape the future of Palestine and Israel. The text itself is short, only 67 words:

> His Majesty's Government view with favour the establishment in Palestine of a national home for the Jewish people, and will use their best endeavours to facilitate the achievement of this object, it being clearly understood that nothing shall be done which may prejudice the civil and religious rights of existing non-Jewish communities in Palestine, or the rights and political status enjoyed by Jews in any other country.

This government decision was transmitted in the form of a brief letter from Foreign Secretary Arthur Balfour addressed to Lord Walter Rothschild, head of the English Zionist Federation.

A mixture of imperial *realpolitik* and religious sentiment combined to help members of the Cabinet respond sympathetically to sustained lobbying efforts by Zionist leaders. Hard-headed political considerations included hopes of gaining international Jewish support for the British war effort and post-war interests. These were combined with the religious beliefs of several influential British statesmen whose reading of Biblical prophecy made them sympathetic to the aspirations of the scattered Jewish people to return to live in the land of their ancestors. The final wording of the Balfour Declaration was the result of several draftings over the course of the preceding five months. Apart from some minor disappointment in the choice of the word "establishment" over "reconstituting" (which would have recognized a *pre-existing* right of Jews to return), Zionists regarded this declaration of great-power support as a major achievement for their movement.[3]

Most problematic in the long term would be the ambiguous phrases outlining what would later become known as a "dual obligation" on the part of the British: a positive commitment to Zionists was conditioned by a negative injunction not to harm the civil and religious rights of the indigenous population of Palestine. This combination contained internal contradictions and a built-in imbalance which contributed to the reasons why it would be rejected by Palestinian and Arab nationalists. Among other things, the latter would point out that the resident population was not referred to as "Arabs" or as "Palestinians," but rather as "non-Jewish," and that it was only their "*civil* and *religious* rights"—not political or national rights—that would be safeguarded.[4]

Much has been written on the question of whether, taken together, these three sets of commitments were inconsistent with each other, and whether the British really believed they would be able to deliver satisfaction on all three promises. Most writers have treated these wartime pledges as the basis for considering Palestine/Israel a "twice promised" or "much too promised land."[5] Others regarded the three overlapping commitments as not necessarily mutually incompatible and as standard international diplomatic practice based on imperial calculations of the day.[6]

British attitudes and behavior contributed to both anti-colonialist resentment among the Arabs and (after some initial euphoria) deep mistrust and suspicion among the Jews. Arab nationalists protested that the British had, despite repeated assurances, betrayed them by not fulfilling commitments enshrined in the McMahon–Husayn correspondence—viz., to recognize Arab independence in specified areas that would include Palestine. The British, in response, claimed that the area that became Mandatory Palestine had been excluded from the promises of Arab independence. Attempts to produce authoritative interpretations of McMahon's territorial commitments (e.g., during the St. James' Palace "round-table" conferences in early 1939) were never totally convincing. Even today, scholars remain divided over the status of this exchange of correspondence and the extent of British promises to, or duplicity towards, the Arabs.[7] One thing was certain: these competing wartime promises led to exaggerated and incompatible expectations among Arabs, Palestinians, and Zionists alike, aggravating already existing tensions and mutual suspicions.

Britain's "Dual Obligation"

In the immediate post-war years the British did attempt to promote their interests in the region while minimally satisfying some of the claims and demands of their French allies, along with those of their new Arab and Zionist clients. During the year of the Paris Peace Conference, for example, British efforts to harmonize relations among these competing factors led to the promotion of an entente, brokered by officials like Colonel T. E. Lawrence ("of Arabia"), between Amir Faysal, (temporarily) enthroned in Damascus, and Dr. Chaim Weizmann of the Zionist Organization. This reconciliation effort actually resulted in the signing of a landmark treaty— but one that remained inoperative partly because of French insistence on ruling in Damascus and ousting Faysal after he proclaimed himself King of Syria in early 1920.[8] In partial recognition of its wartime pledges to King Husayn, Britain during 1921 managed to find thrones for two of his sons: Faysal in Iraq and Abdullah in Transjordan.

Arabs, Palestinians, and Zionists at the time maintained, as their supporters today continue to maintain, different appreciations of the British role and responsibility. As noted, unfulfilled hopes of post-war independence left many Arab nationalists embittered, as the new Mandates appeared to be thinly disguised extensions or modifications of colonial rule. Most Arabs rejected *a priori* the legitimacy of the Balfour Declaration and the terms of the Mandate (see below) which were based on this British pledge. Together with the disappointment and frustration of not enjoying independence in the wake of World War I, Arab nationalists viewed the British role as nefarious and prejudicial to their rights and interests, both in its broader colonialist impact of blocking Arab independence and in its specific implementation in Palestine, with the Mandate's articles fostering a Jewish national home. This thread runs through all official petitions, memoranda, and proclamations issued by the recognized leadership of the Palestinians, the Palestine Arab Congress and its Arab Executive Committee during the 1920s, and the Arab Higher Committee from 1936.

This critical view of the British role can also be found in the writings of analysts and scholars, an early example of which was George Antonius' *The Arab Awakening*, published in 1938. A recent experimental high school curriculum for Palestinian and Israeli students summarized the Palestinian narrative reflecting this view of the British role:

> British imperialism found in Zionism a perfect tool for attaining its own interests in the Arab East, which was strategically and economically important for the Empire. Likewise, Zionism used British colonialist aspirations to gain international backing and economic resources for its project of establishing a Jewish national home in Palestine. This alliance of British imperialism and Zionism resulted in ... the Balfour Declaration[,] ... a conspicuous example of the British policy of seizing another nation's land and resources and effacing its identity. It is a policy based on aggression, expansion and repression of a native people's aspirations for national liberation. ... For the Palestinians, the year 1917 was the first of many ... marked by tragedy, war, disaster, killing, destruction, homelessness and catastrophe.[9]

Needless to say, Zionist and Israeli appreciations of the British role are different. At the time, Zionist leaders expressed gratitude to Britain for becoming the first major power to recognize the Jewish people's claim to return to rebuild their national home in Palestine; they felt further reinforced by similar support expressed by other Western states, both individually and collectively through the League of Nations' adoption of the terms of the Mandate for Palestine. The same recent experimental school curriculum quoted above provided the following summary of the Zionist narrative on the issue of the British contribution:

> The Zionist movement was born in the major centers of Jewish population in Europe, and its purpose was to return the Jewish people to its land and

put an end to its abnormal situation among the nations of the world. ...
[Here follows a description of Zionist immigration and settlement efforts
since 1882.] The first time any country expressed support for Zionism was
in a letter sent by Lord Balfour ... . It expressed the support of the British
Government for establishing a national home for the Jewish people in the
land of Israel.[10]

Notable in this narrative is the emphasis on Jewish self-help, and the
secondary role assigned to the British. This is consistent with the post-
1921 shift in Zionist politics and polemics portraying themselves as an
aggrieved party often having to deal with unfulfilled British commitments,
lukewarm British support on the ground, and a perceived pro-Arab tilt in
British attitudes and policy.

An important turning point in this regard was the mid-1921 creation of
the Amirate of Transjordan in portions of Mandated Palestine territory
east of the Jordan River (in the process of creating a throne for Husayn's
son, Abdullah). The exclusion of this territory from the application of the
Jewish national home provisions of the Mandate was, for many Zionists, a
great disappointment; for followers of Revisionist leader Vladimir
Jabotinsky, it was nothing less than a British "betrayal" and the "first
partition" of their anticipated homeland.[11]

Over the ensuing years, Zionist representatives would address their
complaints and grievances to London and the League of Nations, accusing
the British administration in Palestine of not faithfully implementing
policies that they had expected to promote the growth of the Jewish
national home. This line of argument found moderate and polite expression in the Zionist mainstream, but during the 1930s and 1940s it would
take on more radical (sometimes anti-colonial) rhetoric and action from
militant splinter groups like the *Irgun Zvai Leumi* (the "Irgun," or ETZEL)
and the "Stern Gang" (*Lohamei Herut Israel*, or LEHI).[12]

This critique by Zionists of British betrayal has been carried down
through memoirs and partisan writings.[13] Menachem Begin's memoir,
The Revolt, contains some far-reaching—and far-fetched, if the record
is examined honestly and carefully—accusations of British anti-Jewish
duplicity and a "blueprint" or "Master Plan" for controlling Palestine:

> ... the Arabs, when required, would "rebel" against the "foreign invasion";
> and the Jews would forever be a threatened minority. Each would have to be
> protected from the other—by British bayonets ... . This cycle of events was
> repeated again and again. The Arabs were encouraged, sometimes quite
> openly, to organize attacks on the Jews. Then would come an Inquiry
> Commission with their [sic] reports. A White Paper would be published,
> and immigration stopped or reduced almost to nothing.[14]

Even today one can find on the website of "Christian Action for Israel" a litany of anti-Zionist actions during the Mandate period that were supposedly products of a conspiracy of incitement by British officials.[15]

Therein lay the no-win situation of the British, whose attempts to implement their "dual obligation" under the terms of the Mandate were doomed to disappoint one party or the other—and often both. It would prove impossible for the British to satisfy both the repeated expressions of fears, objections, and resistance by the Arab majority, on the one hand, and Zionist complaints that the British were not fulfilling promised undertakings to them, on the other. Such contested views of the British role have become intertwined with other arguments—e.g., whether Zionists were returning to their homeland or invading someone else's, whether Palestinian objections were genuine or artificially manipulated. While seemingly not as unbridgeable as the first two core arguments outlined above in Chapter 3, the contested versions of the role played by the British only add more fuel to the mix.

In the remainder of this chapter, we will see more evidence of how this divergence is illustrated in the patterns of Palestinian–Jewish–British relations under the Mandate. In the course of this overview we will also encounter and examine the fourth and fifth of our selected core arguments: whether Palestinian nationalism and its opposition to Zionism were authentic, genuine, and based on real grievances, and whether the advent of Zionism brought harm or benefit to the indigenous population.

The Mandate and Its Implementation: Cycle of Protests and Inquiry Commissions

In the wider context of general Arab disappointment with the post-war settlement in which the Middle East was subdivided into French and British spheres of influence under the Mandate system, Arabs from Palestine who had previously been active in nationalist clubs aiming at independence shifted their focus during the immediate post-war years (1918–1921) from a *pan*-Arab struggle to a specifically *local* form of *Palestinian*-Arab nationalism. With the demise of post-war hopes of including Palestine (as "Southern Syria") in an Arab confederation under Faysal in Damascus, the Palestinian Arab leadership focused on resisting the Zionist program in Palestine itself—a program that, if implemented, could certainly block the eventual emergence of an independent Arab state there.[16]

From 1920 onwards, the Palestinian community created—like its rival, the Jewish *yishuv*—a "state within a state." The Palestinian political apparatus consisted at first of two major overarching institutions: the

Palestine Arab Congress, built from local Muslim–Christian associations, and the Supreme Muslim Council. The former elected an Executive Committee, known as the Arab Executive, to represent the spectrum of family, regional, and religious affiliations. Until the mid-1930s, the Arab Executive served as the chief advocate of Palestinian interests in interviews with British officials; it also sent delegations abroad to London and Geneva.[17]

After 1920, both Arabs and Zionists became locked into repeating patterns of complaining to the British colonial officials in Palestine and/or London about the unwarranted or aggressive behavior of the other side, and/or the unfair treatment they were receiving from the authorities in comparison with the other community. Ostensibly insignificant incidents or symbolic gestures took on nationalistic colors as each side jealously sought to maintain and advance its status vis-à-vis the other—as, for example, with the early British decision to recognize Hebrew as one of Palestine's three official languages in government communications, on coins, and on postage stamps.

The Mandate for Palestine, an international legal document consisting of 28 articles, was officially ratified in mid-1922 and came into force a year later. Replicating the same ambivalence and contradictions that were built into the Balfour Declaration, the Preamble and Articles 2, 4, and 6 of the Mandate included some phrasing that was even more favorable to the Zionists than the Balfour Declaration itself—especially the Preamble's recognition of "the historical connexion of the Jewish people with Palestine and ... the grounds for reconstituting their national home in that country." The document provided the three parties with a sort of "constitution" defining Britain's obligations and responsibilities as Mandatory vis-à-vis both the Zionists and the indigenous population, and became a key reference point for official complaints by leaders on both sides.

Throughout the period of British rule, Palestinian representatives rejected the legitimacy of the Mandate itself as being in violation of parts of Article 22 of the League of Nations Covenant. They also pointed out that the Jewish national home provisions of the Mandate were inconsistent with principles of self-determination and pledges enunciated in other British declarations, US president Woodrow Wilson's "Fourteen Points," and the King–Crane Commission Report of August 1919.[18] Over the years, scholars of international law and political commentators have applied their analytical skills to advocating the respective cases for Palestine or the Zionists—attempting to prove, as if in a courtroom, either that the Balfour Declaration and the Mandate for Palestine were illegal documents or that they were legitimate exercises in international (i.e., European) diplomacy and law.[19]

Palestinian protests notwithstanding, the Mandate was adopted and came into force; Great Britain was to administer Palestine much like a Crown Colony, but entrusted with a "dual obligation" to promote the Jewish national home while, at the same time, preparing its population for eventual self-government and independence. The British were required to submit annual reports to the Permanent Mandates Commission of the League of Nations, which also became a forum for representations from Palestinian Arabs and Zionists.

The main issues in contention throughout the Mandate period remained more or less constant, namely: Jewish immigration, land sales to Jews, and the creation of self-governing institutions. Arab representatives called for restriction or elimination of the first two, while pressing for fulfillment of measures to achieve the third (as called for in Article 2 of the Mandate). Zionist representatives argued for support for the first two (as outlined under Article 2 and other terms of the Mandate), claiming that these would bring only benefit and progress to the country and all its inhabitants. They advised and lobbied against steps that would have brought the country closer to full democratic self-government on the grounds that the wishes of the local population could not be used to override the stated objective of creating a Jewish national home.

Looking at the Mandate period as a whole, the following pattern repeats itself at various intervals:

- An administrative measure is adopted implementing an aspect of the Zionist program—e.g., a new government immigration schedule, purchase of lands and establishment of a new Jewish settlement, issuing of a government contract or concession to a Jewish individual or Zionist body.
- Palestinian Arabs express displeasure with such measures as unfairly advancing the interests of the Zionists against their own.
- Periodically, frustrations and other catalysts transform these cumulative complaints and protests into violent outbreaks aimed at the *yishuv* and/or the British administration.
- The British apply police/military measures to restore law and order, and then contemplate (minimal) political steps to deal with the expressed Palestinian grievances.
- A commission of inquiry is created, gathers evidence, and makes recommendations (often issued as a "White Paper") for palliative measures aimed at resolving the most pressing of the complaints presented by the Palestinians.
- Zionists complain about the British handling of the Palestinian complaints.

- Palestinians complain about the inadequacy and/or hypocrisy of British proposed solutions, and/or about Zionist abilities to sidestep or divert plans for recommended changes in British policy in Palestine.

Clashes and Confrontations during the Early Years of the Mandate

This cycle of protest–commission–recommendation could be seen most dramatically in the form of outbreaks of violence in April 1920, May 1921, August 1929, and April 1936. In the first case, three days of anti-Jewish rioting in Jerusalem during the overlapping religious festivals of Nebi Musa, Easter, and Passover left 5 Jews dead and 211 wounded, with 4 Arabs dead and 25 wounded, the latter mostly from British police action. Religious and political tensions at this time had been aggravated by the news from San Remo that Great Britain would indeed be awarded the Mandate for Palestine, and also by defiant protesters waving portraits of Faysal as "King of Syria and Palestine." The reaction of the Zionist leadership was to label the events a "pogrom," blaming "a few Arab agitators" and openly accusing the British administration of complicity and encouragement of the rioters through its indifference and hostility towards the Jews. A military inquiry (the Palin Commission) focused its attention on the failings of the British military administration (shortly to be replaced by a civil one) in the maintenance of law and order.[20]

The 1920 Jerusalem riots, and the subsequent imprisonment of Vladimir Jabotinsky and other Jews involved in attempting to organize armed Jewish defense bands, also marked an important turning point in discussions among *yishuv* and Zionist leaders about the organization of militias to protect Jews from Arab attack. In December of that year, the *Histadrut* (the powerful General Federation of Jewish Labor in Palestine) laid the foundations of the *Hagana* ("defense"), the semi-clandestine Jewish paramilitary force that would be transformed in 1948 into the Israel Defense Forces [IDF]. The *Hagana* built itself on the previous experience and cadres of the watchmen's organizations that had been formed in the pre-1914 period to protect outlying Jewish settlements. Its commanders would be funded by and answerable to the *yishuv* political leadership, and the militiamen would keep a low profile under tacit British acquiescence.[21]

In May 1921, under a new civil administration under Sir Herbert Samuel, Palestinian Arabs attacked Jews in Jaffa and Jewish settlements in the neighboring area. Following factional skirmishes between two Jewish Mayday parades on the outskirts of Tel Aviv, looting and "a general hunting of Jews" in Jaffa spread to a number of places, including a Zionist hostel for new immigrants. After six days of intermittent attacks, some 50 Jews were dead and 150 wounded. In the wake of the riots, Zionist leaders criticized British laxity in protecting Jews, and were extremely concerned with the High Commissioner's decision to suspend Jewish immigration temporarily—a move that they feared would constitute a political precedent that could lead to a *de facto* Arab veto on the progress on the Jewish national home.

In their testimony before the inquiry commission headed by the chief justice of the Palestine Supreme Court, Sir Thomas Haycraft, Zionist and *yishuv* spokesmen stressed the malevolent role played by Arab demagogues, agitators, "effendis" and foreign agents. The Commission's summary of these Zionist submissions merit quotation here as they represent a line of argument that would be used again and again throughout the Mandate period:

> It has been said to us by Jewish witnesses that there was no essentially anti-Jewish question at that time [May 1921], but that a movement against the Jews was engineered by persons who, anxious to discredit the British Government, promoted discontent and disturbance of the peace by stirring up the common people against the Jews. It is argued by them that all the trouble is due to the propaganda of a small class whose members regret the departure of the old regime, because British administration has put an end to privileges and opportunities of profit formerly enjoyed by them. ... These witnesses asseverate that Zionism has nothing to do with the anti-Jewish feeling manifested in the Jaffa disturbances.

Immediately rejecting such an interpretation, the Haycraft Report noted that "the feeling against the Jews was too genuine, too widespread and too intense to be accounted for in the above superficial manner."[22]

This snapshot offers an early example of the recurring argument over the genuineness of Palestinian nationalism and opposition to Zionism, another of the eleven core arguments that make this conflict so contested. During the Mandate period itself, and subsequently in academic and polemical writing, many advocates of Zionism promoted the idea that Arabs living in Palestine were not genuinely opposed to the coming of the Jews—whether because they had no particular political attachment to the country, or because everyone knew that Zionism would bring only great benefit to the local population.

Zionist Responses to Palestinian-Arab Opposition

As we shall see below, those who were on the ground in Palestine could not avoid noticing the periodic expressions of Palestinian Arab opposition to Zionism. How did Zionist and *yishuv* leaders deal with evidence of Palestinian unrest, protest, or resistance? Some have argued that, whether out of arrogance or naïveté, Zionist pioneer settlers had a blind spot and did not see the Palestinian Arabs, who were invisible or a neutral part of the landscape. While it may be true that at some points the contesting claims of the Palestinians were an "unseen question" for many Jews in the *yishuv*, there is ample evidence that not speaking publicly about it was a conscious and tactical decision. For, behind closed doors and notwith-standing the publicly expressed denunciations of agitators and challenges to the credibility of Palestinian protesters, Jews and Zionists did indeed engage in periodic soul-searching and internal debates on the issue of how to deal with Arab rejection.

These stock-taking exercises produced a wide range of explanations and remedies for the opposition Zionists were encountering.[23] The vast majority of Jews and Zionists—inspired by the drive and need for a Jewish homeland in Palestine and believing their own claims to be legitimate and internationally recognized—were unable or unwilling to interpret and accept the outbreaks of 1920 and 1921 as genuine evidence of legitimate Palestinian fears or concerns. Looking back, one is tempted to conclude that those public responses were rationalizations, a form of denial, whether self-serving or self-delusionary.[24]

There were, however, a few Zionist and *yishuv* leaders who did conclude that Palestinian resistance to Zionism was indeed a genuine and natural (rather than artificial or transitory) response. Some were forced to the difficult conclusion that—unfortunately, tragically even—such rejection contradicted and could eventually block the implementation of the Zionist program. A number of possible conclusions flowed from this realization. A minority within this minority concluded that the Zionist dream was therefore unrealizable and had to be abandoned; these individuals "dropped out," became non-Zionists or anti-Zionists.

But there were other, more common, responses. Some, recognizing both the fact and legitimacy of Palestinian opposition, sought ways to adjust their Zionist credo while seeking solutions to the impasse that presented itself. The Zionist Revisionist movement's response to this clash was an unabashedly colonialist one: to proceed to make the Jewish presence an irremovable reality by forcibly overriding the objections of the indigenous population. Those objections were unfortunate and inevitable, in this analysis, but the answer was for Zionists to proceed with immigration, land acquisition, and military strengthening of the *yishuv* until a defensible Jewish state could be created. This has become known as the "iron wall" approach, based on two outspoken articles published in November 1923 by Revisionist leader Vladimir Jabotinsky.

Although they may not have owned up to it, many rival left-wing labor-Zionists shared the same determination to press ahead with immigration, land purchase, and military preparedness (*"hagana"*) as forcefully as needed.[25]

On the other extreme, *Brit-Shalom* (Covenant of Peace), *Ihud* (Unity), and similar organizations dedicated to Arab–Zionist reconciliation proposed that—faced with the reality of rival Arab nationalist demands— Zionists had to downsize or abandon their goal of a Jewish state and pursue other constitutional options instead. One such option was a binational state; others were parity or federal arrangements that would take into account the Palestinian Arabs as a people entitled, equally with Zionist Jews, to share in ruling a future independent state of Palestine.[26] But such deference to the needs of "the other" was reserved to a tiny minority among Zionists and Jews—the majority of whom continued to believe in the legitimacy and historical necessity of their own movement for Jewish statehood.

Psychologically, for many, belief in the inherent goodness and historic necessity of Zionism excluded the logical possibility that rival Palestinian claims and complaints could also be valid. It was therefore comforting to believe that Palestinian protests and objections were temporary or artificially manipulated. Not only for public consumption, as conveyed in testimonies before inquiry commissions, but also in internal correspondence, did Zionist officials invoke evidence and adduce reasons in conscious or subconscious efforts to convince themselves that Palestinian objections were not insurmountable, not driven by genuine popular feeling, discontent, or nationalism, but rather by the manipulation of selfish, special interests—e.g., merchants, landowners, effendis, British pro-Arab conspirators, or anti-British intriguers.

Socialist-Zionists, who were the backbone of the foundational second *aliya* (wave of immigration, 1904–1914), saw the clash through their own ideological prism. In their view, the indigenous society was a feudal one that awaited only the liberation of the Palestinian peasant and working classes—a revolutionary utopia that would arrive with the help of massive Jewish immigration, the assistance and solidarity of a powerful Jewish labor movement, and the creation of a Jewish state. In retrospect, critical scholarship has debunked this vision as naïve at best, hypocritical at worst—fraught with contradictions, such as the insistence on a Jewish majority that meant the exclusion or subservient status of Arab labor. In the end, despite their ideological idealism, labor-Zionists offended and alienated the indigenous population rather than appearing as its saviors or benefactors.[27]

"Making the Desert Bloom"

These *negative* Zionist arguments dismissing Palestinian and Arab objections and resistance were intimately connected to the frequently advanced *positive* argument that Zionism—contrary to Palestinian complaints of dispossession and disenfranchisement—was bringing economic and social benefits to the entire population and the region as a whole. As one Zionist writer explained in 1945,

> The Jews had always hoped that the benefits which their development of Palestine conferred upon the Arabs would naturally result in the process of time in the latter becoming reconciled to the Balfour Declaration. Despite the unprovoked attacks upon them in [1920 and] 1921, they made every effort to live on terms of friendship and goodwill with their Arab neighbours. Not only did they adopt solemn declarations to this effect at Zionist Congresses and on other occasions and reaffirm them in official documents, but they sought to realise them in various spheres of daily life—social, economic, and cultural. Apart from the thousands of Arabs employed in the old Jewish agricultural settlements, hundreds found work in the new industrial undertakings directly due to Jewish enterprise. Arab landowners enriched themselves by selling land to Jews, Arab farmers by disposing of their agricultural produce to them, and Arab landlords by letting houses and other property.[28]

Indeed, such negative and positive arguments were organically linked in the minds of many Zionists who expected—whether naïvely, benignly or cynically—the resident Palestinian population to accept new Jewish immigrants in the same spirit as this fictional exchange in Herzl's 1902 novel, *Altneuland* [Old-New Land], set in a futuristic Palestine of 1923:

> "Just look at that field! [exclaims local Arab leader, Reschid Bey] It was a swamp in my boyhood. The New Society [i.e., Zionist land purchase company] bought up this tract rather cheaply, and turned it into the best soil in the country. It belongs to that tidy settlement up there on the hill. It is a Moslem village—you can tell by the mosque. These people are better off than at any time in the past. They support themselves decently, their children are healthier and are being taught something. Their religion and ancient customs have in no wise been interfered with. They have become more prosperous—that is all."
>
> "You're queer fellows, you Moslems [exclaims Mr Kingscourt, a visiting ex-Prussian nobleman]. Don't you regard these Jews as intruders?"
>
> "You speak strangely, Christian," responded the friendly Reschid. "Would you call a man a robber who takes nothing from you, but brings you

something instead? The Jews have enriched us. Why should we be angry with them? They dwell among us like brothers. Why should we not love them?"[29]

Throughout the Mandate period, Zionist officials knew they had to justify their continued demands for Jewish immigration and opportunities for land purchase by demonstrating that such activity brought benefit, both locally to the Palestinians and also to the British exchequer through revenues that made Palestine a less expensive burden for the British taxpayer. Much effort was devoted to presenting statistics proving this case. Commissions of inquiry during the Mandate period could not but be impressed with the economic and social indicators (e.g., population growth, infant mortality) that showed striking differences between areas within Palestine that had significant vs. insignificant Jewish presence, as well as between Palestine as a whole and the neighboring countries. The Peel Commission (see below, Chapter 5), for example, was impressed by what it saw in 1936:

> The general beneficent effect of Jewish immigration on Arab welfare is illustrated by the fact that the increase in the Arab population is most marked in urban areas affected by Jewish development. A comparison of the census returns in 1922 and 1931 shows that, six years ago, the increase percent in Haifa was 86, in Jaffa 62, in Jerusalem 37, while in purely Arab towns such as Nablus and Hebron it was only 7, and at Gaza there was a decrease of 2 percent.[30]

Academic and popular literature of the time—with titles like *Palestine: Land of Promise* and *Harvest in the Desert*—reinforced this argument for the general public, especially during the 1930s and 1940s.[31]

This emphasis on "Zionism = progress" was often accompanied by disparaging remarks about the ability of the indigenous Arab population to develop the land and the economy. Zionist spokesmen, from Dr. Weizmann on down, frequently likened the Arab–Zionist struggle to one between the "forces of destruction, the forces of the desert" on the one side and "the forces of civilization and building" on the other.[32] Later, in 1947, Zionist representatives would press for the UN partition boundaries of the proposed Jewish state to include the Negev Desert by arguing that

> The largely uninhabited, derelict territory could be developed only by means of bold and comprehensive irrigation schemes, which we alone were ready and able to undertake. Handing over the Negev to the Arabs ... meant abandoning it to eternal neglect and desolation. Only the Jews, who were prepared to invest their full energies and resources in the Negev with no

commercial intent, could redeem the vast arid expanse and uncover the buried mineral deposits.[33]

An interesting corollary to this stress on Zionism as the bearer of economic blessings for Palestine was the argument that the improved economy of Palestine during the Mandate period attracted a significant number of unrecorded or illegal Arab immigrants from the neighboring countries.[34] This not only reinforced the general Zionist claim, but at the same time was used to undermine the genuineness of Palestinian opposition and complaints by implying that (a) Arab as much as Jewish immigration contributed to any apparent overcrowding or landlessness inside Palestine, and (b) that there was nothing particularly distinct about *Palestinian* Arabs, since all residents of the region moved about interchangeably without any particular attachment to a specific country. A variation of these latter claims, clearly aimed at downgrading or discrediting Palestinian and Arab connections to the contested land, surfaced during the 1980s when an American non-specialist published *From Time Immemorial*. The contentious study was seen by one critic as a brazen hoax aimed at perpetuating the "wilderness image" and myth of Palestine being an empty land without a people, waiting only for Zionists to come and civilize it.[35]

From the late 1920s onward, Palestinians and their supporters challenged the economic blessings argument by offering evidence of distress caused by the dispossession of tenant farmers who were forced to migrate to harsh conditions or unemployment in urban areas, even while some people in the Arab sector drew benefits from land sales and from Jewish contributions to the economy of Mandatory Palestine. British and international inquiry commissions throughout the period received submissions and listened to testimonies that described the hardships caused by demographic pressure and economic change wrought by the newcomers, especially in the late 1920s and early 1930s.[36]

On the political level, observers often noted a "disconnect" between economic benefits and political satisfaction. The Peel Commission, for example, found that, though the Arabs had benefited by the development of the country owing to Jewish immigration, this had no impact on lessening their antagonism to Zionism. The Commission's Report paraphrases Arab testimony as follows:

> You say we are better off: you say my house has been enriched by the strangers who have entered it. But it is *my* house, and I did not invite the strangers in, or ask them to enrich it, and I do not care how poor or bare it is [as long as] I am master in it.[37]

Zionist officials, too, had to face the unhappy realization that few if any leaders of the Palestinian community welcomed them in the spirit of Herzl's fictitious Reschid Bey. Vladimir Jabotinsky was one Zionist who was not surprised; he had never shared the mainstream and left-wing view that the "natives" would sell their birthright in exchange for economic benefits.[38] By the 1930s labor leader and newly elected chairman of the Jewish Agency Executive David Ben-Gurion was also aware of the futility of the economic blessings argument in persuading Palestinians to welcome Zionism. "For the Arab leaders," he reported to his colleagues on the Jewish Agency Executive, "there is no value to the economic aspect of the development of the country, even if they admit—and not all of them do—that our immigration brings a *material blessing* to the land. They say—and from an Arab viewpoint I think rightly so—'None of your honey, none of your sting'."[39]

These divergent views on whether Zionism brought economic benefit or damage to Palestine and its people continued throughout the Mandate period to be a crucial part of the representations made in attempts to influence important third-parties. As with other core arguments noted thus far, much effort was expended and continues to be expended in attempts to establish which party is right on this contested point.

The Deceptive Lull

With an eye to defusing tensions and grievances that had threatened the tranquillity of the country during 1920 and 1921, the Colonial Secretary in London (Winston Churchill) and the High Commissioner in Jerusalem (Herbert Samuel) studied the Haycraft Report on the Jaffa riots with a view to establishing Britain's future policy on more solid ground. This they hoped to achieve by taking steps towards setting up (controlled) representative institutions, and by issuing a major statement of policy. In rapid succession, the British presented proposals for a legislative council, an advisory council, and an "Arab Agency"—but these were abandoned after being boycotted by the Palestinian leadership mainly because of their built-in recognition and protections of the Jewish national home and the absence of Arab majority control.[40] In Chapter 11, under the heading of "missed opportunities," we will look at the question of whether the Palestinians, by rejecting these forms of limited self-government, deprived themselves of a tool that might have had some effect in limiting the advance of Zionism.

The Churchill White Paper of June 1922—partly a crisis-management response to the Jaffa riots of May 1921—was an important attempt to clarify and balance both parts of Britain's dual obligation. It would remain in force for the coming fifteen years as the authoritative statement of how Britain planned to rule Palestine. While solemnly reaffirming His Majesty's Government's [HMG] commitment to promoting the Jewish national home, Churchill announced that Jewish immigration would be limited by the country's "economic absorptive capacity"—suggesting that Zionist immigration would not be allowed to strain Palestine's economy but rather only to improve it by bringing progress and prosperity to the land. Further attempts to ease Arab fears included a clarification that the terms of the Balfour Declaration did "not contemplate that Palestine as a whole should be converted into a Jewish National Home, but that such a Home should be founded *in Palestine*" [emphasis in original]—wittingly or unwittingly setting the stage for the possible future partition of the country. Also, in an indirect rebuke to Zionist leader Chaim Weizmann, Churchill affirmed that HMG had no intention of making Palestine "as Jewish as England is English."[41]

The five years following the issuance of Churchill's White Paper and the ratification of the Mandate were uneventful, even peaceful—leading both British and Zionist leaders to conclude that the expressions of Palestinian discontent displayed in 1919–1921 would turn out to be a passing, transitional phenomenon, probably less genuine or deeply felt than had first appeared. Many concluded that this opposition was bound eventually to dissipate as the population came to enjoy the expected economic and other benefits to be brought by European Zionist immigrants. Such, at least, were the optimistic assumptions under which British and Zionist officials operated in the mid-1920s.[42] These assumptions were soon to prove untenable, shattered by renewed tension and violence in 1928 and 1929.

Notes

1   For maps indicating areas promised to the Arabs and those to be shared by the allies under the Sykes–Picot Agreement, see Martin Gilbert, *The Routledge Atlas of the Arab–Israeli Conflict*, 7th ed., London / New York: Routledge, 2002, 5–6.

2   Grey to Cambon, 16 May 1916, reproduced in *The Arab–Israeli Conflict: Readings and Documents*, ed. John Norton Moore, abridged and revised edition, Princeton, NJ: Princeton University Press, 1977, 880–3.

3   The classic examination of the genesis of and politics surrounding the Balfour Declaration is Leonard Stein, *The Balfour Declaration*, London: Valentine Mitchell, 1961. For a legalistic anti-Zionist critique, see W. T. Mallison, Jr., "The Balfour Declaration: An Appraisal in International Law," in *The Transformation of Palestine*, ed. Ibrahim Abu Lughod, 2nd ed., Evanston, IL: Northwestern University Press, 1987, 61–111; W. Thomas Mallison and Sally V. Mallison,

The Palestine Problem in International Law and World Order, Harlow, UK: Longman, 1986, ch. 1.

4 George Antonius, *The Arab Awakening: The Story of the Arab National Movement*, New York: G. P. Putnam's Sons, 1946 [orig. London: Hamish Hamilton, 1938; reprinted New York: Capricorn, 1965], 394–7, 400–2; Rashid Khalidi, *Palestinian Identity: The Construction of Modern National Consciousness*, New York: Columbia University Press, 1997, 22–3, and *The Iron Cage: The Story of the Palestinian Struggle for Statehood*, Boston, MA: Beacon, 2006, 32–3, 36.

5 Aaron David Miller, *The Much Too Promised Land: America's Elusive Search for Arab–Israeli Peace*, New York: Random House (Bantam Dell), 2008; Colin Chapman, *Whose Promised Land? The Continuing Crisis over Israel and Palestine*, Grand Rapids, MI: Baker Books, 2002.

6 See, e.g., Elie Kedourie, *In the Anglo–Arab Labyrinth: The McMahon–Husayn Correspondence and Its Interpretations, 1914–1939*, Cambridge: Cambridge University Press, 1976, reprinted London: Frank Cass, 2000; Julius Stone, *Israel and Palestine: Assault on the Law of Nations*, Baltimore, MD: Johns Hopkins University Press, 1981, ch. 1; Isaiah Friedman, *Palestine, a Twice-Promised Land?* New Brunswick, NJ: Transaction, 2000.

7 Antonius, *Arab Awakening*, chs. VIII, IX, X, XIII; Robert John and Sami Hadawi, *The Palestine Diary*, vol. 1, foreword by Arnold J. Toynbee, New York: New World Press, 1970, 299–312; Kedourie, *In the Anglo–Arab Labyrinth*; Isaiah Friedman, *The Question of Palestine, 1914–1918: British–Jewish–Arab Relations*, London: Routledge and Kegan Paul, 1973, and *Palestine, A Twice-Promised Land?*; Charles D. Smith, "The Invention of a Tradition: The Question of Arab Acceptance of the Zionist Right to Palestine during World War I," *Journal of Palestine Studies* XXII:2 (Winter 1993), 48–61; United Nations, Division for Palestinian Rights, "The Origins and Evolution of the Palestine Problem: 1917–1988—PART I, 1917–1947," posted 30 June 1990, accessed 13 April 2008 at http://domino.un.org/UNISPAL.NSF/561c6ee353d740fb8525607d00581829/aeac80e740c782e4852561150071fdb0.

8 This stillborn agreement has become a landmark, not without some controversy, in the annals of Arab–Zionist diplomatic efforts. See Neil Caplan, *Futile Diplomacy*, vol. I: *Early Arab–Zionist Negotiation Attempts, 1913–1931*, London: Frank Cass, 1983, 36–46, and "Faisal Ibn Husain and the Zionists: A Reexamination with Documents," *International History Review* V:4 (November 1983), 561–614.

9 "PRIME" project ("Palestinians and Israelis Learn the Narrative of 'the Other' "), quoted in Dan Bar-On and Sami Adwan, "The Psychology of Better Dialogue between Two Separate but Interdependent Narratives," in *Israelis and Palestinian Narratives of Conflict: History's Double Helix*, ed. Robert I. Rotberg, Bloomington / Indianapolis: Indiana University Press, 2006, 219–20.

10 Ibid., 219–21.

11 Cf. Map 1.1. Bernard Wasserstein dismisses as right-wing propaganda this interpretation of the British cutting back on territory allegedly promised

for the Jewish national home. See his *Israelis and Palestinians: Why Do They Fight? Can They Stop?* 3rd ed., New Haven, CT / London: Yale University Press / London: Profile Books, 2008, 102–6.

12 On the latter group, see Joseph Heller, *The Stern Gang: Ideology, Politics, and Terror, 1940–1949*, London / Portland, OR: Frank Cass, 1995.

13 E.g., William B. Ziff, *The Rape of Palestine*, New York / Toronto: Longmans, Green and Co., 1938; Samuel Katz, *Days of Fire: The Secret Story of the Making of Israel*, Jerusalem: Steimatsky's [London: W. H. Allen], 1968; Benjamin Netanyahu, *A Durable Peace: Israel and Its Place among the Nations*, rev. ed., New York: Warner Books, 2000, ch. 2 ("The Betrayal").

14 Menachem Begin, *The Revolt [Story of the Irgun]*, foreword by Rabbi Meir Kahane, Los Angeles: Nash Publishing, 1972 [orig. New York: Schuman / London: W. H. Allen, 1948/1951], 30–2. For detailed accusations of British encouragement and manipulation of Arab opposition to Zionism, see Netanyahu, *A Durable Peace*, 55–72.

15 http://christianactionforisrael.org/medigest/june97/backgrnd.html/accessed 13 April 2008.

16 Yehoshua Porath, *The Emergence of the Palestinian Arab National Movement, 1918–1929*, London: Frank Cass, 1974, ch. 2; Khalidi, *Palestinian Identity*, ch. 7.

17 See, e.g., Porath, *Emergence*, chs. 3, 7, 8; Ann Mosely Lesch, *Arab Politics in Palestine, 1917–1939: The Frustration of a National Movement*, Ithaca, NY / London: Cornell University Press, 1979, 90–101, 152–70.

18 E.g., Porath, *Emergence*, 42–9; main documents from 1918–1919 are reproduced in *A Documentary History of the Arab–Israeli Conflict*, ed. and with historical introductions by Charles L. Geddes, New York, etc.: Praeger, 1991, 23–8, 39–78. A smaller sampling can be found in David W. Lesch, *The Arab–Israeli Conflict: A History*, New York / Oxford: Oxford University Press, 2008, 85–90.

19 For the Arab case, see W. F. Boustany, *The Palestine Mandate: Invalid and Impracticable: A Contribution of Arguments and Documents towards the Solution of the Palestine Problem*, Beirut: American Press, 1936; Henry Cattan, *Palestine and International Law: The Legal Aspects of the Arab–Israel Conflict*, 2nd ed. foreword by W. T. Mallison, Jr., London: Longman, 1976, chs. II and III; W. Thomas Mallison and Sally V. Mallison, *The Palestine Problem in International Law and World Order*, Harlow, UK: Longman, 1986, chs. 1 and 2. For the Zionist case, see Nathan Feinberg, *Studies in International Law: With Special Reference to the Arab–Israel Conflict*, Jerusalem: Magnes Press, Hebrew University, 1979; Alan Dershowitz, *The Case for Israel*, New York: John Wiley, 2003, ch. 4.

20 Report of the Court of Inquiry ... regarding the Riots in Jerusalem, 1 July 1920, National Archive, Kew, England (formerly Public Record Office), FO 371/5121, file E9379/85/44; Neil Caplan, *Palestine Jewry and the Arab Question, 1917–1925*, London: Frank Cass, 1978, 57–61.

21 Caplan, *Palestine Jewry*, 76–9; Anita Shapira, *Land and Power: The Zionist Resort to Force, 1881–1948*, transl. William Templer, Stanford, CA: Stanford University Press, 1999, 97–8, 124–5; Yaacov Lozowick, *Right to Exist: A Moral Defense of Israel's Wars*, New York, etc.: Doubleday, 2003, 70–1.

22 Colonial Office, *Palestine: Disturbances in May 1921*, Cmd. 1540, October 1921 (the Haycraft Report), quotation from p. 44; Caplan, *Palestine Jewry*, 85–7, 94.

23 Amos Elon, *The Israelis: Founders and Sons*, New York: Holt, Rinehart and Winston, 1971, 154, 158; Caplan, *Palestine Jewry*, 2–7, 199–203; Anita Shapira, 357.

24 For a comprehensive psychosocial examination of this phenomenon, see Stanley Cohen, *States of Denial, Knowing about Atrocities and Suffering*, Cambridge, UK / Malden, MA: Polity / Blackwell, 2001.

25 V. Jabotinsky, "The Iron Wall" [originally published in Russian *O Zheleznoi Stene*] in *Rassvyet*, 4 November 1923, reprinted in *The Jewish Herald* (South Africa), 26 November 1937, accessed online at http://www.information-clearinghouse.info/article14801.htm; extract reproduced as doc. 11 in *Israel in the Middle East: Documents and Readings on Society, Politics, and Foreign Relations, Pre-1948 to the Present*, 2nd ed., eds. Itamar Rabinovich and Jehuda Reinharz, Lebanon, NH: Brandeis University Press / University Press of New England, 2008, 41–3. Cf. Ian Lustick, "To Build and To Be Built By: Israel and the Hidden Logic of the Iron Wall," *Israel Studies* I:1 (Spring 1996), 196–223; Shapira, *Land and Power*, 154–63; Avi Shlaim, *The Iron Wall: Israel and the Arab World*, London: Allen Lane / Penguin Press, 2000, 11–16.

26 *Dissenter in Zion: From the Writings of Judah L. Magnes*, ed. and introduced by Arthur A. Goren, Cambridge, MA: Harvard University Press, 1982.

27 Gershon Shafir, *Land, Labor, and the Origins of the Israeli–Palestinian Conflict, 1882–1914*, Cambridge / New York: Cambridge University Press, 1989; updated edition, Berkeley / Los Angeles: University of California Press, 1996. For other critiques of labor-Zionism's policies on Arab labor and Jewish–Arab class solidarity, see Michael Shalev, *Labour and the Political Economy in Israel*, Oxford: Oxford University Press, 1992; Zeev Sternhell, *The Founding Myths of Israel: Nationalism, Socialism, and the Making of the Jewish State*, transl. David Maisel, Princeton, NJ: Princeton University Press, 1998.

28 Israel Cohen, *The Zionist Movement*, London: Frederick Muller, 1945, 182 (ch. XII, entitled "Outrages, Enquiries, and Congresses").

29 Theodor Herzl, *Old New Land* [*Altneuland*], transl. from German [1941, 1960] by Lotta Levensohn, with a new introduction by Jacques Kornberg, New York: Markus Wiener and Herzl Press, 1987, 124. Cf. different renderings in Elon, *The Israelis*, 161, and Walter Laqueur, *A History of Zionism*, New York: Schocken, 1976, 133.

30 Palestine Royal Commission, *Report*, 129.

31 Walter Clay Lowdermilk, *Palestine, Land of Promise*, 2nd ed., New York / London: Harper and Bros., 1944; Maurice Samuel, *Harvest in the Desert*, Philadelphia, PA: Jewish Publication Society, 1944; ESCO Foundation

for Palestine, Inc., *Palestine: A Study of Jewish, Arab, and British Policies*, New Haven, CT: 1947.

32 Weizmann speech to Physicians' Conference, Jerusalem, *Palestine Post*, 24 April 1936, p. 1; cf. A. W. Kayyali, *Palestine: A Modern History*, London: Croom Helm, 1978, 191.

33 David Horowitz, *State in the Making*, transl. Julian Meltzer, New York: Alfred A. Knopf, 1953, 268.

34 Fred M. Gottheil, "Arab Immigration into Pre-State Israel: 1922–1931," in *Palestine and Israel in the 19th and 20th Centuries*, eds. Elie Kedourie and Sylvia G. Haim, London: Frank Cass, 1982, 143–52; Arieh L. Avneri, *The Claim of Dispossession: Jewish Land-Settlement and the Arabs, 1878–1948*, New Brunswick, NJ: Transaction Books, 1984 (transl. from the Hebrew [1980] by the Kfar-Blum Translation Group), 30–7.

35 Joan Peters, *From Time Immemorial: The Origins of the Arab–Jewish Conflict over Palestine*, New York: Harper and Row, 1984. For important critiques of this work, see Norman G. Finkelstein, "Disinformation and the Palestine Question: The Not-So-Strange Case of Joan Peters's *From Time Immemorial*," in *Blaming the Victims: Spurious Scholarship and the Palestinian Question*, eds. Edward W. Said and Christopher Hitchens, London: Verso, 2001, 33–69, and his *Image and Reality of the Israel–Palestine Conflict*, new and rev. ed., New York: W. W. Norton [2nd ed., London: Verso], 2003, ch. 2; Yehoshua Porath, "Mrs. Peters's Palestine," *New York Review of Books*, 32:21–2, 16 January 1986, available at http://www.nybooks.com/articles/5249; "Mrs. Peters's Palestine: An Exchange" (Ronald Sanders, Daniel Pipes, Yehoshua Porath), *New York Review of Books*, 35:5, 27 March 1986, available at http://www.nybooks.com/articles/5172.

36 E.g., Arab Executive Committee, Memorandum on the White Paper of October 1930, prepared by Aouni Abdul-Hadi, Jerusalem, December 1930, reproduced [in English] in *Documents of the Palestinian National Movement, 1918–1939: From the Papers of Akram Zuaytir [in Arabic]*, ed. Bayan Nuwayhid al-Hout, Beirut: Institute for Palestine Studies, 1979, doc. 167, pp. 342–50 (land), 350–2 (immigration), and doc. 168 (cover-letter of 5 January 1931), p. 354; Kayyali, *Palestine*, 205; John Ruedy, "Dynamics of Land Alienation," in *The Transformation of Palestine*, ed. Ibrahim Abu-Lughod, 119–38; Janet L. Abu-Lughod, "The Demographic Transformation of Palestine," in ibid., 139–63.

37 Palestine Royal Commission, *Report*, 131. Cf. ibid., 125–30.

38 Jabotinsky, "The Iron Wall," 4 November 1923; also his letter to F. Kisch, 4 July 1925, quoted in Caplan, *Palestine Jewry*, 198–9; Khalidi, *Iron Cage*, 72.

39 David Ben-Gurion, *My Talks with Arab Leaders*, transl. Aryeh Rubinstein and Misha Louvish, ed. Misha Louvish, Jerusalem: Keter, 1972, 80, 15 (for Musa Alami's reported remark "that he would prefer the land to remain poor and desolate even for another hundred years, until the Arabs themselves were capable of developing and making it flower").

40 Porath, *Emergence*, 147–58, 169–78; Lesch, *Arab Politics in Palestine*, ch. 8. For the *yishuv*'s reactions to the same proposals, see Caplan, *Palestine Jewry*, ch. 8.

41 Colonial Office, *Palestine: Correspondence with the Palestine Arab Delegation and the Zionist Organisation*, Cmd. 1700, June 1922 (the Churchill White Paper); reproduced in *The Israel–Arab Reader: A Documentary History of the Middle East Conflict*, 7th revised ed., eds. Walter Laqueur and Barry Rubin, New York: Penguin Books, 2008, 25–9.

42 For a snapshot of British optimism and perceptions of tranquillity, see Colonial Office, *Palestine: Report of the High Commissioner on the Administration of Palestine, 1920–1925*, Colonial No. 15, 1925; Caplan, *Palestine Jewry*, 195–7.

5
Collapse of the Mandate: Rebellion, Partition, White Paper, 1929–1939

Radicalization of Palestinian Politics

The peaceful lull started to unravel after September 1928 owing to an upsurge in religious-incited nationalist tensions. In late August 1929, following a year of incidents, provocations, and demonstrations around Muslim and Jewish holy places, Palestinian worshippers emerged from Friday prayer to attack Jews in Jerusalem. Rumors of Jewish attacks on Muslims sparked similar violence in other places, including savage attacks on the long-established, non-Zionist, ultra-orthodox Jewish communities living in Hebron and Safed. In all, some 133 Jews were killed and 339 wounded, almost all of them by Arabs, with 116 Arab deaths and 232 wounded, caused mostly by British troops and police.[1]

The Hebron massacre, in particular, is still remembered by Jews as the worst of "events of *tarpat*" (the Hebrew acronym for the year corresponding to 1929).[2] In Hebron, 59 men, women, and children were murdered, another 60 wounded, and some mutilated and raped, by mobs. As elsewhere, British police action left something to be desired. Apart from these victims and perpetrators, some 300 Hebronite Jews found protection thanks to the courage of almost two dozen of their Palestinian neighbors. The subsequent evacuation of Hebron's remaining Jews to Jerusalem left a scar for decades. After the 1967 war in which Israel captured the city from Jordanian rule, some Jews sought to restore their ancient community in the midst of hundreds of thousands of Palestinian Arabs.[3]

The 1929 "disturbances" brought the Shaw Commission of Inquiry to Palestine to investigate the underlying causes and to recommend solutions. Between 24 October and 27 December 1929, the commissioners heard evidence from British, Zionist, and Arab counsel and witnesses. Zionist spokesmen sought to incriminate the Mufti of Jerusalem for wilful religious incitement and to indict the British administration for its underpreparedness and laxity in maintaining the firm hand of law and order. Testimony presented by Palestinian witnesses spoke of landlessness and other hardships caused by Zionist immigration and land purchase, as well as their fears of domination by the Jews. While these fears could not have been based on the actual (declining) number of Jews arriving in the country at the time, the Palestinian public was alarmed by nationalist statements and provocations coming especially from members of the Zionist–Revisionist movement, and from other Jews who were making religious claims to take control over the Western (Wailing) Wall, which was also holy to Muslims as *al-Buraq*—the place from which the Prophet Muhammad ascended to Heaven.[4]

To the great disappointment of Zionist and *yishuv* leaders, the Shaw Commission's *Report* published on 31 March 1930 gave more credence to Arab fears and complaints than to their own.[5] A new fact-finding inquiry followed quickly under Sir John Hope Simpson, whose report focused on the economic impact on Palestinian farmers of Zionist immigration and land purchase. Assessment of these reports by the British cabinet led to a new White Paper, issued in October 1930 and bearing the name of Colonial Secretary, Lord Passfield. Meanwhile, an international legal commission appointed by the League of Nations recommended ways of defusing the specifically religious conflict over the Holy Places.

The Passfield White Paper greatly distressed Zionists by focusing on the Arab grievances that it felt needed to be addressed through proposed restrictions on land sales and Jewish immigration. The White Paper also recommended a resumption of suspended discussions towards establishing self-governing institutions in Palestine.[6] But the restrictions envisaged on Zionist immigration, settlement, and land purchase were soon overturned by Prime Minister Ramsay MacDonald, who addressed a letter of reassurance to Dr. Weizmann in February 1931—the product of several months of intensive lobbying in London. What had at first appeared as the worst setback for the Zionists and the greatest victory for the Palestinians vis-à-vis the crucial support of British policy-makers ended in another stalemate. Neither party emerged from the political crisis with much confidence that British policy could be counted on to satisfy its demands.[7]

The years 1929–1931 marked an important turning-point in Arab–Jewish–British relations in Palestine, with each party drawing a number of lessons. Recent events had demonstrated the importance and power of religious symbolism (perceived threats to holy places) in mobilizing the two communities into violent confrontation with distinctly nationalistic overtones. Even if the Shaw and Hope Simpson recommendations were not fully implemented, the door had now been opened to reconsideration of some of the basic premises of the Mandate and the application of its Jewish national home provisions. New ideas for "parity" arrangements in government, cantonization, and other constitutional measures were floated in Zionist circles, while good relations were quietly developed with the Amir Abdullah across the Jordan.[8]

Palestinian leaders took some time to recover from the shock and disappointment of MacDonald's letter to Weizmann, which they considered a betrayal and dubbed the "Black Letter." The Arab Executive's cap-in-hand diplomacy with the British masters of the country was now discredited among a younger generation who would press for more militant forms of resistance.[9] The reports of Development Commissioner Lewis French (December 1931, April 1932) on agricultural development and land settlement confirmed several of the Palestinians' complaints, but left Zionists feeling somewhat vindicated because the extent of the landlessness problem was shown to be less than previously claimed.[10] Wishing to rectify their tactical error of rejecting British proposals in 1922–1923, some Palestinian Arab politicians looked forward to the reopening of discussions towards creating a democratically elected legislative council.

In late October 1933, reflecting a deliberate defiance focused on British rather than Jewish or Zionist targets, Palestinian nationalists organized well-coordinated protests in Jaffa, Haifa, and other towns. British police action against the illegal demonstrations resulted in some 25 deaths and over 200 injuries.[11] The importance of these generally not-well-remembered events lies in their being a forerunner of the 1936 general strike, and in helping to convince a small but growing number of British officials and Zionist leaders that they were now dealing with a genuine national movement and not merely gangs of hoodlums working at the behest of agitators or self-serving, manipulative effendis.

Indeed, Palestinian-Arab politics during the 1930s came to be more effectively organized and directed from below, as a younger and more radical generation grew tired of the political style of the older notables. The Arab Executive Committee became increasingly criticized for its moderation and cooperation with the British, and its ineffective protests against the Mandatory's implementation of Zionist policies. New political parties were formed, not based exclusively on family ties or clan loyalty.[12]

In the northern hill country, an Islamic preacher, Izz ad-Din al-Qassam, embarked on guerilla activities against British and Zionist targets until he was killed in a gun battle in November 1935. Qassam's well-attended funeral channeled and increased the political tensions in the country, which were already rising owing to a number of other factors. London's disappointing response to Palestinian pressure for an elected legislative council contributed to a radicalization of Palestinian political thinking, as did the fears caused by a sharp increase in Jewish immigration during 1933, 1934, and especially 1935, when the highest total (61,854) of Jewish immigrants of any year of the Mandate period was recorded. Political tensions also escalated following disclosures of Jewish arms smuggling activity, while publicity surrounding cases of evicted tenant farmers, especially those from Wadi al-Hawarith in August 1933, focused nationalist criticism of land sales to Jews. The grievances and problems associated with the outbreaks in 1929 had evidently not been solved by intervening inquiry commissions, policy statements, or changes in the Mandate's regulations and administration.

General Strike and Rebellion, 1936

Following several murders, attacks, and counterattacks by Arabs and Jews in mid-April 1936, the British imposed a curfew and declared a state of emergency. The Arab Higher Committee [AHC], a recently formed umbrella grouping of Palestinian political factions, declared a general strike which was accompanied by an armed uprising. What started as "disturbances" soon escalated into what became known as the Palestinian-Arab "revolt" or "rebellion" (*thawra*), seriously challenging British rule and the Zionist policy in Palestine during 1936–1939. While the British civil administration was criticized for its ineffectual response to the violence, including its slowness to empower the military to forcefully pursue the rebels, there can be no doubt that many of the countermeasures taken by police and army—searches, collective fines, curfews, and bulldozing of homes—were indeed harsh, and caused great suffering and bitterness among the Palestinian population.[13]

After more than five months of daily attacks, damage, and disruption caused by the general strike and rebellion, secret diplomacy orchestrated in London yielded identical public statements in early October 1936 by three neighboring Arab rulers (Arabia's Ibn Sa'ud, Transjordan's Abdullah, and Iraq's Ghazi) urging the Palestinians to return to normal life and to put their trust in Great Britain to find a just solution to their grievances. In response (also prearranged), the AHC called off its general strike, and the rebellion subsided. The ceasefire was achieved along with the setting of an important precedent: inviting and allowing regional leaders to intervene in Palestinian affairs. Historians generally portray this turning point as one that harmed, more than it helped, the Palestinians.[14]

During the preceding six months, according to official British accounts, "upward of 1,000 Arab rebels" were killed mostly in clashes with troops and police, along with another 314 dead (including 195 Arabs and 80 Jews) and 1337 wounded (including 804 Arabs and 308 Jews).[15] By all accounts, the zeal and degree of organization (under a network of improvised national committees) had been impressive—albeit accompanied by a degree of violence and intimidation directed against those Palestinians who displayed insufficient commitment and loyalty to the strike and/or to the armed rebels.[16]

Turning Point: The (Peel) Royal Commission

The outbreak gave rise to doubts as to whether the Palestine Mandate was still workable. Important changes during the 1930s contributed to these doubts, notably the deteriorating conditions of European Jews after the rise to power of Adolf Hitler and the successful movement towards greater independence in neighboring Arab countries. Britain's inability to fulfill its dual obligation under the Mandate had become, for some, apparent as the country became torn between two rival, inward-looking and increasingly nationalistic communities.

The lull in the violence paved the way for the British Cabinet to send out a waiting Royal Commission whose terms of reference were more far reaching than any of its predecessors, viz.:

> to ascertain the underlying causes of the disturbances which broke out in Palestine in the middle of April; to inquire into the manner in which the Mandate for Palestine is being implemented in relation to the obligations of the Mandatory towards the Arabs and the Jews respectively; and to ascertain whether, upon a proper construction of the terms of the Mandate, either the Arabs or the Jews have any legitimate grievances upon account of the way in which the Mandate has been, or is being implemented; and if the Commission is satisfied that any such grievances are well founded, to make recommendations for their removal and for the prevention of their recurrence.[17]

On 11 November 1936 the Commission, subsequently known by the name of its chairman, the first Earl of Peel, arrived in Palestine to begin gathering evidence and hearing testimony from British officials and from Zionist and Arab representatives. In Jerusalem the Commission heard from 60 witnesses in public sessions and another 53 in private sessions. In January the Commissioners returned to London and heard two more witnesses in public and another 8 during *in camera* sessions before adjourning to write their report.[18]

The 404-page *Report*, published as a White Paper in early July 1937, stands today as a seminal study of the conflict in all its complexity. In unsentimental and penetrating fashion, the authors paid tribute to the growth and dynamism of the Jewish *yishuv* while acknowledging the deep-seated nationalistic expectations and grievances that motivated both Arabs and Jews to reject each other, as well as continued British rule. Among the Commission's rather daring conclusions was that the Mandate was unworkable. In one of its most quoted lines, the *Report* solemnly affirmed that "[a]n irrepressible conflict has arisen between two national communities within the narrow bounds of one small country." There was, the commissioners went on,

> no common ground between them ... . The Arab community is predominantly Asiatic in character, the Jewish community predominantly European. They differ in religion and in language. Their cultural and social life, their ways of thought and conduct, are as incompatible as their national aspirations. These last are the greatest bar to peace. ... [T]o maintain that Palestinian citizenship has any moral meaning is a mischievous pretence. Neither Arab nor Jew has any sense of service to a single State.[19]

The *Report* proposed partition of the contested country as the only option that offered some hope of a solution:

> Manifestly, the problem cannot be solved by giving either the Arabs or the Jews all they want. The answer to the question "Which of them in the end will govern Palestine?" must surely be "Neither." We do not think that any fair-minded statesman would suppose ... that Britain ought either to hand over to Arab rule 400,000 Jews, whose entry into Palestine has been for the most part facilitated by the British Government and approved by the League of Nations; or that, if the Jews should become a majority, a million or so of Arabs should be handed over to their rule. But, while neither race can justly rule all Palestine, we see no reason why, if it were practicable, each race should not rule part of it.

Recognizing that the idea of partitioning the small country had been considered and rejected previously because of perceived difficulties they did not wish to underestimate, the Commissioners nonetheless concluded

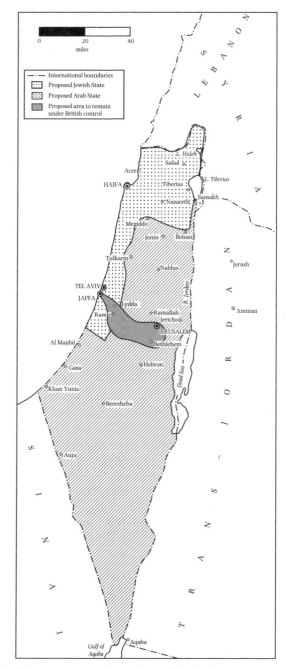

Map 5.1 Peel Commission Partition Plan, July 1937

that "those difficulties do not seem so insuperable as the difficulties inherent in the continuance of the Mandate or in any other alternative arrangement .... . Partition seems to offer at least a chance of ultimate peace. We can see none in any other plan."[20]

This dramatic recommendation was accompanied by proposals for interim restrictions on land sales and a cap on Jewish immigration to be determined, for the first time, not by Palestine's "economic absorptive capacity" (as laid down in the Churchill White Paper of 1922), but rather by the political temperature in the country. The British Government welcomed the *Report* and prepared to take steps towards implementing its main recommendations.

Immediate reactions to the Peel proposals were mostly negative. The Palestinian community was united behind the AHC in rejecting the proposals and repeating its demands for a termination of the Mandate, cessation of Jewish immigration and land purchases, and the creation of an independent Arab state. Particularly offensive to the Palestinian leadership was the Royal Commission's assumption that "the Arabs and the Jews of Palestine stand as opposed litigants with equal rights." Equally objectionable was the Commission's proposed solution which seemed to treat "the Jewish case as the basic issue to be considered and solved without reference to the Arab issues at stake." This represented a clear and unacceptable violation of Arab rights:

> For the Arabs of Palestine are the owners of the country and lived in it prior to the British Occupation for hundreds of years and in it they still constitute the overwhelming majority. The Jews on the other hand are a minority of intruders, who before the war had no great standing in this country, and whose political connections therewith had been severed for almost 2000 years. It is impossible to find either in logic or morality any justification for the attempt to renew this broken connection by the establishment of a so-called Jewish National Home. Such an attempt is without precedent in history, ancient or modern, nor is it based on anything but the force of British Arms and the complete lack of a sense of political reality among the Jews.[21]

The revolt reignited with greater fury, especially after late September 1937 when rebels assassinated the acting British District Commissioner in Nazareth. British countermeasures became more severe, including the outlawing of the AHC; its president, the Mufti al-Hajj Amin al-Husayni, was forced to flee, first to Beirut then to Baghdad, Teheran, and Berlin. Other members of the AHC were either interned or banned from the country, creating a leadership vacuum that would have disastrous consequences for the Palestinian national movement over the coming decade.

In Chapter 11, under our discussion of "missed opportunities," we will examine whether the Palestinians were wise to reject Peel's proposal to partition the country, and whether, by accepting it, they might have contained the further growth of the Jewish national home.

The Peel *Report* and renewed rebellion also had their regional echoes. The Amir Abdullah, who stood to gain territorially by Peel's proposal to incorporate the Arab parts of Palestine into his Transjordanian kingdom, tentatively welcomed the Royal Commission's *Report*; but he soon retreated, as other neighboring Arab leaders echoed each other in denouncing the partition plan. Committees were set up in Damascus, Baghdad, and elsewhere to provide support and solidarity for the Palestinian rebels, culminating in a pan-Arab conference attended by over 400 delegates in Bludan, Syria, in early September 1937. Among the resolutions adopted in support of the Palestinians was one suggesting that the Arab states might be inclined to ally themselves more closely with Britain's European enemies.[22] British leaders had to be concerned with these reactions, as Arab displeasure over Palestine threatened to undermine imperial stability in the Middle East as well as Muslim sympathy in the Indian subcontinent, during a time of growing tensions with European Fascist powers.

With the first overt proposal for a Jewish *state* (rather than a mere "national home"), Zionists were faced with difficult choices that divided the movement as a whole, as well as its various parties and factions. The Zionist Congress meeting in Zurich in July 1937 adopted, by a 2-to-1 majority vote, a set of convoluted resolutions that accepted the principle of partition but sharply criticized many of the details of the plan and mandated the executive to negotiate with the British for a more favorable map.[23] During 1938, the Jewish Agency prepared and submitted elaborate research reports and studies on Palestine's demography and economy to a follow-up "technical" commission (aka the "Palestine Partition Commission") under Sir John Woodhead. Palestinian Arabs boycotted the technical commission, which visited Palestine from late April to early August 1938. The Woodhead Commission *Report* of November 1938 concluded that partition was impractical, and found it impossible to recommend any plan unanimously.[24]

Retreat from Partition

The (not unexpected) inconclusive result of the Woodhead Commission was taken by policy-makers in London as a signal to announce that HMG was no longer wedded to a partition solution. Instead, the British government would invite Arab and Zionist delegates to attend a round-table conference.[25] Strategic calculations regarding the Arab states' loyalty during an imminent confrontation with Germany and Italy played a role in British decisions and attitudes of the day, placing the Zionists at a clear disadvantage as preparations were made for a conference at the St. James' Palace in London. If the conference failed to produce an agreed solution, Colonial Secretary Malcolm MacDonald announced, HMG would take responsibility for promulgating a new policy for Palestine.

Arab and Palestinian delegates in London refused to meet with Zionists, whether as a delegation or as individuals. Predictably, almost three dozen parallel, formal Anglo–Arab and Anglo–Zionist sessions (and three secret tripartite meetings) in early 1939 produced only frustration and no agreement on a future policy for Palestine. Given the deadlock, MacDonald issued a White Paper in May 1939 calling for new restrictions on Jewish immigration and land purchases. Only 75,000 immigrants might enter Palestine over the coming five-year period, after which the Arabs would have to give their consent. The High Commissioner would be given "general powers to prohibit and regulate transfers of land" to Jews with a view to protecting Arab cultivators.[26] Palestine would become independent within ten years, but the final independence of Palestine was to be granted only after a transitional period which, according to MacDonald's original idea, "could not end unless Arabs and Jews were, in practice co-operating and unless there was an assurance that such co-operation would continue."[27]

The MacDonald White Paper, and the London talks leading up to its issue, provided one of the last major examples of the futility of British efforts to play the role of "honest broker" between Arabs and Zionists in their struggle over Palestine. "In the last resort," complained Palestinian leader Awni Abd al-Hadi, the British had cynically placed the Arabs "at the mercy of Jewish co-operation" since they "knew that the Jews would never allow an independent state." Other Arab delegates at St. James' protested that this amounted to placing humiliating (and insuperable) obstacles in the path of the Palestinians' right to self-determination.[28]

For David Ben-Gurion, the British proposals at St. James' amounted to the "handing over [of] the Jews to the mercy of the Arabs"—"a more evil, stupid and shortsighted plan," he wrote to his wife, "cannot be imagined."[29] Following the publication of the White Paper two months later, the *yishuv* reacted with violent protests while Ben-Gurion later vowed to fight the White Paper as if there was no war against Germany, but to fight the war on Britain's side against Nazi Germany as if there were no White Paper.[30]

Both sides found fault with the new British policy. The White Paper outraged Zionists by its immigration restrictions and by its presumption that the promises of the Balfour Declaration and the Mandate were now fulfilled. The new policies seemed to them nothing short of blatant appeasement of the Arab world. Indeed, Palestinians emerged from the St. James' Conference and the White Paper with two distinct political gains:

1 Palestine's right to independence, even though conditional and deferred, was recognized in principle by the Mandatory Power;
2 The right of the Palestinians to safeguard their majority status by preventing the Jews from surpassing a certain proportion of the population was also acknowledged, and the Palestinians would be given an instrument (a veto over immigration after five years) with which to exercise this right.

Still, the exiled Mufti and other Palestinian leaders were adamant in their rejection of MacDonald's new Palestine policy, as it fell short of their demands for full and immediate independence.[31] In retrospect, we can wonder whether Palestinians missed an opportunity to contain or block the further expansion of the Jewish national home at this crucial historical moment by not seizing upon and attempting to operationalize the White Paper's proposals for an independent Palestinian state, which might have emerged within ten years with a clear Arab majority, following limitations on Jewish immigration and land purchases (see also Chapter 11).

The Resort to Force: Violence, Terrorism, and National Struggles

If these two political gains could be called fruits of the rebellion, its costs would prove enormous in terms of the harm done to the Palestinians' potential as a national community to hold their ground against the minority *yishuv* that was struggling for Jewish statehood. In their first sustained uprising against British rule and the Zionist program, the rebels did succeed in inflicting much damage and, at times, were in control of large areas of the country. Official British tallies for 1938, for example, were 5708 incidents of violence, including 986 attacks on the police or military, 651 attacks on Jewish settlements or quarters, 331 bomb throwings, 215 abductions, 720 attacks on telegraph communications, 341 incidents of sabotage on roads and railways, 104 punctures of oil pipelines, and 430 assassinations or attempted assassinations. By the time the second phase of the revolt petered out in mid-1939, the official tally of Arab rebels killed by British military and police forces was another 1000, while the courts had tried and sentenced more than 55 Arabs to death and 3300 to terms of imprisonment. Official figures for other casualties "from terrorist and gang activities" for the 1937–1939 stage of the revolt were 1500 killed (including at least 115 British, 350 Jews and 900 Arabs) and 2000 wounded.[32]

These British figures almost certainly underestimate the real losses, especially among the Palestinians.[33] The high toll of Palestinian Arabs was due in largest part to serious schisms and killings among rival pro-rebel, pro-Mufti and anti-Mufti groups. Referring also to the harsh repression meted out by the British, historian Rashid Khalidi laments the "tragic course that led to the sacrifices of the 1936–1939 revolt, the crushing of which marked the beginning of the end of Arab Palestine."[34] The impact of these losses would be felt most seriously in the leadership vacuum that would handicap the Palestinians during the crucial showdown in the final years of British rule (see Chapter 6).

The second phase of the rebellion also introduced a new element on the *yishuv* side—the increased operations of dissident militias not answering to the official Zionist leadership's strategy of *"havlaga"* (self-restraint). By the Fall of 1937, with the resumption and increase of rebel activity, discipline behind the *yishuv*'s strategy of self-restraint was wearing thin, especially among *Irgun* (IZL, until then known as *"Hagana*-B") militants. In July 1938, two *Irgun* bombings killed 74 Arabs and wounded 129 in Haifa's main market, unleashing a cycle of reprisal attacks targeting Jewish and Arab civilians.[35] Even the mainstream underground *Hagana* adjusted its tactics by taking offensive action against Arab targets, creating "Special Night Squads" under the guidance of an eccentric Christian fundamentalist and Zionist, Orde Charles Wingate, who was seconded for a period to the British military in Palestine.[36] During the coming decade, an even more radical splinter, *LEHI* (aka the "Stern Gang") would join in what would become a major "Jewish revolt" against British rule.[37] (see also below, Chapter 6).

For both Palestinian Arabs and Jews, the 1936–1939 revolt marked the climax of a long-running process of militarization of their respective struggles. From the earliest local skirmishes between Palestinian famers, Bedouin raiders, and Zionist settlers and the creation of *ha-Shomer* (the Jewish watchmen's organization) during Ottoman times, the resort to arms would take on an increasingly important role as the struggle between the two communities became more nationalistic during the Mandate period. From December 1920, as we have noted, the semi-underground *Hagana* organization undertook responsibilities for arming and training Jews who were put to their first tests in May 1921, November 1922, and August 1929.

This brings us to the sixth of the core arguments to be examined: *Is the [Palestinians'] [Arabs'] [Zionists'] [Israelis'] resort to violence justified, or is it to be condemned?* In some ways this contested point can be seen as an offshoot of the core argument over whether Zionists were returning to their land, or invading someone else's. In the cross-fire of argument and counterargument, supporters of one party or the other will attempt to undermine the worthiness of the rival's claim by allegations of its essentially aggressive and violent—and hence "evil"—character. Each party, in its own defense, will assert that it was not initiating violence, but only responding to the violence emanating from the other side. In the post-1948 period, successor versions of these arguments would be launched with rephrased questions: Who is the aggressor, and who is acting in self-defense? Who is the "terrorist," and who is the "freedom fighter"?

Seen from the Palestinians' point of view, the very arrival of Jewish immigrants in what they considered to be their homeland was self-evidently objectionable—especially since these newcomers sometimes openly proclaimed that they intended one day to become a majority and create a sovereign Jewish state within which they, the indigenous inhabitants, would be forced to become a minority. Did this not, they asked, entitle them to object and, if necessary, take up arms to prevent this from happening? Zionism, despite being sanctioned by the international (i.e., European) community, was for the Palestinians an imposition and an intrusion—an inherently aggressive act, even though many of its various small steps may have been carried out by the letter of the law or without actual use of physical force.

Some commentators, advancing the argument made by Palestinians, lay the blame squarely on the British for overlooking and overriding Arab wishes and providing the bayonets without which Zionism could not have implanted itself. In 1970, for example, noted historian Arnold J. Toynbee wrote:

> The reason why the state of Israel exists today and why 1,500,000 Palestinian Arabs are refugees is that, for thirty years, Jewish immigration was imposed on the Palestinian Arabs by British military power until the immigrants were sufficiently numerous and sufficiently well-armed to be able to fend for themselves with tanks and planes of their own.[38]

Back in 1938, George Antonius, a well-to-do intellectual living in Jerusalem, was able to articulate the dilemmas he experienced as the terror and violence of the rebellion continued to inflict their damage on all parties across the country. "No lasting solution of the Palestine problem," he wrote,

> is to be hoped for until the injustice is removed. Violence, whether physical or moral, cannot provide a solution. It is not only reprehensible in itself: it also renders an understanding between Arabs, British and Jews increasingly difficult of attainment. By resorting to it, the Arabs have certainly attracted an earnest attention to their grievances, which all their peaceful representations in Jerusalem, in London and in Geneva had for twenty years failed to do.

Building on his distinction between "moral" and "physical" violence, Antonius went on:

> But violence defeats its own ends; and such immediate gains as it may score are invariably discounted by the harm which is inseparable from it. Nothing can come from the terror raging in Palestine; but the wise way to put an end to it is to remove the causes which have brought it about. The fact must be faced that the violence of the Arabs is the inevitable corollary of the moral violence done to them, and that it is not likely to cease, whatever the brutality of the repression, unless the moral violence itself were to cease.

And, invoking what he called "the path of ordinary common sense and justice," he pointed an accusatory finger in the direction of Zionism:

> There is no room for a second nation in a country which is already inhabited, and inhabited by a people whose national consciousness is fully awakened and whose affection for their homes and their countryside is obviously unconquerable. ... [N]o room can be made in Palestine for a second nation except by dislodging or exterminating the nation in possession.[39]

This sentiment, captured during the peak violent period of the 1936–1939 Palestinian revolt, is still part of the contemporary Palestinian sense of grievance at the definitive loss of their homeland in 1948 to the rival Zionist movement.

From the foregoing one can see how and why Palestinians can and do view themselves, throughout the past 130 years of conflict, as the aggrieved party facing unwarranted Jewish and Zionist aggression. Seen from the Zionists' point of view, the picture is altogether different. They regarded their return to what they considered their homeland, the largely undeveloped and sparsely inhabited *Eretz-Israel* (Palestine), as not only sanctioned by divine promise but also recognized by the world powers and the League of Nations. Hence, when Palestinian objections to their arrival took the form of physical attacks, this constituted for the Zionists an intolerable act of aggression—not unlike the wanton pogroms that Jews faced in eastern Europe and elsewhere. Such threats naturally required Jews in Palestine to defend themselves, especially given the uncertain ability or willingness of the ruling power (after 1917, the British) to provide adequate protection.

Many Israeli and Jewish writers cannot accept the notion of parallels, reciprocity, or symmetry in the violence exhibited by both sides. In setting out his contemporary "moral defense of Israel's wars," Israeli writer Yaacov Lozowick reviews the history and clearly sees no shared responsibility for any "cycle" of violence. What he sees is, rather, a clash between the antithetical forces of "building" (Zionists) and "destroying" (Palestinians) during the Mandate period. For Lozowick and others, the Palestinians' rejection is unwarranted, irrational, total—made even more illegitimate because of its murderous (often antisemitic and genocidal) qualities.[40] This viewpoint is countered by Palestinian historian, Rashid Khalidi, who calls it "the ludicrous but widely believed accusation that the Palestinians were motivated by no more than antisemitism in their opposition to Zionism," whereas in reality they should be viewed as "just ... a colonized people trying to defend their majority status and achieve independence in their own country."[41]

Not all expositions of the Zionist case are so clear cut or one sided as Lozowick's. We can learn much on this tricky question from the analysis of "the Zionist resort to force" between 1881 and 1948 offered by Anita Shapira. The Israeli historian begins her important study *Land and Power* by recreating the worldview of the early pioneers and their Palestine-born offspring, describing the sense of isolation and desperation captured by the phrase *"ein breira"*—there is "no choice," i.e., no choice but to fight the Arabs for control of the country. "Awareness of the existence of an irreconcilable Jewish–Arab conflict," she notes, "contained a subliminal assumption that this was a Gordian knot and could only be cut by the sword."[42]

Unlike Lozowick and others, Shapira has no moral or intellectual difficulty in recognizing and understanding why the Palestinians could choose to reject Zionism. Along with the demographic and economic growth of the *yishuv* during the Mandate period came important changes in Jewish self-perception, radically transformed from that of a weak, defenseless, and easily victimized people to that of a determined and self-confident community able and willing to defend itself. This "growing confidence" and "new self-assurance," Shapira recognizes, were viewed by the Palestinians "as a form of insolence." Increasing Jewish immigration and land purchases, she writes, only demonstrated further to the Palestinians that the Zionist project "naturally harbored an element of aggressiveness."[43] Indeed, the ideological rhetoric of socialist Zionism included phrases like *kibush ha-avoda*, the "conquest of labor."

Shapira notes that Zionist psychology was "molded by the conflicting parameters of a national liberation movement and a movement of European colonization in a Middle Eastern country"[44]—accepting and merging, in effect, both sides of the core argument which we discussed above (Chapter 3) about whether Zionism is a form of colonialism or nationalism. Her examination of the evolution of Zionist attitudes to the Arabs and the use of force yields two distinct approaches. From 1881 to 1936, she believes, Zionist thinking was dominated by a "defensive ethos," which was replaced after 1936 by an "offensive ethos." This transformation reflected the movement's changing fortunes in the real world of international politics and in the regional arena of Arab and Palestinian affairs. The "defensive ethos" had been built on evolutionary and gradualist assumptions regarding the ability of Zionism to flourish under protection of the Turkish and British régimes, ultimately producing a Jewish majority, and thus peacefully take over the country through the power of their critical mass: numbers (immigration), economic infrastructure, newly purchased land, and the creation of colonies and collective settlements.

These optimistic assumptions began to unravel by the early 1930s, as the Palestinians awakened to the dangers that Zionist successes represented to their own aspirations to national self-determination on that same contested territory. By the mid-1930s, Shapira believes, the defensive ethos was already changing, and "functioning as an incubator of enmity and alienation." This allowed *yishuv* political culture to become more influenced by its "nationalist component," which expanded "at the expense of the socialist component" among the youth.[45] The imagery of the stalwart pioneer, worker, and watchman that had been at the core of the mythology and mystique of the earlier defensive ethos was supplanted in the later period of the offensive ethos by that of the intrepid underground fighter or warrior—"the new image of the Jew, proud and courageous, ready to fight back." Young Jews came to believe that "[t]he land was theirs, theirs alone. This feeling was accompanied by a fierce sense of possessiveness, of joyous anticipation of the fight for it."[46]

By the time of the Arab rebellion, and with the deteriorating situation of Europe's Jewish communities, more and more people in the *yishuv* came to the pessimistic conclusion that time was running out for the Zionist project. Increasingly, they became aware of the rising national consciousness of the Arabs in Palestine and the neighboring countries. Equally obvious to these Jews was British self-interest in appeasing these Arab nationalist forces and retreating from the burdensome pro-Zionist commitments enshrined in the Mandate. These factors, made painfully obvious during the Palestinian revolt and the St. James' Conference, combined to force the *yishuv* "to confront the terrifying prospect of a war without any end in sight." One result was "a slow shift in the meaning of the concept of *power* from the sense of a critical mass to physical-military power."[47]

In the internal struggle between left- and right-wing approaches, labor-Zionism's support for a policy of *havlaga* (self-restraint) was pitted against what Shapira describes as the appeal of the *Irgun*'s "[u]nbridled nationalist ideology joined with the sanctification of violence as the exclusive political method."[48]

The challenge was indeed seen as an existential one by followers of Menachem Begin, founder of the *Irgun* and future prime minister of Israel, who unabashedly transformed Descartes's well-known dictum, "I think, therefore I am" from words to action:

[t]here are times in the history of peoples when thought alone does not prove their existence. A people may "think" and yet its sons, with their thoughts and in spite of them, may be turned into a herd of slaves—or into soap. There are times when everything in you cries out: your very self-respect as a human being lies in your resistance to evil.

We fight, therefore we are![49]

This self-understanding of Zionists about the nature and purpose of violence before 1948 has a number of echoes for the wider conflict and for the evolution of parallel attitudes among Palestinians through the 1950s and beyond. One is the logical progression from this militant brand of heroism to the desire to sacrifice oneself for the good of the nation, a willingness to die as well as to kill for the cause—the personal quest for martyrdom. Another is the symmetry and numerous similarities to be found when examining the internal Palestinian debates in the 1960s and afterwards over the role of revolutionary armed struggle in the still unsuccessful quest for Palestinian statehood (see below, Chapter 8).[50]

A third consideration is what political scientist Ian Lustick has called the "solipsistic" use of terror by both sides both before and after 1948. As Lustick convincingly demonstrates, the purposes of resorting to terror include not only drawing attention to one's cause, harming the enemy, and causing the enemy to panic. An equally important function of terror is the liberating and empowering contribution it can make to the identity and self-image of an embattled party.[51] Such views on the inevitability and cleansing power of violence can be viewed as offsetting, in some ways, the demoralizing self-perceptions both parties entertain of their "righteous victimhood."

The overuse and emotional misuse of the very terms "terror" and "terrorism" can create smokescreens that careful analysts need to avoid. For some—including Zionists in the 1930s and 1940s[52]—the label "terrorist" is one to be worn proudly and defiantly. For others—including Israelis and Americans vis-à-vis the Palestine Liberation Organization from the 1960s onward—it is a term of extreme vilification used to discredit one's enemies. Since 11 September 2001 especially, the term has been so liberally applied to discredit opponents and critics as to lose much of its essential meaning.

The parties' resort to violence during the Mandate period has been carried forward to the present day, taking different forms to suit the evolving conflict and improvements in the technologies of war and killing. Arguments over its justification or glorification have continued and remain unresolved, as partisans of both sides follow a predictable script. First, they give eloquent expression to their side's profound and passionate desire for peace, while documenting and denouncing the other party's lack thereof. Then they claim that their resort to violence is in fact legitimate self-defense against the threats and unwarranted aggression perpetrated by the other side. Finally, they supply evidence to dismiss, debunk, or delegitimize claims of the other side that it was merely acting in self-defense. Thus, deeply anchored in a self-evident belief in the rightness of their cause and the purity of their side's intentions and behavior, each side's partisans are locked into a closed-circle argument as they review the history of outbreaks and easily blame the other side for creating the violence that continues to this day.

Notes

1 United Kingdom, *A Survey of Palestine, Prepared in December 1945 and January 1946 for the Information of the Anglo–American Committee of Inquiry*, HMSO: 1946, reprinted 1991 by the Institute for Palestine Studies, Washington, DC, vol. I, 24.

2 Similarly, Zionists and Israelis would recall and refer to the subsequent outbreaks of 1936 by their Hebrew calendar year, *tartzah*.

3 Moshe Kohn, "Massacre Remembered" and "A Belated Thanksgiving," *Jerusalem Post* Intl. Ed., week ending 26 August 1989, pp. 9–10; "Hebron Scroll" [translation of eyewitness report from Aharon Reuven Bernzweig, 2 September 1929], ibid., p. 11; Herb Keinon, "Memories of a Massacre," *Jerusalem Post* Intl. Ed., week ending 9 November 1996, p. 8.

4 Colonial Office, Palestine Commission on the Disturbances of August 1929, *Evidence Heard ... in Open Sittings*, Colonial No. 48, 1930; Porath, *Emergence*, ch. 7; Mattar, *Mufti of Jerusalem*, ch. 3. As can be seen in Table 2.1, official Jewish immigration figures for 1927 and 1928 were –3358 (net emigration) and 10, respectively.

5 Colonial Office, *Palestine: Report of the Commission ... 1929 Disturbances*, Cmd. 3530, April 1930.

6 Colonial Office, *Palestine: Report on Immigration, Land Settlement and Development by Sir John Hope Simpson*, Cmd. 3686, October 1930, extract reproduced in *From Haven to Conquest: Readings in Zionism and the Palestine Problem until 1948*, ed. and introduced by Walid Khalidi, Beirut: 1971 / Washington, DC: Institute for Palestine Studies, 1987, 303–7; *Palestine: Statement of Policy*, Cmd. 3692, October 1930 ("Passfield White Paper"—reproduced in *A Documentary History of the Arab–Israeli Conflict*, ed. and with historical introductions by Charles L. Geddes, New York: Praeger, 1991, 113–40).

7 J. Ramsay MacDonald to Chaim Weizmann, 13 February 1931, reproduced in *The Israel–Arab Reader: A Documentary History of the Middle East Conflict*, 7th rev. ed., eds. Walter Laqueur and Barry Rubin, New York: Penguin, 2008, 36–41; Neil Caplan, *Futile Diplomacy*, vol. I: *Early Arab–Zionist Negotiation Attempts, 1913–1931*, London: Frank Cass, 1983, 84–7.

8 Neil Caplan, *Futile Diplomacy*, vol. II: *Arab–Zionist Negotiations and the End of the Mandate*, London: Frank Cass, 1986, ch. 1.

9 For a good assessment of Arab and Zionist reactions to the crisis of 1929–1931, see Avraham Sela, "The 'Wailing Wall' Riots (1929) as a Watershed in the Palestine Conflict," *The Muslim World* LXXXIV: 1–2 (January–April 1994), 60–94. See also Martin Kolinsky, *Law, Order and Riots in Mandatory Palestine, 1928–35*, London: St. Martin's Press, 1993; Weldon C. Matthews, *Confronting an Empire, Constructing a Nation: Arab Nationalists and Popular Politics in Mandate Palestine*, London / New York: I. B. Tauris, 2006.

10 ESCO Foundation for Palestine, Inc., *Palestine: A Study of Jewish, Arab, and British Policies*, New Haven, CT: Yale University Press, 1947, vol. II, 713–22; Kenneth W. Stein, *The Land Question in Palestine, 1917–1939*, Chapel Hill: University of North Carolina Press, 1984, ch. 5; Bernard Wasserstein, *Israelis and Palestinians: Why Do They Fight? Can They Stop?* 3rd ed., New Haven, CT / London: Yale University Press / London: Profile Books, 2008, 51–3.

11 League of Nations, Permanent Mandates Commission, Minutes of the Twenty-Fifth Session, Geneva, May 30 to 12 June 1934, accessed 14 April 2008 at http://domino.un.org/unispal.NSF/3d14c9e5cdaa296d85256cbf 005aa3eb/eced90aa109e98d40525661600509168; Kolinsky, *Law, Order and Riots*, 172–81; Matthews, *Confronting an Empire, Constructing a Nation*, ch. 7.

12 Yehoshua Porath, *The Palestinian Arab National Movement, 1929–1939: From Riots to Rebellion*, London: Frank Cass, 1977, chs. 2, 5; Ann Mosely Lesch, *Arab Politics in Palestine, 1917–1939: The Frustration of a National Movement*, Ithaca, NY / London: Cornell University Press, 1979, chs. 5, 9; Matthews,

Confronting an Empire, Constructing a Nation, ch. 2; Rashid Khalidi, *The Iron Cage: The Story of the Palestinian Struggle for Statehood*, Boston, MA: Beacon Press, 2006, 82–90.

13 Compare, for example, John Marlowe, *Rebellion in Palestine*, London: Cresset Press, 1946, chs. X, XII, and XIV with A. W. Kayyali, *Palestine: A Modern History*, London: Croom Helm, 1978, ch. 7. For archives-based studies, see Michael J. Cohen, "Sir Arthur Wauchope, the Army, and the Rebellion in Palestine, 1936," *Middle Eastern Studies* IX (1973), 19–34; Tom Bowden, "The Politics of the Arab Rebellion in Palestine, 1936–39," *Middle Eastern Studies* XI:2 (May 1975), 160–9.

14 Marlowe, *Rebellion in Palestine*, 165; Elie Kedourie, "Great Britain and Palestine: The Turning Point," in *Islam in the Modern World and Other Studies*, New York: Holt, Rinehart and Winston, 1980, 93–170; J. C. Hurewitz, *The Struggle for Palestine*, New York: Norton, 1950, 71; Porath, *Palestinian Arab National Movement*, 214; Kayyali, *Palestine: A Modern History*, 198–9; Aaron S. Klieman, "The Arab States and Palestine," in *Zionism and Arabism in Palestine and Israel*, eds. E. Kedourie and S. G. Haim, London: Frank Cass, 1982, 118–36; R. Khalidi, *Iron Cage*, 124.

15 *A Survey of Palestine*, I: 38. For a critical reassessment of these figures, see Walid Khalidi, "Note on Arab Casualties in the 1936–39 Rebellion," in *From Haven to Conquest*, Appendix IV, 846–9.

16 Marlowe, *Rebellion*, ch. X; Hurewitz, *Struggle*, 67–72; Porath, *Palestinian Arab National Movement*, ch. 7; Lesch, *Arab Politics in Palestine*, 217–27. Tom Bowden, in assessing the effectiveness of British counterinsurgency to this insurrection, is less impressed than other scholars and observers by the degree of Palestinian-rebel organization and effectiveness, which he qualifies as "highly developed brigandage" and situates as sitting half-way between "primitive banditry" and a "sophisticated people's revolutionary war." Bowden, "The Politics of the Arab Rebellion in Palestine, 1936–39," 169.

17 Palestine Royal Commission, *Report*, Cmd. 5479, London: HMSO, July 1937, ix.

18 Palestine Royal Commission, *Minutes of Evidence Heard at Public Sessions (with Index)*. Colonial No. 134, London: HMSO, 1937. Reproduced in *The Rise of Israel, vol. 22: The Palestine Royal Commission*, ed. with an introduction by Aaron S. Klieman, New York / London: Garland, 1987.

19 Palestine Royal Commission, *Report*, 370–1.

20 Ibid., 375–6.

21 *Memorandum Submitted by the Arab Higher Committee to the Permanent Mandates Commission and the Secretary of State for the Colonies*, [Jerusalem] dated 23 July 1937, p. 4; reprinted in *The Rise of Israel, vol. 17, Arab–Jewish Relations, 1921–1937*, ed. and introduced by Aaron S. Klieman, New York / London: Garland Publishing, 1987, 218.

22 Bludan resolutions discussed and quoted in Christopher Sykes, *Crossroads to Israel, 1917–1948*, Bloomington / London: Indiana University Press, 1965 [Midland Paperback, 1973], 177. For some interesting primary documents illustrating daily activities, see *Despatches from Damascus: Gilbert MacKereth and*

British Policy in the Levant, 1933–1939, eds. Michael G. Fry and Itamar Rabinovich, Tel Aviv: Dayan Center, 1985, 171–95.

23 Political Resolution of the Twentieth Zionist Congress concerning the Report of the Palestine Royal Commission, reproduced in *The Arab–Israeli Conflict*, ed. John Norton Moore, Princeton, NJ: Princeton University Press, 1974, vol. 3, doc. 25 (pp. 184–6); also quoted and discussed in ESCO Foundation, *Palestine: A Study of Jewish, Arab, and British Policies*, II: 854–6, and Allan Gerson, *Israel, the West Bank and International Law*, London / Totowa, NJ: Frank Cass, 1978, 87–8. For a detailed treatment of the debates, see Yitzhak Galnoor, *The Partition of Palestine: Decision Crossroads in the Zionist Movement*, Albany: State University of New York Press, 1995.

24 Cmd. 5854. See also Yossi Katz, *Partner to Partition: The Jewish Agency's Partition Plan in the Mandate Era*, London / Portland, OR: Frank Cass, 1998.

25 Cmd. 5893.

26 *Palestine: Statement of Policy*, Cmd. 6019, London: HMSO, May 1939.

27 MacDonald, minutes of St. James' Conference meetings with Arabs and with Jews, both 6 March 1939, quoted in Caplan, *Futile Diplomacy* II: 111.

28 Minutes of St. James' Conference meetings with Arabs, 1 and 17 March 1939, quoted in Caplan, *Futile Diplomacy* II: 112.

29 Quoted in Caplan, *Futile Diplomacy* II: 112.

30 Shabtai Teveth, *Ben-Gurion: The Burning Ground, 1886–1948*, Boston, MA: Houghton Mifflin, 1987, 718 and chs. 40–1.

31 Caplan, *Futile Diplomacy* II: 110–13; R. Khalidi, *Iron Cage*, 114–16.

32 *A Survey of Palestine*, I: 43, 46, 49.

33 In his critical reassessment of these figures, Walid Khalidi estimates the total number of Arabs killed at more than 5000, and wounded at just under 15,000. See W. Khalidi, "Note on Arab Casualties in the 1936–39 Rebellion," in *From Haven to Conquest*, Appendix IV, 849.

34 R. Khalidi, *The Iron Cage*, 64, 66–7, 107–8, 111–12.

35 *A Survey of Palestine*, I: 45.

36 On Wingate, see Leonard Mosley, "Orde Wingate and Moshe Dayan," and David Ben-Gurion, "Our Friend: What Wingate Did for Us," *Jewish Observer and Middle East Review*, 27 September 1963, 15–16, both reproduced as ch. 39 in *From Haven to Conquest*, 375–87; Christopher Sykes, *Crossroads to Israel, 1917–1948*, Bloomington: Indiana University Press, 1973, 182–3; Edwin Samuel, *A Lifetime in Jerusalem*, Jerusalem: Israel Universities Press, 1970, 169–71; Samuel Katz, *Days of Fire: The Secret Story of the Making of Israel*, Jerusalem: Steimatzky's [London: W. H. Allen], 1968, 34–5.

37 Yehuda Bauer, "From Cooperation to Resistance: The Haganah 1938–1946," *Middle Eastern Studies* II (1965–1966), 182–210; J. Bowyer Bell, *Terror out of Zion: Irgun Zvai Leumi, LEHI, and the Palestine Underground, 1929–1949*, New York: St. Martin's Press, 1977 [reissued as *Terror out of Zion: The Fight for Israeli Independence*, with a new introduction by the author and a foreword by Moshe Arens, New Brunswick, NJ: Transaction, 1996];

Yigal Elam, *"Haganah, Irgun* and 'Stern': Who Did What?" *Jerusalem Quarterly* 23 (Spring 1982), 70–8.

38   A. J. Toynbee, foreword to Robert John and Sami Hadawi, *The Palestine Diary,* vol. 1, New York: New World Press, 1970, p. xiv.

39   George Antonius, *The Arab Awakening,* London: Hamish Hamilton, 1938, 409–12.

40   Yaacov Lozowick, *Right to Exist: A Moral Defense of Israel's Wars,* New York, etc.: Doubleday, 2003, 63–79. His Chapter 2 is entitled "The British Mandate: The Decisions to Build and Destroy" and Chapter 3 is entitled "1948: Decisions about Genocide."

41   R. Khalidi, *Iron Cage,* 119.

42   Anita Shapira, *Land and Power: The Zionist Resort to Force, 1881–1948,* transl. William Templer, Stanford, CA: Stanford University Press, 1999, 283.

43   Ibid., 107, 139.

44   Ibid., 355.

45   Ibid., 215, 275.

46   Ibid., 186, 275.

47   Ibid., 221–2.

48   Ibid., 248.

49   Emphasis orig. Menachem Begin, *The Revolt [Story of the Irgun],* foreword by Rabbi Meir Kahane, Los Angeles: Nash Publishing, 1972 [orig. New York: Schuman / London: W. H. Allen, 1948/1951], 46.

50   See, e.g., Yezid Sayigh, *Armed Struggle and the Search for State: The Palestinian National Movement, 1949–1993,* Oxford: Oxford University Press / Washington, DC: The Institute for Palestine Studies, 1997.

51   Ian S. Lustick, "Changing Rationales for Political Violence in the Arab–Israeli Conflict," *Journal of Palestine Studies* 20:1 (Autumn, 1990), 54–79, and "Terrorism in the Arab–Israeli Conflict: Targets and Audiences," in *Terrorism in Context,* ed. Martha Crenshaw, University Park, PA: Pennsylvania State University Press, 1995, 514–52. For other perspectives on the role of violence in the conflict, see Lesch, *Arab Politics in Palestine,* ch. 9 ("The Political Use of Violence"); Sheila H. Katz, *Women and Gender in Early Jewish and Palestinian Nationalism,* Gainesville, etc.: University Press of Florida, 2003, ch. 5 ("Politicizing Masculinities: *Shahada* and *Haganah*").

52   E.g., Geula Cohen, *Woman of Violence: Memoirs of a Young Terrorist, 1943–1948,* transl. Hillel Halkin, New York: Holt, Rinehart and Winston, 1966. For a detailed study, see Joseph Heller, *The Stern Gang: Ideology, Politics, and Terror, 1940–1949,* London / Portland, OR: Frank Cass, 1995.

6

Shoah, Atzma'ut, Nakba: 1939–1949

During the course of World War II and the closing years of the Mandate period, the British governed Palestine under the 1939 White Paper's interpretation of their revised obligations to both communities—an interpretation that was challenged and undermined at many turns by both principal parties and their regional and international supporters. The issue of whether Britain unfairly favored one party over the other, in this latest incarnation of Palestine policy as in previous statements, remained and remains one of the unresolved core arguments in the contested histories of Palestine and Israel.

In this chapter we will focus on the impact of the Holocaust in Europe on the situation in Palestine and the creation of Israel. In the course of this momentous decade we note the emergence of several new core arguments between Zionists (soon to become "Israelis"), Palestinians, and Arabs, as the clash between them assumed dramatic and crisis proportions.

The Holocaust and Jewish Immigration to Palestine

In his opening testimony to members of the Peel Commission in Jerusalem on 25 November 1936, Dr. Chaim Weizmann began by elaborating on "the Jewish problem as it presents itself to us today." Citing recent events and unsympathetic or anti-Jewish remarks made by German and Polish leaders, the President of the World Zionist Organization built his case for the Jewish need for immigration to Palestine by pointing to the growing number of Jews "for whom the world is divided into places where they cannot live, and places into which they cannot enter."[1] This was fully two years before the notorious nationwide "Kristallnacht" pogroms in Germany and Austria, which gave notice to the world of the drastic plans the Nazi régime really intended for the Jews of Europe. Within a few years, Jews in Nazi-run territories were subjected to disenfranchisement, round-ups, ghettoization, deportations, firing squads, and ultimately industrial-scale murder which resulted in the death of two-thirds of Europe's 9 million Jews.[2]

In this chapter we explore the connections that have been made between (a) the Holocaust (in Hebrew, *shoah*) and the pre-1948 Zionist–Arab conflict, (b) the Holocaust and the creation of the state of Israel (independence, or *atzma'ut*, in Hebrew), and (c) the Jewish Holocaust (*shoah*) and the Palestinian catastrophe (*nakba*, in Arabic).[3]

From the 1930s until today, Jews, Palestinians, and Arabs have used and misused the Holocaust in their arguments over whose rights are being fulfilled or denied in their contest over Palestine/Israel. In the cross-fire of arguments, there has been no shortage of contentious parallels, comparisons, or "lessons" deduced from that unprecedented event in human history.[4] In our own discussion, we shall try to steer clear of gratuitous misuse and misappropriation—even while conveying accurately how the parties themselves may at times have been guilty of just that.[5]

In Chapter 5 we saw evidence of how events in Europe began to have their impact on Palestine's Arab and Jewish communities, especially with the sharp increase in Jewish immigration in the wake of Hitler's 1933 takeover in Germany. Controversies still persist over a number of issues. Both Jews and Palestinian Arabs, each for their own reasons, raise disturbing questions about why *other* countries—especially the USA and the underpopulated British dominions—were not more generous in easing quotas and visa restrictions, and welcoming Jewish refugees. For example, year-by-year comparisons for Jewish immigration to the US and to Palestine for 1933–1944 are given in Table 6.1[6]

Another question still disputed by observers and historians is whether leaders of the Zionist movement are to be blamed for not placing the elementary humanitarian value of saving lives during the Nazi period ahead of the political advantages of using the Jewish refugee plight as an argument for strengthening the Zionist claim to, and the existing Jewish *yishuv* in, Palestine. These are indeed major controversies worthy of profound ethical and historiographical investigation, but they go beyond the framework of the present study.[7]

In the pages that follow, we shall trace the spillover of the European Jewish crisis onto the situation in Palestine as the nationalist rivalry between the two communities became ever more acute. The immediate impact on Palestine of the rise of Nazism in Europe was plain enough to

Table 6.1 *Jewish immigration to USA and Palestine, 1933–1944*

Year	Jewish immigrants to USA	Jewish immigrants to Palestine
1933	2372	30,327
1934	4134	42,359
1935	4837	61,854
1936	6252	29,727
1937	11,352	10,536
1938	19,736	12,868
1939	43,450	16,405
1940	36,945	4547
1941	23,737	3647
1942	10,608	2194
1943	4705	8507
1944	n.a.	14,464

see. To the mounting insecurity of Jewish communities in various European states was added the huge disappointment that very few countries were willing to intervene to protect the targeted minorities or to welcome refugees. This was especially obvious after the pathetic results of the July 1938 Evian Conference that was convened to mobilize resources for receiving Jews who needed to emigrate from Europe. By this point, Jewish leaders around the globe were left treating Palestine as the main, if not the only, shores of their salvation.[8]

Not surprisingly, the massive increase in the Jewish population sparked Palestinian-Arab fears of being overrun by Jewish newcomers. These fears, as we noted in Chapter 5, were a contributing factor to the outbreak of the 1936 Rebellion. In addition, the appeal of Nazi and Fascist movements and ideologies grew stronger among Arab nationalists who came to view the British and French colonial powers, along with world Jewry and the Zionist movement in Palestine, as their prime enemies. Indeed, within a few years al-Haj Amin al-Husayni, Mufti of Jerusalem and exiled leader of the Palestinian-Arab national movement, would seek to make an alliance with the Third Reich.[9] This constellation of anti-Jewish forces resonated, in its turn, among the Jews of Palestine, increasing their sense of vulnerability and common fate.[10]

In the months and years following the issuance of MacDonald's statement of British policy in May 1939, Zionist representatives and supporters lobbied with increased intensity among Western politicians and diplomats for the abrogation of the White Paper's restrictions on Jewish immigration so that Palestine could better serve as a refuge for those seeking to flee the horrors of Nazi Europe. In May 1942, an emergency Zionist conference was convened at the Biltmore Hotel in New York and passed resolutions calling for immediate mass immigration to *Eretz-Israel*, and also for the postwar creation of a Jewish "commonwealth" (i.e., state) in an undivided Palestine.[11] Going beyond a repetition of the Zionists' official rejection of the 1939 White Paper policy, the Biltmore resolutions constituted the first overt and full Zionist demand for *statehood*—not merely a "national home," and not merely in a *part* of partitioned Palestine.

The Holocaust—then in what would turn out to be its most murderous year for the Jews—was immediate in the minds and hearts of the delegates assembled at this emergency Zionist conference. As American Zionist leader Rabbi Abba Hillel Silver argued at the time:

> We cannot truly rescue the Jews of Europe unless we have free immigration to Palestine. We cannot have free immigration into Palestine unless our political rights are recognized there. Our political rights cannot be recognized unless our historic connection to the country is acknowledged and our right to rebuild our national home is affirmed. The whole chain breaks if one of our links is missing.[12]

This logic of this appeal is an eloquent example of the seventh of our selected core arguments in dispute: *What linkage, if any, should be made between the destruction of European Jewry during the Holocaust and the question of who should rule Palestine/Israel?*

Contrary to the Zionist position outlined above, Arab reaction was to seek to detach, as much as possible, the struggle for Palestine from the European Jewish question. In the concluding pages of *The Arab Awakening*, composed in late 1937 or early 1938, George Antonius was already acutely aware of the impact the Jewish tragedy would have on the struggle for Palestine:

> The relief of Jewish distress must be sought elsewhere than in Palestine, for the country is too small to hold a larger increase of population, and it has already borne more than its fair share. It is for Great Britain who has taken the lead in this work of charity at Arab expense to turn to the vast resources of her empire and to practise there some of the charity she has been preaching . . . .

The treatment meted out to Jews in Germany and other European countries was, in Antonius' words, "a disgrace to its authors and to modern civilisation." But

> [t]o place the brunt of the burden upon Arab Palestine is a miserable evasion of the duty that lies upon the whole of the civilised world. It is also morally outrageous. No code of morals can justify the persecution of one people in an

attempt to relieve the persecution of another. The cure for the eviction of the Jews from Germany is not to be sought in the eviction of the Arabs from their homeland; and the relief of Jewish distress may not be accomplished at the cost of inflicting a corresponding distress upon an innocent and peaceful population.[13]

Seven years later, in the Fall of 1944, at a conference in Alexandria, Egypt, the foundations of the League of Arab States were laid and resolutions in support of the Palestinians were passed, repeating earlier Arab calls for "the cessation of Jewish immigration, the preservation of Arab lands, and the achievement of independence for Palestine." While declaring their regret over "the woes which [had] been inflicted upon the Jews of Europe by European dictatorial states," delegates to the conference echoed Antonius' plea that "the question of these Jews should not be confused with Zionism, for there can be no greater injustice and aggression than solving the problem of the Jews of Europe by another injustice, i.e., by inflicting injustice on the Arabs of Palestine."[14] During a meeting aboard a US warship in the Red Sea in early 1945, President Franklin D. Roosevelt's high-level personal diplomacy sought—in vain—to convince Saudi Arabia's King Ibn Sa'ud to support the opening of the doors of Palestine so as to provide a refuge for Jewish survivors of Nazi Europe. The Arab monarch insisted stiffly that the European Jewish tragedy would have to be solved by the nations of Christian Europe.[15]

Following the defeat of Nazi Germany, the fate of Jewish Holocaust survivors, many of whom were languishing in displaced persons ["DP"] camps, overshadowed all efforts to resolve the already intense intercommunal conflict between Palestinian Arabs and the Jewish *yishuv*. During the three remaining years of the British Mandate, militant Jewish groups experienced a sense of abandonment and desperation, resorting to increasing anti-British and anti-Arab terrorism, declaring their own "Jewish Revolt" against British rule and cooperating with the mainstream *Hagana* to create a temporarily unified "Jewish Resistance Movement."[16] Zionist underground groups also organized secret operations and boatlifts to ferry survivors to the shores of Palestine through a British naval blockade. Only a few ships got through, and many Jewish refugees were caught and sent to be interned in British camps on the nearby island of Cyprus. These events became dramatized for the American and European publics through effective media coverage, especially in the case of the ship *Exodus 1947*, whose passengers were returned to European soil.[17]

As sincerely and as passionately as some came to adopt the view that the only salvation for European Jewish refugees was to throw open the gates of Palestine, Arabs and Palestinians continued to protest that the

Holocaust was a Christian-European and global problem that needed an international solution, one to be undertaken mainly by European powers and their allies. Yet they were unable to win over most Western audiences away from their support for a Zionist/Palestine solution for the survivors of the Holocaust. The Palestinians' main contention, that solving the problem of European Jewish survivors by sending them to Palestine was unjust, fell on deaf ears. The US president commissioned his representative on the Inter-Governmental Committee on Refugees, Earl G. Harrison, to visit the DP camps and to report back on the situation and wishes of the internees. Harrison's report, which unsurprisingly indicated that almost all of them desired to go to Palestine, influenced Truman to press publicly for the immediate admission of 100,000 Jewish refugees to Palestine.[18]

The Anglo–American Committee of Inquiry

In response to growing criticism over their policies on Palestine and Jewish refugees, and coinciding with greater direct American involvement in dealing with the aftermath of war in Europe, British policy-makers in October 1945 agreed to set up an Anglo–American Committee of Inquiry [AACI]. The Committee, jointly chaired by Judge Joseph C. Hutcheson and Sir John E. Singleton and composed of six American and six British members, visited Europe (including displaced persons camps) and Palestine in early 1946, and gathered submissions and testimonies from British, Arab, and Jewish representatives.[19]

Partly because it would be overtaken by events and by a United Nations report sixteen months later, the AACI *Report* of May 1946 is not particularly well remembered today. But its recommendations—surprisingly unanimous, given sharp official Anglo–American disagreements at the time over how to deal with both the refugee and Palestine issues—are worth reviewing here. They offer important insights into the positions of the rival contestants as they stood deadlocked in 1945–1946, especially under the weight of the post-war European situation.[20]

To the great dismay of Arab and Palestinian spokesmen, the AACI clearly and deliberately linked, rather than divorced, the issues of Holocaust survivors and the future of Palestine. The *Report* specifically proposed, as both a humanitarian and political gesture, the immediate entry into Palestine of 100,000 Jewish survivors. As for constitutional arrangements, the Committee sidestepped both partition (as Peel had proposed nine years earlier) and the unitary state (consistently demanded by Arab spokesmen) and recommended instead that the future government of Palestine be based on non-domination and "binational" principles:

(I) That Jew shall not dominate Arab and Arab shall not dominate Jew in Palestine.

(II) That Palestine shall be neither a Jewish state nor an Arab state ... Palestine ... must be established as a country in which the legitimate national aspirations of both Jews and Arabs can be reconciled without either side fearing the ascendancy of the other. In our view this cannot be done under any form of constitution in which a mere numerical majority is decisive, since it is precisely the struggle for a numerical majority which bedevils Arab–Jewish relations... .[21]

Such a radical recommendation testifies to the impact on the commissioners of a small but articulate group of Jewish intellectuals that included world-renowned philosopher Martin Buber and Hebrew University president, Dr. Judah L. Magnes, members of the *Ihud* ("Unity") Association, a successor to the *Brit-Shalom* ("Covenant of Peace") group active in the late 1920s and early 1930s. Today's discussions over the one-state versus the two-state solution for Israelis and Palestinians can look back to the AACI *Report* as the greatest achievement of advocates of what was then called a binational (one-state) solution, although the use of certain terminology has shifted over the years.

As we shall see below, the Committee's proposals were soon overtaken by events, leading to other proposals more palatable to the great powers.

UNSCOP and the Creation of Israel

Even before the outbreak of World War II, Adolf Hitler's successful takeover of Germany helped to convince many formerly non-Zionist and anti-Zionist Jews to appreciate, if not embrace, the Zionist "option" as vital for their physical salvation. For Zionist leaders and ideologues, Hitler and the Holocaust were the terrible proof of the correctness of Herzl's theory and the urgent need for a Jewish state in Palestine. Deriving little comfort from this confirmation of the Zionist thesis, many were overcome with grief by the war's end, knowing that, for millions already murdered, a Jewish state would come too late. From 1946 to 1948, little else seemed to matter to Jewish community leaders as they mobilized for what they treated as a life-and-death campaign to turn Palestine into a Jewish state that could welcome those who managed to survive the horrors of the war.

During the postwar period, the linkage between the questions of Jewish DPs in Europe and the future of contested Palestine was indeed a central focus of public discussion, offering the Zionist movement an unprecedented advantage in garnering world sympathy in a contest that the Palestinian Arabs simply could not win. In February 1947 the British returned the Palestine problem to United Nations General Assembly, which proceeded in May to appoint the final investigative body of the period: an eleven-member Special Committee on Palestine [UNSCOP].

Following the familiar pattern of previous commissions, the Special Committee gathered evidence (some of which was simply updated versions of material submitted a year earlier to the AACI) and heard testimony from mid-June to late July 1947. UNSCOP's visit to Palestine came exactly at the right time for Committee members to witness, firsthand, the arrival and subsequent deportation of survivors aboard the refugee-laden ship *Exodus 1947*.[22] Owing to a boycott declared by Palestinian leaders, the Committee heard testimony only from non-Palestinian Arab representatives in Beirut and Amman. It had been decided in advance that UNSCOP would *not* visit the camps in Europe (as the AACI had done), but several members nevertheless organized their own unofficial side-trip to Indersdorf, Hahne, and other DP camps while the Committee based itself in Geneva to complete the writing of its report.[23]

The majority *Report* submitted by UNSCOP on 31 August 1947 recommended the partition of Palestine into independent Jewish and Arab states and a *corpus separatum* for Jerusalem under international administration, to be bound by economic union.[24] There can be no doubt that Committee members were affected, as the AACI had been, by the plight of European Jewish Holocaust survivors. The determination of which lands, and how much territory, should be accorded to the proposed Jewish state was influenced not only by the vaunted creative abilities of the Jews to "make the desert bloom" but also by the need to absorb the expected hundreds of thousands of Holocaust survivors. In the end, after debate and slight amendments, the boundaries of the proposed Jewish state would comprise 55 percent of the land surface of Mandatory Palestine, including the largely unpopulated Negev Desert. Its population would comprise roughly 500,000 Jews and 400,000 Arabs—an extremely large Arab minority by any standard.

During September, October, and November, 1947, discussions ensued in committees and plenary of the UN General Assembly meeting at Lake Success, NY. Public debates over both technicalities and principles were accompanied by extensive behind-the-scenes lobbying in UN corridors as well as with the foreign ministries and home governments of many member-states. The contrast between pro-Palestinian and pro-Zionist accounts of these fateful months is dramatic. Pro-Arab narratives portray strong-arm tactics ruthlessly used by Zionists and their powerful (often American) supporters to push weak or wavering small states to vote for partition.[25] Pro-Israeli accounts depict the whole process as a campaign waged by "a small, feeble people, without sovereignty or influence"

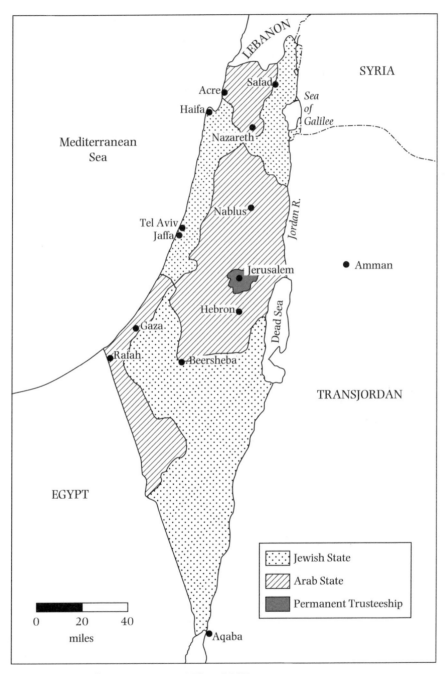

Map 6.1 United Nations Partition Plan, 1947

fighting against "overwhelming" odds to win statehood through the required two-thirds vote in the General Assembly.[26] Even after discounting hyperbolic and propagandistic excesses, there remains a large gap between the contested accounts of how the UN partition plan came to be adopted, with Palestinians and their supporters claiming foul play and Zionists/Israelis viewing the achievement as a valiant uphill struggle against heavy odds. Another question that continues to receive varying answers is the extent to which Western guilt for what had happened to the Jews in the Holocaust was a factor affecting the ultimate voting decisions of UN member-states.[27]

On 29 November 1947, the UNSCOP proposals were finally adopted, with slight modification, in General Assembly Resolution 181 by a vote of 33 in favor, 13 against, with 10 abstentions.[28] Zionists were elated by the result, while Palestinians and Arabs were outraged, vowing to defend Arab Palestine from what they considered the unjust imposition of a Jewish state therein. More than the perceived unfairness and particulars of the proposed plan and map, Palestinians objected in principle to an outside body, the United Nations, forcing the demands of a minority against the wishes of the indigenous majority. This brings us to recognize, as the eighth of our selected core arguments: *Was UNGA Resolution 181 (Partition) a legitimate exercise of the authority of the United Nations in international law, and were the Arab states and the Palestinians wise to reject it?*

Like the earlier unresolved questions over the legality of the Mandate for Palestine and the later dispute over Israel's settlement activity in the territories it occupied during the June 1967 war, the chief protagonists of the first part of this debate tend to be experts in international law. Anyone venturing into the legalistic niceties and Latin principles invoked by these experts should not be surprised to discover the fact that many of these lawyers are only human, and can often be intensely partisan commentators who see few shades of gray between the competing positions. Thus, pro-Palestinian advocates, echoing the minority arguments raised during the debates at Lake Success in the Fall of 1947, challenge the legality of the UN to force a solution that was contrary to the expressed wishes of the majority of the population. The General Assembly, they argue, lacks the power (held by the Security Council) to *enforce* its decisions by applying sanctions; its powers are only to *recommend.*[29] Taking the contrary legalistic position, pro-Israeli experts argue that the Resolution was a just and legitimate one, and register a countercriticism against the Arab states for defying the expressed will of the United Nations when they chose to attack Israel in May 1948.[30] The absence of any UN sanctions against the Arab states for their invasion of Palestine became, for Israel and its supporters, the first example of a litany of criticisms of the alleged anti-Israel biases of the world body, tempering their jubilation at the historic vote of 29 November 1947 which had recognized the Jews' right to a sovereign state in part of Palestine.[31]

Other, more political/historical, arguments flow from this crucial legal debate. Israelis and their supporters criticize the Palestinians and the Arab states by portraying their rejection of the UN partition plan as proof of aggressive attitudes and warlike intentions. A corollary is that, by their refusal to accept a partitioned Arab state in part of Mandatory Palestine and their attempt to block the creation of the Jewish state as proposed by Resolution 181, the Arabs and Palestinians are themselves to blame for the Arab–Israeli war of 1948 and must bear full responsibility for all its negative consequences—i.e., loss of territory to Israel, loss of the opportunity to create a Palestinian state, and especially the lot of the Palestinian refugees. We will discuss this below, and again later (Chapter 11) under the heading of "missed opportunities."

War: *Atzma'ut* and *Nakba*

The outbreak of the war, known to Israelis as the War of Independence (*milhemet ha-atzma'ut*) and to Palestinians as the Catastrophe (*al-nakba*), can be dated alternatively as 30 November 1947 (the day after the UNGA passed Resolution 181) or 15 May 1948, when the Provisional Government of Israel declared its independence on the day of the departure of the British, precipitating an attack by Egyptian, Syrian, and Jordanian forces. Fighting continued, off and on, until early 1949. The war took the lives of some 6000 Israelis—a heavy proportion of the total population; 13,000 to 16,000 Palestinians, and 2000 to 2500 other Arabs, with many additional thousands of wounded.[32]

Israelis and their supporters have often portrayed the crossing by these armies of the frontiers of the former Mandatory Palestine as not only a violation of UN Resolution 181 but also the launching of a war of extermination, with blood-curdling rhetoric about "driving the Jews into the sea." From the perspective of the Palestinians and the Arab states, this external military intervention was an effort to save the Arab portions of Palestine from being overrun by superior Zionist forces.[33] Palestinians themselves participated as members of local militias without much central military or political coordination. Adding to the confusion were troops sent under the auspices of the Arab League (the Arab Liberation Army [ALA], led by Fawzi al-Qawuqji) and bands recruited by the Muslim Brethren in Egypt. The armies of Lebanon and Iraq also took part in the fighting on limited fronts, while Yemen and Saudi Arabia sent token contingents.

The deeper perceptions and self-views of Palestinians, Arabs, and Israelis in this war are starkly different, and have often been oversimplified. In the mainstream Israeli narrative of *milhemet ha-atzma'ut*, the beleaguered and poorly armed few triumphed against the well-armed and better-equipped many, just as the biblical David had bravely taken on and slain the mighty Goliath. The new Israelis, in this narrative, narrowly escaped annihilation only by their own valiant efforts.[34]

Palestinian and Arab accounts of the war show themselves confronting better-organized and highly motivated Zionist militias who had for years been secretly training and arming themselves in preparation for this day, while they themselves were ill prepared, poorly led, and disorganized, also at the mercy of neighboring Arab armies whose motives and maneuvers were, despite official statements, not primarily dedicated to the salvation of Palestine for the Palestinians. Their disastrous military performance during 1947–1949 was, in the words of historian Rashid Khalidi, also "in an important sense no more than ... a tragic epilogue to the shattering defeat of 1936–39." The behavior of the Arab states during the 1947–1949 struggle for Palestine followed the pattern set in the late 1930s, when they assumed the political initiative and responsibility for the Palestine cause—with "each major Arab state ... follow[ing] its own line and seek[ing] to serve its own interests, generally with disadvantageous consequences for the Palestinians."[35]

Recent research by historians has attempted to cut through the competing propaganda and self-views as underdog to establish more accurate and realistic estimates of the balance of forces during various stages of the 1947–1949 Arab–Israeli war for Palestine. Most historians now tend to discount the Israeli myth that they were the "few against the many" in this war. While the entire Arab world by population and land mass does appear overwhelming when juxtaposed with the tiny Jewish *yishuv* numbering between 600,000 and 650,000 in 1947, the effective fighting forces doing battle on the ground were more favorable to the Zionist side. For example, during the first stage of the war (sometimes labeled the "civil war"), before the invasion of regular Arab armies, *Hagana* and other Zionist militias registered some crucial strategic victories over the local Palestinian fighters and ALA forces, benefiting from better motivation, coordination under a central command, and superior numbers of fighters, in the range of almost 50,000 Jews (including reserves) against fewer than 10,000 Arabs.[36] For the first weeks of the fighting, however, Zionist forces were not as well equipped as those fielded by the Arab states.

Another controversy about the conduct of the war takes one step further the core argument over the British role that we examined in Chapter 4. In the Zionist–Israeli view, Britain after 1947 continued to supply and provide diplomatic cover for its main Arab state clients, Jordan and Iraq, thereby encouraging them in their warlike ambitions and ultimate assault on the incipient Jewish state. Yet, among Palestinians there is no corresponding expression of gratitude towards the British for being helpful allies in any way. Was it not British bayonets, Palestinians asked, that had provided three decades of support for the Jewish national home to grow to the point of being able militarily to take over the country? Palestinians also blame the British governor of Haifa for colluding with *yishuv* leaders and *Hagana* officers in helping the latter take over the mixed city in April 1948.[37] An even more serious denunciation is reserved for British collusion with King Abdullah of Jordan (and indirectly with the Zionists) by giving HMG's blessing to his plan to annex portions of the West Bank, thereby preventing the creation of a Palestinian state that might have been led by the Mufti (then in exile in Cairo) or his allies.[38] Arabs also blamed other outsiders for the success of the Zionists in the war: the USA in particular, the Soviet Union to a lesser extent, and Zionist agents operating in both countries who provided manpower and smuggled arms that supported and fueled the Zionist militias in their military takeover of lands beyond the UN-recommended partition borders.[39]

This first Arab–Israeli war resulted in the creation of the sovereign state of Israel, which was accepted into membership of the United Nations in May 1949. After four General Armistice Agreements were signed with Egypt, Jordan, Syria, and Lebanon in 1949, the frontiers of the new state of Israel extended beyond those recommended in the UN partition plan to cover approximately 78 percent of the area of former Mandatory Palestine.

The territory that might have become a Palestinian Arab state under the 1947 UN partition plan now lay in fragments. Although British, American, and United Nations officials would continue for several years thereafter to refer in their documentation and speechmaking to an entity called "Palestine," by mid-1949 the country once known under that name was parceled out among the new state of Israel, Jordan (the West Bank, annexed in 1950), and Egypt (the Gaza Strip).[40]

The Catastrophe, *al-nakba*, left the Palestinians with the loss of a homeland, the destruction of their society, and the displacement, flight, and/or expulsion of more than half the Arab population (between 650,000 and 750,000 people). These latter Palestinians became refugees, stateless, the wards of a new UN agency known as UNRWA.[41] For the next two decades they would be known internationally as the "*Arab* refugees"—with the term "Palestinian" receding into the background. The refugees' right to return to their homes or be compensated was recognized in Article 11 of

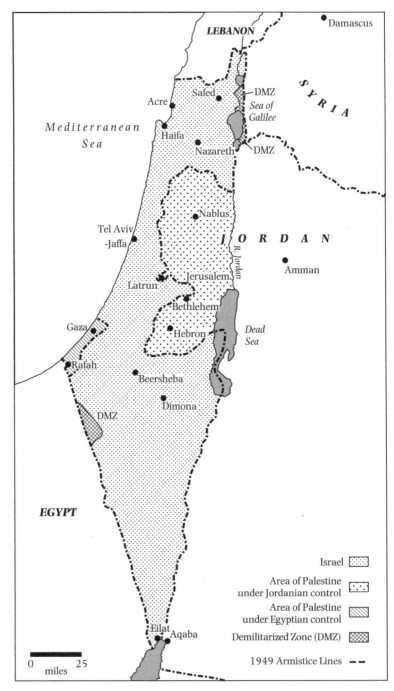

Map 6.2   Israel and Her Neighbours, 1949–1967

UN General Assembly Resolution 194, passed on 11 December 1948.[42] But, for a series of complex reasons summarized below, the Palestinian refugees and their descendants still exist today, and their rights under this resolution remain unimplemented.

One of the most contentious of the core arguments that emerged during the first Arab–Israeli war was: *How did Palestinians become refugees in 1948–1949? And why did they remain refugees for so long?* Politicians, propagandists, and historians have focused much energy over the years trying to establish whether the Palestinians became refugees as a result of voluntary flight, a by-product of war, or deliberate expulsion at the hands of Zionist and Israeli armed forces. Even today opinion remains sharply divided, with the methods and motives of researchers being challenged as much as the historical facts and arguments themselves.

For years, official and unofficial Israeli versions have claimed that most of the Palestinians left their homes voluntarily or under orders from Arab commanders to evacuate temporarily so as to return after the Jews were defeated. This explanation was challenged in the 1960s by an Irish journalist's examination of BBC monitoring of Arabic radio broadcasts, and later by scholars digging through archive files that began to become accessible in the 1980s.[43] Pro-Zionist accounts sometimes cite cases of Jews appealing to Arabs to remain—most prominently in the evacuation of the Arab communities in the mixed towns of Haifa and Tiberias in April 1948. The implication is that these appeals to remain were typical, whereas they were based on unique circumstances and their sincerity remains, to this day, in dispute.[44] Recent research based on oral history testimonies has tended to discount this blanket indictment of the Arab leadership, and to support the contrary version—viz., that in many cases Palestinian and Arab leaders exhorted the population to remain in place.[45]

Apologists on both sides—those dedicated to proving or disproving Arab or Zionist/Israeli moral-political responsibility for the flight and/or expulsion of the Palestinian population—will selectively bring forth supportive parts of the extensive evidence available, while ignoring or discrediting those accounts that undermine or contradict their thesis. Thus, for example, Efraim Karsh revisited the 1948 war after sixty years, selectively drawing on an impressive array of new documentation, including previously unseen files in the *Hagana* and IDF archives, in order to argue that "none of the 170,000 to 180,000 Arabs fleeing urban centers, and only a handful of the 130,000 to 160,000 villagers who left their homes, had been forced out by the Jews" prior to 14 May 1948.[46]

Such research findings are not dispassionate, but rather are geared to serve in the unfinished battles aimed at proving or refuting the currently pervasive view that Zionist militias and Israeli forces deliberately and systematically expelled the Palestinian population. Critics of Israel's actions point to a secret, or not-so-secret, master-plan, the *Hagana's "Tochnit Dalet"* (Plan D), comprehensive and systematic battle orders for seizing Arab-populated areas. Some regard Plan D as proof of the Zionists' intention to "ethnically cleanse" newly captured lands of their Palestinian population (see also Chapter 11).[47] For some observers, this intention to expel Palestinians during the war is intimately connected to hopes and plans, dating back to Herzl and under discussion across the entire Zionist political spectrum, to remove—or "transfer"—the indigenous Arabs to make room for the creation of a Jewish majority population.[48]

One of the most thorough and balanced pieces of research on the refugee question is *The Birth of the Palestinian Refugee Problem*, published by Israeli "new historian" Benny Morris (see also Chapter 11) in 1987, and revised in 2004.[49] Morris' account included revelations of previously unknown massacres, rape, expulsions, and looting committed by Israeli forces that shocked Israeli and pro-Zionist readers and earned him much notoriety on both sides of the Israel–Palestine divide. But his painstaking research did not lead him to support the thesis that the Palestinians became refugees as a result of an overarching Zionist master-plan for the "ethnic cleansing" of Palestine's Arab population. In subsequent debates, Nur Masalha and others criticized Morris for failing to follow his own evidence to what they felt was their logical conclusion.[50] Forced to re-examine his findings and treatment, Morris responded in 2004 to these critics that by admitting that pre-1948 support for the idea of "transfer" was more extensive than he had realized, but replying also that "the connection between that support and what actually happened during the war is far more tenuous than Arab propagandists will allow."[51]

Faced with these contested interpretations, some of which may remain unresolved, we may conclude that between 1947 and 1949 almost three-quarters of a million Palestinians became refugees as a result of a combination of causes, with varying degrees of shared responsibility among the various actors and combatants:

- Many fled to avoid the "normal" cruelties and brutality of war.
- In some locations, *yishuv*–British cooperation and collusion helped to coerce Palestinians to leave.
- Many fled in extreme panic, especially as a result of the widely publicized and originally exaggerated reports of atrocities committed by the *Irgun* and *LEHI* attackers on the Palestinian village of Deir Yasin in early April 1948.[52]

- In certain sectors Zionist militias and IDF units deliberately emptied villages and expelled thousands.
- Many Palestinian Arabs left their homes out of demoralization and confusion caused by an absence of effective leadership and discipline within their community.

As for the supplementary question—*Why have the Palestinians remained refugees for so long?*—it too remains contentious, with all parties pointing the finger of blame at others. While many of the 20th-century's post-war refugee problems have been either resolved or mitigated by combinations of international humanitarian relief and political accommodation, the Palestinian case is an anomaly whose resolution seems, if anything, more difficult today than it ever was. From time to time, international bodies and actors have sought a formula for compensation, repatriation, or resettlement, but with no breakthrough of the impasse.[53]

Israelis and their supporters lay the blame for the non-resolution of this problem squarely on the Arab states, mainly their refusal to sign full peace treaties (see also Chapter 7, below). If they had proceeded with the expected next steps towards peace and normalization, Israel claimed, the signatories to the 1949 armistice agreements could have been able to dispose of outstanding questions including boundaries and refugees. The Arab states' insistence on continuing the state of war and their refusal to recognize and deal with Israel have been, in the Israeli view, a major stumbling block in finding a solution to the Palestinian refugee problem.

In the crossfire of accusations, Israelis and their supporters further blame the Arab states, with the connivance of UNRWA ("a sinecure for bureaucrats and a breeding ground for hatred and irredentism"),[54] for deliberately and cynically perpetuating the condition of the refugees, so as to

- avoid any humanitarian or political responsibility to resettle and integrate them among their own Arab populations;
- maintain the refugees' bitterness and feelings of revenge, so as to prepare them to one day return (if readmitted) as a "fifth column" to destabilize the Jewish state or (if not readmitted) to serve as saboteurs and *feday'un* (commandos) to attack Israel, or
- have the refugees serve as a propaganda tool (if not readmitted) in the Arabs' unfinished war against Israel.[55]

Arabs and Palestinians accuse the Israelis of not only having deliberately expelled large numbers of Palestinians but also callously refusing to recognize the Palestinian refugees' internationally sanctioned right, under Resolution 194, to return to their homes or be compensated.

Israelis, in response, declined to implement this clause in the UN General Assembly resolution, in part pointing out (as the Arabs did regarding GA Resolution 181 on partition) that the Assembly has only the power to *recommend*, not to *enforce*.

But behind this legalistic Israeli position lay more than mere quibbling or tough bargaining tactics. With the same intensity and conviction as the displaced Palestinians believed they had an uncontestable right to return to their homes, the new Israeli leadership in 1948 and 1949 took a clearly defined position against their return.[56] In declining the UN Mediator's late July 1948 personal appeal for a gesture to relieve the hardships being endured by the first waves of Palestinian refugees, Israel's new Foreign Minister, Moshe Shertok (later Sharett) wrote to Count Folke Bernadotte conveying his country's argumentation connecting Arab states' responsibility for the war with the fate of the Palestinian refugees:

> Arab mass flight from within Israel and Israel-occupied areas is a direct effect of Arab aggression from the outside. ... The Arab Governments and the Great Power [the allusion is to the UK] which espoused their cause cannot have it both ways: do everything they can to undermine and destroy the State of Israel, and then, having failed, require the State of Israel to take over the liability for the results of their own reckless action.
>
> ... [T]he Provisional Government [of Israel] is not in a position, as long as a state of war exists, to readmit the Arabs who fled from their homes on any substantial scale.

Sharett, who otherwise embodied a moderate diplomatic approach to Israel's dealings with the Arabs and the Palestinians, went on to elaborate the deeper reasoning behind what soon became the official firm line of Israeli governments against a return of Palestinian refugees:

> The Palestinian Arab exodus of 1948 is one of those cataclysmic phenomena which, according to the experience of other countries, changed the course of history. It is too early to say exactly how and in what measure the exodus will affect the future of Israel and of the neighbouring territories. When the Arab States are ready to conclude a peace treaty with Israel, this question will come up for constructive solution as part of the general settlement and with due regard to our counterclaim in respect of the destruction of Jewish life and property. The long-term interests of the Jewish and Arab populations; the stability of the State of Israel and the durability of the basis of peace between it and its neighbours; the actual position and fate of the Jewish communities in the Arab countries; the responsibility of the Arab Governments for their war of aggression and their liability for reparations [—all these] will be relevant to the question of whether, and to what extent and under what conditions, the former Arab residents of the territory

of Israel should be allowed to return. For such a comprehensive and lasting peace settlement the Provisional Government of Israel is ever ready, but it holds that it cannot in fairness be required to carry through unilateral and piecemeal measures of peace while the other side is bent on war.[57]

Despite the passage of UNGA Resolution 194 and repeated follow-up resolutions over the years, Israel has consistently rejected any massive return of Palestinian-Arab refugees.[58] From an early point the Israeli position was that it would consider only plans for resettlement (outside of Israel) and/or compensation of refugees, and only within the context of Arab moves towards non-belligerency (e.g., cancelling the Arab boycott and blockade of Israel) and eventual comprehensive peace. Israel has offered to consider limited family reunification as a humanitarian issue, but has ruled out any wholesale return by right.

The persistence of the Palestinian refugee issue, unresolved over so many generations, has created a major stumbling block for anyone attempting to find a solution to the Israeli–Arab and/or Israeli–Palestinian conflicts. Since the Oslo breakthrough and the start of direct Israeli–Palestinian negotiations in 1993, the refugees' claimed "right of return" looms large among the obstacles to a comprehensive and durable peace, one of the thorniest unresolved issues in Palestinian–Israeli diplomacy (see also Chapter 10, below).

Nakba and *Shoah*: Victims versus Victims, Once Again

As if the Palestinian refugee issue were not intractable enough on its own, it becomes worse when compounded with arguments about the connection between the Holocaust and the struggle for Palestine, i.e., the interlocking of the tragedies of Jewish and Palestinian Arab refugees.[59] Between 1947 and 1949, during and after the fighting, not one but two forced migrations took place, producing complications that would last for generations. Hundreds of thousands of Palestinian Arabs fled or were expelled, leaving behind homes and property which the new state of Israel, in seeking to alleviate an acute housing shortage, turned over to many of the hundreds of thousands of European Jewish refugees and also to Jews fleeing their homes and abandoning their assets in Arab and Muslim countries during 1948–1951.[60]

Many Israelis at the time hoped that this phenomenon would be treated as an "exchange of populations" (as had happened between Greece and Turkey, for example, following World War I), and thus resolve the refugee problem quickly. The Arab states and the Palestinians refused to see the refugee issue (and its proposed solution) in these terms.[61] Seen from their perspectives, as noted above, innocent Palestinian Arabs were unjustly being made to pay for the Holocaust, to pay for the sins of Europe.

Israelis and Zionists continue, to this day, to differ with Palestinians and Arabs over the extent to which the plight of European Jewry during the 1940s should be linked to the Zionist plan for, and claim to, Palestine— our seventh core argument outlined above. A few intellectuals and academics have been able to break away from the consensus of their respective national communities on this highly emotional issue.[62] But, for the vast majority, one's position on the connection between the two issues is deeply felt and impervious to contradiction or rational persuasion.

Since 1949, these facts and perceptions have become part of the two parties' contrasting national narratives and their reciprocal sense of victimhood. Israel's military victory had brought to the Jews *tkuma* (redemption) following their ultimate victimization, the *shoah*. *Atzma'ut* (independence) and statehood changed these Jews and Zionists into the first Israelis.[63] The Arabs' battlefield defeat brought on their *nakba*: the loss of Palestinian lands, loss of a potential nation-state, and the creation of a sizable refugee population scattered throughout the region and beyond.

This feeling of unfair victimization, caught between the Holocaust and the first Palestine war, has remained deeply rooted among many Palestinians to this day and is highly resistant to explanation or counterargument. Some Palestinians vigorously denounce what they regard as Zionist and Jewish manipulation of post-Holocaust guilt and sympathy in efforts to sidestep or marginalize legitimate Palestinian claims and concerns.[64] Even when addressing Jewish Israelis in a non-confrontational and empathetic manner forty years after the events, leading Palestinian–Israeli writer Emil Habibi nevertheless characterized the Holocaust "as the original sin which enabled the Zionist movement to convince millions of Jews of the rightness of its course" and concluded his essay with the following sentence: "If not for your—and all of humanity's—Holocaust in World War II, the catastrophe that is still the lot of my people would not have been possible."[65]

Most Israelis would fail to see themselves, and Israel's rescue of a part of endangered European Jewry, as the cause of the Palestinian refugee problem. In terms of Deutscher's allegory of the man jumping from the burning building (Chapter 2), they would respond that pre-1948 Jewish immigration had mostly benefited the local Arab population, rather than "falling on" and "crippling" it, and that the Arab "sufferer" did far more deadly things than merely "swear revenge" to spark the cycle of violence that came to mark the conflict. Given the decades-long Arab rejection of

Israel and threats to its existence, along with periodic resurgences of antisemitism around the globe, Israelis view the Holocaust in a different light; for them it is still an "open wound."[66]

Yet such argumentation does little or nothing to earn Arab sympathy or quell Arab resentment on the issue. The promulgation of Israel's Law of Return in 1950,[67] endowing automatic Israeli citizenship to any Jew applying for it, was a belated answer to a hostile or indifferent world which had not offered sanctuary to Jews fleeing for their lives. For the Palestinians, however, this Law confirmed Israeli moves to prevent exiled Palestinians from returning to their pre-1948 homes, and became en-twined in the package of unresolved grievances which increased Arab bitterness. Taken together with Israel's rejection of UNGA Resolution 194, Arabs and their supporters accuse Israeli governments of acting in a racist, discriminatory manner in defiance of the international community.

Social psychologists have rightly identified these parallel and exclusive feelings of victimization over these two issues as key obstacles to mutual understanding between Israelis and Palestinians. "Generally," write Dan Bar-On and Saliba Sarsar,

> both sides mourn their own man-made cataclysm separately. There is an underlying fear that the acknowledgement of the tragedy of the "other" will justify their moral superiority and imply acceptance of their collective [raison d'être]. For the Palestinians, accepting the Jewish pain around the Holocaust means accepting the moral ground for the creation of the State of Israel. For the Israeli Jews, accepting the pain of the 1948 Palestinian refugees means sharing responsibility for their plight and their right of return.[68]

Recognizing this two-pronged, deep-rooted psychological barrier to Israeli–Palestinian reconciliation, some peace activists have developed special activities aimed at sensitizing Palestinians and Jewish Israelis to each other's primal pains and fears. Special programs about the *shoah* and trips to former concentration camps have been geared to educating Israel's Palestinian-Arab citizens not only about the reality and the facts of the Holocaust, but also about the impact this event still has on their Jewish fellow-citizens, generations later (see also Chapter 7).[69] Meanwhile, grass-roots organizations like *Zokhrot* ("they remember") seek to open the minds and hearts of Israeli Jews to acknowledging the Palestinian losses and suffering that are still felt as a result of the *nakba*.[70] Mutual recognition of each other's pain is a difficult first step (see also Chapter 12). Even more difficult is agreeing on the extent to which that pain creates any entitlement.

Notes

1 Chaim Weizmann, "The Jewish Case," 25 November 1936, *The Letters and Papers of Chaim Weizmann*, series B [Papers], December 1931–April 1952, ed. Barnet Litvinoff, Rutgers, NJ: Transaction Books / Jerusalem: Israel Universities Press, 1984, paper #22, 100, 102.

2 On the November 1938 Kristallnacht pogroms and their significance as a turning point in the Holocaust, see Lucy S. Dawidowicz, *The War against the Jews, 1933–1945*, New York, etc.: Bantam Books, 1986, 99–106.

3 Parts of this chapter are drawn from my article, "The Holocaust and the Arab–Israeli Conflict," in *So Others Will Remember: Holocaust History and Survivor Testimony*, ed. Ronald Headland, Montreal: Vehicule Press, 1999, 82–97.

4 I use the term "unprecedented" advisedly, as Professor Yehuda Bauer does, to avoid the problematics and polemics of the "unique-versus-universal" debates regarding the Holocaust. See Yehuda Bauer, *Rethinking the Holocaust*, New Haven, CT / London: Yale University Press, 2001.

5 For a recent contribution to this discussion see Leonard Grob and John K. Roth, eds., *Anguished Hope: Holocaust Scholars Confront the Palestinian–Israeli Conflict*, Grand Rapids, MI: Eerdmans, 2008.

6 Walid Khalidi, *From Haven to Conquest: Readings in Zionism and the Palestine Problem until 1948*, Beirut 1971; 2nd printing, Washington, DC, 1987, Appendix VI, 855.

7 For a sampling of the latter controversies, see ibid., introduction, lviii–lvix, 853–5; Christopher Sykes, *Crossroads to Israel, 1917–1948*, Bloomington / London: Indiana University Press, 1965 [Midland Paperback, 1973], 187–9, 377–80; Tom Segev, *The Seventh Million: The Israelis and the Holocaust*, New York: Hill and Wang, 1993; Shabtai Teveth, *Ben-Gurion and the Holocaust*, New York: Harcourt Brace, 1996; Dina Porat, *The Blue and the Yellow Stars of David: The Zionist Leadership in Palestine and the Holocaust, 1939–1945*, Cambridge, MA: Harvard University Press, 1990; Idith Zertal, *From Catastrophe to Power: Holocaust Survivors and the Emergence of Israel*, Berkeley / Los Angeles: University of California Press, 1998; Idith Zertal, *Israel's Holocaust and the Politics of Nationhood*, Cambridge: Cambridge University Press, 2005.

8 Sykes, *Crossroads to Israel*, 183–9.

9 Yehoshua Porath, *The Palestinian Arab National Movement, 1929–1939: From Riots to Rebellion*, London: Frank Cass, 1977, 76, 119; Francis R. Nicosia, *The Third Reich and the Palestine Question*, Austin: University of Texas Press, 1985; Philip Mattar, *The Mufti of Jerusalem: al-Hajj Amin al-Husayni and the Palestinian National Movement*, rev. ed., New York: Columbia University Press, 1992, ch. 8; Zvi Elpeleg, *The Grand Mufti: Haj Amin al-Hussaini, Founder of the Palestinian National Movement*, transl. David Harvey, ed. Shmuel Himelstein, London: Frank Cass, 1993, ch. 2; Avraham Sela, "Arab Nationalists and Nazi Germany, 1939–1945," in *So Others Will Remember*, ed. Headland, 70–81.

10 For example, the Hebrew national poet Haim Nahman Bialik wrote phrases like "The entire world is my gallows" in his writings about the 1936 Arab

revolt. Anita Shapira, *Land and Power: The Zionist Resort to Force, 1881–1948*, transl. William Templer, Stanford, CA: Stanford University Press, 1999, 225.

11 Biltmore Program, 11 May 1942, reproduced in *The Israel–Arab Reader: A Documentary History of the Middle East Conflict*, 7th rev. ed., eds. Walter Laqueur and Barry Rubin, New York: Penguin, 2008, 55–7; Yehuda Bauer, *From Diplomacy to Resistance: A History of Jewish Palestine, 1939–1945*, Philadelphia, PA: Jewish Publication Society, 1970, ch. 6.

12 Abba Hillel Silver, "Toward American Jewish Unity," in *The Zionist Idea: A Historical Analysis and Reader*, ed. Arthur Hertzberg, New York: Atheneum, 1969, 597. A classic exposition of this case was also made at the time for the general American public by Dr. Chaim Weizmann, "Palestine's Role in the Solution of the Jewish Problem," *Foreign Affairs* 20:2 (1942), 324–38, reprinted in *A Middle East Reader*, ed. Irene L. Gendzier, Indianapolis / New York: Pegasus, 1969, 311–25.

13 George Antonius, *The Arab Awakening: The Story of the Arab National Movement*, New York: G. P. Putnam's Sons, 1946, 411 [orig. London: Hamish Hamilton, 1938]. For a post-facto version of the same arguments, see Walid Khalidi, *From Haven to Conquest*, lv–lvii.

14 Robert W. MacDonald, *The League of Arab States: A Study in the Dynamics of Regional Organization*, Princeton, NJ: Princeton University Press, 1965, 317–18. Cf. Geoffrey Furlonge, *Palestine is My Country: The Story of Musa Alami*, New York: John Murray, 1969, 130–7; Neil Caplan, *Futile Diplomacy, vol. II: Arab–Zionist Negotiations and the End of the Mandate*, London: Frank Cass, 1986, 131, 176–7, 264–7, 326 (n. 83), 333 (n. 44).

15 William Eddy, *FDR Meets Ibn Saud*, New York: American Friends of the Middle East, 1954, quoted in Khalidi, *From Haven to Conquest*, 510–11.

16 Great Britain, The Anglo–American Committee of Enquiry Regarding the Problems of European Jewry and Palestine, *Report, 1946* (Lausanne, 20 April 1946), Cmd. 6808, London: HMSO, 1946, extract on "The Zionist Military Organisations" in Khalidi, *From Haven to Conquest*, 595–600; Great Britain, Colonial Office, *Palestine: Statement of Information Relating to Acts of Violence*, July 1946, Cmd. 6873, London: HMSO, 1946, reproduced in *From Haven to Conquest*, 601–12; Menachem Begin, *The Revolt [Story of the Irgun]*, foreword by Rabbi Meir Kahane, Los Angeles: Nash Publishing, 1972 [orig. New York: Schuman / London: W. H. Allen, 1948/1951]; J. Bowyer Bell, *Terror Out of Zion: Irgun Zvai Leumi, LEHI, and the Palestine Underground, 1929–1949*, New York: St. Martin's Press, 1977 [reissued as *Terror out of Zion: The Fight for Israeli Independence*, with a new introduction by the author and a foreword by Moshe Arens, New Brunswick, NJ: Transaction, 1996]; Bauer, *From Diplomacy to Resistance*; Yigal Elam, "*Haganah, Irgun* and 'Stern': Who Did What?" *Jerusalem Quarterly* 23 (Spring 1982), 70–8; Michael J. Cohen, *Palestine and the Great Powers, 1945–1948*, Princeton, NJ: Princeton University Press, 1982, ch. 4.

17 These events became immortalized in Leon Uris' best-selling 1958 novel, *Exodus*, and in the 1960 Oscar-winning Otto Preminger Hollywood film of

the same name. For some first-person accounts of these refugee-smuggling operations, see Ephraim Dekel, *Briha: Flight to the Homeland*, transl. from the Hebrew by Dina Ettinger, ed. Gertrude Hirschler, New York, Herzl Press, 1973; Ehud Avriel, *Open the Gates: The Dramatic Personal Story of "Illegal" Immigration to Israel*, preface by Golda Meir, New York: Atheneum, 1975; I. F. Stone, *Underground to Palestine, and Reflections Thirty Years Later* [reprint of the original 1946 edition], New York: Pantheon, 1978; Yoram Kaniuk, *Commander of the Exodus*, transl. Seymour Simckes, New York: Grove Press, 1999; Dov Freiberg, *To Survive Sobibor*, transl. Barbara Doron, Jerusalem / New York: Gefen, 2007, 559–99.

18 Preliminary Report to President Truman on Displaced Persons in Germany and Austria, August 1945, *Dept of State Bulletin* 13 (30 September 1945), 456–63, reproduced in J. C. Hurewitz, *Diplomacy in the Near and Middle East: A Documentary Record 1535–1956*, Cambridge: Cambridge University Press, 1987; Cohen, *Palestine and the Great Powers*, 56–8, 62. For a cynical British account of Zionist propaganda and manipulation of the "DPs," see Lieut.-General Sir Frederick Morgan, "A 'Displaced Person' in Post-War Germany, 1945–1946," extract from *Peace and War: A Soldier's Life*, London: Hodder and Stoughton, 1961, in Khalidi, *From Haven to Conquest*, 1987, 527–48.

19 For firsthand accounts of the activities of the AACI, see Bartley Crum, *Behind the Silken Curtain: A Personal Account of Anglo–American Diplomacy in Palestine and the Middle East*, New York: Simon and Schuster, 1947; Richard Crossman, *Palestine Mission: A Personal Record*, New York: Harper and Bros., 1947; David Horowitz, *State in the Making*, transl. Julian Meltzer, New York: Alfred A. Knopf, 1953. Official submissions to the AACI can be found in United Kingdom, *A Survey of Palestine, Prepared in December 1945 and January 1946 for the Information of the Anglo–American Committee of Inquiry*, HMSO: 1946, reprinted 1991 by the Institute for Palestine Studies, Washington, DC; Laqueur and Rubin, *The Israel–Arab Reader*, 57–62; "The Case against a Jewish State in Palestine: Albert Hourani's Statement to the Anglo–American Committee of Enquiry of 1946," *Journal of Palestine Studies* 35:1 (Autumn 2005), 80–90. See also J. C. Hurewitz, *The Struggle for Palestine*, New York: Norton, 1950, chs. 17–18; Cohen, *Palestine and the Great Powers*, 60–7 and ch. 5.

20 Anglo–American Committee of Inquiry: Recommendations and Comments, 1 May 1946, reproduced in Laqueur and Rubin, *The Israel–Arab Reader*, 62–5.

21 Recommendation No. 3, in ibid., 63–4.

22 Jorge Garcia-Granados, *The Birth of Israel: The Drama as I Saw It*, New York: Knopf, 1948, 172–82; Horowitz, *State in the Making*, 178–9; Abba Eban, *An Autobiography*, New York: Random House, 1977, 79–80.

23 Garcia-Granados, *The Birth of Israel*, 216–33; Evan M. Wilson, *A Calculated Risk: The U.S. Decision to Recognize Israel*, foreword by William B. Quandt, Cincinnati, OH: Clerisy Press, 2008 [reprint of *Decision on Palestine: How the U.S. Came to Recognize Israel* (1979)], 216–18.

24 UN Special Committee on Palestine, Summary Report, 31 August 1917, in Laqueur and Rubin, *The Israel–Arab Reader*, 65–9. For personal accounts of

some of the UNSCOP members and contemporaries, see Garcia-Granados, *The Birth of Israel*; Daniel Mandel, *H. V. Evatt and the Establishment of Israel: The Undercover Zionist*, London: Frank Cass, 2004; Horowitz, *State in the Making*; Wilson, *A Calculated Risk*, 218–24.

25 For a sampling, see Sir Muhammad Zafrullah Khan, "Thanksgiving Day at Lake Success, November 27, 1947," in Khalidi, *From Haven to Conquest*, 709–22; General Carlos P. Romulo, "The Philippines Changes its Vote," in ibid., 723–6; Kermit Roosevelt, "The Partition of Palestine: A Lesson in Pressure Politics," in ibid., 727–9; Wilson, *A Calculated Risk*, 224–47.

26 Horowitz, *State in the Making*, 237. For a sampling of first-person accounts of the debates and lobbying for votes on the UNSCOP proposals, see ibid., 239–304; Abba Eban, "Tragedy and Triumph," in *Chaim Weizmann, A Biography by Several Hands*, eds. Meyer W. Weisgal and Joel Carmichael, foreword by David Ben-Gurion, New York: Atheneum, 1963, 299–303; Abba Eban, *Personal Witness: Israel through My Eyes*, New York: G. P. Putnam's Sons, 1992, ch. 5.

27 See, e.g., David Arnow, "The Holocaust and the Birth of Israel: Reassessing the Causal Relationship," *Journal of Israeli History* 15:3 (Autumn 1994), 257–81.

28 UNGA, Resolution on the Future Government of Palestine (181), 29 November 1947, in Laqueur and Rubin, *The Israel–Arab Reader*, 69–77.

29 Henry Cattan, *Palestine and International Law: The Legal Aspects of the Arab–Israel Conflict*, 2nd ed., London: Longman, 1976, ch. IV; W. Thomas Mallison and Sally V. Mallison, *The Palestine Problem in International Law and World Order*, Harlow, UK: Longman, 1986, ch. 3; Walid Khalidi, "Revisiting the UNGA Partition Resolution," *Journal of Palestine Studies* 27:1 (Autumn 1997), 5–21; John Quigley, *The Case for Palestine: An International Law Perspective*, rev. and updated ed., Durham, NC / London: Duke University Press, 2005, ch. 6 ("Whose Land to Give? The UN Power over Palestine"). Privately, Ambassador Abba Eban conceded that on this point the Arabs "were on stronger ground than we were." Eban, *Personal Witness*, 128–31.

30 E.g., Nathan Feinberg, "The Question of Sovereignty over Palestine," from *On an Arab Jurist's Approach to Zionism and the State of Israel*, reproduced in *The Arab–Israeli Conflict: Readings and Documents*, abridged and rev. ed., ed. John Norton Moore, Princeton, NJ: Princeton University Press, 1977, 63–5.

31 See, e.g., Neil Caplan, "'Oom-Shmoom' Revisited: Israeli Attitudes towards the UN and the Great Powers, 1948–1960," in *Global Politics: Essays in Honour of David Vital*, eds. Abraham Ben-Zvi and Aharon Klieman, London: Frank Cass, 2001, 167–99; Benny Morris, *1948: A History of the First Arab–Israeli War*, New Haven, CT: Yale University Press, 2008, 402–4.

32 Morris, *1948: A History of the First Arab–Israeli War*; Philip Mattar, "al-Nakba," *Encyclopedia of the Palestinians*, rev. ed., ed. Philip Mattar, New York: Facts on File, 2005, 328–30.

33 For an interesting compendium of the war as seen from various perspectives, see *The War for Palestine: Rewriting the History of 1948*, eds. Eugene L. Rogan and Avi Shlaim, Cambridge: Cambridge University Press, 2001.

34 As an epigraph to his book *1948: The First Arab–Israeli War*, Benny Morris reproduces a poem, "David," by the late American-Zionist essayist and publicist, Marie Syrkin, inviting the reader to "suppose, this time, that Goliath shall not fail," i.e., that the Arabs had won the war in 1948.

35 Rashid Khalidi, *The Iron Cage: The Story of the Palestinian Struggle for Statehood*, Boston, MA: Beacon Press, 2006, 123–4.

36 W. Khalidi, *From Haven to Conquest*, 858–71; Simha Flapan, *The Birth of Israel: Myths and Realities*, New York: Pantheon, 1987, 9–10, 187–99; Ilan Pappé, *The Making of the Arab–Israeli Conflict, 1947–51*, London: I. B. Tauris / New York: St. Martin's Press, 1992, ch. 2; Benny Morris, *Righteous Victims: A History of the Zionist Arab Conflict, 1881–1999*, New York: Alfred A. Knopf, 1999 / London: John Murray, 2000, 191–6, 215–18; Morris, *1948, A History of the First Arab–Israeli War*, 81–93, 199–207, 398–402; R. Khalidi, *Iron Cage*, 131–5.

37 Walid Khalidi, "The Fall of Haifa," *Middle East Forum* 35:10 (December 1959), 22–32, reproduced in "The Fall of Haifa Revisited," *Journal of Palestine Studies* 37:3 (Spring 2008), 30–58.

38 Avi Shlaim, *Collusion across the Jordan: King Abdullah, the Zionist Movement, and the Partition of Palestine*, Oxford: Clarendon Press, 1988; R. Khalidi, *Iron Cage*, 127–9.

39 Ilan Pappé, *Britain and the Arab–Israeli Conflict, 1948–51*, London: Macmillan Press / St. Antony's College, 1988.

40 Note the polemical slants of two other versions of this map: "The Frontiers of the State of Israel, 1949–1967" in Martin Gilbert, *The Routledge Atlas of the Arab–Israeli Conflict*, 7th ed., London / New York: Routledge, 2002, 50 (which makes no mention of "Palestine"), and the condemnatory "Arab Territories Seized by Israel in 1948 and 1949 in Violation of the U.N. Partition Plan" http://www.passia.org/palestine_facts/MAPS/Arab_territories_seized_by_Israel_in_194849.htm

41 United Nations Relief and Works Agency for Palestine Refugees in the Near East, established 8 December 1949 by UN General Assembly Resolution 302. Official website at http://www.un.org/unrwa/. See Edward H. Buehrig, *The UN and the Palestinian Refugees: A Study in Nonterritorial Administration*, Bloomington: Indiana University Press, 1971; Milton Viorst, *Reaching for the Olive Branch: UNRWA and Peace in the Middle East*, Washington, DC: Middle East Institute, 1989.

42 UNGA Resolution No. 194 (III), 11 December 1948, reproduced in Laqueur and Rubin, *Israel–Arab Reader*, 85. See also *United Nations Resolutions on Palestine and the Arab–Israeli Conflict*, vol. I: 1947–1974, rev. ed., ed. George J. Tomeh, Washington, DC: Institute for Palestine Studies, 1988, 16.

Article 11 reads as follows: "11. Resolves that the refugees wishing to return to their homes and live at peace with their neighbours should be permitted to do so at the earliest practicable date, and that compensation should be paid for the property of those choosing not to return and for loss or damage to property which, under principles of international law or in equity, should be made good by the Governments or authorities responsible."

43   Erskine B. Childers, "The Other Exodus," *The Spectator* (London), 12 May 1961, reproduced in W. Khalidi, *Haven to Conquest*, 795–806; Flapan, *Birth of Israel*, 81–118; Christopher Hitchens, "Broadcasts," in *Blaming the Victims: Spurious Scholarship and the Palestinian Question*, eds. Edward W. Said and Christopher Hitchens, London: Verso, 2001, 73–83.

44   W. Khalidi, "The Fall of Haifa"; Efraim Karsh, "*Nakbat Haifa*: the Collapse and Dispersion of a Major Palestinian Community," *Middle Eastern Studies* 37:4 (October 2001), 25–70; Mustafa Abbasi, "The End of Arab Tiberias: The 1948 Battle for the City," *Journal of Palestine Studies* 37:3 (Spring 2008), 6–29; Morris, *1948*, 140–7.

45   Saleh Abdel-Jawad, "The Arab and Palestinian Narratives of the 1948 War," in *Israeli and Palestinian Narratives of Conflict: History's Double Helix*, ed. Robert I. Rotberg, Bloomington / Indianapolis: Indiana University Press, 2006, 72–114.

46   Efraim Karsh, "1948, Israel, and the Palestinians: Annotated Text," *Commentary* May 2008, accessed June 2008 online at http://www.commentarymaga zine.com/viewarticle.cfm/1948–israel–and-the-palestinians–annotated-text-11373.

47   Walid Khalidi, "Plan Dalet Revisited: Master Plan for the Conquest of Palestine," *Journal of Palestine Studies* 18:1 (Autumn 1988), 3–37; Walid Khalidi, *All That Remains: The Palestinian Villages Occupied and Depopulated by Israel in 1948*, Washington, DC: Institute for Palestine Studies, 1992; Pappé, *Making*, ch. 3; Ilan Pappé, *The Ethnic Cleansing of Palestine*, Oxford: Oneworld Publications, 2006.

48   Erskine B. Childers, "The Wordless Wish: From Citizens to Refugees," in *The Transformation of Palestine*, ed. Ibrahim Abu Lughod, 2nd ed, Evanston, IL: Northwestern University Press, 1987, 165–202; Chaim Simons, *International Proposals to Transfer Arabs from Palestine, 1895–1947: A Historical Survey*, Hoboken, NJ: Ktav Publishing, 1988; Nur Masalha, *Expulsion of the Palestinians: The Concept of "Transfer" in Zionist Political Thought, 1882–1948*, Washington, DC: Institute for Palestine Studies, 1992; Pappé, *Ethnic Cleansing*, ch. 2; Rashid Khalidi, *Iron Cage*, 126.

49   Benny Morris, *The Birth of the Palestinian Refugee Problem, 1947–1949*, Cambridge: Cambridge University Press, 1987, and *The Birth of the Palestinian Refugee Problem Revisited*, Cambridge, UK / New York: Cambridge University Press, 2004.

50   Nur Masalha, "A Critique of Benny Morris," *Journal of Palestine Studies* 21:1 (Autumn 1991), 90–7; Benny Morris, "Response to Finkelstein and Masalha," *Journal of Palestine Studies* 21:1 (Autumn 1991), 98–114; essays by Shlaim, Morris, and Masalha in *The Israel/Palestine Question*, ed. Ilan Pappé, London / New York: Routledge, 1999, 171–220; comments by Edward Said and by Abdo al-Asadi, quoted in Mustafa Kabha, "A Palestinian

Look at the New Historians and Post-Zionism in Israel," in *Making Israel*, ed. Benny Morris, Ann Arbor: University of Michigan Press, 2007, 309; Norman G. Finkelstein, *Image and Reality of the Israel–Palestine Conflict*, new and rev. ed., New York: W. W. Norton [2nd ed., London: Verso], 2003, ch. 3; Roane Carey, "Dr. Benny and Mr. Morris: The Historian and the Twisted Politics of Expulsion," *CounterPunch* 19–20 July 2008, accessed 23 July 2008 at http://www.counterpunch.org/carey07192008.html.

51 Morris, *Birth of the Palestinian Refugee Problem Revisited*, 5–6, 39–64. At the same time Morris also responded to Israeli critics Shabtai Teveth and Anita Shapira, who argued that there was "no connection between the occasional propagation of the idea" of "transfer" and what happened in 1947–1948. He chose not to respond, however, to the more egregious accusations of intellectual dishonesty leveled at him by Efraim Karsh, *Fabricating Israeli History: The "New Historians,"* 2nd rev. ed., London: Frank Cass, 2000, ch. 2.

52 R. Khalidi, *Iron Cage*, 133.

53 For example, the special mission of Dr. Joseph E. Johnson, president of the Carnegie Foundation, who went to the region in 1961 under a mandate from the UN Conciliation Commission for Palestine. See David P. Forsythe, *United Nations Peacemaking: The Conciliation Commission for Palestine*, Baltimore, MD / London: Johns Hopkins University Press, 1972, ch. V; extract from his report on the Israel Ministry of Foreign Affairs website, accessed 3 September 2008 at http://www.mfa.gov.il/MFA/Foreign%20Relations/Israels%20Foreign%20Relations%20since%201947/1947–1974/16%20Palestine%20Conciliation%20Commission-%20Nineteenth%20P.

54 Alvin Z. Rubinstein, "Transformation: External Determinants," in *The Arab–Israeli Conflict: Perspectives*, 2nd ed., ed. Alvin Z. Rubinstein, New York: HarperCollins, 1991, 82.

55 E.g., Marie Syrkin, *The State of the Jews*, Washington, DC: New Republic Books / Herzl Press, 1980, 119–46; Marie Syrkin, "The Palestinian Refugees: Resettlement, Repatriation or Restoration?" [from *Commentary* magazine 41:1 (1966)], in *Israel, the Arabs and the Middle East*, eds. Irving Howe and Carl Gershman, New York: Bantam, 1972, 157–85; Jonathan Spyer, "UNRWA: Barrier to Peace," *BESA Perspectives Papers* No. 44, 27 May 2008, accessed online at http://www.biu.ac.il/SOC/besa/perspectives44.html.

56 Benny Morris, "The Crystallization of Israeli Policy against a Return of the Arab Refugees: April–December, 1948," *Studies in Zionism* 6:1 (Spring 1985), 85–118.

57 M. Shertok to Count Folke Bernadotte, 1 August 1948, *Documents on the Foreign Policy of Israel*, vol. I, 14 May–30 September 1948, ed. Yehoshua Freundlich, Jerusalem: Israel State Archives, 1981, 443–4 [doc. 406].

58 See also Morris, *Birth of the Palestinian Refugee Problem*, ch. 4; Abba Eban statement at the UN, 4 May 1949, *Documents on the Foreign Policy of Israel, vol. 4* (May–December 1949), ed. Yemima Rosenthal, Jerusalem: Israel State Archives, 1986, 14–16 (doc. 5).

59 For a thoughtful compilation of academic studies on these intertwined questions, see *Exile and Return: Predicaments of Palestinians and Jews*, eds. Ann M. Lesch and Ian S. Lustick, Philadelphia: University of Pennsylvania Press, 2005.

60 See, e.g., Tom Segev, *1949: The First Israelis*, New York: Free Press, 1986, chs. 5–6. The tragedy of individual Jewish and Palestinian families' interlocking stories of loss and displacement has been conveyed most poignantly in literary form. See, e.g., Ghassan Kanafani, "Returning to Haifa," in *Palestine's Children: Returning to Haifa and Other Stories*, transl. Barbara Harlow and Karen E. Riley, Boulder, CO: Lynne Rienner, 2000, 149–96; Yehuda Yaari, "The Judgment of Solomon," in *Modern Jewish Stories*, ed. Gerda Charles, London: Faber and Faber, 1963 [Englewood Cliffs, NJ: Prentice-Hall, 1965], 21–43. Kanafani's Arabic novella was adapted, with the late author's family's permission, as a play in Hebrew by playwright Boaz Gaon and directed by Sinai Peter at Tel Aviv's Cameri Theatre Company in 2008. See a review by Etty Diamant, "Return to Haifa Confronts Holocaust Victims with Palestinian Refugees," *Palestine–Israel Journal of Politics, Economics and Culture* 15:1–2 (2008), 210–12. See also Chapter 8, below.

61 For a critique of the exchange of populations approach, see Yehouda Shenhav, "Arab Jews, Population Exchange, and the Palestinian Right of Return," in *Exile and Return*, eds. Lesch and Lustick, 225–45.

62 For examples of Israelis, see Boaz Evron, "The Holocaust: Learning the Wrong Lessons," *Journal of Palestine Studies* 10:3 (Spring 1981), 16–25; A. B. Yehoshua, "The Holocaust as Junction," in *Between Right and Right*, New York: Doubleday, 1981, 1–19; Avraham Burg, *The Holocaust is Over: We Must Rise from Its Ashes*, London: Macmillan, 2008.

63 Segev, *1949: The First Israelis*.

64 Joseph Massad, "Palestinians and Jewish History: Recognition or Submission?" *Journal of Palestine Studies* 30:1 (Autumn 2000), 52–67. Cf. Yoav Gelber, quoted above, page 48.

65 Emil Habibi, "Your Holocaust, Our Catastrophe," *The Tel Aviv Review* I:1 (January 1988), 332–6.

66 Amos Elon, *The Israelis: Founders and Sons*, New York: Holt, Rinehart and Winston, 1971, ch. 8.

67 Israel, Law of Return, 5 July 1950, reproduced in Laqueur and Rubin, *Israel–Arab Reader*, 87.

68 Dan Bar-On and Saliba Sarsar, "Bridging the Unbridgeable: The Holocaust and al-Nakba," *Palestine–Israel Journal* 11:1 (2004), 63–70.

69 On an unusual visit of 250 Israeli Jews and Arabs to Auschwitz in Spring 2003, see Yoav Peck, "When They Learn Our Past," *Jerusalem Report* 7 April 2003, 54; Eetta Prince-Gibson, "Arabic in Auschwitz," *Jerusalem Post* 20 June 2003, 15–16.

70 See, e.g., Eitan Bronstein, "The Nakba in Hebrew: Israeli-Jewish Awareness of the Palestinian Catastrophe and Internal Refugees," in *Catastrophe*

Remembered: Palestine, Israel and the Internal Refugees: Essays in Memory of Edward W. Said, ed. Nur Masalha, London / New York: Zed Books, 2005, 214–41. Also the Zokhrot website at http://www.nakbainhebrew.org; "Healing Israel's Birth Scar," 9 April 2008, accessed online at http://tonykaron.com/2008/04/09/healing-israels-birth-scar/.

7
Israel and the Arab States, 1949–1973

The conflict that we saw unfolding in the previous chapters was largely one between Zionists and Palestinians for the control of Palestine/*Eretz-Israel*. After 1949, the Palestinians—following a decline that had begun with the suppression of their 1936–1939 revolt—were a spent force, dispersed, leaderless, many living as dependent refugees, and without a territorial base. Their disappearance from the scene as autonomous political actors allowed most people in Israel to focus attention on the Arab states in the aftermath of the war that had just ended. For the foreseeable future, a list of issues and grievances—some longstanding, others of recent vintage—came to constitute an *Arab–Israeli* (rather than an Israeli–*Palestinian*) conflict.

For the next two decades, specifically Palestinian issues were relegated to the back burner and were treated as secondary to this new inter-state conflict involving mainly Israel, Syria, Jordan, and Egypt. Indeed, some came to believe that, since there was no longer a distinct Palestinian people organized in a national movement seeking to create an independent Arab state, there was no longer any Palestinian problem or question. For Israelis, political, military-strategic, and other calculations were now treated in the context of bilateral and multilateral relations among sovereign states. The contest between Zionists/Israelis and Palestinian Arabs—the two rival national communities that had until 1948 been seeking sovereignty over the same territory—rested dormant during this period, and would be revived only in the years after 1967 (below, Chapter 8).

In this chapter we examine the changed structure and dynamics of this Arab–Israeli conflict during the quarter-century between 1949 and 1973—a period marked by three major inter-state wars: October 1956 (Israel and Egypt), June 1967 (Israel, Egypt, Jordan, and Syria), and October 1973 (Israel, Egypt, and Syria). The international dimensions of the conflict also changed. Before 1948 the main protagonists had vied with each other under a largely unchallenged British Mandatory power, with the European states and the USA in the background. After World War II, British, French, Americans, and Russians jockeyed with each other in efforts to secure and extend their influence in the region. Indeed, the post-1949 period witnessed a heightened superpower rivalry during the "Cold War" in which the US and the USSR courted states and peoples, seeking alliances in the strategic Middle East. As was happening elsewhere around the globe, small nations had to make decisions regarding how far to compromise their nominal sovereignty in becoming client states beholden to their American or Soviet patrons for diplomatic, economic, and/or military aid. A new global dimension and ideological schisms were superimposed onto existing rivalries and conflicts in the region (of which the Arab–Israeli dispute was but one). Powerful external actors pursued their interests in ways that overshadowed and often overrode those of the local parties.

The Palestinian Issue after 1949

As we have seen, the involvement of the Arab states in the affairs of Palestine that began during the 1936 rebellion brought about, in its wake, a series of progressively more adverse consequences for the Palestinians, leading up to and including the Arab states' ineffective diplomatic performance at the United Nations in 1947 and 1948 and the defeat of their armies (along with Palestinian militias) in 1948–1949. The diplomatic and battlefield victories of the new Jewish state and the loss of Arab Palestine left the post-1948 Arab world marked by political instability, feelings of aftershock and humiliation, but also some self-criticism.[1] The most visible scars could be seen in the loss of territory, the vanished opportunity to create an independent Palestinian Arab state and—most painfully—the continuing existence of Palestinian refugees in Lebanon, Syria, Jordan, and Gaza, mainly in camps run by the United Nations Relief and Works Agency [UNRWA].

In the international arena the "Palestine question" receded almost totally from the agenda and was replaced by a relief and humanitarian issue known as "the Arab refugees." At the General Assembly, the debates on UNRWA's annual reports and the votes allocating new funding for its refugee relief and educational budgets served as the main platform for considering Palestinian issues. Except for local and regional committees established to represent Palestinian refugees and press for their repatriation (or family reunification), the recovery of their assets (businesses, blocked bank accounts, etc.), or compensation for their abandoned or destroyed property, Palestinians as a community were without recognized or effective leadership.

Two attempts to express Palestinian national consensus and create national institutions were short-lived and flawed, reflecting the near-total dependency of the Palestinians on the existing Arab régimes. In late September 1948, the exiled Mufti and the remnants of his Arab Higher Committee proclaimed the existence of the "All-Palestine Government" based in Gaza, but soon moved its offices to Cairo.[2] Several months later, a Palestinian congress convened in Jericho to express a "popular demand"—orchestrated by Abdullah's supporters—for the Hashemite Kingdom's annexation of the West Bank (which came about in 1950).[3]

The real initiative and responsibility in the political and diplomatic sphere now lay in the hands of the leaders of the Arab states. For the Palestinians, all this amounted to "Arab tutelage," in the words of Palestinian-American historian Rashid Khalidi. Palestinians "lost agency."

> [I]f they were spoken for at all, they were spoken for by the Arab states, each of which had its own considerations and calculations, all of which were weak ... Even such limited Palestinian efforts to speak for themselves internationally as took place were entirely dependent on the support of the Arab states.[4]

The recovery of Palestine and the return of the refugees became entangled in the inter-Arab politics of the region—the "Arab cold war" described by historian Malcolm Kerr.[5] Arab politicians and régimes used the Palestine issue as a litmus test of their nationalist and patriotic standing, or in efforts to boost their regional leadership aspirations. This usually resulted in leaders attempting to "outbid" each other in taking a hard line against Israel, creating additional pressure for radicalization of their political stances.[6]

In the post-1949 period, the phrase "Palestine cause" carried with it both positive and negative associations. On the one hand, the Arab states' loss in the war against the Jews in 1948–1949 stood out as a badge of shame for the old régimes, several of which were soon replaced. On the other, it represented the Arab states' pledge to restore Palestinian rights, return the Palestinians to their land, (perhaps) drive the Jews out, and, generally, undo the injustice of 1948.

This heated rhetoric translated into a number of concrete expressions. One was the maintenance of a strict taboo against actions or contacts that would imply recognition of the legitimacy of Israel as a sovereign state. In this spirit, the Arab League created an office in Damascus to promote and monitor an economic boycott (originated by the League in December 1945) of the Jewish state.[7] During the early 1950s, Arab régimes sometimes found themselves affording limited support for cross-border raids (see below) executed by displaced Palestinians living in their midst. These early *feday'un* (guerillas) caused death and injury to Israelis and sabotage of property, periodically provoking reprisals by Israeli forces against villages and military installations of the host countries—thereby testing the generosity and hospitality of their Arab hosts. The ambivalent and often tense relationships created between the governments of Egypt, Jordan, and Syria and these largely disorganized Palestinians during the 1950s[8] previewed the even more complicated relations that would develop between guerilla groups that, in later decades, would form the Palestine Liberation Organization [PLO]. The escalation of this low-level cross-border fighting during 1954–1956 was also a contributing factor to the outbreak of the second Arab–Israeli war in late 1956.

From Armistice to Non-Peace

On 24 February 1949, on the Greek Island of Rhodes, Egypt and Israel signed what would turn out to be the first of four successive General Armistice Agreements [GAAs] governing the belligerent states' military disengagement from the war. At the time, everyone involved in the drawing-up of the armistice accords had anticipated that their duration would be short.[9] But, as the months and years went by without the expected movement towards peace treaties, the frustrated protagonists would return to wrangle over their interpretations of the 1949 agreements they had signed. Much of the argumentation was legalistic, as the texts of the GAAs offered sufficient ambiguity to allow the parties to draw diametrically opposed conclusions.[10]

The inability to transform the 1949 armistice agreements into peace treaties—a deviation from the normal sequence of *ceasefire→ armistice→ peace*—was a special feature of the new Arab–Israeli conflict, making it appear more intractable than other similar international disputes. Six issues dominated the tense relations between Israel and the Arab states in the period of "non-peace" following 1949:

1 recognition, legitimacy
2 boundaries, territory
3 refugees
4 Jerusalem
5 freedom of passage through the Suez Canal
6 water.

Given the parties' obstinacy following the signing of the GAAs, Arab and Israeli positions hardened on these six issues, leaving the leaderless Palestinians sidelined and the refugees without hope of a speedy settlement. From early 1949 to late 1951, the United Nations offered several mechanisms under which the parties were invited to work out their differences. But all efforts undertaken by the Conciliation Commission for Palestine [PCC], created by UNGA Resolution 194 of December 1948, eventually floundered.

Why were the ex-belligerents not able to transform their armistice agreements into peace treaties? And is any party to blame for "missing opportunities" and not converting the Armistice Agreements into more stable peace treaties? We will look at the second question in Chapter 11, and examine the first here.

In the absence of any progress towards signing Israeli–Arab peace treaties, the UN undertook responsibility for keeping a lid on an inherently unstable situation along the frontiers through the creation of United Nations Truce Supervisory Organization [UNTSO], an umbrella monitoring agency for the Mixed Armistice Commissions [MACs] operating under the terms of each of the four GAAs. Skirmishes and incidents often occurred along the frontiers, especially in disputed areas or zones designated as "demilitarized," leading Israel, Egypt, Jordan, and Syria to submit numerous complaints to their respective MACs, which became inundated with investigations and issuing rulings.[11]

But it was political, rather than legal or military, considerations that were paramount in characterizing the nature of the new Arab–Israeli conflict and in explaining the inability of the parties to move from armistice to peace. Predictably, the Arab governments and Israel all adopted hardline positions on the issues of boundaries, refugees, Jerusalem, and recognition during PCC conferences convened at Lausanne (1949), Geneva (1950) and Paris (1951). But all United Nations post-war Middle East diplomatic efforts seemed doomed to fail, given the deadlock over the preconditions set down by each party:

- The Arabs regarded the signed armistice agreements as their recognition that the war had ended, but argued that Israel needed to retreat from territory captured beyond the 1947 UN partition map in the 1948–1949 fighting (see Map 6.2) and allow the return or compensation of refugees *before* they would consider moving to peace and recognizing the new Israeli state, while
- The Israelis viewed their signed armistice agreements as not only having put an end to fighting, but also requiring the next step to be for the parties to negotiate a *comprehensive* peace package; only in this

context would Israel agree to consider territorial adjustments, war reparations, and the question of refugees.

Such was the shape of the stalemate undermining all efforts at negotiation and peacemaking after 1949. For UN purposes, this meant that Arab representatives might cooperate with, and attend conferences convened by, the PCC, but they would refuse to sit at the same table, or affix their signatures to the same document, as Israeli delegates.[12] In these early tests, the only success the Conciliation Commission could record was in the area of its technical work on preparation of the dossier for compensation for refugee assets, the facilitation of some family reunification, and an agreement for the unfreezing of blocked Palestinian bank accounts.[13]

Israel tried to build upon its armistice agreements and its admission to membership in the United Nations in May 1949, hoping these would lead to recognition by most states and normalization within the world body. By late 1949, 47 states (out of 58) had granted recognition and/or established diplomatic relations with the Jewish state.[14] Israeli leaders referred to the GAAs, among other things, as *de facto* validation of their claims to territory captured during the war and as justification for denouncing Arab actions which implied the continuation of a state of belligerency. Arab spokesmen, for their part, underlined the limited military scope of the documents while bemoaning the imbalance of forces which had produced humiliating or otherwise unsatisfactory agreements.[15] In terms of diplomatic feelers during the 1950s, all overtures from potential Arab negotiators ignored the GAAs and were based either on the November 1947 partition plan or the plan submitted by UN Mediator Count Folke Bernadotte just before his assassination in September 1948.[16] The Israelis, for their part, rejected both these proposals as starting-points, insisting that any negotiations take the status quo, as enshrined in the GAAs, as the appropriate *point de départ*.[17]

The list of post-1949 contested issues, in terms of the six unresolved disputes enumerated above, festered for decades with only unsatisfactory attempts at solutions. Chief among them, the Palestinian refugees became a political football *par excellence*. Their case, along with consideration of the final delineation of mutually recognized frontiers, became stalemated and sidelined as Israel and the Arab states bickered and could not be brought together to negotiate a comprehensive peace. The status of Jerusalem also remained contested, as a PCC subcommittee's recommendations on internationalization and disarmament submitted in September 1949 ran counter to the interests of both Israel and Jordan; the two states that effectively occupied the divided Holy City simply chose to ignore international opinion. Egypt denied free passage through the

Suez Canal to ships bound to or from Israel, despite an authoritative UN Security Council ruling in September 1951 backing Israel's interpretation of its rights to freedom of navigation through this international waterway. UNSC Resolution 95 was never enforced against the Egyptians, who insisted that the armistice had not ended the state of belligerency between themselves and the Israelis but had merely "suspended" the war.[18] On a number of occasions Israel attempted, without success, to test the Egyptian blockade by commissioning a ship to pass through the Suez Canal. On other occasions, it pressed the powers (who proved unenthusiastic) to raise the issue in the UN Security Council.

Only one success can be recorded for this period. A secret and tacit agreement for allocating shares of the Jordan River waters was reached thanks to the laborious efforts of a team of Americans headed by Eric Johnston, a personal emissary of US president Dwight D. Eisenhower. Shuttling between various Middle East capitals between 1953 and 1956, Johnston registered this major practical achievement which had to be kept deliberately low-key and under the political radar during a tense period that would eventually produce the second Arab–Israeli war.[19]

Low-Intensity Border Warfare, 1949–1956

With Israel and the Arab states in near-permanent diplomatic deadlock, border friction and bellicose rhetoric escalated from year to year. Each party seemed to be holding firm, not feeling compelled to engage in any peace discussions, waiting it out until such time as the great powers or the United Nations might move to attempt to cajole or coerce them to consider diplomacy. Some were waiting for a new, more favorable, situation to be created in the wake of the next war which, they felt, was sure to break out sooner or later.

An important backdrop for the 1949–1956 period was a pattern of increasing cross-border Palestinian infiltration and raids by *feday'un* (or *feday'in*; "self-sacrificers"), mainly from Egyptian-controlled Gaza, matched by Israeli reprisals of increasing severity. Both *feday'un* and Israeli attacks included military and civilian targets, the latter sometimes targeted deliberately, sometimes hit as "collateral damage." Both Israelis and Arabs suffered civilian casualties and damage to property; the tactics and weapons used by the cross-border raiders were often horrific, seldom as "gentlemanly" as those used in conventional warfare between armies.[20]

Every year thousands of incidents were reported, along with dozens of deaths and injuries from cross-border raids.[21] Motives for Arab infiltration into Israel were varied: economic (e.g., harvesting crops on family owned land that ended up on the Israeli side of the armistice lines), sabotage of water pipelines or electricity (politically inspired, to destabilize the new Jewish state), criminal marauding, and terrorist killings of civilians (sometimes "revenge," sometimes to terrorize). A pattern of unceasing, low-level, cross-border terror attacks increased the level of fear and insecurity in the Israeli public and further hardened existing attitudes in which Arabs were seen as congenital murderers whose aggressive actions had to be countered by stern measures. Among the more gruesome attacks on Israeli civilians were the March 1954 ambush at Maaleh Akrabim of a Tel Aviv bus to Eilat in which the passengers were executed, one by one, and the grenade attack a year later on a wedding party celebrating in the settlement of Patish.

Among Israel's political and military leaders, a policy of retaliation evolved in which the elements of punishment, revenge, and deterrence were all entangled in a primitive "eye-for-an-eye" approach, becoming the latest incarnation of the pattern of violence we explored during the Arab revolt of the 1930s in Chapter 5, when we examined the core argument: *Is the [Palestinians'] [Arabs'] [Zionists'] [Israelis'] resort to violence justified, or is it to be condemned?* A series of major Israeli cross-border operations proved to be decisive steps in the countdown to the Suez/Sinai War of 1956: Qibya (October 1953), Nahhalin (March 1954), Gaza (February 1955), as-Sabha (November 1955), Syrian positions along the Sea of Galilee (December 1955), and Qalqilya (October 1956).[22] Each was a response to a provocation (e.g., an attack inside Israel), and each represented a major escalation in terms of death toll, the scale of force used, and the level of military sophistication.

The Qibya raid, a little known but crucial turning-point, offers a good illustration of the security dilemmas and explosiveness of the unstable, no-war-no-peace character of Israel–Arab relations of the 1950s.[23] In response to a terrorist attack that killed a mother and two children in the Israeli village of Kfar Yahud, a specially trained Israeli commando force ("Unit 101") under a young captain, Ariel Sharon, mounted a massive reprisal attack on the West Bank village of Qibya, from which the infiltrators were suspected to have come. During the night of 14–15 October 1953, the Israeli raiders killed between 50 and 60 inhabitants of the village and wounded another 15. Reports disagreed as to whether most of casualties had occurred while people hid in their houses which the Israeli attackers (presuming them empty?) blew up, or whether they had been deliberately massacred by machine-gun fire and grenades, and their houses subsequently blown up.

On the international stage, the scale and brutality of the massacre led to an unprecedented level of condemnation of Israel. Although he loyally used all his rhetorical skills to defend his country's actions before the UN General Assembly, Israel's silver-tongued Ambassador Abba Eban admitted privately that he considered Qibya the worst blow to Israel's standing in world public opinion since the creation of the state, making an even more serious stain on Israel's reputation than the pre-state massacre of Arabs by Jewish terrorists at the village of Deir Yasin.[24]

But another segment of Israeli opinion was not so critical of the Qibya raid. While regretting the loss of innocent lives, David Ben-Gurion justified the action in a cabinet statement broadcast over Israel Radio. The Israeli prime minister and defense minister (who would shortly begin a brief period of retirement) described the raid as a legitimate retaliation that he hoped would end four years of repeated armed infiltrations, which had by their imperceptible day-by-day nature taken their toll without drawing much serious attention in world capitals.[25]

The Qibya raid also became the subject of vigorous internal debate and helped propel a crisis within the Israeli political élite, pitting the activist David Ben-Gurion against the (soon-to-be-deposed) Foreign Minister, Moshe Sharett. In congratulating Ariel Sharon, Ben-Gurion felt that it didn't "make any real difference what will be said about [Qibya] around the world. The important thing [was] how it [would] be looked at here in this region." The raid, Ben-Gurion was reported as saying, would "give us the possibility of living here."[26]

Sharett, who favored diplomacy and the maintenance of world sympathy ahead of knee-jerk, tit-for-tat military retaliations, believed that decisions on reprisals had always to be viewed in the larger context of "the question of peace .... We have to curb our reactions. And the question always remains: Has it really been proven that reprisals bring about the security for which they were planned?" He favored a measured response over excessive retaliation that would only lead, in his view, to inflaming a thirst for revenge and an escalation of violence.[27]

In the halls of the United Nations Israel's Qibya raid was also the subject of weeks of impassioned speeches and the drafting of resolutions.[28] Other border flare-ups followed a similar pattern. Receiving reports of complaints through the channels of UNTSO, the UN Security Council became the scene of dreary and predictable political theater: listening to speeches, complaints, accusations, and counteraccusations, followed by backroom drafting of resolutions and lobbying among members, sometimes concluded by a vote censuring one or both parties for violating the truce. The United Nations invariably took a critical view of Israel's state-sanctioned retaliatory responses while routinely urging Israel's neighbors to do more to control their frontiers and prevent infiltration. Such attempts at even-handedness did not sit well with many Israelis, who became convinced that the world body was tilting unfairly against them and favoring the Arabs.

The effectiveness of the retaliations policy as a deterrent remained a subject of recurring debate among decision-makers in Israel, among Israel's defenders and detractors abroad, as well as among social scientists.[29] Despite the apparent short-term quiet achieved along the frontiers following a particular action, the long-term effect seems to have been to exacerbate the conflict.[30] One of the few benefits, from an internal Israeli point of view, was that these reprisal actions relieved the sense of victimization and outrage on the Israeli street by exacting from the Arabs a "price for spilling Jewish blood." Such a result, of course, only contributed to a cycle of revenge and the deepening of mutual animosities.

It has become an enduring pattern of the Arab–Israeli conflict, from the 1950s until today, for Israel's political and military decision-makers to face frequent choices of how to respond to raiders—whether designated "freedom fighters," "martyrs," or "terrorists"—from across the border. Debates over tactics and ethics in the repeating cycles of violence have become a permanent feature of the Israeli–Arab and Israeli–Palestinian conflicts. Each new cross-border raid, bombardment, or attack almost guarantees a future response from the victim, and is also sure to provide more ammunition for those attempting to prove which party is the aggressor and which is merely trying to defend itself against the other's aggression. Comically and cynically, it can be seen as a question of complaining: "He hit me back first!"

From War to War, I (1949–1956)

A number of other factors—some external to the region or with little connection to the core struggle for Palestine/Israel—contributed to the outbreak of the second Arab–Israeli war in late October 1956. A crucial change in the regional balance of power came in the Summer of 1952 when the bloodless Free Officers revolution overthrew the corrupt Egyptian monarch. Led by General Muhammad Neguib and Colonels Gamal Abd al-Nasir and Anwar al-Sadat, a popular new régime began an experiment in Arab socialism, land reform, and realignment away from the West. Following snubs from the Americans and British (who began the process of withdrawing from their bases in the Suez Canal Zone), Nasir became a spokesman of the Non-Aligned Movement of developing countries that did not want to have to choose between the capitalist West and the communist East.

The change of régime in Egypt also afforded a brief, and quickly lost, window of opportunity when secret peace feelers were exchanged between Nasir and Moshe Sharett via Egyptian and Israeli emissaries in Paris. But by mid-1954 Egyptian–Israeli relations soured considerably in the wake of the uncovering of a spy ring in Alexandria and Cairo in which Israeli secret agents and Egyptian Jews attempted to undermine Egypt's relations with Britain and the US. Following the humiliation of Egyptian troops in Gaza during a heavy punitive Israeli reprisal operation in February 1955, the two countries appeared on a collision course, headed for war. The build-up of the Egyptian military with Soviet armaments (sent via Czecho-slovakia) during 1955 and 1956 was a matter of great concern to the Israelis, who appealed to the Western powers to provide the Jewish state with defensive weapons to match, along with a security treaty.[31]

Only with France did the Israelis manage to establish clandestine co-operation in the areas of arms procurement, intelligence sharing, and nuclear development. The Americans and British did everything possible to stall their usually negative answers to Israel's pleas for arms or a treaty, hoping at all costs to avoid an arms race in which the USSR backed the Arab world aligned against them and Israel. Their secret attempts during 1955 and 1956 to have Egyptian and Israeli leaders meet to discuss terms of an Anglo–American peace plan known as "Project Alpha" came to naught, as Nasir, Ben-Gurion, and Sharett successfully avoided making commitments, each for his own reasons.[32]

Neither Nasir nor Ben-Gurion wished to be seen by the international community as the initiator of a new war, but both sides did everything possible along their common frontier to provoke the other into launching full-scale hostilities. From the Israeli vantage point, the ongoing cycle of infiltration and reprisal—and the absence of significant arms or a security guarantee from the three Western powers—led to internal pressures from activist army officers and politicians to consider a pre-emptive attack on Egypt before it could completely absorb its new Soviet armaments in preparation for an attack on Israel. Even while David Ben-Gurion, serving then as prime minister and minister of defense, resisted such pressures, the chief of staff, Moshe Dayan, and others sought ways to provoke Egypt into attacking, hopefully also drawing in the Jordanians, so that the IDF might have an opportunity also to "straighten out" the West Bank boundaries of 1949 which some of them found indefensible.[33]

In the context of inter-Arab rivalries, the one-upmanship between Iraqi, Syrian, and Egyptian régimes played upon lingering Palestinian discontent, and during 1956 a slide to war was discernable. Pro-Nasir agents stirred up Arab nationalist feeling and unrest among Palestinian refugees in Jordan, leading to the dismissal by the young King Hussein of General

Glubb, the British founder and commander of the (Jordanian) Arab Legion, and further Arabizing his country's army by dismissing almost all of its British officers.[34] In January and April of 1956 UN Secretary-General Dag Hammarskjöld undertook personal visits to the region with the aim of restoring both parties' respect for the terms of their 1949 armistice agreement and heading off the feared outbreak.

Meanwhile, in response to Nasir's surprise nationalization of the Suez Canal Company in July, an international crisis developed with maritime states forming a coalition (the Suez Canal Users Conference) that attempted without success to pressure the Egyptian leader into retracting his defiant action. This external development augured well for Israel's top leadership who, historian Benny Morris claims, had already set their own course for war, "prodded by the persistent pinpricks of the infiltrators, by militant public opinion, by an officer corps bent on hostilities, by the vision of the potential 'second round' threat from Egypt and the rest of the Arab world, and by France."[35] During a top-secret high-level meeting in Sèvres, outside Paris, on 22–24 October 1956, Britain joined France and Israel in a tripartite conspiracy to recapture the Suez Canal and overthrow Nasir.[36]

On 29 October Israeli paratroopers were dropped into the Mitla Pass, deep in the Egyptian Sinai Desert, within striking distance of the Suez Canal—providing the first part of planned pretext for British and French intervention. Under the guise of protecting the Suez Canal from the belligerents, the British and French intervened militarily, destroying almost all of the Egyptian air force and landing paratroops in Port Said. But very quickly the invading troops were obliged by a UN cease-fire resolution to call a halt to their unfinished conquest of the Suez Canal Zone.[37]

By this time the tripartite collusion had become an open secret and was seized upon by the Soviet Union, whose prime minister issued dire threats in letters to American, French, British, and Israeli leaders. Anti-colonial anger reignited in Egypt, the Middle East, and throughout the developing world, dealing a blow to Israel's efforts to be welcomed among the non-aligned nations, most of whom now clearly identified Israel with the dying colonial powers. The Sinai/Suez war also caused strains in the Anglo–French–American alliance, as the Eisenhower administration was surprised and felt betrayed by this aggressive behavior on the part of its transatlantic allies.

Fighting between Egyptian and Israeli forces in the Sinai ended on 5 November, with both sides agreeing to a cease-fire brokered through the United Nations. After seven days of fighting, several thousand Egyptians, 500 Palestinians (mostly civilians in the Gaza Strip), and 190 Israelis had been killed; 800 Israeli soldiers were wounded, and about 4000 Egyptians taken prisoner.[38] Frenzied diplomacy undertaken at the UN by

Hammarskjöld and Canadian Foreign Affairs Minister Lester B. Pearson resulted in the General Assembly's creation and dispatch of a United Nations Emergency Force [UNEF] to take up positions along the Egyptian–Israeli border. After strong pressure from the Americans and the UN, the IDF finally retreated in early March 1957, handing over to UNEF contingents its last positions in the Gaza Strip and Sharm el-Sheikh. Having tried to hold out for firm guarantees, Israelis were left with little choice but to trust in the UNEF's monitoring capabilities to prevent *feday'un* infiltration into Israel from Gaza and to oversee shipping lanes in the Straits of Tiran, and to rely on US promises to assist Israel in assuring free navigation.

From War to War, II (1957–1967)

Following a familiar pattern, each of the series of Arab–Israeli wars since 1948–1949 left a trail of consequences and unfinished business that would carry forth the seeds of the next war.[39] Some issues were not resolved by the fighting; others were new controversies or irritants created by the warfare.

For eight years following the 1956 Suez/Sinai war, cross-border raiding subsided, providing short-term fulfillment of one of Israel's chief war aims. During the post-1956 period Israel went on to develop and expand economic and political relations with many emerging nation-states in Africa and Asia, as well as solidifying alliances with Turkey, Iran, and Ethiopia. But little else changed in ways that promised reconciliation and peace between the Arab states and Israel. "Paradoxically," notes Benny Morris, "the political outcome of the [1956] war was a clear and substantial radicalization of the conflict."[40]

Despite humiliation at the hands of British, French, and Israeli military forces, Nasir was acclaimed in Egypt and the Arab world for having registered "a moral and political victory over Israel and imperialism."[41] This led to an upsurge in his popularity throughout the Arab world; regaining lost Arab pride became a motive force in Nasir's new role as anti-colonialist hero.[42] A number of Arab states experienced military coups and revolutionary changes, with the threatened pro-Western régimes in Lebanon and Jordan requiring American and British military intervention in 1958. Nasirist elements in Syria, Iraq, and Jordan mobilized public enthusiasm for pan-Arab unity, and there were several short-lived attempts at unification and confederation. Although he cooperated with the UN in keeping Palestinian *feday'un* from resuming their infiltration from Gaza into Israeli territory, the Egyptian leader's ardor for defeating Israel in a "third round" seemed to grow stronger as he assumed the mantle of pan-Arab savior. His new confidence was based in part on Soviet help in rebuilding, re-equipping, and training his armed forces, as well as providing economic assistance, including the prestige project of the High Aswan Dam to promote industrialization in Egypt.

Skirmishes on the Israeli–Syrian border carried over from pre-1956 patterns, increasing in frequency and seriousness. Unresolved disputes and minor frictions over rights on the Sea of Galilee and usage of the DMZs along the Israeli–Syria frontier periodically exploded into violence involving artillery and mortar exchanges. Israel's decision to proceed with its National Water Carrier project—and especially to channel water from Sea of Galilee (also known as Lake Kinneret, or Lake Tiberias) through central Israel to help irrigate farms in the Negev Desert—triggered Arab League objections. In a minor "war over water" between Israel and Syria, Lebanon and Syria began preparing plans to divert the Jordan headwaters on their own Hasbani and Banias Rivers. Threats of violence loomed as both parties declared that the other's proposed water projects would be considered a "threat to the peace."[43]

Palestinian activism re-emerged during this period after a hiatus of a decade, finding its way onto the agenda of inter-Arab politics. Each Arab régime offered mostly verbal and some material support to the Palestinian cause as a pan-Arab issue, seeking to protect its own interests and freedom of action. The creation of the Palestine Liberation Organization [PLO] at the Arab League Summit in Cairo in January 1964 was an important step in returning the Palestinians to a more prominent, if not yet central, role in regional affairs. The Palestine National Council, the PLO's parliament, convened for the first time in Jerusalem in May 1964 and adopted a National Charter calling for the elimination of Israel and the restoration of Palestine to the Palestinians.[44] On 1 January 1965, the "Fatah" movement—the largest single constituent group within the PLO— mounted the first of many cross-border raids, an unimpressive sabotage attempt on Israel's recently inaugurated National Water Carrier. Over the next two and a half years, Fatah and other groups mounted some 122 raids into Israel; without access to Israel from Egypt, they now operated mainly from bases in Lebanon, Jordan, and Syria.[45]

After the killing of three Israeli paratroops by a mine near the Jordanian border in November 1966, Israeli forces mounted a major reprisal raid on the village of as-Samu. This action had a destabilizing effect on the Hashemite kingdom with its large Palestinian population and contributed to inter-Arab calls for action against Israel.[46] To these local incidents— pin-pricks adding to Israel's insecurity and provoking cross-border incursions—were added international and regional factors that would ultimately combine to bring about the next Arab–Israeli war. An arms race had developed between Soviet clients Syria and Egypt, on the one hand, and Israel as a largely French but now also an American client, on the other. In the pan-Arab context of displaying support for the Palestinian cause, Egypt found itself ridiculed for "hiding behind the skirts of the UNEF" while the rival Syrian régime struck a more militant pose. Syrian shelling of northern Israeli settlements and towns from bunkers perched on the Golan Heights had provoked occasional retaliations and air strikes by Israel. Overflights ended up in dogfights in early April 1967 in which Israeli pilots shot down six Syrian MiG-21 fighter jets, including two over Damascus.[47]

Threats and blood-curdling rhetoric escalated accordingly. Although the Israeli military may have been confident about its superiority, a feeling of panic developed among sectors of the public: as Abba Eban recalls, many people "were afraid that a great massacre was sweeping down upon us. And in many places in Israel there was talk of Auschwitz and Maidanek."[48] During May 1967 Israel, Egypt, and Syria mobilized and deployed their troops as open warfare loomed, waiting only for one side to fire the first shot. Soviet intelligence reports transmitted to both Egypt and Syria indicated that Israel was amassing troops on the Syrian border with the aim of invading Syria and toppling the radical Ba'th rulers in Damascus. In fact, no such build-up occurred. In a diversionary effort to threaten Israel's southern flank, Nasir moved more troops into the Sinai. His subsequent request for the removal of UNEF observers from the frontier with Israel was speedily approved and executed by UN Secretary-General U Thant, to the consternation and surprise of many observers, and possibly even of the Egyptian president himself.

Nasir's blockade of the Straits of Tiran to Israeli shipping on 23 May 1967 was designated by Israel as a *casus belli*. Blood-curdling rhetoric from Arab capitals contributed to a feeling of siege and doom among Israelis, whose prime minister and minister of defense, the uncharismatic Levi Eshkol, proved unable to inspire confidence among the public. Last-ditch international efforts to head off an expected outbreak of war through political discussions, or the demonstrative dispatch of a multinational flotilla to the Israeli port city of Eilat, proved fruitless.[49]

In a surprise attack on the morning of 5 June 1967, Israeli fighter jets bombed Egyptian airfields, destroying most of the aircraft on the tarmac while IDF tanks and troops advanced into Gaza and the Sinai Peninsula. Bound by a recently signed mutual defense pact and with its army placed (on paper at least) under Egyptian military command, Jordan opened fire on Israeli positions in and around Jerusalem, leading Israelis to expand their fighting onto two fronts. In lightning fashion, the Israelis destroyed the remaining air forces in Syria and Jordan, and achieved victory after victory against Egyptian and Jordanian ground forces. On 9 June, Israeli forces were ordered to undertake a massive assault to conquer the Syrian-controlled Golan Heights. After six days of fighting, Israeli casualties totaled approximately 780 dead and 2500 wounded; Egypt lost perhaps 10,000 to 15,000 killed and 5000 taken prisoner; Jordan lost 800 killed and over 600 were taken prisoner; Syria lost 500 dead, with 2500 wounded and almost 600 taken prisoner.[50]

Historians of the Arab–Israeli wars continue to debate several questions associated with the 1967 outbreak. One is whether, in the high-level consultations between Israeli representatives and the US Johnson administration in late May, the Americans gave a "green light"—or an "amber light"—to the IDF to attack Egypt in June. Another is whether (and, if so, why) the Soviets knowingly provided false intelligence information to the Syrians and Egyptians, wittingly or unwittingly contributing to increasing the belligerence of the Arab states that ultimately provoked Israel's preemptive strike.[51]

More noteworthy are some of the after-effects and consequences of the lop-sided Israeli victory, which changed the geopolitical balance and map of the Middle East. The IDF's rapid conquest of the Sinai Peninsula, the Gaza Strip, the West Bank, and the Golan Heights added 430,000 sq. km. to Israel's territory—an area three an a half times larger than Israel proper. The war also altered the shape of the conflict in several ways. Significantly, the new map removed Egypt and Jordan from their "tutelage" over the Palestinians in the Gaza Strip and the West Bank, reuniting all the pieces of former Mandatory Palestine under Israeli rule.

Following weeks of apocalyptic gloom, the Israeli public savored the thrill and relief of victory. For some people, the decisive Israeli victory was "the Holocaust that didn't happen"—largely because, this time, the tough Israeli Jews chose not to behave like their supposedly passive diaspora cousins.[52] Some wondered, optimistically at the time, whether an opportunity had been created for a new partition plan for sharing or re-dividing the disputed land between Israelis and Palestinians.[53] This apparent opening proved illusory and fleeting.

At the other end of the political spectrum in Israel, many religious Jews saw the victory as miraculous, and viewed the capture of the Holy Places inside the ancient walls of Jerusalem as a messianic sign of divine intervention and approval for the liberation of all of *Eretz-Israel* within its full Biblical boundaries. "A messianic, expansionist wind swept over the country," noted historian Benny Morris. "Secular individuals were also swept up."[54] Several years later the *Gush Emunim* ("Bloc of the Faithful") was created, a fundamentalist movement dedicated to the (re)settlement of

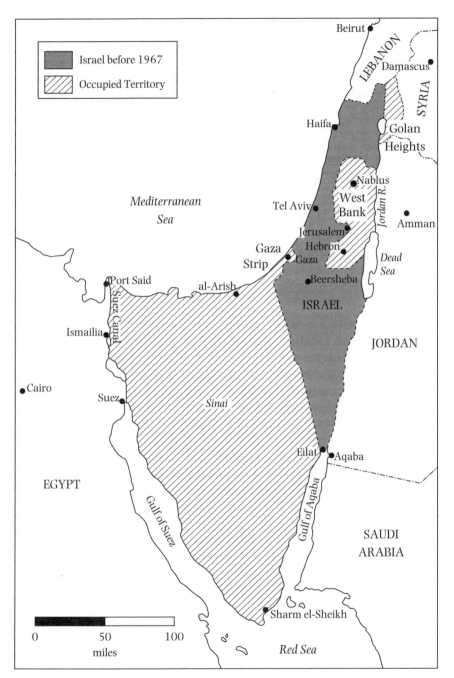

Map 7.1   Israel and Occupied Territories, 1967

Jews throughout the newly acquired territories of what they considered *Eretz-Israel ha-Shlema*—the "complete land of Israel," or "greater Israel."

Those in the Arab world and elsewhere who regarded Israel's creation in 1948 as the illegitimate product of violent conquest and ethnic cleansing viewed the triumphant Israelis and the new 1967 map of greatly enlarged Israel as proof of Zionism's inherent aggressiveness and expansionism. Between 200,000 and 250,000 Palestinians, almost a quarter of the West Bank's population, were displaced, some during the war but most in expulsions immediately afterwards, many becoming refugees for the second time since 1948.[55] Those who remained in their homes came under Israeli military occupation, which would prove to be more than temporary as deadlock once again set in between the belligerents of the third major Arab–Israeli war.

Israel's conquest of the Egyptian Sinai, Jordanian West Bank, and Syrian Golan created potential bilateral bargaining situations, giving rise to the formula of exchanging "land for peace"—which was soon elevated into a sacred principle as the required starting-point for seeking ways to end the Arab–Israeli conflict. The dispute, in its newly revised form, also cast Israel as the new regional superpower, waiting smugly for a "phone call" from Nasir in Cairo, Hussein in Amman, and/or Salah Jadid in Damascus, suing for terms of peace. In the international arena, Egypt and Syria (backed by the USSR) and Israel (backed by the US) each sought to bring appropriate United Nations pressure to bear on the other party.

After months of public debate and backroom negotiations at the United Nations, the Security Council on 22 November 1967 adopted Resolution 242, based on a consensus of what the drafters considered would make possible some movement toward peace. The resolution, built on the land-for-peace idea, would become a benchmark for all future efforts to resolve the conflict. In the immediate months and years following November 1967, officials of the UN, the US government, and the Soviet Union undertook diplomatic efforts to get each of the parties to declare its acceptance of the resolution's principles and recommendations.[56]

From War to War, III (1967–1973)

Often cited as a masterpiece of diplomatic ambiguity, UN Security Council Resolution 242 called for the "withdrawal of Israeli armed forces from territories occupied in the recent conflict," but (significantly, some would argue) not the "withdrawal of Israeli armed forces from *the* [i.e., *all the*] territories occupied in the recent conflict." This omission of the definite article "the" gave tremendous bargaining leverage to the Israelis, who did not consider themselves obliged to withdraw from every inch of territories captured during the war. Arab interpretations stressed the resolution's firm reiteration of the principle of the inadmissibility of acquiring territory by war and, given their view of Israel as the unquestioned aggressor in June 1967, they believed Israeli withdrawal from *all* territories captured should be unconditional, and not related to any diplomatic *quid pro quo*. None of the Arab leaders, especially after the humiliation of their battle-field defeats, was about to "pick up the phone" to call Tel Aviv to begin peace talks. All this signaled the prospect of more years of boycott, non-recognition, diplomatic stalemate, and probably future wars.

Resolution 242 also affirmed the necessity of tackling three longstand-ing sore points, namely: (a) freedom of navigation (backing Israeli com-plaints since 1949 about Egypt's refusal to allow passage of Israeli shipping through the Suez Canal); (b) "achieving a just settlement of the refugee problem"; and (c) guaranteeing of "the territorial inviolability and political independence of every State in the area." Equipped with this resolution, Swedish diplomat Gunnar Jarring accepted the job of UN Special Representative and attempted to move the ex-belligerents along a path to peace. Given the tough stance of the Arab states to offer nothing until Israel committed itself to full withdrawal from territories seized in the June 1967 war,[57] Jarring was unable to get the parties to meet face-to-face and his mission took the form of shuttling between Middle Eastern capitals. His efforts, in the end, came to naught, as did those of US Secretary of State William Rogers.[58]

Beginning in December 1968, Egypt and Israel found themselves locked into increasingly deadly exchanges of artillery fire along the Suez Canal. Israeli planes carried out many sorties, sometimes deep into Egyptian territory, resulting in the Egyptian deployment of new Soviet missile batteries along the Canal and the use of Soviet pilots to bolster Egyptian air defenses. Between March 1969 and August 1970, this low-level Egyptian–Israeli "War of Attrition" kept the pot boiling, with many fragile ceasefires negotiated only to be broken. In the end, this mini-war cost the lives of thousands of Egyptians (military and civilian) and 367 Israeli soldiers. It demonstrated Arab dissatisfaction with the status quo and kept post-war tensions high, not only between the main protagonists on the ground but also between their Soviet and American patrons.[59] It also helped to position Israel and Egypt for one more major war before the conditions for bilateral peace arrangements would be favorable within the next decade.

The non-resolution of the post-1967 stalemate and the legal ambigu-ities about the status of the territories captured by the Israelis became fertile ground for the development of the tenth of our *core arguments*, one that remains part of the Arab–Israeli conflict to this day. *Is the land conquered by Israel in June 1967 on the West Bank of the Jordan to be considered "occupied territory," and does Israel have the right to build Jewish settlements there?*

For religious Zionists, the answer is clear. The territories in question are, for them, an integral part of the Biblically promised *Eretz-Israel.* The residence there by non-Jewish inhabitants for centuries or millennia was considered a temporary "occupation" which the state of Israel had now corrected by "liberating" those territories and returning them to their rightful Jewish owners. *Gush Emunim* and other settlers' movements proceeded to implement their own "return to Zion" by moving into these territories and lobbying for active government support for what they considered a supreme endeavor commanded by the Lord. These groups claimed to be continuing the pioneering work of Zionism begun during the first and second *aliyot* but, in their view, abruptly and artificially stopped by the borders of 1949; this ideological stance appealed to some and was criticized by others.[60] Israeli governments had their own secular rationale for allowing or encouraging the settlement enterprise—chiefly to apply pressure on Jordan to move more quickly towards considering a land-for-peace swap.[61]

Arab, Palestinian, and other spokesmen challenged Israeli settlement activities by invoking the Fourth Geneva Convention, under which (Art. 49) the "Occupying Power shall not deport or transfer parts of its own civilian population into the territory it occupies." Most nations of the world support this straightforward reading of the situation and of the international convention, accepting that the lands in question are indeed "occupied" by Israel as a result of the 1967 war and should be treated accordingly.[62]

The official Israeli interpretation, however, is based on a different understanding of the legal status of the West Bank as being "disputed" but not "occupied" territory. The reasoning behind this stance stems from the status of the lands that devolved from the termination of the British Mandate, with Israel being seen as the only state to inherit sovereignty over (most of) those lands in 1949. Sovereign authority over the West Bank and Gaza is less clear-cut from a legal point of view because (a) Jordan's 1950 annexation of the West Bank was never internationally recognized, except by two countries (Britain, Pakistan), and (b) Egypt never claimed or assumed sovereignty over the Gaza Strip, but chose only to administer the area.[63]

Based on this interpretation, successive Israeli governments have authorized the acquisition of lands and the building of new settlements in the territories primarily on the basis of its own domestic political and economic considerations, often invoking debatable security imperatives. Relatively less heed was given to the impact of expanding settlements on the indigenous Palestinian population, on the neighboring states, or on international (or American) public opinion. At first "dovish" Israeli leaders did not object to the creation of new settlements, seeing them as bargaining chips and levers with which to pressure the Arabs into agreeing to negotiate. But as the occupation continued with no political agreement in sight, the growth of Jewish settlements in the territories continued apace, bringing in their wake not only human rights abuses (see Chapter 9) but also the necessary infrastructure that signaled a certain permanency rather than a temporary occupation: road networks, electricity grids, water access, and adequate security and protection.

Adding uncertainty to the local, regional, and international tensions during the post-1967 period were leadership changes in Israel (hardline Golda Meir replacing the dovish Levi Eshkol), Egypt (pragmatic Anwar al-Sadat replacing charismatic ideologue Gamal Abd al-Nasir), and Syria (military strongman Hafez al-Asad replacing Ba'athist functionary Nureddin al-Atasi). A kind of internal coup also occurred in 1969 within the recently created PLO, when Fatah's Yasir Arafat was elected chairman, effectively ending Egypt's manipulation of the organization. The latter development testified to the growing centrality and autonomy of the Palestinians as an actor in inter-Arab and Israeli–Arab relations, a trend we shall examine in Chapter 8.

The battle of Karameh, Jordan, in March 1968, was an important engagement during which Palestinian fighters, with the support of the Jordanian Army, held out against units of the IDF, leading to a new self-confidence which in turn contributed to an increased radicalization and militarization of the conflict. An excess of Palestinian assertiveness subsequently led to "Black September" of 1970. Some radical Palestinian groups went too far in challenging the authority of the Jordanian régime, provoking violent confrontations in which the King's army killed between 3000 and 5000 Palestinians (of whom only some 1000 were fighters), wounding or expelling many more. In the years following, PLO factions were forced to relocate and conduct their operations against Israel from bases in Lebanon.[64]

Arabs in Egypt, Syria, Jordan, and elsewhere experienced post-war despair at their inability to hold their ground against the Israelis.[65] Following the death of Gamal Abd al-Nasir in 1970, Anwar Sadat sought to wean Egypt away from its dependence on the Soviet Union and to create a new relationship with the Americans, who he felt might offer, among other things, diplomatic leverage on Israel to return occupied Sinai to Egypt. After some unanswered peace feelers in 1970 and 1971, Sadat and the Syrians prepared instead to force a break in the stalemate by military means. Their forces were initially successful in launching a surprise attack, on the Jewish holy day of Yom Kippur (which fell on 6 October 1973), against thinly manned Israeli lines along the Suez Canal and on the Golan Heights, driving the IDF back and recapturing some of the land occupied by Israel in the previous war.

Soviet and American resupply of weaponry during the war were crucial to the three belligerents. Other Arab states briefly exercised their new economic clout by announcing a total embargo on oil sales to the US and on other states according to their support for Israel. After three weeks of fighting, Israeli troops regained their ground and a cease-fire was established with the intimate involvement of the US and USSR—neither of whom wished to see any of the protagonists decisively humiliated. Losses of war matériel and human casualties were high on all sides: more than 2800 Israelis died, almost 9000 wounded; Arabs lost about 8500 dead and 20,000 wounded.[66] Soviet and American diplomatic efforts produced a new Security Council Resolution (338), one that reaffirmed 242 but called additionally for "negotiations ... between the parties concerned under appropriate auspices aimed as establishing a just and durable peace in the Middle East."

The shock of being caught off-guard caused much soul-searching in Israel, just as the early successes of Syrian and Egyptian forces allowed them a renewed sense of honor and victory, creating an entirely new psychological environment for post-war diplomatic efforts.[67] The impact of the oil embargo also signaled a new factor enhancing inter-Arab cooperation and giving the Arabs an improved bargaining position. The US announcement of a nuclear alert in the eastern Mediterranean during the fighting had sent a chilling message not only to the Soviet Union but also to the local actors. As a near-miss, it was a sobering warning for all concerned of the dangers of allowing regional warfare to explode into something more ominous.

Notes

1   For a firsthand Palestinian auto-critique, see, e.g., Musa Alami, "The Lesson of Palestine," *Middle East Journal* 3:4 (October 1949), 373–405. Other important re-evaluations were published by Beirut scholar Constantine K. Zurayk, *The Meaning of the Disaster*, transl. R. Bayly Winder, Beirut: Khayat's, 1956, and Lebanese diplomat Charles Malik, "The Near East: The Search for Truth," *Foreign Affairs* 30 (January 1952), reprinted in *Arab Nationalism: An Anthology*, ed. with an introduction by Sylvia G. Haim, Berkeley / Los Angeles: University of California Press, 1962, 189–224, esp. 200–5.

2   Avi Shlaim, "The Rise and Fall of the All-Palestine Government in Gaza," *Journal of Palestine Studies* 20:1 (Autumn 1990), 37–53; Rashid Khalidi, *The Iron Cage: The Story of the Palestinian Struggle for Statehood*, Boston, MA: Beacon Press, 2006, 135–6.

3   Avi Plascov, *The Palestinian Refugees in Jordan, 1948–1957*, London: Frank Cass, 1981; Mary Wilson, *King Abdullah, Britain and the Making of Jordan*, Cambridge, UK / New York, etc.: Cambridge University Press, 1987, 181–4; Joseph Nevo, *King Abdallah and Palestine: A Territorial Ambition*, London / New York: Macmillan [St. Antony's Series], 1996, 166–71; Adnan Abu-Odeh, *Jordanians, Palestinians and the Hashemite Kingdom in the Middle East Peace Process*, Washington, DC: United States Institute of Peace Press, 1999, 45.

4   Khalidi, Iron Cage, 125–6, 136.

5   Malcolm Kerr, *The Arab Cold: Gamal Abd al-Nasir and His Rivals, 1958–1970*, 3rd ed., London / New York: [for the Royal Institute of International Affairs] Oxford University Press, 1971.

6   Itamar Rabinovich, *The Road Not Taken: Early Arab–Israeli Negotiations*, New York / Oxford: Oxford University Press, 1991, 82.

7   Robert W. MacDonald, *The League of Arab States: A Study in the Dynamics of Regional Organization*, Princeton, NJ: Princeton University Press, 1965, 118–23; Aharon Cohen, *Israel and the Arab World*, New York: Funk and Wagnalls, 1970, 348–9, 484–6; Dan S. Chill, *The Arab Boycott of Israel: Economic Aggression and World Reaction*, New York: Praeger, 1976; Walter Henry Nelson and Terence C. F. Prittie, *The Economic War against the Jews*, New York: Random House, 1977; Sami Hadawi, *Arab Boycott of Israel: Peaceful, Defensive and Constructive*, Ottawa: Arab League Information Center, 1977.

8   See, e.g., Rashid Khalidi, *The Iron Cage*, 136–8, 141.

9   See, e.g., Nathan A. Pelcovits, *The Long Armistice: UN Peacekeeping and the Arab–Israeli Conflict, 1948–1960*, foreword by Samuel W. Lewis. Boulder, CO / San Francisco / Oxford: Westview Press, 1993, 40–3.

10 See, e.g., Shabtai Rosenne, *Israel's Armistice Agreements with the Arab States: A Judicial Interpretation*, Tel Aviv: Blumstein's [for the International Law Assn., Israel Branch], 1951; articles by Henry Cattan, Nathan Feinberg, and the Seminar of Arab Jurists, reproduced in Moore, *The Arab–Israeli Conflict* I: 221, 246f., 339.

11 For excellent firsthand and other accounts of the armistice regime, see E. H. Hutchison, *Violent Truce: A Military Observer Looks at the Arab–Israeli Conflict, 1951–1955*, New York: Devin-Adair, 1956; E. L. M. Burns, *Between Arab and Israeli*, New York: Ivan Obolensky, 1963; Carl von Horn, *Soldiering for Peace*, London: Cassell, 1966; Earl Berger, *The Covenant and the Sword: Arab–Israeli Relations, 1948–56*, Toronto: University of Toronto Press [London: Routledge and Kegan Paul], 1965; N. Bar-Yaacov, *The Israeli–Syrian Armistice: Problems of Implementation, 1949–1966*, Jerusalem: Magnes Press (Hebrew University), 1967; Aryeh Shalev, *The Israeli–Syria Armistice Regime, 1949–1955*, Boulder, CO: Westview Press /Jerusalem: The Jerusalem Post [Jaffee Center for

Strategic Studies, Study No. 21], 1993; Pelcovits, *Long Armistice*; Neil Caplan, *Futile Diplomacy*, vol. III: *The United Nations, the Great Powers and Middle East Peacemaking, 1948–1954*, London: Frank Cass, 1997, ch. VIII.

12   On the unsuccessful UN diplomacy of the period, see Neil Caplan, "A Tale of Two Cities: The Rhodes and Lausanne Conferences, 1949," *Journal of Palestine Studies* 21:3 (Spring 1992), 5–34; Caplan, *Futile Diplomacy* III: chs. III–VII and IX–X.

13   On the work of the PCC, see David P. Forsythe, *United Nations Peacemaking: The Conciliation Commission for Palestine*, Baltimore, MD / London: Johns Hopkins University Press, 1972.

14   http://www.mfa.gov.il/MFAHeb/General+info/About+us/foreign_relation. htm. Cf. Aaron S. Klieman, *Israel and the World after 40 Years*, Washington, etc.: Pergamon-Brassey's, 1990, 8, who gives the probably incorrect number of 54 countries affording recognition by May 1949.

15   See, e.g., Caplan, *Futile Diplomacy* III: 54–5; Pelcovits, *Long Armistice*, 42; John Quigley, *The Case for Palestine: An International Law Perspective*, rev. and updated ed., Durham, NC / London: Duke University Press, 2005, 90–3; Israel State Archives, *Documents on the Foreign Policy of Israel* vol. 6 (1951), ed. Yemima Rosenthal (Jerusalem: 1991), 66f., 201.

16   Bernadotte Plan, in *Futile Diplomacy* III: 28–33, 279–83. See also Amitzur Ilan, *Bernadotte in Palestine: A Study in Contemporary Humanitarian Knight-Errantry*, New York: St. Martin's Press, 1989, 177–91, 242–7.

17   See, e.g., Sharett address to National Press Club, Washington, 21 November 1955, quoted in Caplan, *Futile Diplomacy* III: 55.

18   UNSC Resolution 95, 1 September 1951, reproduced in *The Israel–Arab Reader: A Documentary History of the Middle East Conflict*, 7th rev. ed., eds. Walter Laqueur and Barry Rubin, New York: Penguin, 2008, 88–9 (given erroneously as resolution 619). For Egyptian responses, see Michael B. Oren, *Origins of the Second Arab–Israel War: Egypt, Israel and the Great Powers: 1952–56*, London: Frank Cass, 1992, 39–42; Caplan, *Futile Diplomacy* III: 54.

19   On the Johnston mission, see Samir N. Saliba, *The Jordan River Dispute*, The Hague: Martinus Nijhoff, 1968, 89–107; Michael Brecher, *Decisions in Israel's Foreign Policy*, New Haven, CT: Yale University Press, 1975, 192–7; Miriam R. Lowi, *Water and Power: The Politics of a Scarce Resource in the Jordan River Basin*, New York / Cambridge, UK: Cambridge University Press, 1993, 86–91; Arnon Sofer, *Rivers of Fire: The Conflict over Water in the Middle East*, transl. Murray Rosovsky and Nina Copaken, Lanham, MD: Rowman and Littlefield, 1999, 158–61.

20   Benny Morris, *Israel's Border Wars, 1949-1956: Arab Infiltration, Israeli Retaliation, and the Countdown to the Suez War*, Oxford: Clarendon Press, 1993, chs. 4–5.

21   Ibid., 97–9.

22   The fighting at Qalqilya, which left some 70 Arabs and 17 Israelis dead, was described by Bar-On as "the bloodiest and bitterest battle ... since the end of the 1948 war." For details of the fighting and the political and military

aftermath, see Mordechai Bar-On, *The Gates of Gaza: Israel's Road to Suez and Back, 1955–1957*, transl. Ruth Rossing, New York: St. Martin's Press, 1994, 213–18; Moshe Dayan, *Diary of the Sinai Campaign*, New York: Harper and Row, 1966, 52–7; Morris, *Israel's Border Wars*, 397–402.

23 Morris, *Israel's Border Wars*, ch. 8; Caplan, *Futile Diplomacy* III: 220–9; "The 1953 Qibya Raid Revisited: Excerpts from Moshe Sharett's Diary," special document introduced by Walid Khalidi, annotated by Neil Caplan, *Journal of Palestine Studies* 31:4 (Summer 2002), 77–98.

24 Eban to Sharett, 26 November 1953, Israel State Archives, *Documents on the Foreign Policy of Israel*, vol. 8 (1953), ed. Yemima Rosenthal, Jerusalem: 1995, 906–7 [doc. 539]. Cf. Abba Eban, *An Autobiography*, New York: Random House, 1977, 173; Eban, *Personal Witness: Israel through My Eyes*, New York: G. P. Putnam's Sons, 1992, 236; Gideon Rafael, *Destination Peace: Three Decades of Israeli Foreign Policy: A Personal Memoir*, New York: Stein and Day, 1981, 34; Caplan, *Futile Diplomacy* III: 222–4.

25 ISA, Cabinet minutes, 19 October 1953, reprinted in *Davar*, 20 October 1953; Eng. transl. in Livia Rokach, *Israel's Sacred Terrorism: A Study Based on Moshe Sharett's Personal Diary and Other Documents*, Belmont, MA: Association of Arab-American University Graduates, 1980, 61f.; Caplan, *Futile Diplomacy* III: 224; Morris, *Israel's Border Wars*, 252–8.

26 See Caplan, *Futile Diplomacy* III: 224, and sources cited there.

27 Neil Caplan, "The 'Sharettist Option' Revisited," in *Arab–Jewish Relations: From Conflict to Resolution? Essays in Honour of Prof. Moshe Ma'oz*, eds. Elie Podeh and Asher Kaufman, Brighton: Sussex Academic Press, 2005, 69, 73 (n. 6). On the two contrasting worldviews and approaches of Ben-Gurion and Sharett, see Michael Brecher, *The Foreign Policy System of Israel: Setting, Images, Process*, London / Toronto / Melbourne: Oxford University Press, 1972, ch. 12.

28 In the end, UNSC resolution 101 (1953) censuring Israel was adopted by a vote of 9–0–2 on 24 November 1953. See *United Nations Resolutions on Palestine and the Arab–Israeli Conflict*, vol. I: 1947–1974, rev. ed., ed. George J. Tomeh, Washington, DC: Institute for Palestine Studies, 1988, 135–6.

29 See, e.g., J. B. Glubb, "Violence on the Jordan–Israel Border: A Jordanian View," *Foreign Affairs* 32:4 (July 1954), 552–62; Moshe Dayan, "Israel's Border and Security Problems," *Foreign Affairs* 33:2 (January 1955), 250–67; Fred J. Khouri, "The Policy of Retaliation in Arab–Israeli Relations," *Middle East Journal* 20:4 (Autumn 1966), 435–55; Barry M. Blechman, "The Impact of Israel's Reprisals on Behavior of the Bordering Arab Nations Directed at Israel," *Journal of Conflict Resolution* 16:2 (June 1972), 155–81; Jonathan Shimshoni, *Israel and Conventional Deterrence: Border Warfare from 1953 to 1970*, Ithaca, NY / London: Cornell University Press, 1988, 48–51, 65–8; Morris, *Israel's Border Wars*, chs. 5–6.

30 Fred J. Khouri, "Friction and Conflict on the Israeli–Syrian Front," *Middle East Journal* 17:1–2 (Winter–Spring 1963), 24; Khouri, "The Policy of Retaliation," 438.

31 On this period see Michael B. Oren, "Secret Egypt–Israel Peace Initiatives Prior to the Suez Campaign," *Middle Eastern Studies* 26:3 (July 1990), 351–70, and *Origins of the Second Arab–Israel War*; M. Bar-On, *Gates of Gaza*; Neil Caplan, *Futile Diplomacy*, vol. IV: *Operation Alpha and the Failure of Anglo–American Coercive Diplomacy in the Arab–Israeli Conflict, 1954–1956*, London: Frank Cass, 1997; Avi Shlaim, *The Iron Wall: Israel and the Arab World*, London: Allen Lane / Penguin Press, 2000, chs. 3–4.

32 Shimon Shamir, "The Collapse of Project Alpha," in *Suez 1956: The Crisis and Its Consequences*, eds. Wm. Roger Louis and Roger Owen, Oxford: Clarendon Press, 1989, 73–100; Caplan, *Futile Diplomacy* IV.

33 On the build-up to war, see the analyses offered by M. Bar-On, *Gates of Gaza*; Morris, *Israel's Border Wars*; Motti Golani, *Israel in Search of War: The Sinai Campaign, 1955–1956*, Brighton: Sussex Academic Press, 1998; and Mordechai Bar-On, Benny Morris, and Motti Golani, "Reassessing Israel's Road to Sinai/Suez, 1956: A Trialogue," in *Traditions and Transitions in Israel Studies: Books on Israel, volume 6*, eds. Laura Zittrain Eisenberg, Neil Caplan, Naomi B. Sokoloff, and Mohammed Abu-Nimer, Albany: State University of New York Press, 2002, 3–41.

34 Uriel Dann, "Glubb's Ouster and its Aftermath," in U. Dann, *King Hussein and the Challenge of Arab Radicalism: Jordan, 1955–1967*, New York / Oxford: Oxford University Press, 1989, 31–8.

35 Benny Morris, *Righteous Victims: A History of the Zionist Arab Conflict, 1881–1999*, New York: Alfred A. Knopf, 1999 / London: John Murray, 2000, 288–9. See also Golani, *Israel in Search of War*.

36 M. Bar-On, *Gates of Gaza*, ch. 15; S. Ilan Troen, "The Protocol of Sèvres: British/French/Israeli Collusion against Egypt, 1956," *Israel Studies* I:2 (Fall 1996), 122–39; Avi Shlaim, "The Protocol of Sevres: Anatomy of a War Plot," in *The 1956 War: Collusion and Rivalry in the Middle East*, ed. David Tal, London: Frank Cass [Cummings Center Series], 2001, 119–44; Mordechai Bar-On, "Three Days in Sèvres, October 1956," *History Workshop Journal* 62 (2006), 172–86.

37 Among the many studies devoted to the Sinai/Suez war of 1956, the following are recommended: Kennett Love, *Suez: The Twice-Fought War*, New York / Toronto: McGraw-Hill, 1969; Wm. Roger Louis and Roger Owen, eds., *Suez 1956: The Crisis and Its Consequences*; Selwyn Ilan Troen and Moshe Shemesh, eds., *The Suez–Sinai Crisis 1956: Retrospective and Reappraisal*, London: Frank Cass, 1990; Keith Kyle, *Suez: Britain's End of Empire in the Middle East*, New York: I. B. Tauris, 2003 [orig. 1991]; David Tal, ed., *The 1956 War*.

38 Morris, *Righteous Victims*, 295–6.

39 For an overview, see Itamar Rabinovich, "Seven Wars and One Peace Treaty," in *The Arab–Israeli Conflict: Perspectives*, 2nd ed., ed. Alvin Z. Rubinstein, New York: HarperCollins, 1991, ch. 2.

40 Morris, *Righteous Victims*, 301.

41 Elie Podeh, "Regaining Lost Pride: The Impact of the Suez Affair on Egypt and the Arab World," in *The 1956 War*, ed. Tal, 221.

42 Yoram Meital, "Egyptian Perspectives on the Suez War," in *The 1956 War*, ed. Tal, 195–207; Podeh, "Regaining Lost Pride," ibid., 209–24.

43 See, e.g., Khouri, "Friction and Conflict on the Israeli–Syrian Front," 14–34; Morris, *Righteous Victims*, 303–4; Ami Gluska, " 'The War over the Water' during the 1960s," in *A Never-Ending Conflict: A Guide to Israeli Military History*, ed. Mordechai Bar-On, Westport, CT / London: Praeger, 2004, 109–31.

44 The Palestine National Charter: Resolutions of the Palestine National Council, 1–17 July 1968, accessed March 23 2008 online at http://www.yale.edu/lawweb/avalon/mideast/plocov.htm.

45 Sayegh, *Armed Struggle*, 104–8; Morris, *Righteous Victims*, 303.

46 Michael B. Oren, *Six Days of War: June 1967 and the Making of the Modern Middle East*, Oxford: Oxford University Press, 2002, 33–8; Morris, *Righteous Victims*, 303.

47 Morris, *Righteous Victims*, 304.

48 Abba Eban, *An Autobiography*, New York: Random House, 1977, 400.

49 Morris, *Righteous Victims*, 304–11; Richard B. Parker, *The Politics of Miscalculation in the Middle East*, Bloomington: Indiana University Press, 1993, ch. 4.

50 Morris, *Righteous Victims*, 311–29; *The Six Day War: A Retrospective*, ed. Richard B. Parker, Gainesville: University Press of Florida, 1996; Oren, *Six Days of War*, 305.

51 Morris, *Righteous Victims*, 305–10; Parker, *The Politics of Miscalculation*, chs. 1, 2, 5; Ze'ev Schiff, "The Green Light," *Foreign Policy* 50 (Spring 1983), 73–85; Avner Cohen, *Israel and the Bomb*, New York: Columbia University Press, 1998, ch. 14; Roland Popp, "Stumbling Decidedly into the Six-Day War," *Middle East Journal* 60:2 (Spring 2006), 281–309; Isabella Ginor, "The Cold War's Longest Cover-up: How and Why the USSR Instigated the 1967 War," *MERIA* 7:3 (September 2003); Isabella Ginor and Gideon Remez, "The Spymaster, the Communist, and Foxbats over Dimona: The USSR's Motive for Instigating the Six-Day War," *Israel Studies* 11:2 (Summer 2006), 88–130; Isabella Ginor and Gideon Remez, "The Six-Day War as a Soviet Initiative: New Evidence and Methodological Issues," *MERIA* 12:3 (September 2008).

52 Jay Y. Gonen, *A Psychohistory of Zionism*, New York: Mason-Charter, 1975, 166–7; Simon N. Herman, *Israelis and Jews: The Continuity of an Identity*, Philadelphia, PA: Jewish Publication Society, 1971, 211–12, and "In the Shadow of the Holocaust," *Jerusalem Quarterly* 3 (Spring 1977), 89–90.

53 See, e.g., Abba Eban, "Some Unsystematic Thinking About the Arab–Israeli Conflict," in *Dynamics of a Conflict: A Re-examination of the Arab–Israeli Conflict*, ed. Gabriel Sheffer, Atlantic Highlands, NJ: Humanities Press, 1975, 361–2; Bernard Wasserstein, *Israelis and Palestinians: Why Do They Fight? Can They Stop?* 3rd ed., New Haven, CT / London: Yale University Press / London: Profile Books, 2008, 122–5.

54 Morris, *Righteous Victims*, 329–36.

55 Some expulsions, like those from the (immediately razed) villages of Imwas, Yalu, Beit Nuba, and Deir Ayyub in the Latrun Salient displayed "an element of revenge for 1948." Morris, *Righteous Victims*, 328.

56 Among the many discussions of this landmark resolution, see the Washington Institute publication, *UN Resolution 242: Building Block of Peacemaking*, accessed online at http://www.washingtoninstitute.org/templateC04.php? CID=151; commentary by Yossi Beilin, Daoud Kuttab, Rana Sabbagh-Gargour, and Abdel Monem Said Aly; see bitterlemons.org, Middle East Roundtable, 22:6, 5 June 2008, "The Land for Peace Formula Revisited," accessed online 30 August 2008 at http://www.bitterlemons.org. PalestineFacts.org accessed on line at http://www.palestinefacts.org/pf_1948to1967_un_242. php; Israel Ministry of Foreign Affairs accessed online at http://www.mfa.gov. il/MFA/Peace%20Process/Guide%20to%20the%20Peace%20Process/State ments%20Clarifying%20the%20Meaning%20of%20UN%20Security%20C

57 Khartoum Arab Summit resolutions of 1 September 1967, text reproduced in *The Israeli–Palestinian Conflict: A Documentary Record, 1967–1990*, ed. Yehuda Lukacs, Cambridge: Cambridge University Press, 1992, 454–5.

58 On the Jarring (UN) and Rogers (US) mediation episodes, see Saadia Touval, *The Peace Brokers: Mediators in the Arab–Israeli Conflict, 1948–1979*, Princeton, NJ: Princeton University Press, 1982, chs. 6 and 7; Norman G. Finkelstein, *Image and Reality of the Israel–Palestine Conflict*, new and rev. ed., New York: W. W. Norton [2nd ed., London: Verso], 2003, ch. 6.

59 On the War of Attrition, see Yaacov Bar-Siman-Tov, *The Israeli–Egyptian War of Attrition, 1969–1970*, New York: Columbia University Press, 1980; David A. Korn, *Stalemate: The War of Attrition and Great Power Diplomacy in the Middle East, 1967–1970*, Boulder, CO: Westview Press, 1992; Morris, *Righteous Victims*, 347–63; Parker, *Politics of Miscalculation*, chs. 6–7; Dan Shueftan, "The Israeli–Egyptian 'War of Attrition,' 1969–1970," in *A Never-Ending Conflict*, ed. Bar-On, 147–59; Isabella Ginor, "Under the Yellow Arab Helmet Gleamed Blue Russian Eyes: Operation *Kavkaz* and the War of Attrition," *Cold War History* 3:1 (October 2002), 129–56; Zeev Maoz, *Defending the Holy Land: A Critical Analysis of Israel's Security and Foreign Policy*, Ann Arbor: University of Michigan Press, 2006, ch. 4.

60 Gershon Shafir, "Zionism and Colonialism: A Comparative Approach," in *The Israel/Palestine Question*, ed. Ilan Pappé, London / New York: Routledge, 1999, 91–5; Geoffrey Aronson, *Creating Facts: Israel, Palestinian and the West Bank*, Washington, DC: Institute for Palestine Studies, 1987; Ian Lustick, *For the Land and the Lord: Jewish Fundamentalism in Israel*, New York: Council on Foreign Relations, 1988; Robert I. Friedman, *Zealots for Zion: Inside Israel's West Bank Settlement Movement*, New York: Random House, 1992; Gershom Gorenberg, *The Accidental Empire: Israel and the Birth of the Settlements, 1967–1977*, New York: Times Books, 2006.

61 See, e.g., Wasserstein, *Israelis and Palestinians*, 125–8.

62 Legal arguments are presented by W. Thomas Mallison and Sally V. Mallison, *The Palestine Problem in International Law and World Order*, Harlow, UK:

Longman, 1986, ch. 6, and John Quigley, *The Case for Palestine: An International Law Perspective*, rev. and updated ed., Durham, NC / London: Duke University Press, 2005, chs. 23–4.

63   Allan Gerson, *Israel, the West Bank and International Law*, London: Frank Cass, 1978, 76–82 and ch. IV; Julius Stone, *Israel and Palestine: Assault on the Law of Nations*, Baltimore, MD: Johns Hopkins University Press, 1981, 51–6, 118–20.

64   Yezid Sayigh, *Armed Struggle and the Search for State: The Palestinian National Movement, 1949–1993*, Oxford: Oxford University Press / Washington, DC: The Institute for Palestine Studies, 1997, 262–81, 312–17; Adnan Abu-Odeh, *Jordanians, Palestinians and the Hashemite Kingdom in the Middle East Peace Process*, Washington, DC: United States Institute of Peace Press, 1999, ch. 8; Morris, *Righteous Victims*, 373–5; Rex Brynen, *Sanctuary and Survival: The PLO in Lebanon*, Boulder, CO: Westview Press [London: Pinter Publishers], 1990.

65   The defeat sparked a new round of intellectual debate and self-criticism. See, e.g., Constantine Zuraik, "Today and Yesterday—Two Prominent Aspects of the New Meaning of the Disaster," *Middle East Forum* XLIII:2–3 (1967), 13–20; Nissim Rejwan, "Arab Advocate of Westernization," *New Outlook* 15 (October 1972), 27–34; Cecil A. Hourani, "The Moment of Truth: Towards a Middle East Dialogue," *Encounter* 29:5 (1967), 3–14, reproduced in *A Middle East Reader*, ed. Irene L. Gendzier, Indianapolis / New York: Pegasus, 1969, 384–405.

66   Casualty figures in Ian J. Bickerton and Carla L. Klausner, *A History of the Arab–Israeli Conflict*, 5th ed., Upper Saddle River, NJ: Pearson / Prentice Hall, 2007, 170, citing Trevor N. Dupuy, *Elusive Victory: The Arab–Israeli Wars, 1947–1974*, New York: Harper and Row, 1978, 609. On the 1973 war, see Mohamed Heikal, *The Road to Ramadan*, New York: Quadrangle, 1975; Morris, *Righteous Victims*, ch. 9; Chaim Herzog, *The War of Atonement: The Inside Story of the Yom Kippur War*, London: Greenhill Books, 2003; Abraham Rabinovich, *The Yom Kippur War: The Epic Encounter that Transformed the Middle East*, New York: Schocken, 2005.

67   For a cultural-historical-psychological interpretation of the new Arab openness to negotiations with Israel, see Raphael Patai, *The Seed of Abraham: Jews and Arabs in Contact and Conflict*, Salt Lake City: University of Utah Press, 1986, 336.

8

Back to the Core: Israel and the Palestinians

Primal Fears, New Militancy

The decades of no war, no peace, following 1949 left both Palestinians and Israelis feeling embittered, uneasy, and emotionally battered. The non-resolution of the refugee problem contributed to Palestinian feelings of dejection and despair as second and third generations were born into statelessness, without authentic or effective political leadership, dependent on the machinations of cynical or bombastic politicians. Palestinian anger was aimed in three directions: the Israelis whom they accused of expelling them in 1947–1949, the Arab host governments for their begrudging hospitality and less-than-generous support, and the international community for its indifference to their plight, except for the UN's annual philanthropic handouts.[1] Memories of pre-1948 home and homeland were passed down from parents to children. Poetry and education inculcated dreams of "the Return"—al-awda—with a mystique and power akin to the hopes and longings promoted earlier among diaspora Zionists for their *Eretz-Israel*. Why, it was asked, should the world expect the Palestinian refugees to forget in several decades what the Jews had failed to forget in two thousand years?[2]

Such deep-seated feelings of helplessness would soon give way to a new generation of Palestinians willing to martyr themselves in efforts to end their diaspora existence and refugee status by regaining their homeland through their own actions. We get a vivid sense of this generational change in the self-view of Palestinians during this period through the fictional protagonist of Ghassan Kanafani's novella, *Returning to Haifa*, published in 1969. Said and his wife, who had been forced to flee in April

1948, return to their family home which is now occupied by an Israeli couple (Holocaust survivors, as it happens). Comparing himself disparagingly to his son who is about to run off to join the *feday'un*, Said comes to the end of his emotionally charged visit to Haifa:

> At that moment he felt a deep longing for [his son] Khalid [back in Ramallah] and wished he could fly to him and embrace him and kiss him and cry on his shoulder, reversing the roles of father and son in some unique, inexplicable way. "This is the homeland." He said it to himself, smiling ....

Out loud, Said continues, to his wife Safiyya:

> "... I'm looking for the true Palestine, the Palestine that's more than memories .... I was just saying to myself: What's Palestine with respect to Khalid? He doesn't know the vase or the picture or the stairs or Halisa or Khaldun [in the Haifa being revisited after 19 years that Khalid, born in exile, has never seen]. And yet for him, Palestine is something worthy of a man bearing arms for, dying for. For us, for you and me, it's only a search for something buried beneath the dust of memories .... We were mistaken when we thought the homeland was only the past. For Khalid, the homeland is the future. That's how we differed and that's why Khalid wants to carry arms. Tens of thousands like Khalid won't be stopped by the tears of men searching in the depths of their defeat for scraps of armor and broken flowers. Men like Khalid are looking toward the future, so they can put right our mistakes and the mistakes of the whole world ...."[3]

At the same time, a toughness and aggressiveness developed among Israelis that would prove an enduring obstacle to de-escalating the conflict. Despite the successes of the heroic generation that was victorious in 1948, fear of destruction had become a central factor in the self-image of the Israelis as "weak—victimized but righteous." In the Israeli psyche was buried "the belief—at times hidden, at times overt—that 'the whole world is against us'," as well as a "strange admixture of a sense of power accompanied by a willingness to defy the entire world with the sense of helplessness and profound apprehension."[4] During the 1950s and 1960s, many Jews looked back on the *shoah* and saw a dichotomy between previously defenseless, passive diaspora "sheep" who had supposedly been herded to their slaughter without resisting and the proud, macho *sabras*—native-born Israelis—around whom a new mystique of militancy was built.[5]

Relations with the Palestinians and the Arabs were seen through this prism, which was in many ways a cover for primal insecurity. Far from being a forgotten chapter of history, the Holocaust, noted veteran journalist Amos Elon in 1971, continued to help explain "the fears and prejudices, passions, pains, and prides that spin the plot of public life [in Israel] and will likely affect the nation for a long time to come. The lingering memory of the holocaust makes Arab threats of annihilation sound plausible." The memory of the Holocaust "accounts for the prevailing sense of loneliness, a main characteristic of the Israeli temper since Independence. It explains the obsessive suspicions, the towering urge for self-reliance at all cost in a world which permitted the disaster to happen."[6]

As noted above, the Israeli victory in June 1967 was for many Jews and Israelis "the Holocaust that didn't happen," thanks, they believed, to the new Israelis' initiative and assertiveness—qualities that were presumably lacking among the Jews of Europe a generation earlier.[7] Both prior to and even following its lightning victory, Israel continued to see and portray itself as little David facing the Arab giant Goliath—a stereotypical caricature at variance with the superiority demonstrated by the Israeli army and air force on the battlefield and in the skies. The post-1967 reality of Israeli prowess managed to coexist, however incongruously, with this persisting self-image as endangered and besieged victims.

In the Arab world, the unexpectedly humiliating defeat in 1967 after a decade of development, modernization, and Soviet aid gave rise to both increased feelings of bitterness against the alien usurpers of Palestine and also new soul-searching about the deeper societal ills revealed by this second *nakba*.[8] Only the relative success of Egyptian and Syrian forces in October 1973 seemed to offer a new climate of self-esteem that might prove more conducive to fruitful negotiations between Israel and the Arab states.

The Re-emergence of the Palestinian National Movement after 1967

The re-emerging Palestinian-Arab national movement received new impetus from the Arab defeat in the 1967. The recently created PLO channeled and gave new voice to the accumulated grievances and resentments of a dispersed people who had, before 1948, been the majority indigenous population of British Mandatory Palestine and, before that, of the provinces and districts of the Muslim Ottoman Empire. A surge of Palestinian national self-awareness and militancy was nourished by solidarity with other liberation movements around the world. Exploiting the mystique of revolutionary armed struggle with its freedom fighters, the *kufiyyah*-clad Palestinian *feda'yun* generated an enthusiasm that counteracted the despair and humiliation of the recent military defeat of three Arab armies.

For a short period after June 1967 the PLO attempted to establish cells of fighters to attack Israeli targets from forward bases on the West Bank recently occupied by Israel, but this effort collapsed,[9] leaving Palestinians forced to revert to their previous pattern of launching attacks from external bases that depended on the hospitality of Arab states for logistical and political support.

The 1970s witnessed changes to the shape of the Arab–Israeli conflict, and an important refocusing on its specifically *Palestinian*–Israeli core. The immediate issues on the agenda were Israeli withdrawal to June 1967 lines and Arab recognition and peace with the Jewish state, as called for in the land-for-peace formula promoted by UNSC Resolution 242 (1967) and reinforced by 338 (1973). Yet, despite the fact that neither of these international documents mentioned the Palestinians by name, the Palestinians managed during the 1970s to bring their quest for recognition of their right to national self-determination to the world's attention, using both violence and political means.

The decade began with a number of acts of international terrorism undertaken against Israeli and Jewish targets by factions within and outside the PLO. Airplane hijacking became the weapon of choice in the arsenal of Palestinian groups attempting to hit Israeli targets abroad and draw the world's attention to their cause. As with earlier forms of violence used by both sides, the terror of the 1970s also performed vital inner-directed functions as well, establishing a pecking order among competing factions but, above all, restoring the morale and self-esteem of exiled Palestinians everywhere.[10] On 6 September 1970, members of the Popular Front for the Liberation of Palestine [PFLP] simultaneously hijacked three Western commercial aircraft (from TWA, Swissair, and Pan Am) and flew two of them to an unused airfield outside Amman, Jordan— eventually freeing most of the hostages and blowing up the planes. By one count, between 1968 and 1977, Palestinian groups hijacked or attempted to hijack 29 aircraft.[11]

May 1972 brought two daring assaults to Israel's Lydda Airport, one a hijacked plane (which was stormed and recaptured with minimal loss of life) and the other a bloodbath perpetrated by Japanese Red Army terrorists, acting on behalf of the PFLP, on passengers (mostly Christian pilgrims) in the arrivals lounge. The most sophisticated and spectacular attack of the period was on the Israeli athletes' apartment at the Olympic Games in September of that year in Munich, West Germany; a rescue attempt botched by German police resulted in the deaths of all nine Israeli captives and five kidnappers.

Although international targets were usually "softer" than those inside Israel proper, terrorists from across the Lebanese border were periodically able to penetrate defenses, inflict destruction, and sow panic inside Israel. In May 1974, for example, attackers belonging to the Popular Democratic Front for the Liberation of Palestine [PDFLP] entered the nursery in the northern kibbutz of Ma'alot, holding 90 children hostage until a gun battle ended with the deaths of the terrorists and 20 of their hostages.

One factor contributing to the surge in recruitment and operations of these terrorist/guerilla groups was the fact that many Palestinians had, by this time, despaired of ever finding satisfaction of their claims and grievances through the standard avenues of international diplomacy. Those channels were, after all, the very ones responsible for creating (illegitimately, they believed) the state of Israel in 1948, following which the United Nations and its member-states had relegated Palestinians to the status of a pitiful "Arab" refugee population, offering them no standing as primary participants in world affairs. Most recently, the newly created PLO had watched the members of the United Nations Security Council draft and endorse Resolution 242 which—like the Balfour Declaration exactly fifty years earlier—made no reference at all to Palestinians' national existence or national rights, referring to them only indirectly in the phrase about "achieving a just settlement of the refugee problem."

Within Palestinian institutions at this time much internal debate was devoted instead to questions regarding the delicate web of Palestinian relations with various Arab states; means versus ends, tactics versus strategy; politics versus revolutionary armed struggle; legitimacy of targeting Israeli and/or Jewish civilians or military personnel, inside or outside of Palestine/Israel; and the true meaning and application of various articles in the National Charter. Splinter groups, like the Marxist PFLP under George Habash and the PDFLP under Nayyef Hawatmeh, prioritized armed struggle over politics, making common cause with other revolutionary liberation movements that favored the tactics of kidnapping, bombing, and hijacking of civilian aircraft. Activists debated ideology, tactics, strategy, and the role of armed struggle within their factions and under the PLO umbrella organizations, displaying the same intensity and passion as the Zionist splinter groups had done with the mainstream *Hagana* during the 1930s and 1940s. Some actively rejected the compromising stances sometimes adopted by mainstream Fatah leaders, resulting in much disunity within the ranks and also competitive "outbidding" that only intensified the pattern of terrorism and violence.[12]

Many Palestinians, of course, rejected the "terrorist" label, feeling justified in engaging in armed struggle in the same manner that other liberation movements had done and were doing. They viewed violence as a perfectly legitimate tool for resisting the occupation of lands they lost in 1948 and again in 1967, as well as for drawing the world's urgent attention to their neglected cause—even if the chances of physically destroying the usurping Zionist state seemed remote.[13] In choosing this route, radicals and rejectionists were being true to the words of the PLO's 1968 National Charter, which called for the "elimination of Zionism in Palestine" by "armed struggle" as the only method ("strategy," not "tactics") of regaining Palestine as an Arab state for its original Palestinian inhabitants, using "fedayeen action" as "the nucleus of the popular Palestinian war of liberation" (arts. 15, 9, 10).

During this period, Israelis and their supporters highlighted the violent and what some called the "politicidal" nature of the PLO and its National Charter, condemning and refusing to deal with a "terrorist organization." Going beyond statements of denunciation, Israeli responses included violent reprisals and special operations, including assassinations of suspected terrorists, attacks on the offices and headquarters of militant groups, and the bombing of refugee camps (mostly in Lebanon) in which terrorists were said to be hiding and from which they were operating.[14] Not surprisingly, these Israeli counterinsurgency measures and aerial attacks only increased the level of Palestinian determination and thirst for revenge, and had little deterrent effect.

The violent cycles of the 1970s and 1980s unleashed an updated version of the unresolved core argument that we examined in the 1936–1939 Arab Rebellion and the Israeli reprisals in the 1950s over the resort to force, its effects, and its justification. IDF historian Netanel Lorch denounced PLO violence as just a continuation of Arab aggressiveness based on "principles that had been laid down several decades before," while Zionist and Israeli responses were, in his view, in no way symmetrical:

> From the outset [Zionist military organization] came as a reaction to the Arab resort to violence, in self-defense against attacks from both irregular and regular military forces. The very names of the successive organizations—Hashomer ("The Watchman"), Haganah ("Defense"), I.D.F. ("Israel Defense Forces")—denote their basic mission. It may thus be paradoxical that a movement, and subsequently a State, which has never envisaged violence as a means for the achievement of its objectives, has been engaged almost continuously in violent struggle.[15]

In the decades following the 1967 war, the Americans generally supported Israel's position that the PLO should be excluded from the diplomatic process until it signed on to Resolution 242, recognized Israel's right to exist, and explicitly renounced terrorism.[16] Ostracizing the PLO involved many awkward incidents over the coming years, during which Israelis or Americans tried to promote and deal with "non-PLO"

Palestinians as part of a campaign to discredit the PLO's claim to be the legitimate spokesman for the Palestinian people. Palestinians, meanwhile, rejected references to their struggle as "terrorism"; the American/Israeli precondition for them to renounce it seemed grossly unfair. As Rashid Khalidi observed sarcastically, Palestinians "were required by the United States and Israel to cease their resistance to an illegal occupation as a precondition for being allowed to negotiate for an end to that occupation."[17] For the next decade and a half, the PLO stood firm in officially rejecting Security Council Resolution 242 for not addressing Palestinian needs and the minimum requirements of a just and lasting peace.[18] Almost as stubbornly as the Israelis and Americans kept it excluded from the diplomatic game, the PLO drew a clear red line, until 1988, against any compromise or acceptance of Resolution 242, and seemed committed to regaining Palestine almost exclusively by armed struggle.

During the early 1970s there emerged faint signals that the PLO might abandon the categorical rejection of Israel inherent in its National Charter and, according to some analysts, move "gradually [to] accept ... a two-state solution."[19] Yet, as Rashid Khalidi acknowledges, this shift was either imperceptible to, or seen differently by, the US and Israel, who looked at other evidence—continuing armed struggle on the ground and the fighting words of new PNC resolutions—and came to more negative conclusions about Palestinian intentions. This brings us to consider the last on our list of unresolved *core arguments* besetting the contested histories of Israel and Palestine: *What are the true intentions of the Palestinians and the PLO: To eliminate the Jewish state of Israel and replace it with an Arab state of Palestine? Or to create a Palestinian Arab state in part of historic Palestine, to coexist alongside an Israeli Jewish state?*

For years much of the debate centered round Resolution 2 of the PNC Political Program adopted in Cairo on 9 June 1974: "The PLO will employ all means, and first and foremost armed struggle, to liberate Palestinian territory and to establish the independent combatant national authority for the people over every part of Palestinian land that is liberated."[20] Many commentators have interpreted this last phrase as signaling the PLO's willingness to accept a mini-state in the West Bank and Gaza—i.e., something less than total liberation of all of Palestine. The earlier reference to employing "all means" was seen to hint at a retreat from the uncompromising goal of eliminating Zionism only through armed struggle.

Many writers today look back to this moment uncritically as if it constituted an unambiguous shift in PLO policy.[21] At the time, however, the reality of the change was not at all obvious; indeed, it was hotly contested. Former military intelligence analyst, Yehoshafat Harkabi— who after 1978 would radically modify his deterministic and negative reading of Arab hostility and intentions[22]—argued vigorously at the time that this formulation was nothing but a clever deception cloaking the PLO's unchanged goal of liberating *all* of Palestine. If not all in one go, then the Palestinians would do so in "stages," beginning with any pieces of territory acquired by armed struggle or through negotiation.[23]

Those who believed this interpretation of Palestinian intentions pointed to the unceasing campaign of violent attacks inspired or organized by the PLO or its offshoots against Israelis and Jews around the world. They also cited the 1968 National Charter and the uncompromising character of its goals as expressed, inter alia, in Article 21: "The Palestinian Arab people, in expressing itself through the armed Palestinian revolution, rejects every solution that is a substitute for a complete liberation of Palestine ... ."

Yezid Sayigh does not share this interpretation, or the argument that the 1974 resolution disguised a strategy of total liberation by stages. In his detailed examination of the history of the movement, he credits the PLO for showing diplomatic flexibility in "its willingness to modify its objectives and strategy," but admits that this "fell far short of offering recognition to the Jewish state, let alone coexistence." It did, however, imply a "readiness both to enter into indirect negotiations and to put off the total liberation of Palestine, if not abandon it altogether." This tentative diplomatic opening was, however, to be accompanied by "demonstrative military action against Israel" in order to "underlin[e] the ability of the PLO to spoil any peace initiative that excluded it."[24]

There are many who believe, like Sayigh, that the true goal of the Palestinians is coexistence with Israel. The bellicose rhetoric, they point out, is intended chiefly to placate militant factions. They argue that a close reading of internal Palestinian debates shows a gradual evolution of Palestinian goals in the direction of an accommodation with Israel. These changes are expressed through subtle wording changes in the authoritative resolutions adopted by meetings of the Palestinian parliament-in-exile, the National Council.[25] Unfortunately, these ambiguous changes of phrasing fail to convince skeptics, with the result that both parties and their supporters resort to much inconclusive parsing of phrases and hairsplitting squabbles over the true meaning of various PNC resolutions.[26]

The November 1988 PNC meeting in Algiers (below, Chapter 10) would be an important marker in the evolution of Palestinian attitudes, although it would still not be enough to lay to rest, once and for all, the core argument over Palestinian intentions. The question remains among the most troubling unresolved questions, re-emerging again to obstruct a breakthrough in generating mutual trust among the parties during the Oslo period after 1993.

The Palestine Question at the United Nations

During the 1970s the PLO and the Palestinian cause continued to benefit from greater attention and solidarity in the regional and international arena. The Arab summit meeting in Rabat, Morocco, in October 1974 affirmed not only "the right of the Palestinian people to return to their homeland and to self-determination," but (echoing the recent PNC resolutions) also their "right to establish an independent national authority, under the leadership of the PLO in its capacity as the sole legitimate representative of the Palestine people." The latter phrase represented an important achievement for the PLO, undermining Jordan's self-proclaimed trusteeship over the Holy Places of Jerusalem and the Palestine issue through its occupation of the holy city and the West Bank between 1948 and 1967.[27]

During this period Palestinian leaders scored their greatest successes at broadening support for their cause in the international arena. In November 1974, PLO chairman Yasir Arafat was invited to deliver an address to the UN General Assembly,[28] which proceeded afterwards to adopt Resolution 3236, expressing its deep concern that no just solution had yet been achieved for the problem of Palestine, which continued "to endanger international peace and security." The landmark resolution, going beyond recent UN declarations favoring Palestinian rights,[29] reaffirmed by a vote of 89 in favor, 7 against, with 37 abstentions, the "inalienable rights" of the Palestinian people to "self-determination without external interference" and to "national independence and sovereignty." Reinforcing its routine annual calls since December 1948, the General Assembly further reaffirmed "the inalienable right of the Palestinians to return to their homes and property from which they have been displaced and uprooted, and call[ed] for their return."[30] In an accompanying resolution, the UN granted the PLO "observer status" and in 1975 went on to establish a "Committee on the Exercise of the Inalienable Rights of the Palestinian People" which continues to serve, with its secretariat (the Division for Palestinian Rights), as an international base for documentation and pro-Palestinian advocacy.

In vain did the Israeli Ambassador denounce the world body for its invitation to Arafat, thereby "capitulat[ing] to a murder organization which aims at the destruction of a Member State of the UN" and "prostrat[ing] itself before the PLO, which stands for premeditated, deliberate murder of innocent civilians, denies to the Jewish people its right to live, and seeks to destroy the Jewish State by armed force."[31] Adding to Israel's feelings of alienation and isolation, the General Assembly in November 1975 adopted an omnibus resolution against racial discrimination containing a closing line determining that "zionism" was "a form of racism and racial discrimination." To Jews and Zionists, this UN stance was an example of egregious bias, selectively singling out and chastising the Jews and their national liberation movement and associating it with the unmitigated evils of South Africa's apartheid régime. The political machinations involved in mobilizing votes for this resolution in the UNGA were also criticized for their crass cynicism.[32]

Among its various pronouncements, UNGA Resolution 3626 of 1974 had recognized the Palestinian people as "a principal party in the establishment of a just and durable peace in the Middle East." While this (re-) "Palestinization" of the conflict enjoyed a sympathetic hearing at the UN and especially among its developing member-states, UN focus on the specifically *Palestinian*–Israeli core was not without its critics. One professor complained, for example, about "a cascade of pro-Palestinian sentiments and the 'PLO-ization of the U.N.' which intensified invective against Israel and efforts to isolate it."[33] Legal scholar Julius Stone devoted an entire volume to a scathing attack on these developments at the UN from an international law perspective.[34] For these critics, the crux of the conflict was not the unfulfilled Palestinian quest for self-determination but rather the inability of the Arabs to accept the reality and legitimacy of Israel's very existence.

Official spokesmen, media commentators, advocates, and academics alike went on the counterattack, broadening the debate to cast doubt on the authenticity of Palestinian nationalism generally. Some members of the American Academic Association for Peace in the Middle East, for example, sought to undermine or delegitimize any forms of distinct Palestinian national claims.[35] In many publications and public forums the following arguments, some of which relate to familiar core arguments we have seen in earlier years, were adapted to the circumstances of the 1970s and 1980s:

1   Historically, there was no such thing as a separate, distinct Palestinian people, who after World War I were calling themselves "southern Syrians."

2   There was never much positive content to Palestinian nationalism, which was based primarily on negative reactions to the efforts and successes of the Zionists.

3   The Arab states' support for the PLO and the demand for the creation of a Palestinian state were self-serving and only a tool to be used (like the refugees) in their battle against Israel—"the continuous exploitation of these questions as a weapon of Arab belligerency against Israel," in the words of Israel's ambassador to the UN in November

1974.[36] If Arab support for this claim to independent Palestinian statehood were genuine, it was asked, why didn't Jordan and Egypt, who controlled parts of Mandatory Palestine between 1949 and 1967, move to create a Palestinian state in those areas while they had the power to do so?

4   There was no current need for a separate Palestinian state, as Jordan was already a Palestinian state. Again, as the Israeli ambassador proclaimed before the UN General Assembly: "Geographically and ethnically Jordan is Palestine."[37] To support this claim, reference is made to the fact that greater Mandatory Palestine was originally partitioned by Winston Churchill in 1922, to create Abdullah's Amirate of Transjordan east of Jordan River, with the Jewish national home policy thereafter reduced in its application to Palestine west of the Jordan.[38]

5   The creation of a Palestinian state would be giving a state structure and forward bases to a terrorist organization dedicated to the destruction of Israel: "The question," quoting Israel's ambassador again, was: "should there be peace between Israel and its eastern neighbour [i.e., Jordan/Palestine], or should an attempt be made to establish a Palestine Liberation Organization base to the east of Israel from which the terrorist campaign against the Jewish State's existence could be pursued?"[39]

These arguments were advanced against the backdrop of almost daily Palestinian guerilla/terrorist incursions into Israel or against Israeli and Jewish targets abroad; frequent Israeli reprisal attacks on Palestinian targets in Lebanon, Syria, and Jordan, often with devastating "collateral damage" to civilian populations; and periodic complaints, and defenses, brought before the UN about Israeli violations of human rights in the territories occupied since 1967.

Going beyond these day-to-day concerns, heated discussions and learned treatises not only second-guessed the legitimacy of UN decisions regarding Israel's creation, but also reopened the contested narratives over basic Palestinian and Jewish rights to sovereignty and national self-determination.[40] Just as many Jews and Israelis took offense at Arab and Palestinian denials of Israel's right to exist as a Jewish state,[41] so too were Palestinians and other Arabs offended by Israeli Prime Minister Golda Meir's 1969 remarks—however moderately expressed or interpreted in subsequent years—that

> There were no such thing as Palestinians. When was there an independent Palestinian people with a Palestinian state? It was either southern Syria before the First World War, and then it was Palestine including Jordan. It was not as though there was a Palestinian people in Palestine considering

itself as a Palestinian people and we came and threw them out and took their country away from them. They did not exist.[42]

Palestinians and Jordanians, each for different reasons, also recoiled at the implications of both the Israel Labor Party's "Jordanian option" and the Likud Party's harsher "Jordan is Palestine" political slogan. Considering Jordan already a Palestinian state, Likud leader Yitzhak Shamir proclaimed in 1982 that there was no room west of the Jordan River for a *second* Palestinian state; it would be "a prescription for anarchy, a threat to both Israel and Jordan, and a likely base for terrorist and Soviet penetration."[43] Seen from a Jordanian perspective, this was nothing less than an Israeli "conspiracy ... to establish a Palestinian state outside the Palestinians' historical homeland in the West Bank and the Gaza Strip— against Palestinians' wishes and at Jordan's expense."[44]

Those who rejected the five arguments listed above found appropriate counterarguments to promote Palestinian efforts to be recognized as legitimate claimants to national self-determination on the soil of the contested territory of Palestine west of the Jordan River. Some of these counterarguments were based on positions adopted by the UNGA and developed in publications of the newly created UN Division for Palestinian Rights.[45] For example:

1 Palestinian advocacy of the "southern Syrian" option after World War I does not contradict their authentic Palestinian national identity focused on the country called "Palestine," but was rather a strategic and transitory episode seeking to develop ties with neighboring Arab countries.

2 Palestinian nationalism is an authentic expression of an indigenous people seeking sovereign control over the land they have considered their homeland for centuries, despite the colonial imposition on them of an alien people claiming rights to the same land.

3 The non-creation of a Palestinian state between 1949 and 1967 can be explained by a number of internal Palestinian and external Arab-state causes that combined to make such a plan unworkable, rather than being attributed to cynical manipulation of an inauthentic national cause.

4 Most of the Palestinians living in the Hashemite Kingdom of Jordan are there because they were displaced from their real homes in Palestine west of the Jordan River. The land between the Mediterranean Sea and the western boundary of Iraq was arbitrarily labeled "Palestine" by the British after World War I; the land east of the Jordan River has never been viewed by Palestinian Arabs as their national home, nor seriously conceived by the British as part of a future Jewish national

HISTORIES IN CONTENTION

home. The indigenous population of the Hashemite Kingdom of Jordan, to which Palestinians emigrated or fled after 1948 and 1967, is made up of Bedouin, Circassians, Chechens, Armenians, and other Arabic-speaking groups.

5 The creation of a Palestinian state would bring an end to the need for armed struggle. In the context of a peace settlement, the new government would be absorbed in the creative work of building up a state and restoring Palestinian society and infrastructures that were destroyed in 1948.

Point 5 on both lists was, and has remained to this day problematic, bringing us back, full circle, to the eleventh core argument highlighted above—whether the true aim of Palestinians and the PLO is the ultimate elimination of Israel and its replacement by an Arab Palestinian state, or rather the creation of a Palestinian-Arab state on only *part* of historic Palestine/*Eretz-Israel*, to coexist alongside a Jewish-Israeli state.

Finally, it should be noted that, despite firm US support of Israel in its refusal to recognize or deal with the PLO until certain conditions were met, American opinion during this period did show signs of movement towards greater recognition of a central role for the Palestinians[46]—although many were still averse to any official contact with or recognition of the PLO. Those arguing for the rights of the Palestinians to be treated on at least equal footing with those of Israelis in the diplomatic arena had to overcome the negative fallout from two sources: the continued acts of international terrorism perpetrated by Palestinians during this period, and the bellicose anti-Zionist rhetoric in the Palestine National Charter. The frequent association between the words "PLO," "Palestinians," and "terrorism" made it difficult for pro-Palestinian advocates to plead their case for a PLO seat at the negotiating table to discuss the future of their contested homeland with the Israelis or at an international conference in which the US was involved. It would take almost a generation before the political positions of PLO, American, and (to a lesser extent) Israeli leaders would evolve and align themselves to open a way towards, first, a US–PLO dialogue in 1988, and subsequently the inclusion of a Palestinian sub-delegation at the Madrid peace conference in 1991 (see Chapter 10, below).

Notes

1 For an eloquent firsthand account of these times and mood, see Fawaz Turki, *The Disinherited: Journal of a Palestinian Exile*, 2nd ed., London / New York: Monthly Review Press, 1974.

2 A. L. Tibawi, "Visions of the Return: The Palestine Arab Refugees in Arabic Poetry and Art," *Middle East Journal* 17:5 (Autumn 1963), 507–26.

3   Ghassan Kanafani, *Palestine's Children: Returning to Haifa and Other Stories*, transl. Barbara Harlow and Karen E. Riley, Boulder, CO: Lynne Rienner, 2000, 186–7.

4   Anita Shapira, *Land and Power: The Zionist Resort to Force, 1881–1948*, transl. William Templer, Stanford, CA: Stanford University Press, 1999, 369–70.

5   On the evolution of this phenomenon, see Amnon Rubinstein, *The Zionist Dream Revisited: From Herzl to Gush Emunim and Back*, New York: Schocken Books, 1984, ch. 8; Bernard Wasserstein, *Israelis and Palestinians: Why Do They Fight? Can They Stop?* 3rd ed., New Haven, CT / London: Yale University Press / London: Profile Books, 2008, 32–7.

6   Amos Elon, *The Israelis: Founders and Sons*, New York: Holt, Rinehart and Winston, 1971, 199.

7   Benny Morris, *Righteous Victims: A History of the Zionist Arab Conflict, 1881–1999*, New York: Alfred A. Knopf, 1999 / London: John Murray, 2000, 311.

8   See, e.g., Ali E. Hillal Dessouki, "Arab Intellectuals and al-Nakba: The Search for Fundamentalism," *Middle Eastern Studies* IX (1973), 187–95 and sources cited there; Raphael Patai, *The Arab Mind*, New York: Charles Scribner's Sons, 1973, 258–67.

9   Yezid Sayigh, *Armed Struggle and the Search for State: The Palestinian National Movement, 1949–1993*, Oxford: Oxford University Press / Washington, DC: The Institute for Palestine Studies, 1997, 207–10 (quotation from p. 210); Morris, *Righteous Victims*, 365–70.

10 Ian S. Lustick, "Terrorism in the Arab–Israeli Conflict: Targets and Audiences," in *Terrorism in Context*, ed. Martha Crenshaw, University Park, PA: Pennsylvania State University Press, 1995, 537–47.

11 Details in this and the following paragraph are from Benny Morris, *Righteous Victims*, 376–81.

12 Sayigh (*Armed Struggle*, 339–57) discusses "Political Rivalry, Military Outbidding" and "Military Jockeying for Diplomatic Position."

13 E.g., John Quigley, *The Case for Palestine: An International Law Perspective*, rev. and updated ed., Durham, NC / London: Duke University Press, 2005, chs. 26–7. For a detailed discussion of internal Palestinian debates over the use of guerilla warfare, both inside and outside Israel/Palestine, see Sayegh, *Armed Struggle*, ch. 8.

14 Fictional and semi-autobiographical portrayals of these battles (and the motivations of their complex protagonists) became very popular in novels and films, notably John Le Carré's spy novel, *The Little Drummer Girl*, London: Hodder and Stoughton, 1983, and George Jonas' cloak-and-dagger journalistic account, *Vengeance: The True Story of an Israeli Counter-Terrorist Team* (1984), reissued New York: Simon and Schuster, 2005. Both were made into successful Hollywood films, the first in 1984, directed by George Roy Hill and starring Diane Keaton, and the latter, released as *Munich* in 2005, directed by Stephen Spielberg and starring Eric Bana.

15 Netanel Lorch, *One Long War: Arab Versus Jew since 1920*, New York: Herzl Press, 1976, xiv–xv.

16   Washington's commitment was made as part of a package leading to the 1975 Israeli–Egyptian disengagement in Sinai. See Steven L. Spiegel, *The Other Arab–Israeli Conflict: Making America's Middle East Policy, from Truman to Reagan*, Chicago: University of Chicago Press, 1985, 300–3. For a critical assessment of this US commitment to Israel, see Donald Neff, "Nixon's Middle East Policy: From Balance to Bias," in *US Policy on Palestine from Wilson to Clinton*, ed. Michael W. Suleiman, Normal, IL: AAUG Press, 1995, 156. The US commitment was reiterated, inter alia, in the US–Israel Memorandum of Agreement, 1 September 1975, reproduced in *The Israeli–Palestinian Conflict: A Documentary Record, 1967–1990*, ed. Yehuda Lukacs, Cambridge: Cambridge University Press, 1992, 60–1.

17   Rashid Khalidi, *The Iron Cage: The Story of the Palestinian Struggle for Statehood*, Boston, MA: Beacon, 2006, 156.

18   PLO Statement rejecting UN Resolution 242, Cairo, 23 November 1967, reproduced in Lukacs, *Israeli–Palestinian Conflict*, 290–1. The PLO's position was reiterated regularly in resolutions adopted at subsequent meetings of the PNC.

19   R. Khalidi, *Iron Cage*, 154–6; Sayigh, *Armed Struggle*, 684; Hussein Agha, Shai Feldman, Ahmad Khalidi, and Zeev Schiff, *Track-II Diplomacy: Lessons from the Middle East*, Cambridge, MA: MIT Press, 2003, 10.

20   PNC Political Programme for the Present Stage, Cairo, 9 June 1974, translation reproduced in Y. Harkabi, *The Palestinian Covenant and Its Meaning*, London: Valentine Mitchell, 1979, 147. Cf. other translations in *The Israel–Arab Reader: A Documentary History of the Middle East Conflict*, 7th rev. ed., eds. Walter Laqueur and Barry Rubin, New York: Penguin, 2008, 162; Lukacs, *Israeli–Palestinian Conflict*, 309; Benjamin Netanyahu, *A Durable Peace: Israel and Its Place among the Nations*, rev. ed., New York: Warner Books, 2000, 441–2, where it is printed as an appendix under the title "The Phased Plan."

21   E.g., "Palestinians want an independent state in the West Bank and Gaza, and to live in peace and cooperation with Israel. This has been the paramount Palestinian national objective since the mid-1970s and has not changed since." Khalili Shikaki, "Ending the Conflict: Can the Parties Afford It?" in *The Israeli–Palestinian Peace Process: Oslo and the Lessons of Failure: Perspectives, Predicaments and Prospects*, eds. Robert L. Rothstein, Moshe Ma'oz, and Khalil Shikaki, Brighton, UK / Portland, OR: Sussex Academic Press, 2002, 45; also ibid., 39.

22   Mordechai Nisan, "Harkabi's Despair" *Midstream* XXV:5 (May 1979), 9–17; Yehoshafat Harkabi, "A Policy for the Moment of Truth," *Jerusalem Post International Edition*, w/e 13 February 1988, 9–10; Yehoshafat Harkabi, "The Last Reminiscence, January 14, 1994" an interview with Pinhas Ginossar and Zaki Shalom, *Israel Studies* I:1 (Spring 1996), 171–95.

23   Harkabi, *The Palestinian Covenant*, 86–7. The incremental intention of the quoted Article 2, "aimed at Israel's demise," becomes clearer when read together with Articles 3 and 4 of the Program (reproduced in ibid., 147–8).

See also Harkabi's detailed essays "The Meaning of 'a Democratic Palestinian State'" (April 1970) and "The Debate at the Twelfth Palestinian National Council" (July 1974), in his collection, *Palestinians and Israel*, New York: John Wiley (Halsted Press), 1974, 70–106 and 269–83. The 1970 essay cited above was also reprinted, with a postscript, in Laqueur and Rubin, *Israel–Arab Reader*, 182–94.

24 Sayigh, *Armed Struggle*, 322. Sayigh further notes that, to "placate rejectionist sentiment and prevent an open split, the mainstream inserted a militant tone into the concluding statement." Ibid., 342–3.

25 Muhammad Muslih, "Towards Coexistence: An Analysis of the Resolutions of the Palestine National Council," *Journal of Palestine Studies* 19:4 (Summer 1990), 3–29; reprinted in *From War to Peace: Arab–Israeli Relations 1973–1993*, eds. Barry Rubin, Joseph Ginat, and Moshe Ma'oz, New York: New York University Press, 1995, 265–91; Khalidi, *Iron Cage*, 154–6, 169–70, 192–5.

26 See, e.g., Harkabi, *Palestinians and Israel*, and *The Palestinian Covenant*, for critiques of the deceptive meanings of ostensibly positive resolutions of various PNC meetings and statements of Palestinian leaders.

27 Arab Heads of State Declaration at Rabat, 28 October 1974, reproduced in Ian J. Bickerton and Carla L. Klausner, *A History of the Arab–Israeli Conflict*, 5th ed., Upper Saddle River, NJ: Pearson / Prentice Hall, 2007, 176; Adnan Abu-Odeh, *Jordanians, Palestinians and the Hashemite Kingdom in the Middle East Peace Process*, Washington, DC: United States Institute of Peace Press, 1999, 209–13; R. Khalidi, *Iron Cage*, 144.

28 UNGA Address, 13 November 1974, reproduced in Laqueur and Rubin, *Israel–Arab Reader*, 171–82.

29 Growing out of the annual deliberations on renewing the mandate and budget of UNRWA, UNGA Resolutions became more and more explicit and extensive in defining and affirming Palestinian rights. See the wording changes in Resolutions 2535 (XXIV), 10 December 1969; 2672 (XXV), 8 December 1970; 2787 (XXVI), 6 December 1971; 2963 (XXVII), 13 December 1972; and 3089 (XXVII), 7 December 1973. Texts available in *United Nations Resolutions on Palestine and the Arab–Israeli Conflict*, vol. I: 1947–1974, rev. ed., ed. George J. Tomeh, Washington, DC: Institute for Palestine Studies, 1988; Henry Cattan, *Palestine and International Law: The Legal Aspects of the Arab–Israel Conflict*, 2nd ed., foreword by W. T. Mallison, Jr., London: Longman, 1976, appendices.

30 UNGA Res 3236 (XXIX), 22 November 1974, "Concerning the Question of Palestine," accessed online 17 July 2008 at http://domino.un.org/UNISPAL. NSF/9a798adbf322aff38525617b006d88d7/025974039acfb171852560-de00548bbe.

31 Speech to the UN General Assembly, 13 November 1974, in Yosef Tekoah, *In the Face of the Nations: Israel's Struggle for Peace*, ed. David Aphek, New York: Simon and Schuster, 1976, 145–52.

32 Text of UNGA Resolution 3379 (XXX), "Elimination of all forms of racial discrimination," 10 November 1975, was adopted by a vote of 72 in favor,

35 against, with 32 abstentions. Text accessed online 17 July 2008 at http://domino.un.org/UNISPAL.NSF/0a2a053971ccb56885256cef0073c6d4/761 c1063530766a7052566a2005b74d1; Bernard Lewis, "The Anti-Zionist Resolution," *Foreign Affairs* 55:1 (October 1976), 54–64; Alvin Z. Rubinstein, "Transformation: External Determinants," in *The Arab–Israeli Conflict: Perspectives*, 2nd ed., ed. Alvin Z. Rubinstein, New York: HarperCollins, 1991, 83. The determination about Zionism was revoked sixteen years later. For text and commentary on UNGA Resolution 46/86 of 16 December 1991, see Israel Ministry of Foreign Affairs website, http://www.mfa.gov.il/MFA/Foreign%20Relations/Israels%20Foreign%20Relations%20since%201947/1988-1992/260%20General%20Assembly%20Resolution%2046-86-%20Revocation, accessed 17 July 2008.

33 Rubinstein, "Transformation," 83.

34 Julius Stone, *Israel and Palestine: Assault on the Law of Nations*, Baltimore, MD: Johns Hopkins University Press, 1981.

35 Michael Curtis, Joseph Neyer, Chaim I. Waxman, and Allen Pollack, eds., *The Palestinians: People, History, Politics*, New Brunswick, NJ: Transaction Books [prepared under the auspices of the American Academic Association for Peace in the Middle East], 1975—especially essays by Marie Syrkin (199–208) and Terrence Prittie (213–27). See also Marie Syrkin, "Who Are the Palestinians?" in *People and Politics in the Middle East*, ed. Michael Curtis, New Brunswick, NJ: Transaction Books / E. P. Dutton [proceedings of the annual conference of the American Academic Association for Peace in the Middle East], 1971, 93–110.

36 Tekoah remarks, UNGA debates, 13 November 1974, *In the Face*, 154.

37 Ibid., 155–6; Paul S. Riebenfeld, "The Integrity of Palestine," *Midstream*, August–September 1975, 7–27; Stone, *Israel and Palestine*, 22–5.

38 For a legal presentation of this claim, see Allan Gerson, *Israel, the West Bank and International Law*, London / Totowa, NJ: Frank Cass, 1978, 44–5. Cf. the counterarguments of Bernard Wasserstein, *Israelis and Palestinians*, 102–6.

39 Tekoah remarks, UNGA debates, 13 November 1974, quoted in Bickerton and Klausner, *A History*, 197.

40 Henry Cattan, *Palestine and International Law: The Legal Aspects of the Arab–Israel Conflict*, 2nd ed., foreword by W. T. Mallison, Jr., London: Longman, 1976, ch. 6; Stone, *Israel and Palestine*.

41 Palestine National Charter, Arts. 19, 20 (cited above, page 18), 22 (cited below, page 188).

42 Interview in the *Sunday Times*, London, 15 June 1969, quoted in Marwan Muasher, *The Arab Center: The Promise of Moderation*, New Haven, CT: Yale University Press, 2008, 292 (n. 11). Cf. Baruch Kimmerling and Joel S. Migdal, *The Palestinian People: A History*, Cambridge, MA: Harvard University Press, 2003, xxvi–xxvii.

43 Yitzhak Shamir, "Israel's Role in a Changing Middle East," *Foreign Affairs* 60:4 (Spring 1982), 791; cf. Muasher, *The Arab Center*, 21.

44 Muasher, *The Arab Center*, 21. On the politics and polemics of the Jordan–
   Palestine debates, see, e.g., Raphael Israeli, "Is Jordan Palestine?" in *Israel, the
   Hashemites and the Palestinians: The Fateful Triangle*, eds. Efraim Karsh and
   P. R. Kumaraswamy, London: Frank Cass, 2003, 49–66.
45 E.g., United Nations, Division for Palestinian Rights, "The Origins and Evolution of the Palestine Problem: 1917–1988—PART I, 1917–1947," posted
   30 June 1990, accessed 13 April 2008 at http://domino.un.org/UNISPAL.
   NSF/561c6ee353d740fb8525607d00581829/aeac80e740c782e4852561
   150071fdb0.
46 Two important markers were the statement of Deputy Assistant Secretary for
   Near East and South Asian Affairs, Harold Saunders, to the US Congress
   House Foreign Affairs Subcommittee on the Middle East, 12 November 1975,
   reproduced in Laqueur and Rubin, *Israel–Arab Reader*, 203–6, and the Brookings Institution Report of a Study Group, *Toward Peace in the Middle East*,
   December 1975, accessed online at the Israel Ministry of Foreign Affairs
   website: http://www.mfa.gov.il/MFA/Foreign%20Relations/Israels%20For-
   eign%20Relations%20since%201947/1974–1977/144%20Toward%20
   Peace%20in%20the%20Middle%20East-%20report%20of%20the. Several co-
   authors would soon become Middle East advisers to incoming US president
   Jimmy Carter.

9
From Camp David to the West Bank to Lebanon

Camp David and the Israel–Egypt Peace Process

In the wake of the October 1973 war, the main actors of international diplomacy went into high gear in pursuit of a settlement of the Arab–Israeli conflict, although without inviting the Palestinians, as now represented by the PLO, to join the process. Despite the perception of victory in surprising the Israelis, crossing the Suez Canal, and overrunning their front lines, Egypt and the Arab states were beginning to realize that there might be no purely military solution to their dispute with Israel and that diplomatic means needed to be employed as well. The Arab states meeting in Algiers in late November 1973 registered the usual declarations demanding full Israeli withdrawal from lands occupied in 1967 and affirming support for the Palestinians, but also hinted that the long-stymied movement from cease-fire to peace might be possible if two preconditions were met: (1) the evacuation by Israel of the occupied Arab territories, including Jerusalem, and (2) the re-establishment of full national rights for the Palestinian people.[1]

International efforts towards a settlement during this period were stage-managed by the United States, more specifically by Secretary of State Henry Kissinger. With unusual tenacity, cleverness, and energy, Kissinger made the US the pre-eminent broker and mediator in the Middle East, effectively sidelining the USSR which was, under a United Nations façade, a co-convener of the December 1973 Geneva Conference. This conference, at which the Arab states and Israel were invited to sit down to discuss peace, opened with some predictably stiff and formulaic statements, and was promptly adjourned *sine die*. The idea of getting the parties to resume discussions in an international conference at Geneva or elsewhere was periodically floated without result until 1991 (see Chapter 10).

Under the umbrella of this adjourned Geneva Conference, Kissinger went on to perfect the art of "shuttle diplomacy" between Middle Eastern capitals, hammering out the terms of two disengagement agreements between Israel and Egypt (signed 17 January 1974 and 1 September 1975), and one between Syria and Israel (31 May 1974). Not unlike the General Armistice Agreements brokered by Ralph Bunche in 1949, these accords were limited to military matters but nonetheless served as useful bases for future attempts to negotiate peace. Although Israeli leaders were not always pleased with the concessions Kissinger pressed them to make, they did benefit from (and the Arab states were correspondingly disappointed by) his acceptance of two of Israel's preferred negotiating strategies: to deal with each of the Arab states one by one, rather than together in a multilateral or multinational conference, and to exclude the PLO, despite its growing standing and popularity at the United Nations.

Egyptian president Anwar al-Sadat engaged in negotiations with Kissinger with an eye to maneuvering Egypt closer to the US, in hopes of getting the Americans to exert some pressure on Israel. Correspondingly, Kissinger's mediation activities positioned the US for the first time as the ideal "honest broker" between the Arab states and Israel. Following his inauguration as president in 1977, Jimmy Carter became personally involved in meeting individually with Israeli and Arab leaders in hopes of bringing them together in the search for peace. But when he started to coordinate efforts with the USSR for reconvening the Geneva Conference, he found himself upstaged by Israel's new right-wing prime minister, Menachem Begin, and Egypt's president, both of whom preferred to open their own bilateral channel so as to avoid bringing in a wider circle of actors.

After some top-secret diplomatic feelers with Israelis via Morocco, Sadat surprised friends and foes alike by dramatically announcing in the Egyptian National Assembly on 9 November 1977 that he was prepared to go anywhere—even the Israeli Knesset—to discuss the return of occupied Arab lands, a solution to the Palestinian problem and peace. Prime Minister Begin immediately issued an invitation. With the stalemate of 1967 broken and some measure of Arab dignity restored by the 1973 war, Sadat felt confident enough to break the taboo of direct dealings with the enemy and to engage in some "heroic diplomacy."[2]

The dramatic visit of Sadat to Jerusalem (19–21 November 1977) included eloquent speeches in the Knesset,[3] broadcast throughout the region, and important backroom discussions which served as preliminary clarifications of the parties' positions on the issues in dispute. The daring gesture posed by Sadat had the effect of breaking some psychological barriers, and provided an important opening and direct contact that had been previously lacking. But the visit and the initial exchanges of views could not, in themselves, bring the parties closer together on many of the concrete and existential issues in dispute, illustrating the truth of Yehoshafat Harkabi's 1974 remark:

> The day negotiations start will indeed be a great occasion for celebration. Yet let us remember the lessons psychologists teach—that direct contacts between human groups do not always draw them together, but may make them realize how far apart they are and thus lead to further estrangement.[4]

Difficult negotiations, in venues alternating between the two countries, ensued over the coming months and revealed some common ground but also frequent deadlocks and misunderstandings. It was becoming clear that there were two levels of difficulty to overcome: those bilateral issues between Egypt and Israel, on the one hand, and the wider and deeper ones between the Arab world, the Palestinians, and Israel, on the other.[5] As talks began to bog down, each party turned more and more to the US to lean on the other to behave more reasonably. When the negotiations seemed stalled and in danger of collapse, President Carter invited both heads of state to the secluded presidential retreat at Camp David, Maryland, in September 1978 for what turned out to be eight days of intensive high-level talks.[6]

Reflecting the emerging dichotomy between broader Israeli–Palestinian/ Arab issues and more limited Israeli–Egyptian concerns, the historic breakthrough that became known as the "Camp David Accords" consisted of two documents: "A Framework for Peace in the Middle East" and "A Framework for the Conclusion of a Peace Treaty between Egypt and Israel," accompanied by a series of short American–Egyptian and American–Israeli side-letters in which additional conditions and commitments were laid out. The signatories were hoping (in vain, as it turned out) that the first framework document would serve as an opening for other Arab states and representatives of the Palestinians to come on board and expand the peace process beyond the bilateral. This document became the vehicle for launching "autonomy talks" dealing with the West Bank and the Gaza Strip, the outcome of which talks was supposed to "recognize the legitimate rights of the Palestinian people and their just requirements. In this way, the Palestinians will participate in the determination of their own future."[7] The second framework document was translated into a formal treaty of peace, signed on the White House lawn on 26 March 1979 amid much festivity and joy, but not without some heckling from protesting supporters of the Palestinians outside the gates.[8]

Sadat's "separate peace," as it was denounced by most Arab leaders, reflected Egypt's weariness for having shouldered more than its fair share of the Arab world's burden of fighting the Palestine cause in three major wars, and signaled the country's temporary disengagement from the pan-Arab fold. Sadat was immediately vilified for breaking ranks and treasonous action.[9] But he had succeeded, unlike his more militant brothers, in liberating at least some Arab soil from Israeli control. For going it alone Egypt paid the penalty of being ostracized for a decade from pan-Arab forums, while Sadat paid the supreme personal price of being assassinated while reviewing a military parade in October 1981.[10]

In April 1982, the Israeli army completed the forced evacuation of resisting Jewish settlers from the Sinai settlement of Yamit, fulfilling the main territorial obligations under the treaty. Despite a number of external pressures on Egyptians and complaints of non-compliance with treaty commitments, this first ever Israel–Arab peace treaty has endured to this day. But the quality of the people-to-people relations between the two countries—diplomatic, economic, touristic—has been uneven, mostly described as a "cold peace." It would only be in Madrid in 1991 that the original Camp David participants would see other Arab states and the Palestinians agreeing to join in their "circle of peace."

The West Bank and Gaza after Camp David

In retrospect, it may seem easy to criticize the authors of the Camp David accords for not finding a successful formula for including the Palestinians. Yet, given the firmly entrenched positions of both Israel (and its US backers) and the PLO (and its Arab, Soviet, and other backers) regarding their conditions for agreeing to recognize and negotiate directly with each other, it is likely that no amount of creative diplomacy at Camp David could have brought the Palestinians into the authors' chosen "Framework for Peace in the Middle East."

In the West Bank and Gaza, captured by Israel in the June 1967 war, relations were becoming increasingly strained as the number of Israeli settlers jumped sharply under Likud prime minister Menachem Begin from 3200 living in 24 settlements in 1977 to 42,600 in over 100 settlements by 1984,[11] encroaching on Palestinian lands and requiring enhanced protection from army and border police. By this time many of the more than 1 million Palestinians in these areas had become dependent on work as day laborers travelling back and forth from their towns and villages to sites inside Israel. The quality of these Israeli–Palestinian relationships on the ground—between occupier and occupied, between master and servant, between boss and worker—was problematic, harsh, and sometimes brutal.[12] Years continued to go by, nullifying initial expectations that the occupation would end with politicians' acceptance of the land-for-peace formula and sitting down to work out the details. Human rights abuses became common as the Israeli authorities, military in essence but with a civilian veneer, ruled over a largely peaceful, but resentful, population.

Despite the necessities of public relations to portray the occupation as enlightened and benign to the Israeli public and to the world, and despite Israelis' aspirations to behave and be perceived as sensitive and respectful human beings, the truth, as Israeli historian Benny Morris described it, "was radically different":

> Like all occupations, Israel's was founded on brute force, repression and fear, collaboration and treachery, beatings and torture chambers, and daily intimidation, humiliation, and manipulation. True, the relative lack of resistance and civil disobedience over the years enabled the Israelis to maintain a façade of normalcy and implement their rule with a relatively small force ....[13]

American political scientist Alan Dowty agrees: "Military occupation was still military occupation, even when carried out by a democratic state and even if it included material benefits."[14] Many of the measures required by military occupation are, by definition, inconsistent with the usual rights and freedoms espoused by democratic states and enjoyed by their citizens. Although limited by certain international legal norms, the occupying power is allowed considerable leeway for security measures if deemed necessary for the protection of the (supposedly temporary) occupation forces and the maintenance of general public order. And so expulsions, curfews, checkpoints, restrictions on movement, deportations, school or business closures, administrative detention, house demolitions, requisitioning of land for often questionable "military" purposes—all these became part of the daily lives of Palestinians under Israeli rule on the West Bank and in the Gaza Strip.[15]

Given the absence of negotiation and the continuation of the occupation into the 1970s, through the 1980s, and beyond, tensions were further aggravated by two factors. One was the rise of a violent form of vigilantism among a portion of the Jewish settler population; the other was a basic ambiguity regarding Israel's ultimate intentions. Generating a cycle of attacks and counterattacks, Palestinians terrorized Jewish settlers by targeting their vehicles traveling to and from West Bank settlements and by occasional ambushes on them when they entered towns like

Hebron, where Jewish and Muslim holy places overlapped.[16] Jewish settlers depended not only on protection from the military, but they also carried their own arms. Often these armed settlers became an unruly and intimidating presence, taking revenge as they saw fit. The army was called upon to intervene to rein in some of the more aggressive settlers who took to bullying Palestinian farmers, villagers, and townspeople near their settlements.[17]

In the early 1980s some radical settlers formed an underground gang named "TNT" (Hebrew acronym for "terror against terror") which planted bombs on Palestinian buses and targeted the vehicles of several prominent mayors. Justifying the vigilante violence were not only the familiar arguments of deterrence (especially where the army was criticized for failing to provide adequate protection) and retaliation. The latter was given additional religious sanction by some rabbis who regarded the land as Biblically promised to Jews; strangers (i.e., Arabs), therefore, should leave or be made to leave. Some fundamentalist settlers also came to view Palestinians as 20th-century embodiments of Amalek of the Bible—the tribe mentioned in Exodus 17:14–16, Deuteronomy 25:17–18, and elsewhere as deserving to be forever pursued until they were wiped off the face of the earth.[18]

A deeper and broader contributor to the tensions was a basic ambiguity regarding Israel's intentions. Would the government, especially (but not only) if the rightist-nationalist Likud were in power, accede to the wishes of a vocal fundamentalist minority of its citizens and, happy to enjoy the fruits of additional real estate, move gradually towards annexing the territories and making them part of the greater Land of Israel (*Eretz-Israel ha-Shlema*), as per Biblical prophecies? Or would the government—moved by the secular worldview of the majority of its citizens under a left-leaning Labor government employing pragmatic, strategic calculations—ultimately agree to return most of the occupied areas, withdrawing its troops, settlers, and other presence as a soon as acceptable peace arrangements could be made (preferably with the previous "owner" or "occupier," the Hashemite Kingdom of Jordan, rather than the despised "terrorist" PLO)? In other words, was Israel treating the territories captured in 1967 as future parts of an expanded Land of Israel, or as bargaining chips to be traded for peace in accordance with Resolution 242? Government policies and statements seemed, at times, to be saying both.

In the absence of clear or consistent signals from Israel's leaders, time did not stand still, and facts—notably the expansion of Jewish settlements and the infrastructure needed to maintain and protect them—continued to be created on the ground. Tension and violence became the common language between Israelis and Palestinians in the occupied territories, while Israel and the PLO maintained their mutual boycott in the political sphere. There was, however, the occasional maverick in both camps who risked legal, political, or physical sanctions and dared to talk to the enemy secretly or on neutral ground, in defiance of the national consensus. Conflict fatigue and the quest for reconciliation motivated the dialogue attempts of these "peaceniks," some of whom, like Palestinian activists Issam Sartawi and Said Hamami, took an assassin's bullets for their treason and willingness to talk to the enemy. In a way, these precursors of the 1970s and 1980s helped to pave the way for the higher-level Israeli–Palestinian dialogue when that taboo was finally broken in Oslo in 1993.[19]

The main Palestinian-related follow-up of Camp David was the attempt to conduct negotiations about Palestinian autonomy in the West Bank—known to the Israelis by their Hebrew Biblical names, *Yehuda ve-Shomron* (Judaea and Samaria)—and the Gaza Strip. For two years from the middle of 1980, about twenty meetings were convened among Israeli, Egyptian, and US delegates. But these dissolved with no real Palestinian involvement and no result other than increased bitterness and cynicism on the part of participants. The whole enterprise was plagued by a wide gap of interests and interpretations, underlying which was a determined pattern of Israeli–Palestinian mutual non-recognition, expressed in the following ways:

1   The Israeli, Egyptian, and Palestinian concepts of autonomy and definitions of self-rule were wildly divergent in spirit and in application. By recognizing only autonomy of the *people*, but not applying to the *land*, Begin's autonomy plan deliberately sought to avoid treating the Palestinians as a national community. To Egyptians and Palestinians, the very idea of self-rule presupposed an evolution towards self-determination—if not a Palestinian state, then an entity of some kind—precisely the red line that Begin would not cross.[20]

2   The Israeli insistence on excluding the PLO and people affiliated with it was matched by the PLO's refusal to participate in the talks, which it denounced as a "Camp David plot" to co-opt Palestinians in a sham autonomy that would never lead to self-determination.

3   Those Palestinians who showed any interest in this process were treated as traitors, as the PLO managed to enforce, sometimes using brute intimidation, a boycott against participation.

4   Arab and Palestinian bitterness hung like a cloud over the talks as it became clear that the Begin government—contrary to what both President Carter and Anwar Sadat had understood at Camp David—had no intention of freezing plans for building new Jewish settlements in the territories.

Fifteen years later, the difficult transition to creating a "Palestinian Interim Self-Government Authority" called for under the 1993 Israeli–Palestinian "Declaration of Principles" (see Chapter 10 below) would display some uncanny parallels to the deadlocks and attitudes encountered during these preliminary discussions about Palestinian autonomy. Also, some commentators would also look back to Palestinian rejection of the Begin plan as a "missed opportunity" for advancing their goal of statehood (see Chapter 11).

The autonomy talks episode overlapped with ongoing Israeli policies in the territories that sought to strengthen leaders from rural villages into an anti-PLO political force known as the "Village Leagues." This effort was seen as fostering so-called moderates against extremists, and recalled Zionist support for anti-Mufti political groups during the 1920s in Mandatory Palestine.[21] These Israeli tactics fed existing political rivalries within the Palestinian community. As in earlier periods, struggles among competing factions and individuals claiming to speak on behalf of all Palestinians constituted a weakness of the national movement in its confrontation with the pre-1948 *yishuv* and Israel. Ultimately, pro-PLO forces won the credibility and leadership battle among West Bank and Gaza Palestinians.[22] This evolution was, for many Israelis, a slow and unwelcome lesson about the impossibility of selecting one's peace-partner, and the need to make peace with one's enemies, however unworthy or detestable their official representatives may appear.

The Lebanon War, 1982–

With southern Lebanon serving as the main staging area both for Palestinian raids into and shelling of Israel after 1970, the Israeli–Lebanon frontier became a war zone with a steady escalation of attacks and counter-attacks. After completing its evacuation of Sinai in April 1982, Israel actively considered forceful military action to remove the military threat from "Fatahland," as some called the southern zone of Lebanon which seemed to be ruled by PLO forces rather than by the weak Beirut government.

The assassination attempt on an Israeli diplomat in London was the provocation Israel used for launching a full-scale invasion of southern Lebanon on 6 June 1982. Beyond the declared military goal of driving back Palestinian bases and artillery to a distance of 40 km, an important political aim was to expel the PLO from Lebanon altogether. More ambitious Israelis hoped also to engineer a régime change in Beirut, realigning internal Lebanese politics (with its heavy Syrian influences) in a way more favorable to Israeli interests, and to sign a peace treaty with Lebanon's future rulers.

In an effort to force the departure of PLO and other Palestinian offices and fighters from Beirut, the IDF laid siege to the Lebanese capital for seven weeks. The precise end date of the war is difficult to pin down (perhaps late August or early September). Numerous cease-fire agreements, partial redeployments, and tactical arrangements resulted in the retreat, some three years later, of Israeli forces south of a line several kilometers north of the international frontier. In the name of protecting its towns and settlements in the north, Israel declared these Lebanese border areas to be a security zone, which the IDF controlled for the next fifteen years with the help of a proxy force, the South Lebanese Army, created expressly for the purpose of excluding or controlling Palestinian fighters and artillery.[23]

The 1982 war cost Israel 650 deaths initially; the toll rose to 1000 by the time Israel finally withdrew its last soldiers from the security zone in mid-2000. According to official Lebanese statistics, 17,825 Lebanese and Palestinians, 84 percent of whom were civilians, were killed in Israel's "Operation Peace for Galilee." It had several significant political ramifications and aftershocks, including:

1 The evacuation of more than 14,000 Palestinian activists and fighters from southern and central Lebanon, and the transfer of PLO offices from Beirut to Tunis.

2 The intensification of a longstanding tacit Israeli alliance with a faction of the Maronite Christians, leading to an Israeli–Lebanese peace agreement, signed on 17 May 1983 but abrogated by the Lebanese within a year.[24]

3 Unprecedented sharp polarization within Israel. A large portion of the population remained unconvinced about the security and moral justifications for the war, and questioned the wisdom of the country's political and military leaders.[25]

4 Massacres at Sabra and Shatilla. Taking advantage of the departure of the PLO, Lebanese Christian militias on 16–18 September settled old scores by entering these two refugee camps and massacring between 800 and 2000 Palestinians (estimates vary widely), mostly civilians. The complicity of the Israeli forces in assisting the Phalangist marauders led to years of dispute over the extent of political or moral responsibility to be accorded to individual Israelis, or collectively to the IDF.[26]

Righteous Victimhood in the 1980s

With the expulsion of the PLO headquarters from Beirut and guerilla bases from south Lebanon, Palestinian political and military affairs were directed from Tunis and elsewhere. Although Israel's northern frontier areas remained relatively quiet, terrorist operations continued to be directed at Israeli and Jewish targets, largely by rejectionist factions defying the PLO's caution and efforts at respectability (see below, Chapter 10). After September 1982, the names Sabra and Shatilla were added to Deir Yasin (1948) and Kafr Qassem (1956)[27] on the list of atrocities that have been seared into the memories of Palestinians, increasing their sense of vulnerability and victimhood at the receiving end of Israeli power, and as a fragmented community, many of whose members lived as an unwelcome refugee population dispersed through-out the Arab world.

This latest victimization of Palestinians in Lebanon serves to remind us of the important undercurrent of righteous victimhood that animates both Israelis and Palestinians, contributing to each party's almost unique focus on its own suffering, in effect reducing its ability to empathize with and recognize any legitimate claims or fears of the other. Paradoxically, Israelis continued—even while on the offensive and displaying great military superiority during the latest war—to perceive themselves as endangered victims, still as little David facing the mighty Arab Goliath. Not accepted by a resentful Arab world bent on justice or revenge for Israel's victories in the wars of 1948, 1956, 1967 and 1973, Israelis were entering a fourth decade of economic boycott, hostility, and relentless cross-border terrorist attacks, producing what some psychologists have called a siege mentality, "Masada complex," or "Samson syndrome."[28] Strangely, perhaps, the Israeli-Jewish self-perception of *powerlessness* coex-ists along with the reality of near-hegemonic Israeli *power* when measured comparatively or in regional and global perspective.[29]

As a survivor of the Holocaust, Prime Minister Menachem Begin made a major contribution to this particularly Jewish-Israeli way of viewing the world—not only believing "the whole world is against us," but also saying "to hell with the Goyim" [non-Jews].[30] Begin intro-duced into Israeli foreign relations his own personal testament, making it almost a policy objective during his tenure that "never again" would Jews—and especially Israeli Jews living in their own sovereign state—be allowed to become victims.[31] In his public utterances Begin was not averse to plainspoken displays of Holocaust remembrance, whether on ostensibly joyous occasions, such as the signing of the Egypt–Israel peace treaty in March 1979, or on menacing ones, e.g., when justifying Israel's risky bombing of the Osirak nuclear facility near Baghdad in 1981.[32]

Both sides have also crassly resorted to the "nazification" of the enemy. In the course of defining Zionism, Article 22 of the PLO's National Charter referred to the movement's "essentially fanatical and racialist" nature and described its methods as being "those of the Fascists and the Nazis."[33] In the wake of Israel's battlefield victories, Arabs and their supporters often depicted the Israelis as behaving towards them as the Nazis had behaved towards the Jews of Europe, with political cartoonists cleverly twisting the Star of David into the shape of a swastika. This motif was also present in the 1982 portrayals of Menachem Begin and Ariel Sharon as cruel Nazis in their treatment of Lebanese and Palestinian civilians during Israel's invasion of Lebanon.

Zionists and Israelis, for their part, focused on the wartime record of the exiled Mufti of Jerusalem. Even today, some publications, websites, and journalists are obsessed with presenting the ex-Mufti as a demonic, Hitler-like figure, suggesting an equation between Hitler's all-out war against world Jewry and the contemporary Palestinian and Arab nationalist struggles against Zionism and Israel.[34] In 1982, Prime Minister Begin viewed his "Operation Peace for Galilee" not as an aggressive attack on a neighboring country but rather as a defensive war in which Jewish soldiers were not only protecting the northern villages of their homeland by driving back the PLO, but also entering Lebanon to protect defenseless Christians from their Muslim-"Nazi" oppressors. For Begin, Yasir Arafat was "a latter-day Hitler" and the Palestine National Charter was another *Mein Kampf*. The pre-1967 borders of Israel were, in Begin's rhetoric, "Auschwitz borders," and the PLO was "the Arab S.S." The alternative to a massive Israeli attack on the PLO in Lebanon in June 1982, the prime minister reportedly told his Cabinet colleagues, would have been nothing less than "Treblinka"—"and we have decided that there will not be another Treblinka." Similarly, the IDF's siege of the PLO's Beirut head-quarters was likened by Begin and others to the 1945 bombardment of Hitler's Berlin bunker.[35]

These deeply felt, parallel Israeli and Palestinian senses of victimhood remain inextricable psychological obstacles to resolving the conflict. To an outside observer they may seem far-fetched, and those who employ geno-cidal motifs as fear-mongers and demagogues. Yet our efforts to under-stand the conflict will not be advanced by wishing away these perceptions of victimhood, or by advising the parties to get over them, move on, and put the past behind them. We will return to grapple with this obstacle again in Chapter 12.

Notes

1   Declaration of the Arab Summit Conference at Algiers, 28 November 1973, accessed online 18 July 2008 at http://www.jewishvirtuallibrary.org/jsource/ History/arabsum73.html.

2   Kenneth W. Stein, *Heroic Diplomacy: Sadat, Kissinger, Carter, Begin and the Quest for Arab–Israeli Peace*, New York: Routledge, 1999. Two of the best critical and analytical treatments of this historic episode are Saadia Touval, *The Peace Brokers: Mediators in the Arab–Israeli Conflict, 1948–1979*, Princeton, NJ: Princeton University Press, 1982, ch. 10, and William B. Quandt, *Camp David: Peacemaking and Politics*, Washington, DC: The Brookings Institution, 1986.

3   Sadat's speech ("Peace with Justice") before the Israeli Knesset, 20 November 1977, reproduced in *The Israel–Arab Reader: A Documentary History of the Middle East Conflict*, 7th rev. ed., eds. Walter Laqueur and Barry Rubin, New York: Penguin, 2008, 207–15, and in *The Israeli–Palestinian Conflict: A Documentary Record, 1967–1990*, ed. Yehuda Lukacs, Cambridge: Cambridge University Press, 1992, 136–46. Begin's speech in Lukacs, *The Israeli–Palestinian Conflict*, 147–53.

4   Y. Harkabi, *Palestinians and Israel*, New York: John Wiley, 1974, 209.

5   One scholar has argued that there is a third, perhaps more important, dimension of the Israel–Egypt relationship, namely a cultural divide, which meant that their negotiations efforts resembled a "dialogue of the deaf." See Raymond Cohen, *Culture and Conflict in Egyptian–Israeli Relations: A Dialogue of the Deaf*, Bloomington / Indianapolis: Indiana University Press, 1990.

6   Some of the firsthand accounts of what happened prior to and during the Camp David summit in September 1978 include: Quandt, *Camp David*; Mohamed Ibrahim Kamel, *The Camp David Accords: A Testimony*, New York: KPI, 1986; Boutros Boutros-Ghali, *Egypt's Road to Jerusalem*, New York: Random House, 1997; Moshe Dayan, *Breakthrough: A Personal Account of the Egypt–Israel Peace Negotiations*, London: Weidenfeld and Nicolson, 1981; Ezer Weizman, *The Battle for Peace*, New York: Bantam, 1981; Jimmy Carter, *Keeping Faith: Memoirs of a President*, New York: Bantam, 1982; Zbigniew Bzrezinski, *Power and Principle: Memoirs of the National Security Advisor, 1977–1981*, New York: Farrar, Straus, Giroux, 1983; Cyrus Vance, *Hard Choices: Critical Years in America's Foreign Policy*, New York: Simon and Schuster, 1983.

7   The frameworks are reproduced, in abridged form, in Laqueur and Rubin, *Israel–Arab Reader*, 222–7. A more complete version can be found in Quandt, *Camp David*, 376–87, and Laura Zittrain Eisenberg and Neil Caplan, *Negotiating Arab–Israeli Peace: Patterns, Problems, Possibilities*, Bloomington / Indianapolis: Indiana University Press, 1998, 169–79.

8   The treaty is reproduced, in abridged form, in Laqueur and Rubin, *Israel–Arab Reader*, 227–8. A more complete version can be found in Quandt, *Camp David*, 397–401, and Eisenberg and Caplan, *Negotiating*, 180–3.

9   For Palestinian statements denouncing Sadat's moves (4 and 21 December 1977), see Lukacs, *The Israeli–Palestinian Conflict*, 335–7; Arab League Summit Communique, Baghdad, 31 March 1979, in ibid., 463–7, extract in Laqueur and Rubin, *Israel–Arab Reader*, 228–9; Arafat interview, 19 November 1979, translated extract in Laqueur and Rubin, *Israel–Arab Reader*, 230–1.

10 For a retrospective discussion and tribute to the late Egyptian president by eighteen scholars and diplomats, see *Sadat and His Legacy: Egypt and the World, 1977–1997*, ed. and introduced by Jon B. Alterman, Washington, DC: Washington Institute for Near East Policy, 1998.

11 Ilan Peleg, *Begin's Foreign Policy, 1977–1983: Israel's Turn to the Right*, Westport, CT: Greenwood, 1987, 110–11, 137.

12 See, e.g., the Karp Report: An Israeli Government Inquiry into Settler Violence on the West Bank, 7 February 1984, extract in Ilan Peleg, *Human Rights in the West Bank and Gaza: Legacy and Politics*, Syracuse, NY: Syracuse University Press, 1995, 147–51, discussed ibid., 90–1; David Shulman, *Dark Hope: Working for Peace in Israel and Palestine*, Chicago: University of Chicago Press, 2007.

13 Benny Morris, *Righteous Victims: A History of the Zionist Arab Conflict, 1881– 1999*, New York: Alfred A. Knopf, 1999 / London: John Murray, 2000, 341.

14 Alan Dowty, *The Jewish State: A Century Later*, Berkeley / Los Angeles / London: University of California Press, 1998, 221.

15 For a sampling of descriptions of Palestinian life and Israel's behavior in the territories, especially during the first two decades, see Raymonda Hawa Tawil, *My Home, My Prison*, New York: Holt, Rinehart and Winston, 1979; Raja Shehadeh, *Samed: Journal of a West Bank Palestinian*, New York: Adama Books, 1984; Dowty, *The Jewish State*, 217–26; Peleg, *Human Rights in the West Bank and Gaza*; John Quigley, *The Case for Palestine: An International Law Perspective*, rev. and updated ed., Durham, NC / London: Duke University Press, 2005, 168–88; W. Thomas Mallison and Sally V. Mallison, *The Palestine Problem in International Law and World Order*, Harlow, UK: Longman, 1986, 240–75; Michael Bruno, "Israeli Policy in the 'Administered Territories'," in *Israel, the Arabs and the Middle East*, eds. Irving Howe and Carl Gershman, New York: Bantam, 1972, 249–65; Alan Dershowitz, "Civil Liberties in Israel: The Problem of Preventive Detention," in Howe and Gershman, *Israel, the Arabs and The Middle East*, 266–99; Allan Gerson, *Israel, the West Bank and International Law*, London / Totowa, NJ: Frank Cass, 1978, ch. III; Alan Dershowitz, *The Case for Israel*, New York: John Wiley, 2003, ch. 19, 22, 24, 25.

16 See, e.g., David K. Shipler, *Arab and Jew: Wounded Spirits in a Promised Land*, rev. ed., New York: Penguin, 2002, ch. 3.

17 For a disturbing and credible eyewitness account of this pattern of violence in recent years, see Shulman, *Dark Hope*.

18 For detailed discussion and analyses of the fundamentalist ideological basis for claims to the land and justification for violence against Arabs, see, e.g., Ian S. Lustick, *For the Land and the Lord: Jewish Fundamentalism in Israel*, New York: Council on Foreign Relations, 1988; Uriel Tal, "Foundations of a

Political Messianic Trend in Israel," *Jerusalem Quarterly* 35 (Spring 1985), 36–45; Henry Siegman, "The Perils of Messianic Politics" (1988), in *Wrestling with Zion: Progressive Jewish–American Responses to the Israeli–Palestinian Conflict*, ed. and with an introduction by Tony Kushner and Alisa Solomon, New York: Grove Press, 2003, 114; Bernard Wasserstein, *Israelis and Palestinians: Why Do They Fight? Can They Stop?* 3rd ed., New Haven, CT / London: Yale University Press / London: Profile Books, 2008, 165–7.

19 See, e.g., *When Enemies Dare to Talk: An Israeli–Palestinian Debate (5/6 September 1978)*, ed. Simha Flapan, London: Croom Helm, 1979; Uri Avnery, *My Friend, the Enemy*, Westport, CT: Lawrence Hill, 1986; Mohamed Heikal, *Secret Channels: The Inside Story of Arab–Israeli Peace Negotiations*, London: HarperCollins, 1996, 321–5; [PLO] Committee for the Occupied Homeland Report on Contact with Jews, Damascus, 21 April 1981, in Lukacs, *The Israeli–Palestinian Conflict*, 357; Hussein Agha, Shai Feldman, Ahmad Khalidi, and Zeev Schiff, *Track-II Diplomacy: Lessons from the Middle East*, Cambridge, MA: MIT Press, 2003, ch. 2; Walid Salem and Edy Kaufman, "Palestinian–Israeli Peacebuilding: A Historical Perspective," in *Bridging the Divide: Peacebuilding in the Israeli–Palestinian Conflict*, eds. Edy Kaufman, Walid Salem, and Juliette Verhoeven, foreword by N. Chazan and H. Siniora, Boulder, CO: Lynne Rienner, 2006, 22–31.

20 Begin's ideas on autonomy were given for the first time in a Knesset speech, 28 December 1977, in Lukacs, *The Israeli–Palestinian Conflict*, 153–5 (extracts in Laqueur and Rubin, *Israel–Arab Reader*, 218–20). An Egyptian and a later Israeli autonomy proposal can be found in Lukacs, *The Israeli–Palestinian Conflict*, 160–70. For critical discussions, see Ilan Peleg, *Begin's Foreign Policy*, ch. 4; Zeev Maoz, *Defending the Holy Land: A Critical Analysis of Israel's Security and Foreign Policy*, Ann Arbor: University of Michigan Press, 2006, 436–42. For a participant's view of the work of the Israeli–Egyptian autonomy committee, see Ephraim Dowek, *Israeli–Egyptian Relations, 1980–2000*, foreword by Yitshak Shamir, London: Frank Cass, 2001, ch. 15.

21 For background, see, e.g., Neil Caplan, *Palestine Jewry and the Arab Question, 1917–1925*, London: Frank Cass, 1978, ch. 7, and "Arab–Jewish Contacts in Palestine after the First World War," *Journal of Contemporary History* XII:4 (October 1977), 635–68; Hillel Cohen, "Why Do Collaborators Collaborate? The Case of Palestinians and Zionist Institutions, 1917–1936," in *Arab–Jewish Relations: From Conflict to Resolution? Essays in Honour of Prof. Moshe Ma'oz*, eds. Elie Podeh and Asher Kaufman, Brighton: Sussex Academic Press, 2005, 43–63.

22 For an insider Israeli account of these developments, see Shlomo Gazit, *Trapped Fools: Thirty Years of Israeli Policy in the Territories*, introduced by Shimon Peres, London: Frank Cass, 2003, 208–38. For a critical look at the Village Leagues, see Salim Tamari, "In League with Zion: Israel's Search for a Native Pillar," *Journal of Palestine Studies* 12:4 (Summer 1983), 41–56; Yezid Sayigh, *Armed Struggle and the Search for State: The Palestinian National Movement, 1949–1993*, Oxford: Oxford University Press / Washington, DC:

The Institute for Palestine Studies, 1997, 483–4; Sari Nusseibeh, with Anthony David, *Once upon a Country: A Palestinian Life*, New York: Farrar, Straus and Giroux, 2007, 197–201, 208–9. See also Statement of West Bank Palestinians, 30 August 1981, reproduced in Laqueur and Rubin, *Israel–Arab Reader*, 235–7; Moshe Ma'oz, *Palestinian Leadership on the West Bank: The Changing Role of the Mayors under Jordan and Israel*, with a contribution from Mordechai Nisan, London: Frank Cass, 1984, 176–83.

23 On the 1982 war, see Ze'ev Schiff and Ehud Ya'ari, *Israel's Lebanon War*, ed. and transl. Ina Friedman, New York: Simon and Schuster, 1984; Rashid Khalidi, *Under Siege: P.L.O. Decisionmaking during the 1982 War*, New York: Columbia University Press, 1986; Peleg, *Begin's Foreign Policy*, ch. 5; Morris, *Righteous Victims*, ch. 11; Eyal Zisser, "The 1982 'Peace for Galilee' War: Looking Back in Anger—Between an Option of a War and a War of No Option," in *A Never-Ending Conflict: A Guide to Israeli Military History*, ed. Mordechai Bar-On, Westport, CT / London: Praeger, 2004, 193–210.

24 Eisenberg and Caplan, *Negotiating*, ch. 2 and 192–4; Morris, *Righteous Victims*, 549–50.

25 For the Government's justifications, see Begin's speech, "The Wars of No Alternative and Operation Peace for Galilee," in Laqueur and Rubin, *Israel–Arab Reader*, 254–7. See also Zisser, "The 1982 'Peace for Galilee' War" and Peleg, *Begin's Foreign Policy*, 165–75.

26 Yitzhak Kahan, Aharon Barak, and Yona Efrat, *Report of the Commission of Inquiry* into the atrocity carried out by a unit of the Lebanese Forces against the civilian population in the Shatilla and Sabra camps; Jerusalem, 7 February 1983. Extracts in Laqueur and Rubin, *Israel–Arab Reader*, 269–74. Full text accessed online 22 July 2008 at http://www.mideastweb.org/Kahan_report. htm. In 2000, using new international conventions for the punishment of war criminals, pro-Palestinian and human rights workers initiated action to pursue the minister of defense at the time (and later prime minister), Ariel Sharon, in the courts, but with no success.

27 On Deir Yasin, see page 116. In October 1956, during a build-up of tension along the Israeli–Jordanian frontier and as Israel was secretly preparing for war against Egypt, farmers returning to their village of Kafr Qassem were callously gunned down by IDF troops for violating a curfew that was imposed on short notice without their knowledge.

28 Benjamin Z. Kedar, "Masada: The Myth and the Complex," *Jerusalem Quarterly* 24 (Summer 1982), 57–63; Nachman Ben-Yehuda, *The Masada Myth: Collective Memory and Mythmaking in Israel*, Madison: The University of Wisconsin Press, 1995; Jay Y. Gonen, *A Psychohistory of Zionism*, New York: Mason Charter, 1975, ch. 13; Shulamith Hareven, "Identity: Victim," in *The Vocabulary of Peace: Life, Culture and Politics in the Middle East*, San Francisco: Mercury House, 1995, 148–54. For a recent study of the resonance of Masada as emitting a new warning against Jewish extremism, see Ted Sasson and Shaul Kelner, "From Shrine to Forum: Masada and the Politics of Jewish Extremism," *Israel Studies* 13:2 (Summer 2008), 146–63.

29   See, e.g., David Biale, *Power and Powerlessness in Jewish History*, New York: Schocken, 1986. See also Anita Shapira, *Land and Power: The Zionist Resort to Force, 1881–1948*, transl. William Templer, Stanford, CA: Stanford University Press, 1999, 369–70 (quoted above, page 161).

30   Mordechai Bar-On, "Historiography as an Educational Project: The Historians' Debate in Israel and the Middle East Peace Process," in *The Middle East Peace Process: Interdisciplinary Perspectives*, ed. Ilan Peleg, Albany: State University of New York Press, 1998, 27–8. A similar, more elegantly expressed sentiment was attributed to the David Ben-Gurion, whose dictum was "What matters is not what the *goyim* say, but what the Jews do."

31   For a discussion of the impact of the Holocaust on Begin's thinking and political behavior, see Peleg, *Begin's Foreign Policy*, 63–8.

32   Neil Caplan, "The Holocaust and the Arab–Israeli Conflict," in *So Others Will Remember: Holocaust History and Survivor Testimony*, ed. Ronald Headland, Montreal: Vehicule Press, 1999, 90–2.

33   Palestine National Covenant, Cairo, 17 July 1968, reproduced in Yehoshafat Harkabi, *The Palestinian Covenant and Its Meaning*, London: Valentine Mitchell, 1979, 123, following the English translation given in a volume produced by Institute for Palestine Studies in 1971. Another translation of the Palestinian National Charter, published by the PLO Research Center in 1969 (ibid., p. 117; also reproduced in Laqueur and Rubin, *Israel–Arab Reader*, 119) offers a different version: viz., "fascist in its methods," omitting the word "Nazi." For other examples, see Y. Harkabi, *Arab Attitudes to Israel*, Jerusalem: Keter, 1972, 176–7. See also Articles 20 and 31 of the Charter of the Islamic Resistance Movement (Hamas), which refer to the Nazi-like qualities and behavior of the Jews. For the text, see Shaul Mishal and Avraham Sela, *The Palestinian Hamas: Vision, Violence and Coexistence*, New York: Columbia University Press, 2000, 188, 195 (and various websites).

34   E.g., Benjamin Netanyahu, *A Durable Peace: Israel and Its Place among the Nations*, rev. ed., New York: Warner Books, 2000, 206–16; David Pryce-Jones, "Their Kampf: Hitler's Book in Arab Hands," *National Review*, 18 July 2002, accessed online 12 August 2008 at http://www.nationalreview.com/nr_comment/nr_comment071802a.asp. For a few examples of websites, see http://www.zionism-israel.com/dic/Haj_Amin_El_Husseini.htm; http://www.palestinefacts.org/pf_mandate_grand_mufti.php; Chuck Morse, "The Faisal–Weizmann Agreement, the Mufti and Hitler, Nazism and Islamic Terror," *The Jewish Magazine*, accessed online 11 August 2008 at http://www.jewishmag.com/116mag/chuckmorse/chuckmorse.htm; "Hitler, The Mufti of Jerusalem and Modern Islamo Nazism," accessed online 11 August 2008 at http://www.youtube.com/watch?v=d51poygEXYU; David G. Dalin and John F. Rothmann, *Icon of Evil*, New York: Random House, 2008, reviewed by David Pryce-Jones, "Malevolence and the Mufti," *Wall Street Journal*, 26 June 2008.

35   Ze'ev Schiff and Ehud Ya'ari, *Israel's Lebanon War*, New York: Simon and Schuster, 1984, 39, 220; Peleg, *Begin's Foreign Policy*, 65, 67; Morris,

Righteous Victims, 514. For contemporary criticism of Begin's use of the Holocaust by leading Israeli intellectuals, see ibid. 514–15; A. B. Yehoshua, "The Holocaust as Junction," in *Between Right and Right*, New York: Doubleday, 1981, 1–19.

10
From Boycott to Mutual Recognition, 1982–2008

The longstanding mutual boycott between Israelis and Palestinians, and between Israel and most of the Arab world, continued to be the dominant pattern of their relations into the 1980s. This major taboo of non-recognition had been broken in the case of the largest Arab state, Egypt, leading to the resolution, albeit slow and halting,[1] of many specific bilateral issues. But a residue of unresolved core (pre-1948) and post-1967 grievances continued to fester among the Palestinians and Israel's other Arab neighbors. The spillover effects of the non-resolution of the Palestinian aspects of the conflict were felt mostly in Lebanon, Syria, and Jordan, as well as by Israeli civilians and Palestinian refugees, both suffering their toll from cross-border attacks and reprisals. Nonetheless, the parties during the 1980s and early 1990s inched closer towards mutual recognition—a minimal prerequisite for any attempt at resolving their century-old conflict.

Peace Plans and Planting Seeds

The 1980s witnessed several international and regional efforts to engage the parties in discussing peace plans. Although there was no immediate result from the succession of proposals, a number of ideas considered and rejected or abandoned during the 1980s would resurface in the following decade with more positive results.

On 1 September 1982 US president Ronald Reagan sought to transform the debris of Israel's Lebanon war into a resumption of the unfinished business of broadening the Camp David peace process. Reagan called upon the Arab states, Palestinians, and Israelis to begin discussions under American mediation, but his suggestion for an autonomous West Bank federated with Jordan were unacceptable to Palestinians and anathema to Israel's Likud government, leading to the quick failure of his initiative.[2] Not wishing to be outdone, Soviet premier Leonid Brezhnev issued his own peace plan for the Middle East several weeks later.[3] At the same time, leaders of the Arab states at a summit meeting in Fez, Morocco, considered proposals by Saudi Arabia's King Fahd to fine-tune their conditions for peace with Israel.[4] But there was little new or attractive enough to elicit a positive Israeli response that would open up a diplomatic process at this time.

During the mid-1980s the Israeli–Lebanon frontier cooled down somewhat, but the Arab–Israeli conflict continued to simmer with cross-border violence, punctuated by the occasional high-profile international terrorist and counterterrorist operation. For example, Israeli planes attacked Arafat's Tunis headquarters on 1 October 1985, and one radical faction (working to outbid rivals with spectacular operations) followed shortly thereafter with the hijacking of an Italian cruise liner, throwing overboard a wheelchair-bound American Jewish tourist in the process.[5] In 1988, Israeli hit squads also penetrated PLO leaders' compounds in Tunis and assassinated high-ranking PLO official Khalil al-Wazir, aka Abu Jihad. Members of the United Nations Security Council found themselves again handling complaints dealing with breaches of, or threats to, the peace submitted by, or against, Israel, Arab states and the Palestinians.

The new American president George H. W. Bush, and his Secretary of State George Shultz, continued US policy of considering the Palestinians on two levels: one, the population living under Israeli occupation and in refugee camps, and the other, the shunned PLO, although it was now recognized by many other countries as the "sole legitimate representative" of the Palestinian people. At various times during his tenure as Secretary of State, Shultz visited the area in attempts to engage Jordanian, Israeli, and unofficial (non-PLO) Palestinian leaders from Jerusalem and the West Bank in American-sponsored discussions about peace.[6] During 1987 he tried to resuscitate plans to convene an international conference under joint US–USSR chairmanship, and in March 1988 he sought to defuse the Palestinian *intifada* (see below) by having the parties consider his own "Shultz initiative."[7] Although none of his proposals bore immediate fruit, a number of his ideas would reappear several years later in the Madrid Conference format.

During this period, informal interpersonal contacts—illegal for Israelis, dangerous for Palestinians, and unpopular for both—multiplied, mainly outside the Middle East. A growing number of academics and public figures came to see the futility and the damage of continuing their mutual boycott and non-recognition. The circle widened of those who dared to talk to the enemy, gradually including people near the center of power in Tunis and Jerusalem. Some of these dialogue projects were conducted in academic settings and behind the curtains of anonymity;[8] others were indirectly connected with Palestinian efforts to foster better relations with the US administration.[9] Imperceptibly, below the radar of high politics and military confrontations, individuals did what they could to prepare the ground for eventual reconciliation and mutual recognition between long-time foes.

The 1980s also witnessed Jordanians engaging in difficult negotiations with the PLO in attempts to fashion a common strategy regarding the ultimate destiny of the West Bank.[10] In April 1987 Israel sought to repeat its success with Egypt when acting Foreign Minister Shimon Peres met secretly with Jordan's King Hussein to discuss conditions for bilateral negotiations under the diplomatic cover of an American-sponsored international conference. Both the Hussein–Arafat (Amman) accord of February 1985 and the Peres–Hussein initiative (known also as the "London Document")[11] were short-lived episodes, overtaken by events and with no immediate results. But they too would turn out, in retrospect, to be markers for future gradual progress to breakthroughs, contributing some elements to the Madrid Conference of 1991 and the eventual Israel–Jordan peace treaty of 1994.

The First *Intifada* and the Gulf War, 1987–1991

As the end of the decade approached, several important events on both the local and global levels significantly altered the structure of the Israeli–Arab and Palestinian–Israeli conflicts and helped to create, for the first time since the mid-1970s, some movement towards their resolution. One was the outbreak of a popular uprising by Palestinians against Israeli occupation in the West Bank and Gaza Strip in December 1987, taking the Arabic name *intifada* (for "shaking off" the occupation). The other was the end of the Cold War followed by the first Gulf War in early 1991.

Economic and social conditions on the ground in the Gaza Strip and on the West Bank continued to deteriorate for the Palestinians—despite rosy official statistics published by the territorial administration. If we juxtapose the self-congratulatory Israel Ministry of Defense official twentieth anniversary publication on the administration of "Judaea, Samaria [i.e., the West Bank] and the Gaza District" with the almost simultaneous eruption of the *intifada*, we can see, as Alan Dowty demonstrates, "the hollowness of the occupation's social and economic benefits. ... [M]ore refrigerators and more schools would not buy Arab acquiescence to continued Israeli control of their lives."[12] Once again, we see evidence of the longstanding unfulfilled Zionist assumption and expectation (Chapter 4) that bringing ostensible material blessings to the Palestinians would win their hearts and eliminate their resistance to having their homeland taken over by another people.

With no relief or political solution imminent, popular disillusionment now extended also to the ineffectual Fatah and PLO leadership working from exile in Tunis. New, more radical, popular, and Islamist forces began to emerge inside the occupied territories as active competitors for the loyalty of the Palestinian public. Notably, the Palestinian Islamic Jihad (founded in 1986) and Hamas (Islamic Resistance Movement, founded in 1988) appealed to Palestinians' religious identity while simultaneously filling a much-neglected gap by providing social, educational, and health services in the territories. Drawing on the teachings of the Muslim Brotherhood (founded in Egypt in the 1920s) and the example of heroic resistance offered by Shaikh Izz ad-Din al-Qassam in the 1930s, these movements also offered a new hope and a different worldview, with a clearly defined objective: the removal of Israel by whatever means necessary, and its replacement by an Islamic Palestinian state.[13]

On 8 December 1987 an accident in which an IDF tank transport vehicle in Gaza killed four Palestinians and wounded seven as they were returning from work was followed by anti-Israel demonstrations and rioting that spread rapidly throughout the territories. Stone-throwing youth came face to face with Israeli soldiers and police on a daily basis, with curfews and closures leading to hardship but also greater defiance among the population, especially the disaffected youth. The level of violence quickly escalated from stones and slingshots to occasional incendiary devices ("Molotov cocktails") which brought Israeli responses in the form of tear gas, rubber bullets, and live ammunition. Tens of thousands were arrested; hundreds of homes were blown up or sealed. During the first year almost 300 Palestinians were killed and more than 11,000 wounded in violent confrontations with Israeli troops and police; by the end of 1991 the Palestinian death toll had risen to more than 800.[14]

The regular appearance of communiqués indicated that actions by local committees were coordinated by an effective grass-roots rebel leadership. The determination and degree of organization among the protesters and rioters surprised everyone, even the PLO and especially Israelis, and drew extensive international media attention. This, in turn, moved the conflict from the back burner to the front, providing dramatic clashes on television screens around the world. A young generation of Palestinians who had lived their whole lives under occupation stepped forward to take control of the *intifada*, introducing a new element and presenting a challenge to the traditional PLO leadership based in far-away Tunis.[15]

Caught off-guard, Palestinian leaders abroad sought to take political and diplomatic advantage of the popular uprising in the territories, and the Palestine National Council meeting in Algiers on 14–15 November 1988 became the scene of important new formulations of PLO policies. Significantly, the PNC adopted resolutions finally accepting UN Security Council Resolutions 242 and 338, thereby acceding to one of American and Israeli conditions for the PLO to be recognized as a viable diplomatic partner. The PNC also issued a Palestinian Declaration of Independence—symbolic, in the absence of control over any sovereign territory—implying coexistence with the state of Israel.[16] Shortly after this historic meeting, Yasir Arafat addressed a special session of the UN General Assembly in Geneva. Responding to a somewhat awkward application of US pressure, and with the involvement of some American-Jewish peace activists, Arafat also read out a carefully prepared press statement renouncing the use of terrorism—thereby opening the door to a US–PLO dialogue.[17]

This was another juncture at which the eleventh of our unresolved core arguments reappears: What are the Palestinians' and the PLO's true intentions vis-à-vis Israel? Skeptical Israelis wondered whether "the leopard had really changed its spots,"[18] while Palestinian commentators underlined the significance of this "new Palestinian diplomacy." Veteran historian Walid Khalidi welcomed the historic decisions as the product of "intensive Palestinian soul-searching" and a "long drawn-out trend towards pragmatism." On the basis of a "mature reading of local, regional and international realities," the Algiers PNC decisions were, he declared,

> a triumph of compassion for one's people over hatred of one's enemy. It thus opened wide the gate towards a historic reconciliation while spelling out its irreducible minimum condition of statehood. It offers an integrated cluster of ideas on which an infrastructure of peace can be built through quiet and purposeful dialogue, preferably with Israel, but otherwise with Washington. ... A vital core demand is involved on each side and is non-negotiable. This is the continued communal and national survival of each protagonist. An outcome that concedes this to one side but denies it to the other will not work.[19]

While these declarations were indeed historic in terms of the evolution of PLO thinking, the flow of diplomatic activity in their wake fell far short of creating any major breakthrough. Mistrustful Israelis, led by a right-wing government under Yitzhak Shamir, continued to focus on quelling the unrest of the *intifada* without being lured into any negotiations with the "new" PLO.

Despite Israeli attempts to put down the *intifada* by repressive military measures and police action, the uprising continued at decreasing levels of intensity until 1993. Its overall impact on Israeli public opinion was significant.[20] Along with the embarrassment and outrage at the harmful international media coverage depicting cruel Israeli soldiers beating protesting women and children, on a deeper level more and more Israelis—including Yitzhak Rabin and other leading figures who had initially advocated the use of maximum force to crush the rioters—began to recoil from the idea of continuing the occupation which did terrible damage to IDF morale and Israel's own democratic value system.

Indeed, for many Israelis, this first *intifada* was a wake-up call. Under the impact of seething Palestinian bitterness and daily violence, many Israelis now felt forced to make a choice: annex the territories, or leave them. If one chose the annexation option, then there were three possibilities regarding the large Palestinian Arab population living there:

1   They could continue to reside there and become full citizens of the state of Israel, with full democratic rights—at some point in the foreseeable future becoming a majority vis-à-vis the country's Jewish population and undoing the raison d'être of Zionism, a demographically "Jewish" state.

2   They could remain as residents but not be granted citizenship in the state of Israel, living as a separate second-class people with limited rights, as in South Africa's former apartheid régime—thereby abandoning any semblance of Israel being a democratic state.

3   They could be encouraged, or forced, to leave their homes and relocate in one of the neighboring Arab countries—i.e., expulsion, or as the proposal became known in Hebrew, *"transfer."*[21]

The third, drastic, option enjoyed a growing popularity among a minority of Israeli Jews during this period, seeming to promise a logical, if brutal, way around the contradictions in options #1 and #2. But the unattractiveness of any of the three alternatives led a far greater number of Israeli Jews to the realization that, sooner rather than later, Israel should contemplate abandoning many of the settlements and disengaging itself—whether by negotiation or unilaterally—from those territories.

The *intifada* helped many Israelis reach the conclusion that the Jewish settlements had been a strategic mistake from the point of view of Israel's vital interests. Against those who advocated annexation and/or transfer as a solution to the Israeli–Palestinian impasse, an increasing number of Israeli political and military figures began calling for "separation" of the two populations—a return to the idea of partition that we examined during the 1930s and 1940s. Public discussion of the idea of separation (and subsequently of "disengagement") would become widespread and more intense over the coming decade.[22]

In July 1988, wishing to extricate his kingdom from the complications of dealing with a rebellious Palestinian population that bore him no particular loyalty, King Hussein announced the severance of Jordan's legal and administrative ties with the West Bank, handing over to local committees and municipal authorities most of the administrative functions and budgets that had been Amman's responsibility since the June 1967 war. The King's motives seem to have been a combination of frustration over Palestinian ingratitude and a resignation that, in the end, only the PLO could really speak for Palestinian concerns.[23] Whatever his motives, Hussein's dramatic act clearly signaled to the Israelis that they could no longer consider the Jordanian leader as an *interlocutor valable* for discussing the future of the West Bank; neither could they continue to consider solutions built around the slogan that "Jordan is Palestine." Instead, Israel—despite the firm ideological stances of Likud prime minister Yitzhak Shamir on settlements, territories, and terrorism—would soon find itself having to engage the Palestinians via the "terrorist" PLO.

In response to Saddam Hussein's claim to Kuwait being a province of Iraq and his invasion of the pro-American sheikdom in late 1990, the US created an American-led coalition of Arab and other armed forces and set up bases in Saudi Arabia. During an air and ground war that lasted several weeks in January and February of 1991, allied forces drove Saddam's troops out of Kuwait. One of the paybacks for the Arab states' cooperation with American plans in dealing this blow to Iraq was the promise of greater US involvement in finding a satisfactory solution to the unresolved Palestine problem. With the recent collapse of the Soviet Union as protector and patron of Syria and other Arab states, the US became an especially worthy target of courtship as the world's "sole remaining superpower"—and especially the only one with any power to influence the government in Tel Aviv.

As for the PLO itself, it had encountered setbacks in its recent diplomatic dialogue aimed at winning American understanding and sympathy. During 1989 and 1990, it was unable to curb terrorism by some of its rebellious factions. During the Gulf crisis in 1990–1991, Yasir Arafat committed a serious tactical blunder by siding with Saddam—thereby losing precious pan-Arab funding for his own coffers and also undermining the standing of the Palestinian diaspora communities that had been living and working in Kuwait and other Gulf states, many of whom were expelled to Jordan and elsewhere.

Madrid and Oslo: A New Peace Process

In the months following the Iraqi defeat, US Secretary of State James Baker returned to the 1970s path taken by Henry Kissinger and, seeking to reconvene the international conference adjourned in Geneva in 1973, engaged in some strenuous shuttling among Middle Eastern capitals. Using diplomatic and economic pressure, borrowing some of the ideas floated by his immediate predecessor, and offering letters of assurances to create procedures and conditions that would satisfy each party's minimal conditions, Baker succeeded in getting each of the main parties to commit itself to attending an international conference. Additional advance efforts had to be devised for Palestinian participation, including a formula (including making the Palestinians officially part of the Jordanian delegation) for bridging Prime Minister Shamir's insistence on *not* meeting with any PLO representatives, on the one hand, and the unwillingness of any credible Palestinian to appear at the conference *unless* he or she had the blessing of PLO headquarters in Tunis, on the other.

Amid much fanfare, a historic gathering opened on 30 October 1991 in Madrid's Royal Palace, breaking decades of taboos about Arabs and Israelis never appearing in the same room or at the same negotiating table. Following the opening speeches, several of which were inflammatory and hardly conciliatory, the plenary adjourned into smaller parallel bilateral working sessions where the ice was broken and key issues of contention laid out on various tables. After several days delegates left Madrid with nothing in the way of substantial breakthroughs, except the dramatic fact of having met, along with some procedures for continuing talks elsewhere.

For more than a year thereafter, delegations continued to meet bilaterally under US State Department auspices in Washington, while a number of multilateral committees convened in different venues around the world to discuss topics of regional concern, including water resources, economic development, arms control, environmental issues, and refugees.[24] Only slight progress could be reported from the many rounds of bilateral Israeli–Syrian and Israeli–Jordanian (which quietly gave birth to separate Israeli–Palestinian) talks in Washington. Minor advances were made at the cost of much frustration, stalling, and posturing for the media back home.[25]

It took an unorthodox gambit by the senior PLO and Israeli leadership—the opening of a secret "back-channel" in Oslo, unknown even to the official delegations meeting in Washington—before a real breakthrough took place in 1993. Under Norwegian mediation, Israelis and Palestinians secretly broke another historic taboo by agreeing to recognize and negotiate with each other. Much careful word-crafting went into the texts of an exchange of brief letters between Prime Minister Yitzhak Rabin and the Chairman of the Palestine Liberation Organization, along with an agreed 17-article "Declaration of Principles on Interim Self-Government Arrangements" [DOP].[26]

The historic signing ceremony and exchange of letters took place on 13 September 1993 on the White House lawn, hosted by a beaming US president, Bill Clinton, who would remain an active third-party facilitator and guarantor of subsequent Israeli–Palestinian negotiations. The DOP was soon followed by interim Palestinian–Israeli agreements signed in Jericho and Cairo, while the toughest bones of contention—designated at the "permanent status" issues (borders, settlements, refugees, Jerusalem, security arrangements)—were reserved for a final series of negotiations scheduled to begin once the interim arrangements were in place. Along the way, the process of Israeli redeployments from West Bank and Gaza population centers, to be replaced by Palestinian administration and new security forces, was expected to create some momentum and help the parties develop a sense of mutual trust.[27]

One of the earliest positive spin-offs of the signing of the Palestinian–Israeli DOP was the green light it gave to Israel and several Arab states to openly devote themselves to drafting and concluding treaties of peace to end the state of war between them. An Israeli–Syrian peace process opened and led to several rounds of negotiation, with heavy US involvement, but each collapsed amid disappointment and recrimination, without successful consummation to date (2009).[28] By contrast, reflecting a much more positive background of previous secret negotiating experience, a Jordanian–Israeli peace treaty was drafted and duly signed, also in the presence of the US President, along the Israeli–Jordanian border on 26 October 1994.[29]

The early 1990s—captured in the tale of two European cities, Madrid and Oslo—was a period of hope and optimism after decades of stalemate, resentment, fears, and frequent explosions of violence. While the post-1978 Camp David peace process had failed in its day to widen the "circle of peace," the changed global and regional circumstances, and perhaps a certain level of conflict fatigue among the parties, augured well for progress under the new peace process begun at Madrid and Oslo. The very fact that talks had begun reduced Israel's sense of isolation and vulnerability, with a noticeably beneficial spin-off effect on Israeli attitudes. Labor Party leader Yitzhak Rabin defeated his right-wing Likud rivals in June 1992, elected on a platform promising a breakthrough on the stalled negotiations. Reviewing his first year in office, the prime minister expressed his optimism and a determination to overcome all obstacles:

The train that travels towards peace has stopped this year at many stations that daily refute the time-worn canard—"the whole world is against us." The United States has improved its relations with us.... In Europe, our dialogue with the E[uropean] C[ommunity] has been improved and deepened. We have been inundated by visiting heads of state—and we have responded to them with friendship and with economic and other links. We are no longer "a People that dwelleth alone."[30]

Indeed, in December 1991 "a completely different constellation of forces at the United Nations" voted to revoke the 1975 "zionism equals racism" resolution, and within two years of Madrid 34 countries established (or re-established severed) diplomatic relations with the Jewish state.[31] Reflecting the new spirit of international acceptance, Rabin's appeals to his countrymen began to incorporate some of the rhetoric previously confined to peace activists and liberal spokesmen who had been arguing that Israelis should stop thinking like outnumbered and beleaguered ghetto fighters, but should rather visualize themselves as strong and secure enough to take some calculated risks for peace.[32] One manifestation of this new positive atmosphere was that visiting foreign dignitaries were no longer obliged, as before, to stop at the country's Holocaust memorial, Yad Vashem, although most continued to make the recommended pilgrimage.

There was also cause for optimism on the Palestinian side. The transition from the Madrid Conference format to the Washington talks and the Oslo back-channel meant that, for the first time, the Palestinian issue was not being ignored, sidetracked, or handled by others. Diplomatic players were now working with—rather than trying to work around—the Palestinians and their recognized leaders in the PLO. And now that the Cold War was over, the absence of superpower rivalry meant that local conflicts might be managed or settled better without being manipulated or magnified to serve the needs of external powers.

As mentioned, Israelis and Palestinians began to see the future in terms of partitioning the area of former Mandatory Palestine between themselves. But much had changed on the ground since partition plans were first floated in the 1930s and 1940s. After decades of blood and destruction, now all the area to be divided was not in neutral but Israeli hands. Indeed, areas claimed by the Palestinians were still being populated by Jewish settlers. The populations of the rival communities were now approximately equal in number, but the two societies were hardly of equal strength or vibrancy—the Palestinians having been dispersed and exiled for almost half a century, while the population of Israel had grown, consolidated, and evolved into a dynamic and highly developed society, a success story by many yardsticks. It would be no easy task for the

Oslo peace process to produce, following its many scheduled steps of implementation, the two-state solution wished for by many, including peace advocates, on all sides.[33] But, despite the radically changed circumstances, the partition concept seemed worth trying and better than any of the alternatives.

Unfortunately, after a few years of attempting to implement the commitments outlined in the DOP, it became painfully obvious that the new Israeli–Palestinian peace process was in trouble. Many deadlines were missed, talks frequently broke down, and cooperation lapsed; mutual trust eroded and was replaced by deeper suspicions. Too-frequent appeals to the US for intervention weakened the entire process. Jewish settlements continued to be built and expanded in the territories that were supposedly subject to final negotiation. The size and shape of the "cake" was, in the words of one Palestinian observer, "quickly shrinking while the two sides negotiated its fate," leading the "overwhelming majority of Palestinians" to lose "all confidence in the peaceful intentions of Israel."[34]

Terrorism returned with a vengeance, in more deadly forms and more often in Israeli population centers. "Anti-Oslo militants on both sides discovered a dirty little secret: they had virtual veto power over the negotiations, because every outrageous act that they perpetrated brought yet another interruption, another setback to the peace process."[35] Among the Palestinians, the Islamist factions of Hamas and Islamic Jihad gained popularity as they accused the official leadership of the Palestine Authority [PA] of serving as "Israel's policeman" in the territories, having shamefully sold out their legitimate rights to the powerful Israelis and their American backers. Charges of corruption, nepotism, and anti-democratic suppression of dissent plagued the new PA administration, undermining its credibility internationally and public confidence domestically.[36]

Neither Arafat nor the multiple security forces created since 1994 seemed able, or willing, to take aggressive action to effectively rein in extremists still bent on terrorizing, killing, and injuring Israelis. Critics of the "strategic incoherence" between PLO policy and action pointed to the leadership's "equivocation about a two-state solution and an end to armed violence long after that course had supposedly been conclusively decided upon," and its inability "to understand the limits of violence."[37] Arafat's failure to control the violence contributed to growing Israeli doubts as to the sincerity of their designated peace partner under Oslo. Israeli opponents of the peace process used the upsurge in Palestinian terror to agitate against further troop redeployments or concessions to the Palestinians.

In November 1995 a Jewish religious fanatic assassinated Prime Minister Yitzhak Rabin to punish him for having ostensibly turned over Jews to their enemies and to prevent him from continuing negotiations with the PA.[38] This high-profile murder sent the nation into shock, and leaders reverted from optimistically and self-confidently engaging the world at large to once again drawing on negative lessons of the Holocaust in their public utterances. Opposition leader Benyamin Netanyahu reflected and played to public fears when referring to Israel's 1949 frontiers as "Auschwitz borders," while Shimon Peres, in his prime ministerial address on the annual *Yom ha-Shoah* (Holocaust Remembrance Day) commemoration, reminded his listeners that the establishment of the state of Israel was "the Jewish people's victory over Nazi Germany."[39]

More broadly, the assassination of Yitzhak Rabin was emblematic of the collapse of peace hopes that were being undermined and undone on a daily basis by numerous negative encounters and experiences associated with the Oslo process.[40] In retrospect, the late 1990s were like a time bomb waiting to explode. The deadline for moving from transitional arrangements to serious negotiations on the permanent status issues was approaching with many unfulfilled or partially completed steps, and much accumulated mistrust and dissatisfaction among the negotiators. Rapid turnover among Israeli prime ministers—Yitzhak Rabin (d. 1995), Shimon Peres (1995–1996), Benjamin Netanyahu (1996–1999), Ehud Barak (1999–2001)—contributed to delays, backtracking, and unfulfilled promises of redeployment of troops and handover of territory, increasing Palestinian frustration and suspicions of Israeli intentions. In October 1996, the Clinton administration invested much energy and resources in convening Israelis and Palestinians to top-level negotiations at the Wye Plantation in Maryland for the purpose of getting them to recommit themselves, with slight modifications, to fulfill their lapsed Oslo obligations.[41]

Camp David Revisited; *Intifada* Redux

The faltering of the Madrid and Oslo peace process led to some last-ditch attempts to revive efforts at reconciling the needs and interests of both Palestinians and Israelis. Ehud Barak won the June 1999 elections on a pledge to bring back Israeli troops from southern Lebanon and to fulfill Rabin's legacy by delivering the unconsummated peace deal with Syria, as well as negotiating the remaining permanent status issues with the Palestinians. After failing with the Syrians, Barak convinced the US president that the situation was so crucial that a high-level, make-or-break

Israeli–Palestinian summit was worth the risk of failure. The July 2000 meetings at Camp David, like the original 1978 version, were full of dramatic tension, went on for fifteen days, but did not replicate the historic success achieved by Sadat, Begin, and Carter.

Instead, Barak and Arafat returned home empty-handed, and a mood of nervous disillusionment set in. A new set of contested narratives was soon created attempting to explain what went wrong at Camp David and who was to blame for the failure. According to one version, Ehud Barak made Yasser Arafat an unprecedented generous offer for ending the conflict, which Arafat rejected without counterproposals, proving he was not a serious partner for peace. According to the second account, Barak, backed by American power, attempted unsuccessfully to dictate an unattractive and non-negotiable deal to Arafat.[42]

Despite the collapse of the July 2000 summit, Barak and Arafat allowed their appointed negotiators to continue talks in attempts to bridge gaps. In late December, just before leaving office, Bill Clinton made an eleventh-hour attempt to force the parties towards an agreement by outlining a set of "Parameters" based on his own personal understanding of where they stood apart and where they might find common ground.[43] Teams of Palestinian and Israeli negotiators reconvened several weeks later in the Egyptian resort town of Taba to discuss and fine-tune Clinton's latest suggestions.

By most accounts, gaps were further narrowed at Taba, but still without any clear-cut agreement ready for initialing or signing. On two important basic issues—Palestinian refugees and their "right of return," and sovereignty over Jerusalem—agreement seemed unachievable in the climate of frustration and mistrust that had developed.[44] The thorny refugee issue (including the claims of Jewish refugees from Arab lands[45]) touches at the heart of Palestinian and Israeli identity and survival.[46] The sensitivity of Israeli and Palestinian opinion on the Jerusalem issue—both as the site of holy places and as a national capital—caught many negotiators at Camp David by surprise and (re-)established itself as one of the most difficult issues to resolve, despite a plethora of creative proposals for sharing or dividing the Holy City.[47]

In the aftermath of the high-stakes disappointments at Camp David and Taba, leaders on both sides retreated into self-serving justification of their recent activity, heaping doubt upon the good faith and intentions of their erstwhile peace partners. By the turn of 2000–2001, all hopes and activity about reviving the diplomatic process were overtaken and overshadowed by an outburst of Palestinian violence, the second *intifada*. In September 2000, opposition Likud leader Ariel Sharon undertook a provocative visit to the Temple Mount to demonstrate Jewish rights to pray there. The site, as we know from the events of 1928–1929, is also holy to Muslims as *al-Haram al-Sharif* (the Noble Sanctuary), the plaza on which stand the golden-domed Mosque of Omar and the nearby (less-photographed, but holier) al-Aqsa Mosque. Angered by the visit, on the following day a crowd of rock-throwing Palestinian protesters was shot at, tear-gassed, and dispersed violently by Israeli police, who killed four and wounded 160 of the demonstrators. Some accounts suggest that Palestinian militants had already been preparing for such an uprising, and that Sharon's visit was an opportune spark rather than the cause of the outbreak.

The second *intifada* was marked by widespread rioting, attacks, and counterattacks of a much bloodier nature than the first *intifada*, which was characterized primarily by stone-throwing, Molotov cocktails, and rubber bullets. In 2000 and after, Israeli troops and police used lethal force, even against peaceful solidarity protests organized by Israel's own Palestinian-Arab citizens. As was the case in the late 1920s, Muslim fears of Jewish encroachment on their holy places added to the intensity of the confrontations during what became known as the al-Aqsa *intifada*.[48]

Israel–PA efforts at rapprochement and negotiation languished as the toll of dead and wounded mounted, victims of daily stabbings, shootings, bombings, and harsh military repression. By September 2004 some 3000 Palestinians and 1000 Israelis had lost their lives, and thousands more were wounded. Palestinians fielded a steady flow of suicide bombers, mainly youngsters willing to detonate themselves against Israeli civilians on buses and in shopping areas, while Israel used home demolitions, its control of the roads at checkpoints, and its superior military forces and equipment in actions against terrorists that harassed, humiliated, and severely disrupted the day-to-day lives of innocent Palestinians.[49]

Two controversial Israeli responses to the Palestinian violence were targeted assassinations to hunt down militants and terrorists, and the construction of a security barrier (in many places fences, in others high concrete walls) to separate the Jewish and Palestinian populations. Israel defended its fence/wall as a legitimate form of self-protection against the suicide bombers, and pointed to the resultant drop in terrorist infiltrations in areas where the barrier was in place. Palestinians protested against the great inconveniences and disruptions caused by the wall which criss-crossed villages, towns, and access roads. Advocacy groups helped to submit legal complaints regarding many places where the wall allegedly encroached on Palestinian-owned land, or where the wall stretched beyond Israeli territory as defined by the 1949 armistice boundaries (the "Green Line"). Some commentators saw the path of the security barrier as a preview of the *de facto* final borders between Jewish Israel and Arab

Palestine, as a preparation for Israel's eventual disengagement from the territories. Many believed that, in the existing climate of hostility, such a separation of populations would be carried out unilaterally to suit Israel's own interests and needs.

Partly due to its high degree of militarization, the al-Aqsa *intifada* proved to be a costly and politically unproductive rebellion.[50] The escalation of Palestinian violence against Israeli targets helped bring a hardline prime minister, Ariel Sharon, to power. The soldier-politician—already well known for his exploits at Qibya in 1953, across the Suez in October 1973, and in Lebanon in 1982—responded by destroying a large part of the PA's security apparatus, administrative offices, and economic infrastructure, and by besieging a humiliated and flabbergasted President Arafat in the ruins of his personal compound in Ramallah. Palestinian suicide bombings against Israeli civilians also resulted in a loss of international support for the Palestinian struggle for statehood, especially after 11 September 2001.

After initially trying to distance himself from his predecessor Bill Clinton's hands-on dedication to pursuing a Palestinian–Israeli breakthrough, President George W. Bush found it impossible to remain disengaged from the deadlocked and still bickering Israelis and Palestinians. American diplomats and CIA officials returned to the Middle East to become embroiled in efforts to arrange ceasefires during the *intifada*, with hopes of thereafter paving the way to renewed political negotiations.[51] US policy statements became more unequivocal about supporting a two-state solution, but stopped short of backing Yasir Arafat and the PA, which the Americans suspected on being soft on "terrorism" and engaging in secret dealings with Iran, Syria, and other enemies of the US and its Western allies.

On the international level, the US endorsed UN Security Council Resolution 1397 (12 March 2002)[52] in support of a two-state solution, and collaborated with Russia, the European Union, and the United Nations to create the "Quartet" under whose auspices a "Performance-Based Roadmap to a Permanent Two-State Solution to the Israeli–Palestinian Conflict" was produced in April 2003.[53] Although all its deadlines have long since expired, this Roadmap stands as one of three possible bases upon which to resume the search for peace, once the contesting parties can be brought together.

A second possible basis for a producing a breakthrough of the latest phase of the Israel–Palestine deadlock comes from the conflict's regional players. A peace initiative promoted by Saudi Arabia received the backing of the Arab League during its Beirut meeting in late March 2002. The Saudi initiative went further than previous Arab plans in offering Israel full diplomatic recognition in exchange for full Israeli withdrawal from the territories captured in June 1967; apparent Arab flexibility in not insisting on an absolute "right of return" for Palestinian refugees should have added to the attractiveness of the plan for most Israelis.[54] Yet, owing partly to the intensification of Palestinian *intifada* during 2002, Israel's initial response to the Arab League initiative was cool. The Saudi initiative remained on the back burner for several years, waiting for new promoters (like US president Barack Obama) and new opportunities to be reconsidered as a basis for breaking the Israeli–Palestinian stalemate.

At the close of 2003 a third blueprint for peace emerged from a group of Palestinian and Israeli ex-negotiators working in their own personal capacity, without government authority. The Geneva Accord of October 2003 was a remarkable document synthesizing, with detailed provisions, the various partial agreements reached during the official negotiations that ended at Taba in January 2001. As a grass-roots effort, it attempted to gain public support among both the Palestinian and Israeli publics by bypassing the recognized leaderships of both camps, who were reluctant to take any political risks for peace.[55] At the time of writing (2009), the Geneva Initiative stands ready as a third set of proposals, waiting for the next group of Palestinian or Israeli leaders who feel the time is right to re-engage in the diplomatic process (see below, Chapter 12).

Perhaps the most significant of the events that have taken place since 2003 have been Israel's unilateral disengagement from Gaza in 2005 and the rise to power of Hamas in the Palestinian elections of 2006. The former is important as a possible precedent for future Israeli moves out of the West Bank. The latter dealt a severe blow to the declining old-school politics and leadership of Fatah and the PLO. The victory of this Islamist party, fervently dedicated to armed struggle and non-recognition of the Jewish state, created new uncertainties both for the negotiating process and for the future of Palestine as an embryo of a state under a unified national leadership. The challenges raised by these two events will be the subjects of analyses by historians looking back on the current decade.

Many unanswered current-events questions linger. Underneath such questions the basic dispute between Israelis and Palestinians—and many of its intertwined core arguments—remain unresolved, mired in an uneasy stalemate. True, the parties have come a long way from their pre-Oslo mutual boycott towards mutual recognition, however incomplete or hesitant on the Palestinian side. But the key issues separating them and the lack of trust in each other's intentions still present formidable obstacles to mutual understanding and a negotiated peace.

Notes

1   For a firsthand account of an Israeli diplomat posted to Cairo during the difficult early years, see Ephraim Dowek, *Israeli–Egyptian Relations, 1980–2000*, foreword by Yitshak Shamir, London: Frank Cass, 2001.

2   On Reagan's initiative, see Ronald J. Young, *Missed Opportunities for Peace: U.S. Middle East Policy, 1981–1986*, Philadelphia, PA: American Friends Service Committee, 1987, chs. 6–7; Laura Zittrain Eisenberg and Neil Caplan, *Negotiating Arab–Israeli Peace: Patterns, Problems, Possibilities*, Bloomington / Indianapolis: Indiana University Press, 1998, 48–51. The text of the Reagan plan (1 September 1982) and talking points for Menachem Begin (8 September) are reproduced in ibid., 184–91; the plan is also reproduced in *The Israel–Arab Reader: A Documentary History of the Middle East Conflict*, 7th rev. ed., eds. Walter Laqueur and Barry Rubin, New York: Penguin, 2008, 257–63.

3   Brezhnev Peace Plan, 15 September 1982, excerpts in *The Israeli–Palestinian Conflict: A Documentary Record, 1967–1990*, ed. Yehuda Lukacs, Cambridge: Cambridge University Press, 1992, 20–1. More elaborate follow-up plans were announced in July 1984 (ibid., 21–4).

4   Final Statement, Twelfth Arab Summit Conference, Fez, Morocco, 9 September 1982, extracts in Laqueur and Rubin, *Israel–Arab Reader*, 263–5.

5   Yezid Sayigh, *Armed Struggle and the Search for State: The Palestinian National Movement, 1949–1993*, Oxford: Oxford University Press / Washington, DC: The Institute for Palestine Studies, 1997, 585–6; Rashid Khalidi, *The Iron Cage: The Story of the Palestinian Struggle for Statehood*, Boston, MA: Beacon, 2006, 146.

6   Cheryl A. Rubenberg, "The Bush Administration and the Palestinians: A Reassessment," in *US Policy on Palestine from Wilson to Clinton*, ed. Michael W. Suleiman, Normal, IL: AAUG Press, 1995, 195–221; Samuel Segev, "The Arab–Israeli Conflict under President Bush," in *From Cold War to New World Order: The Foreign Policy of George H. W. Bush*, eds. Meena Bose and Rosanna Perotti, Westport, CT: Greenwood, and Hofstra University, 2002, 113–36; Kathleen Christison, "The Arab–Israeli Policy of George Shultz," *Journal of Palestine Studies* 18:2 (Winter 1989), 29–47.

7   For details of Shultz's involvement in the Peres–Hussein document (below) and his own plans, see Shultz Plan, 6 March 1988, reproduced in Laqueur and Rubin, *Israel–Arab Reader*, 321–2; Eisenberg and Caplan, *Negotiating*, 2nd ed, ch. 3.

8   See, e.g., the innovative dialogue work by Herb Kelman at Harvard University: Herbert C. Kelman, "Creating the Conditions for Israeli–Palestinian Negoti-ations," *The Journal of Conflict Resolution* 26:1 (March 1982), 39–75; Herbert C. Kelman, "Overcoming the Barriers to Negotiation of the Israeli–Palestinian Conflict," *Journal of Palestine Studies* 16:1 (Autumn 1986), 13–28; Hussein Agha, Shai Feldman, Ahmad Khalidi, and Zeev Schiff, *Track-II Diplomacy: Lessons from the Middle East*, Cambridge, MA: MIT Press, 2003, 25–7; Kelman interview on the website Beyond Intractability: A Free Knowledge Base for

Constructive Approaches to Destructive Conflict, accessed 1 September 2008 at http://www.beyondintractability.org/audio/10637/.

9   See, e.g., Uri Avnery, *My Friend, the Enemy*, Westport, CT: Lawrence Hill, 1986; Mohamed Rabie, *US–PLO Dialogue: Secret Diplomacy and Conflict Resolution*, Gainesville: University Press of Florida, 1995, chs. 3, 8, 12; Bassam Abu-Sharif, "Prospects of a Palestinian–Israeli Settlement," Algiers, 7 June 1988, reproduced [dated 18 June] in Lukacs, *Israeli–Palestinian Conflict*, 397–9; the Abu-Sharif document is also reproduced, along with "Response by Prominent American Jews to the Abu Sharif document," 30 June 1988, in *JPS* 18:1 (Autumn 1988), 272–5, 302–3; Bassam Abu-Sharif and Uzi Muhnaimi, *Best of Enemies: The Memoirs of Bassam Abu-Sharif and Uzi Mahnaimi*, Boston, MA: Little, Brown, 1995, 257–62; Mahmoud Abbas [Abu Mazen], *Through Secret Channels: The Road to Oslo: Senior PLO Leader Abu Mazen's Revealing Story of the Negotiations with Israel*, Concord, MA: Paul [Reading: Garnet], 1995, 4–8, 13–8; Mohamed Heikal, *Secret Channels: The Inside Story of Arab–Israeli Peace Negotiations*, London: HarperCollins, 1996, 343–51; Yossi Beilin, *Touching Peace: From the Oslo Accord to a Final Agreement*, transl. from the Hebrew by Philip Simpson, London: Weidenfeld and Nicolson, 1999, 7–46; Agha et al., *Track-II Diplomacy*, 20–7; Walid Salem and Edy Kaufman, "Palestinian–Israeli Peacebuilding: A Historical Perspective," in *Bridging the Divide: Peacebuilding in the Israeli–Palestinian Conflict*, eds. Edy Kaufman, Walid Salem, and Juliette Verhoeven, foreword by N. Chazan and H. Siniora, Boulder, CO: Lynne Rienner, 2006, 26–31.

10   Jordanian–Palestinian Plan of Action (11 February 1985), reaffirmed by the PLO's Executive Committee, 19 February 1985, statement in Lukacs, *Israeli–Palestinian Conflict*, 368–9; Adnan Abu-Odeh, *Jordanians, Palestinians and the Hashemite Kingdom in the Middle East Peace Process*, Washington, DC: United States Institute of Peace Press, 1999, 221–2; Ilan Pappé, "Jordan between Hashemite and Palestinian Identity," in *Jordan in the Middle East: The Making of a Pivotal State*, eds. Joseph Nevo and Ilan Pappé, London: Frank Cass, 1994, 78–85; Avi Shlaim, *Lion of Jordan: King Hussein's Life in War and Peace*, London: Penguin, 2007, ch. 20; Khalidi, *Iron Cage*, 148.

11   See Eisenberg and Caplan, *Negotiating*, 60–74, 195; Shlaim, *Lion of Jordan*, ch. 21.

12   Alan Dowty, *The Jewish State: A Century Later*, Berkeley, etc.: University of California Press, 1998, 220–1.

13   On the background of the Hamas movement and its emergence in Palestinian society and politics, see, e.g., Ziad Abu-Amr, "Hamas: A Historical and Political Background," *Journal of Palestine Studies* 22:4 (Summer 1993), 5–19; Shaul Mishal and Avraham Sela, *The Palestinian Hamas: Vision, Violence and Coexistence*, New York: Columbia University Press, 2000; Khaled Hroub, *Hamas: Political Thought and Practice*, Washington, DC: Institute for Palestine Studies, 2000; Jeroen Gunning, *Hamas in Politics: Democracy, Religion and Violence*, New York: Columbia University Press, 2008. For the text of its

Charter, see Mishal and Sela, *Palestinian Hamas*, 175–99 (extracts in Laqueur and Rubin, *Israel–Arab Reader*, 341–8), or the Yale University Avalon Documentation Project website, http://www.yale.edu/lawweb/avalon/mideast/ hamas.htm.

14 Mark Tessler, "Intifada, 1987–1993," *Encyclopedia of the Palestinians*, rev. ed., ed. Philip Mattar, New York: Facts on File, 2005, 226.

15 On the *intifada*, see also Ze'ev Schiff and Ehud Ya'ari, *Intifada: The Palestinian Uprising—Israel's Third Front*, New York: Simon and Schuster, 1990; *Intifada: The Palestinian Uprising against Israeli Occupation*, eds. Zachary Lockman and Joel Beinin, Boston, MA: South End Press, 1989; Kenneth W. Stein, "The Intifada and the 1936–39 Uprising: A Comparison," *Journal of Palestine Studies* 19:4 (Summer 1990), 64–85.

16 Palestinian Declaration of Independence, Algiers, 15 November 1988, text in Laqueur and Rubin, *Israel–Arab Reader*, 354–8; *The Palestinian–Israeli Peace Agreement: A Documentary Record*, rev. 2nd ed., Washington, DC: Institute for Palestine Studies, 1994 [hereafter *PIPA*], 268–72; Lukacs, *Israeli–Palestinian Conflict*, 411–5; Palestine National Council, Political Communiqué, Algiers, 15 November 1988, in Laqueur and Rubin, *Israel–Arab Reader*, 349–53; *PIPA*, 273–82; Lukacs, *Israeli–Palestinian Conflict*, 415–20.

17 Arafat speech, UNGA, Geneva, 13 December 1988, text in *PIPA*, 283–97; Lukacs, *Israeli–Palestinian Conflict*, 420–34; Arafat, Press Conference Statement, Geneva, 14 December 1988, text in *PIPA*, 298–9; Ronald Reagan, Statement Authorizing US–PLO Dialogue, Washington, DC, 14 December 1988, text in *PIPA*, 300. See also http://www.mideastweb.org/arafat1988. htm and http://www.mfa.gov.il/MFA/Foreign%20Relations/Israels%20Foreign%20Relations%20since%201947/1984-1988/419%20Statement% 20by%20Yasser%20Arafat-%2014%20December%201988. For background on this episode, see Mohamed Rabie, *US–PLO Dialogue: Secret Diplomacy and Conflict Resolution*, foreword by Harold H. Saunders, Gainesville: University Press of Florida, 1995, esp. ch. 9; Gidon D. Remba, interview with Stanley Scheinbaum, discussed in "Self-Appointed, Arrogant American Jewish Interlopers Offer Illusions of Peace," 17 August 2007, available at http:// www.ameinu.net/perspectives/current_issues.php?articleid=252, accessed 29 August 2007.

18 See, e.g., Benjamin Netanyahu, *A Durable Peace: Israel and Its Place among the Nations*, rev. ed., New York: Warner Books, 2000, 228–42.

19 Walid Khalidi, "The United States and the Palestinian People" (Georgetown University, March 1989), reproduced in Walid Khalidi, *Palestine Reborn*, London / New York: I. B. Tauris, 1992, 157–8. For similar assessments, see Muhammad Muslih, "Towards Coexistence: An Analysis of the Resolutions of the Palestine National Council," *Journal of Palestine Studies* 19:4 (Summer 1990), 3–29; reprinted in *From War to Peace: Arab–Israeli Relations 1973– 1993*, eds. Barry Rubin, Joseph Ginat, and Moshe Ma'oz, New York: New York University Press, 1995, 265–91; Rashid Khalidi, *Iron Cage*, 189–95.

20 Alan Dowty, *Israel/Palestine*, 2nd ed., Malden, MA / Cambridge, UK: Polity Press, 2008, 134–6.

21 The English word was imported into the Hebrew and pronounced *trans-fehr'*. On the concept see Chapter 6 and sources cited in note 48. See also Benny Morris, "A New Exodus for the Middle East?" *The Guardian*, 2 October 2002.

22 E.g., Dowty, *The Jewish State*, 232–48; Bernard Wasserstein, *Israelis and Palestinians: Why Do They Fight? Can They Stop?* 3rd ed., New Haven, CT / London: Yale University Press / London: Profile Books, 2008, 130–40.

23 King Hussein's Speech, 31 July 1988, available at http://www.kinghussein. gov.jo/88_july31.html; reproduced in Harold H. Saunders, *The Other Walls: The Arab–Israeli Peace Process in a Global Perspective*, rev. ed., Princeton, NJ: Princeton University Press, 1991, 197–203 and in William B. Quandt, ed., *The Middle East: Ten Years after Camp David*, Washington, DC: The Brookings Institution, 1988, 494–8; extract in Laqueur and Rubin, *Israel–Arab Reader*, 338–41. Cf. Asher Susser, "Jordan, the PLO and the Palestine Question," in *Jordan in the Middle East: The Making of a Pivotal State*, eds. Joseph Nevo and Ilan Pappé, London: Frank Cass, 1994, 218–21; Abu-Odeh, *Jordanians, Palestinians*, 224–9; Marwan Muasher, *The Arab Center: The Promise of Moderation*, New Haven, CT: Yale University Press, 2008, 23.

24 On the Madrid Conference, see Eisenberg and Caplan, *Negotiating*, 75–89, 196–204.

25 For some documentary exchanges between Israeli and Palestinian delegations and memoranda submitted to the Americans during these talks (January 1992–August 1993), see *The Palestinian–Israeli Peace Agreement: A Documentary Record*, rev. 2nd ed., Washington, DC: Institute for Palestine Studies, 1994, 39–109. For a firsthand account by members of the Jordanian delegation, see Abdul Salam Majali, Jawad A. Anani, and Munther J. Haddadin, *Peacemaking: The Inside Story of the 1994 Jordanian–Israeli Treaty*, foreword by HRH Prince El Hassan Bin Talal of Jordan, preface by David L. Boren, Norman: University of Oklahoma Press, 2006, 23–232.

26 On the Oslo negotiations and the DOP, see Eisenberg and Caplan, *Negotiating*, 103–26, 210–16. For firsthand accounts of some of the participants, see Shimon Peres, *Battling for Peace: A Memoir*, New York: Random House, 1995; Mahmoud Abbas [Abu Mazen], *Through Secret Channels: The Road to Oslo: Senior PLO Leader Abu Mazen's Revealing Story of the Negotiations with Israel*, Concord, MA: Paul / Reading, UK: Garnet, 1995; Yossi Beilin, *Touching Peace: From the Oslo Accord to a Final Agreement*, transl. Philip Simpson, London: Weidenfeld and Nicolson, 1999; Jane Corbin, *Gaza First: The Secret Norway Channel to Peace between Israel and the PLO*, London: Bloomsbury, 1994; Uri Savir, *The Process: 1,100 Days that Changed the Middle East*, New York: Random House, 1998; Dennis Ross, *The Missing Peace: The Inside Story of the Fight for Middle East Peace*, New York: Farrar, Straus, and Giroux, 2004; Ahmed Qurie (Abu Ala), *From Oslo to Jerusalem: The Palestinian Story of the Secret Negotiations*, London: I. B. Tauris, 2006.

27 On the Oslo negotiations and the DOP, see Eisenberg and Caplan, *Negotiating*, 103–26, 210–16.

28 On the Syrian–Israeli negotiations, see Jeremy Pressman, "Mediation, Domestic Politics, and the Israeli–Syrian Negotiations, 1991–2000," *Security Studies* 16:3 (July–September 2007), 350–81; Eisenberg and Caplan, *Negotiating*, 2nd ed., ch. 6.

29 On the Jordanian–Israeli negotiations and treaty, see Eisenberg and Caplan, *Negotiating*, 90–102, 217–28.

30 Rabin address to the Knesset, 27 June 1993. Almost identical phrasing appears in Rabin's inaugural speech of 13 July 1992, reproduced in Laqueur and Rubin, *Israel–Arab Reader*, 403–4.

31 Aharon Klieman, "New Directions in Israel's Foreign Policy," *Israel Affairs* 1:1 (Autumn 1994), 98–9. The number of states with whom Israel had diplomatic relations jumped from 110 in 1992 to 163 in 1998. Israel Ministry of Foreign Affairs website, accessed 5 September 2008 at http://www.mfa.gov.il/MFAHeb/General + info/About + us/foreign_relation.htm.

32 E.g., Abba Eban, "Why Hysteria on a Mideast Parley?" *New York Times*, 3 April 1988. On the evolution of Rabin's thinking, see Hemda Ben-Yehuda, "Policy Transformation in the Middle East: Arms Control Regimes and National Security Reconciled," in *Review Essays in Israel Studies: Books on Israel*, vol. V, eds. Laura Zittrain Eisenberg and Neil Caplan, Albany: State University of New York Press, 2000, 178–87.

33 On the socioeconomic differences and interdependencies between the Israel and Palestine, see Wasserstein, *Israelis and Palestinians*, 57–68. On the evolution of the two-state solution during the preceding decade, see, e.g., Mark A. Heller, *A Palestinian State: The Implications for Israel*, Cambridge, MA: Harvard University Press, 1983; Mark A. Heller and Sari Nusseibeh, *No Trumpets, No Drums: A Two-State Settlement of the Israeli–Palestinian Conflict*, New York: Hill and Wang, 1991.

34 Khalil Shikaki, "Ending the Conflict: Can the Parties Afford It?" in *The Israeli–Palestinian Peace Process: Oslo and the Lessons of Failure: Perspectives, Predicaments and Prospects*, eds. Robert L. Rothstein, Moshe Ma'oz, and Khalil Shikaki, Brighton, UK / Portland, OR: Sussex Academic Press, 2002, 40. See also ibid., 41; Khalidi, *Iron Cage*, 196. Khalidi also stresses that the strategic placement of Jewish settlements and road networks prejudiced the possible *shape* and *viability* of any future Palestinian state wanting to include contiguous areas of Palestinian population.

35 Baruch Kimmerling and Joel S. Migdal, *The Palestinian People: A History*, Cambridge, MA: Harvard University Press, 2003, 378.

36 In 1999 a group of insider intellectuals published what became known as the "Petition of the Twenty," accusing the PA of corruption and the neglect of basic human rights. The PA promptly arrested several of the signatories and intimidated others. See comments by Dr. Adel Samara, accessed online 18 July 2008 at the website of the British International Socialist Group, http://www.isg-fi.org.uk/spip.php?article179 and http://www.isg-fi.org.uk/

spip.php?article178. I am grateful to Ahmad Hamad for this information. Generally, see Khalidi, *Iron Cage*, 151–2.

37 Khalidi, *Iron Cage*, 146, 178.

38 See, e.g., Yoram Peri, ed., *The Assassination of Yitzhak Rabin*, Stanford, CA: Stanford University Press, 2000.

39 Ali Abunimah, "Israel's 'Auschwitz Borders' Revisited," *Desertpeace*, 8 December 2008, accessed online 14 February 2009 at http://desertpeace.word-press.com/2008/12/08/israels-auschwitz-borders-revisited/; remarks by Prime Minister Shimon Peres at Holocaust Martyrs' and Heroes' Remembrance Day Opening Ceremony, Yad Vashem, Jerusalem, 15 April 1996.

40 For critical overview treatments of the ups and downs of the Oslo years, see Ron Pundak, "From Oslo to Taba: What Went Wrong?" in *The Israeli–Palestinian Peace Process*, eds. Rothstein, Ma'oz, and Shikaki,, 88–101; Kimmerling and Migdal, *The Palestinian People*, chs. 10–11; Yoram Meital, *Peace in Tatters: Israel, Palestine, and the Middle East*, Boulder, CO: Lynne Rienner, 2006, ch. 3; Galia Golan, *Israel and Palestine: Peace Plans and Proposals from Oslo to Disengagement*, Princeton, NJ: Markus Wiener, 2007, ch. 2.

41 For a summary of the text of the Wye Agreement, see the Israel Ministry of Foreign Affairs website: http://www.mfa.gov.il/MFA/Peace%20Process/Guide%20to%20the%20Peace%20Process/The%20Wye%20River%20Memorandum, accessed 2 September 2008. For a firsthand account, see Dennis Ross, *The Missing Peace: The Inside Story of the Fight for Middle East Peace*, New York: Farrar, Straus, and Giroux, 2004, chs. 16–17; for a discussion, see Golan, *Israel and Palestine*, 29–33.

42 Jeremy Pressman subjects both of these duelling narratives to critical scrutiny in his "Visions in Collision: What Happened at Camp David and Taba?" *International Security* 28:2 (Fall 2003), 5–43. Rabinovich distinguishes among four narratives, the first two of which (the "orthodox" and the "revisionist") correspond roughly with the two presented here: Itamar Rabinovich, *Waging Peace: Israel and the Arabs, 1948–2003*, rev. and updated ed., Princeton, NJ: Princeton University Press, 2004, 160–76. For discussions of the Camp David summit, see Akram Hanieh, *The Camp David Papers*, Ramallah: Al-Ayyam Newspaper, 2000; an abbreviated version appears in the *Journal of Palestine Studies* 30:2 (Winter 2001), 75–97; Clayton E. Swisher, *The Truth about Camp David: The Untold Story about the Collapse of the Middle East Peace Process*, New York: Nation Books, 2004; Ross, *The Missing Peace*, chs. 24–5; *The Camp David Summit—What Went Wrong? Americans, Israelis, and Palestinians Analyze the Failure of the Boldest Attempt Ever to Resolve the Palestinian–Israeli Conflict*, eds. Shimon Shamir and Bruce Maddy-Weitzman, Brighton, UK / Portland, OR: Sussex Academic Press, 2005; Meital, *Peace in Tatters*, ch. 5; David Matz, "Reconstructing Camp David," *Negotiation Journal* 22:1 (January 2006), 89–103; Golan, *Israel and Palestine*, chs. 3–4; Eisenberg and Caplan, *Negotiating*, 2nd ed., ch. 9.

43 The text of Clinton's "Parameters" of 23 December 2000 is reproduced in Ross, *The Missing Peace*, 801–5; also available online at http://domino.un.

org/unispal.NSF/1ce874ab1832a53e852570bb006dfaf6/d57afcdd6e-b1445585256e37006655e4, accessed 2 September 2008.

44 On the Taba negotiations, see the Moratinos Document, as given in Akiva Eldar, "The Peace that Nearly Was at Taba," *Ha-Aretz*, 15 February 2002 and available online at www.mideastweb.org/moratinos.htm; Pressman, "Visions in Collision"; Golan, *Israel and Palestine*, ch. 5; David Matz, "Trying to Understand the Taba Talks (Part I)," *Palestine–Israel Journal of Politics, Economics and Culture* 10:3 (2003), 96–105, and "Why Did Taba End?" Part II, *Palestine–Israel Journal of Politics, Economics and Culture* 10:4 (2003), pp. 92–8.

45 Justice for Jews in Arab Countries (JJAC), conference in London July 2008, Nathan Jeffay, "The Other Middle East Refugees," *Jerusalem Report*, 4 August 2008, 33–4; Michael R. Fischbach, "Palestinian Refugee Compensation and Israeli Counterclaims for Jewish Property in Arab Countries," *Journal of Palestine Studies* 38:1 (Autumn 2008), 6–24.

46 See "The Refugee Problem at Taba: Akiva Eldar interviews Yossi Beilin and Nabil Sha'ath," *Palestine–Israel Journal of Politics, Economics and Culture* 9:2 (2002), 12–23; *Exile and Return: Predicaments of Palestinians and Jews*, eds. Ann M. Lesch and Ian S. Lustick, Philadelphia: University of Pennsylvania Press, 2005; Khalil Shikaki, "Refugees and the Legitimacy of Palestinian–Israeli Peace Making," in *Arab–Jewish Relations from Conflict to Resolution: Essays in Honour of Professor Moshe Ma'oz*, eds. Elie Podeh and Asher Kaufman, Brighton: Sussex Academic Press, 2006, 363–74; Wasserstein, *Israelis and Palestinians*, 157–61; Akiva Eldar and Avi Issacharoff, "Abbas to Haaretz: Peace Deal Would Have to Include Right of Return," *Ha-Aretz*, 9 September 2008.

47 See, e.g., Elisa Efrat, "Jerusalem: Partition Plans for a Holy City," in *Israel: The First Hundred Years*, vol. 2, *From War to Peace?* ed. Efraim Karsh, London: Frank Cass, 2000, 238–57; Menachem Klein, *Jerusalem: The Contested City*, transl. Haim Watzman, New York: New York University Press, 2001, and *The Jerusalem Problem: The Struggle for Permanent Status*, transl. Haim Watzman, Gainsville: University Press of Florida, 2003; Reuven Merhav, "Planning for Jerusalem," in *The Camp David Summit*, eds. Shamir and Maddy-Weitzman, 167–75; Bernard Wasserstein, *Divided Jerusalem: The Struggle for the Holy City*, 3rd ed., New Haven, CT: Yale University Press, 2008; Michael Dumper, *The Politics of Sacred Space: The Old City of Jerusalem in the Middle East Conflict*, Boulder, CO: Lynne Rienner, 2002; Wasserstein, *Israelis and Palestinians*, 161–4; "Jerusalem in the Current Final Status Talks," bitterlemons.org, Palestinian–Israeli crossfire, Edition 35, 8 September 2008.

48 On the al-Aqsa *intifada*, see Jeremy Pressman, "The Second Intifada: Background and Causes of Israeli–Palestinian Conflict," *Journal of Conflict Studies* 22:2 (Fall 2003), 114–41; Meital, *Peace in Tatters*, ch. 6.

49 Philip Mattar, "al-Aqsa Intifada," *Encyclopedia of the Palestinians*, rev. ed., ed. Philip Mattar, New York: Facts on File, 2005, 23–4.

50 For a critique of Palestinian strategy during the second *intifada*, see Yezid Sayigh, "Arafat and the Anatomy of a Revolt," *Survival* 43:3 (Autumn

2001), 47–60, and "The Palestinian Strategic Impasse," *Survival* 44:4 (Winter 2002), 7–21.

51 The Sharm el-Sheikh Fact-finding Committee Final Report (The Mitchell Report), 30 April 2001; The Tenet Work Plan, 13 June 2001, accessed 5 September 2008 online at http://www.yale.edu/lawweb/avalon/mideast/mitchell_plan.htm and http://www.yale.edu/lawweb/avalon/mideast/mid023.htm.

52 UNSC Resolution 1397, 12 March 2002, accessed 5 September 2008 at http://daccessdds.un.org/doc/UNDOC/GEN/N02/283/59/PDF/N0228359.pdf.

53 A Performance-Based Roadmap to a Permanent Two-State Solution to the Israeli–Palestinian Conflict, 30 April 2003, reproduced in Golan, *Israel and Palestine*, 189–97. Available online at http://www.yale.edu/lawweb/avalon/mideast/roadmap.htm, accessed 5 September 2008.

54 The text of the Beirut Declaration on the Saudi Peace Initiative, 28 March 2002, is available online at http://www.al-bab.com/arab/docs/league/peace02.htm, and in Golan, *Israel and Palestine*, Appendix III. For an insightful Jordanian account of the inter-Arab and other negotiations surrounding the initiative, see Muasher, *The Arab Center*. For other discussions and analyses, see Golan, *Israel and Palestine*, 69–71; Meital, *Peace in Tatters*, 149–56; Elie Podeh, *From Fahd to Abdallah: The Origins of the Saudi Peace Initiatives and Their Impact on the Arab System and Israel*, Jerusalem: Truman Institute of the Hebrew University, 2003.

55 The website of the Geneva Initiative is at http://www.geneva-accord.org/HomePage.aspx?FolderID=11&lang=en. The October 2003 text can be found at http://www.geneva-accord.org/Accord.aspx?FolderID=33&lang=en; extracts reproduced in Golan, *Israel and Palestine*, 199–207. For a firsthand account and analysis, see Menachem Klein, *A Possible Peace between Israel and Palestine: An Insider's Account of the Geneva Initiative*, transl. Haim Watzman, New York: Columbia University Press, 2007.

Part III
Towards a More Useful Discussion of the Arab–Israeli Conflict

11
Writing about the Conflict

In the foregoing chapters, I have presented an overview history of almost 130 years of Israeli–Palestinian and Arab–Israeli conflict in fewer than 180 pages. The intention was to offer readers

- a sense of how the conflict evolved from its early beginnings to one of regional and global dimensions;
- an awareness of changes in the historical context, and repeating patterns of attitudes and behavior, over this period;
- some understanding of the parties, their motivations, and the emotional content of their conflicting views;
- an appreciation of why the conflict is so resistant to a resolution, especially when one singles out a number of core unresolved, perhaps irresolvable, arguments; and
- a basic notion of the main issues in contention among the conflict's various protagonists and among historians who have written about it.

Chapters 3 through 10 are an attempt at presenting the history of the conflict fairly and judiciously, based on an openness to conflicting evidence and the variety of interpretations that have been offered. Neither Zionists, Israelis, Palestinians, nor Arabs have emerged, I hope, as possessing a monopoly of truth, villainy, virtue, or vice.

One of the conclusions to be drawn from the preceding overview is that each of the parties has been operating, and still today operates, with weighty historical baggage. This baggage contains (a) an accumulation of unresolved grievances against, and perceived injustices committed by, the other party, (b) a constantly renewed and refreshed sense of righteousness in its own cause, (c) a constantly renewed and refreshed sense of its victimization at the hands of others, and (d) a degree of pessimism, cynicism, and despair produced by a succession of disappointments over failed efforts and missed opportunities for a just and/or peaceful resolution.

The differing versions of Palestinians and Israelis of their shared history of conflict—their competing narratives—are not easily bridged. Accepting this reality, I have tried to be faithful to the multiple versions and let each of the contested narratives speak in the preceding pages, with a minimum of editorializing of my own.

There are number of different ways of presenting the past 130 years of this conflict, none of which is a neutral recounting of mere facts or a simple chronology of events. In this first of two concluding chapters, we look at how historical and political writing about this conflict not only reports and describes the conflict, but actually reflects and takes part in it—and often distorts it, too.

On the Shortcomings of "Myths versus Facts"

In the preceding pages we have seen examples of how the same events can be interpreted in widely different ways by Israelis and their supporters, on the one hand, and by Palestinians and theirs, on the other. Each party clings to the accuracy of its own narrative and is quick to dismiss contesting versions by designating their components as myth, propaganda, or lies.

Unfortunately, this presentation of the history of the dispute by lining up and reinforcing one party's (true) "facts" against the other's (false) "myths" has also become a popular, but simplistic, way of explaining the conflict to beginners, eliminating inconvenient doubts among the faithful, and trying to win over uncommitted observers. Often buttressed by legitimate scholarship, this approach has its appeal but should be carefully scrutinized for its many flaws. Too much in the complex history of this dispute becomes reduced to a battle between *our* side's truth and the lies or propaganda produced by *their* side. Likewise, our side's virtue is pitted against their evil intentions, our side's resistance (self-defense) against their aggression, our side's desperation and weakness against their overwhelming strength or unfair advantage.

Over the past 130 years both Zionists/Israelis and Arabs/Palestinians have exhibited repeated examples of this mindset. Coming from the protagonists themselves in the heat of their struggle, there is something genuine about such adversarial closed-mindedness. These attitudes are real obstacles to be overcome among real combatants. For professional and lay people involved in peace education, interpersonal sensitivity training, and similar bridge-building activities,[1] these attitudes are precisely the obstacles on which they focus their energies.

But what happens when writers, journalists, scholars, and other interpreters—who stand one or more steps removed from the actual conflict—choose to present the conflict in this binary way, carrying over and mimicking one or the other of these diametrically opposed versions of history? Over the decades many one-sided books, pamphlets, and articles, displaying varying levels of sophistication and often great pretensions to even-handedness, have been published. A sampling of titles, through the decades, is revealing: *Palestine: The Reality* (1939), *Palestine through the Fog of Propaganda* (1946), *Myths and Facts: A Concise Record of the Arab–Israeli Conflict* (1964/1976/1985 etc.), *The Case for Israel* (1967), *True and False about Israel* (1972), *Battleground: Fact and Fantasy in Palestine* (1973/1985), "Zionist Mythinformation: The PLO Replies" (c. 1980), "Palestine & Zionism: Ten Myths" (1981), *Know the Facts* (1985), *The Case for Palestine* (1990/2005), *The Case for Israel* (2003).[2]

Critical readers soon discover that the real intention of these publications is to score points in the ongoing public relations wars between the Israeli/Zionist and Palestinian/Arab viewpoints. Today's heated campus skirmishes between pro-Palestinian and pro-Israeli student groups are only the latest incarnation of this battle which is as old as the conflict itself. Although technology and formats change, many of today's products follow the familiar pattern of "our facts versus their myths." The internet abounds with such adversarial tit-for-tat ways of presenting the issues in dispute, with precious few honest or successful attempts at even-handed presentation.[3]

For those interested in honing debating and advocacy skills, this adversarial way of presenting the conflict is no doubt appealing and useful.[4] But its merits for non-partisan people—those seeking greater understanding of why the parties fight, and whether and under what conditions they will ever be able to reconcile their differences—are dubious. One troubling feature of the myths-versus-facts publications and websites is the degree of certitude they exhibit—often unmatched by anything in real life. The truth is seldom as simple, and the facts seldom as straightforward, as the purveyors of myths-versus-facts make them seem. Also characteristic of this sort of writing is a pervasive tendency to make unflattering presumptions about the motives of the other. Experienced social scientists warn us, however, how difficult it is to know and judge a party's motives: "Our capacity to know the motives of other people is minimal, unreliable, and subject to the powerful seductions of self-justification and projection."[5]

Those seeking factual accuracy and an honest appraisal of the forces at work will be ill served by the myths-versus-facts approach because it is methodologically flawed. By its very essence it marshals facts selectively, and manipulates data using the whole gamut of rhetorical tricks and tools for the sole purpose of advancing a cause—hardly conducive to achieving dispassionate knowledge or critical understanding. Nor is it likely to be helpful for peace activists searching for a way out of the Israeli–Palestinian impasse, because by its confrontational format it fuels a never-ending cycle of polarization, self-justification, and vilification of the other.

The Role of the Academic

What about the halls of academe? Unfortunately, even here—where professional standards should maximize objectivity and accuracy in writing about the Arab–Israeli and Israeli–Palestinian conflict—we encounter many of the problems of distortion or misrepresentation described above. Some scholars willingly choose to lend their credentials to one version of the conflict over the other, and offer their support for educational–public-relations enterprises whose research publications are often little more than sophisticated versions of the myths-versus-facts materials described above.[6]

The problems of scholarly objectivity in writing about the conflict are by no means new, but have surfaced in different ways over the years. In the early 1950s, for example, Sylvia Haim took issue with George Antonius' 1938 publication, *The Arab Awakening*, which we cited earlier (Chapter 3). "It may be argued," she wrote,

> that no historian can work without having a definite point of view, that Antonius adopts a nationalist one, and that in such a case he has to be assessed as a nationalist historian. The phrase "nationalist historian" denotes someone who devotes his abilities and scholarship to the greater glorification of his nation or community. The phenomenon is no doubt widely prevalent, but it is nonetheless to be condemned. A historian may indeed have prejudices and preferences, but these have to be of a kind permissible to him. Seeing that he deals with the actions of men in power, with right and wrong, and generally with what human beings do to each other, he is not permitted to set himself up as the defender of one imperfect cause against another—and all political causes are imperfect. Should he attempt to do so, this but shows a failure in his professional integrity ... .[7]

Much of the published scholarship on the Arab–Israeli and Israeli–Palestinian conflicts—perhaps more than in other contested topics—is written by people who would qualify as "nationalist historians." Nowadays we would call them academics who identify with, and advocate on behalf of, a particular national narrative. As the editor of the *Encyclopedia of the Palestinians* lamented, there is too much "fusion of ideology and scholarship" in a field that "is dominated by partisans ... who have used scholarship and journalism to galvanize their people, to gain world support, and as a weapon against one another in their struggle over Palestine."[8]

Twenty years ago, the editors of a compendium of articles on the conflict described the problems of academic bias in similar terms:

> Even among scholars who are supposed to be objective observers, the conflict has engendered emotional intensity .... Scholars are not immune to the passions that animate the belligerents, who adhere to differing versions of history to support their respective claims. This tug-of-war between scholars ... has manifested itself in contradictory arguments along the same lines which the belligerents themselves use.[9]

These observations echo one of the premises of the *Contesting Histories* series, namely that historians of a conflict often mirror its protagonists and their arguments. Since the late 1980s when those words were written, academics have become even more intensely embattled in ways that reflect the non-resolution and exacerbation of the conflict. Unfortunately, distorted and polemicized presentations of the conflict seem more frequent than ever in scholarly writing and lecturing.[10] Nowadays a non-threatening climate for calm and open-minded discussion of this conflict is a rare commodity on campuses around the world. One manifestation of the heated battles waged in North American universities is the creation and operation of Campus-Watch, a controversial "watch-dog" website dedicated to exposing anti-Israel bias in professors' course materials and lectures.[11] Normal academic politics involving egos, personality clashes, the need to impress those who have power over one's advancement, and genuine ideological battles become even more complicated and embittered when the Arab–Israeli conflict is involved. Accusations of bias, unprofessional behavior, McCarthyite witch-hunting, and suppression of academic freedom have increased and spilled over the walls of academe in a number of *causes célèbres* involving sometimes sordid nationwide campaigns waged to destroy academic reputations or deny people tenure.[12]

It is almost a truism, but it bears repeating that there can be no pure objectivity in discussing human affairs, and that "bias" is a very subjective and relative term. As with any subject, the challenge to both writers and readers is to be alert to and conscious of *which* biases are at work in any piece of research. Readers should be highly skeptical of writers who claim they have no biases at all or who pretend that they can keep their biases from intruding upon their scholarship. Such writers may themselves be unaware of, or in denial about, these unavoidable influences; often they clothe their nationalist history in academic garb, righteously convinced that what they write is professionally sound. A lack of critical self-awareness may leave them unable to detect where ideology or partisanship intrude upon their scholarly tasks.

What can we say, generally, about the optimal role of academics and scholars in their professional research, publication, lecturing, and teaching on this conflict? The following checklist might enjoy a broad consensus—although certainly no unanimity—among historians:

- to provide basic factual accuracy and help establish the historical record based on credible (and multiple, where available) sources;
- to establish causality, where it is warranted, between one action and another, and to offer alternative hypotheses explaining links between events;
- to provide contextualized information helping readers to understand and empathize with the motivations, attitudes, decisions, and behavior of the actors;
- to identify patterns that deepen our understanding of the forces that contribute to causing and maintaining conflict;
- to scrutinize beliefs and myths of all the protagonists even-handedly, without becoming the advocate on behalf of any particular narrative;
- to challenge distortions and misrepresentations, whatever their provenance, by presenting credible counterevidence.

Scholars and Public Intellectuals

Where, then, and under what conditions, can historians of this conflict display their personal opinions? Few will take the extreme position of arguing that academics should or can remain neutral as between master and slave, oppressor and oppressed, victimizer and victim, making no judgments whatsoever between what they consider right and wrong. And most will agree that a historian should display empathy for his/her subjects. But where does one draw the line between acceptable and unacceptable injection of a scholar's personal opinions?

Simplistic critiques based on denouncing a writer's perceived bias or partisanship and praising alleged objectivity or neutrality are themselves problematic, often telling us more about the biases of the critic than the criticized.[13] Instead, let me suggest that it might be more productive to consider academic approaches to this conflict along a spectrum, based on the extent of *reluctance* and the contrasting *willingness* of scholars to disclose their personal opinions. Below I will attempt to define a range of degrees of reluctance/willingness as I see them, from minimalist through moderate to maximum disclosure. The spectrum may also be seen as ranging between those whose personal views are *implicit* in their writing to those who are more *explicit* in providing their evaluations and judgments.

At one end of the spectrum are academics who regard their basic task as being limited to establishing or clarifying the factual record. Who did what to whom? When? How many died? Their chief materials are archival and other primary sources, and they see their main intellectual task as being to uncover and present facts and evidence in a coherent manner. Discussions of the protagonists' motives are cautious and tentative, in some ways secondary to setting down a reliable record and letting the facts speak for themselves.

These academics are reluctant to express their personal opinions on the rights and wrongs committed by the parties. Recognizing that their own gender and socioeconomic, religious, and ethnic backgrounds already have some bearing on their work, they are careful not to "over-process" their research findings by putting too personal a spin on them. Although sometimes criticized as ivory-tower intellectuals, they are content to provide useful and credible raw material, leaving it to other academics and commentators to explore and exploit. They prefer to keep a low profile and not venture into public debates or take stands on controversial issues.

I see myself as following, in most of my scholarly output, this approach, having worked mostly with what some might consider dry diplomatic documents. I want my readers to draw their own conclusions and register their own criticisms based on the historical record that I and others are laying out. If I interject my own personal judgments, they are usually to criticize what I consider to be one party's or another's erroneous appraisals, self-delusions, or wishful thinking. My own personal biases are already implicit in the choices I make: Which topics do I write about? Where do I seek and find my raw material and secondary readings? How do I sift through masses of research material with the aim of using some (judged more credible and pertinent) and setting aside other (less credible or pertinent) documents and readings for discussion? How do I present and structure the historical data? What do I provide as appropriate context?

My personal reluctance to offer personal opinions on some of the larger issues is also motivated by deference towards both the subjects and the consumers of my research, as well as a desire to avoid possible pitfalls of my own fallible perceptions. As Tamil scholar and Israeli peace activist David Shulman has written: "We read the world as best we can, and we are often wrong."[14]

But, surveying the field, it is obvious that the above restraint is a minority approach. There are far more academics who conceive their role in more activist terms. Avi Shlaim, one of the original "new historians" (see below), has offered his view that "the historian's most fundamental task is not to chronicle but to evaluate. The historian's task is to subject the claims of all the protagonists to rigorous scrutiny and to reject all those claims, however deeply cherished, that do not stand up to such scrutiny."[15] Unlike the minimal approach described above, such views presume a professional responsibility to offer opinions and judgments, and not just the facts, to readers. Many in this group are also comfortable contributing, both on campus and off, to ongoing debates and discussions. Their scholarly production leads them to take stands on historical issues and current events close to their hearts or areas of expertise.

Benny Morris may serve as an outspoken example of this type of academic. His published scholarly works on difficult subjects reflect a professional commitment and strict discipline to call the shots as he sees them, and he does not hold back from including harsh criticism based on his reading of the evidence. The 1987 publication of his findings on the expulsion and flight of Palestinian refugees, based mainly on Zionist and Israeli primary sources, was truly ground-breaking and eye-opening. Morris received both praise and criticism for his account, which was accompanied by severe judgments that challenged a number of self-serving myths held by Jews and Israelis about the alleged voluntary exodus of Palestinians and the behavior of Zionist militias and Israeli fighters during 1947–1949, as we saw above in Chapter 6. He was among the first of a generation of "new historians" to challenge the received narrative for 1948 in Israel (see below).

In a critical review of a book published by a fellow "new historian," Morris describes his own striving for objectivity and attempts to keep his personal views out of his scholarship:

> [W]hile historians, as citizens, ha[ve] political views and aims, their scholarly task [is] to try to arrive at the truth about a historical event or process, to illuminate the past as objectively and accurately as possible. [Unlike postmodernists, like Ilan Pappé] I ... believe that there is such a thing as historical truth; that it exists independently of, and can be detached from, the subjectivities of scholars; that it is the historian's duty to try to reach it by using as many and as varied sources as he can. When writing history, the historian should ignore contemporary politics and struggle against his political inclinations as he tries to penetrate the murk of the past.[16]

But keeping a separation between one's professional work as historian and one's beliefs and activities as concerned citizen is easier said than done.

This was vividly illustrated in Morris's case in 2002. Like many Israelis then living through the daily violence of the second *intifada* and embittered over the recent near-miss talks at Camp David and Taba, Morris despaired of the chances of reconciliation. Publicly he vented his frustration against the Palestinians for their unrealistic aims and hostile attitudes and joined Ehud Barak in attacking Arafat as the main cause for the failure of recent peace efforts.[17] In *The Guardian*, fellow new historian Avi Shlaim, who considered the Israelis as the real obstacle to peace, sought to distance himself from his erstwhile comrade-in-arms.[18]

Then, in the course of a January 2004 interview, Morris uttered highly unflattering remarks about Muslim and Arab society and culture, comments that some considered stereotypical and racist.[19] This outburst raised an important question: Can a historian continue to write sound, credible history on the Israeli–Palestinian conflict after having publicly disclosed such a lack of empathy for one of the subjects of his research, and having expressed his belief that "the Arabs are after our state, and they are after our blood."[20] At least some of the reviewers of his latest book on the 1948 war credit Morris for keeping his scholarship separate from, and untainted by, his personal opinions on people and current events.[21]

As a maverick and controversialist by nature, Benny Morris may not be a typical example of how historians of the Arab–Israeli conflict convey their opinions along with their research findings to the general public. But there are many scholars who, like Morris, not only publish about the past but also contribute insightful commentary on current events and take part in contemporary controversies. They see it as a natural part of their job to offer informed opinions and judgments on the attitudes and behavior of the parties in conflict, then as now, to their readers, students, and the media.

Finally, there are a smaller number of academics and commentators who might be described as *engagé* intellectuals. These people usually treat the Israel–Palestine conflict as a subject of study and interest that falls under a larger umbrella—e.g., commitment to a cause, or belief in an ideological system. Many in this category would reject any separation between a narrow professional focus and their broader duties as citizen or human being. Among other things, their wider frame makes it easier for them to take clear-cut positions on the rights and wrongs committed by the parties to the Arab–Israeli conflict. These scholars feel free—some may even feel obliged—to pass judgment on the actions, inaction, and/or motives of the protagonists, and to apportion blame and responsibility for hostilities, the perpetuation of injustice, and/or the absence of a solution.

Such scholars are often also activists, working outside of academia, for example as advisers to policy-makers, NGOs, or advocacy groups. They contribute their energies, expertise, and credibility to struggles for human rights, or peace and reconciliation. This engagement often translates into advocacy on behalf of one of this conflict's protagonists whom they see as being the aggrieved party and whose cause they embrace. In so doing they accept the risks of being accused of allowing their scholarship to be driven by their ideology, or being labeled as advocates, polemicists, or partisans.

Ilan Pappé is an example of this approach to researching and writing about the Israel–Palestine conflict. A self-defined disciple of the late Edward Said, he is an Israeli historian formerly based at Haifa University who moved to the University of Exeter. Pappé's early work followed the standard published-PhD style of being guarded about disclosing personal opinions; his 1988 *Britain and the Arab–Israeli Conflict*[22] exhibited all the markings of the restrained, minimalist scholar described above. Since then, however, his work has reflected far more explicitly some of his personal views. Atypical among Israeli intellectuals, he has gone beyond merely criticizing the Zionist narrative to openly adopting the rival, Palestinian, narrative which he promotes in his work.

In *A History of Modern Palestine: One Land, Two Peoples* (2004, revised 2006) Pappé reveals his credo as follows:

> My bias is apparent despite the desire of my peers that I stick to facts and the "truth" when reconstructing past realities. I view any such construction as vain and presumptuous. This book is written by one who admits compassion for the colonized not the colonizer; who sympathizes with the occupied not the occupiers; and sides with the workers not the bosses. He feels for women in distress, and has little admiration for men in command. He cannot remain indifferent towards mistreated children, or refrain from condemning their elders. In short, mine is a subjective approach, often but not always standing for the defeated over the victorious.[23]

This unusually honest declaration of bias and subjectivity[24] is a product of the current postmodern cultural-studies worldview and lines up clearly on one side of a wider and deeper (and unfinished) debate about how one ought to study and write history. For a subsequent major work on the expulsion of the Palestinians, Pappé chose as his title *The Ethnic Cleansing of Palestine*[25]—a title (like Jimmy Carter's 2007 *Palestine: Peace not Apartheid*[26]) that was bound to rattle all supporters, and even mild critics, of Israel. A close look at the volume reveals that the title is more than an attention-grabbing device, but rather a serious indication of the author's deliberate use of accusatory terminology—ethnic cleansing, like genocide, being a war crime under international law—as a paradigm through which the entire conflict, and not just the 1948 war, he believes, should be understood. Following upon earlier writing on "transfer" described in

Chapter 6, Pappé's 2006 publication selectively adduces additional historical data to present the Israel–Palestine dispute as being the product of Zionism's deliberate intention, from the start, of creating a Jewish state by ethnically cleansing the Palestinian Arab population.

A visible and vocal minority of scholars have, like Ilan Pappé, publicly revealed enough of their personal beliefs and worldviews in their publications on this conflict to be considered *engagé* academics on this spectrum. Their activism propels them, in many cases, into heated polemics as well. They see themselves as "public intellectuals ... invok[ing] their scholarly responsibility and/or authority to express themselves on issues of public concern."[27] But in their passionate engagement it is sometimes difficult to know when devotion to their ideology or worldview may cause them to select and present their facts so as to accord with the dictates of their commitments.[28]

In a sophisticated discussion and powerful disclosure of her personal approach and beliefs, Sara Roy argues in favor of what she calls "humanistic scholarship" on the Palestinian–Israeli conflict. Drawing on her own self-awareness as the daughter of a Holocaust survivor, Roy feels morally compelled to expose the causes and agents of repression while giving an empathetic voice to the victims of oppression and dispossession.[29] The result for Roy is an advocacy for the restoration of Palestinian rights abrogated by Zionism and Israel. Some critics may be unimpressed, and dismiss such a position as anti-Israel propaganda, ideologically motivated and dressed up in academically respectable phraseology. But for the scholar herself, it is overarching humanism that self-consciously drives her lines of inquiry and research in this very troubled field of study.

Readers and students, whatever their partisan leanings or ideological commitments, are in the end *consumers* of scholarly writing. As such, they should develop a critical ability to interpret not only the facts, events, and explanations relating to the conflict, but also the differences among the various human filters through which these facts, events, and explanations are being presented to them. Personal integrity and academic professionalism must be taken as givens for all teachers, scholars, and authors; but day-to-day implementation of these ideals is subject to the usual human imperfections. Careful readers are therefore wise to be aware that all writing on this controversial subject contains the personal opinions of the authors, whether implicit or explicit, in the texts relating to these contested histories.

I have stated my own preference for writing wherein academics keep expressions of their personal views to a minimum. I stand by a more traditional, "positivist" approach to historical facts, objectivity, and bias[30] and remain dubious about the merits of scholarship built on explicit rejection of academic detachment and the corresponding frank identification with either of the embattled parties in the contested histories of Palestine/Israel. But, for better or for worse, the field is dominated by scholars who disagree and who tend to be more explicit, activist, and *engagé*. In defense of my own minority preference, let me conclude by quoting the words of Northrop Frye:

> The scholar ... has all the moral dilemmas and confusions of other men, perhaps intensified by the particular kind of awareness that his calling gives him. But *qua* scholar what he is is what he offers to his society, which is his scholarship. If he understands both the worth of the gift and the worth of what it is given for, he needs, so far as he is a scholar, no other moral guide.[31]

Israel's "New Historians"

With the opening of 1948 materials in many archives, a new generation of scholars eagerly probed the past through these primary sources, producing a wave of revisionist PhD theses and monographs. A particular brand of activist and committed scholarship emerged in Israel in the late 1980s, led by Benny Morris, Avi Shlaim, and Ilan Pappé—scholars with a "mission"[32] who, despite their differences in methodology and ideological leanings, were lumped together as being on a "crusade"[33] under the banner of "new historians."

One mission undertaken by these scholars was to challenge myths, especially those associated with the accepted Zionist *milhemet ha-atzma'ut* narrative of 1948, looking back after forty years. Among other things, these writers wrote with great empathy for the Palestinian victims of the Zionist success story, while criticizing their own leaders for being somewhat intoxicated by their victories and hardened in their new-found power. Some inside Israel, along with many Palestinians and Israel's critics abroad, welcomed the appearance of these new historians—each for different reasons. Some Israelis looked forward to the corrective effect this new scholarship could have in revising mainstream histories that had displayed an overdose of self-glorification, a lack of self-criticism, or unduly myopic perspectives. Many agreed that the very launching of these debates could only be good for the continued study and writing about the history of the conflict.

But many in Israel and the Jewish world were taken aback to see their erstwhile heroes and heroines portrayed in such unflattering ways. Not many were happy to be told that their Zionist saga and the birth of Israel were tainted by original sin because of the way the Palestinians were treated. New research on 1948 seemed to show the state's very foundation as something other than a miraculous victory of beleaguered underdogs, challenging Israelis' self-view as "the few against the many," as David against Goliath.

During the late 1980s and through the 1990s, the Israeli public's displeasure with the new historians (often mistakenly lumped together with avowedly "post-Zionist" and anti-Zionist Israeli and Jewish scholars[34]) was palpable and provoked many counterattacks.[35] Some criticized them for reflecting the imbalance in the availability of their source materials, which naturally led to a disproportionate criticism of the Israeli-Zionist decision-makers while saying little or nothing about what Arab and Palestinian leaders were thinking and doing at the time. Others, less charitably, accused the new historians of engaging in an irresponsible slaughter of sacred cows in selfish pursuit of notoriety and their own career advancement. Others dismissed the scholars for exhibiting an arrogant contrariness or, worse still, a "suicidal" self-loathing.[36]

Beyond stirring up these lively, sometimes vicious, public debates about history among Israelis and Jews, the phenomenon of the new historians had other repercussions. The remainder of this chapter will be devoted to two of them, namely:

1 the use of the "missed opportunities" approach in studying the elusiveness of Arab–Israeli peace, and
2 the spillover of this specifically Israeli phenomenon concerning trends in historiography on the Palestinian side.[37]

Missed Opportunities

It is the business of statesmen and leaders to discover and exploit windows of opportunity for advancing the interests of their people. Similarly, it is the business of academics and other analysts, albeit from the comfort of their armchairs and with the wisdom of hindsight, to review the history of conflicts and point out "missed opportunities" for peace or advancing one's cause.

There are two main purposes for such *post facto* exercises: to allocate blame for failed leadership, and to learn more about the nature of the conflict and the chances for its resolution. Polemical and partisan writing abounds with the former purpose, while academics and policy advisers tend to aim more for the latter. In the following pages we examine both tendentious and effective utilizations of the "missed opportunities approach" by Israelis and Palestinians.

Some authors, especially among Israel's new historians, have portrayed the Israeli–Arab conflict as if it were primarily a series of missed opportunities for peace. For those who frame the discussion in this way, the main purpose of research is to understand the failure to reach peace by exposing and censuring the party or parties considered responsible for missing those presumed opportunities. But narrowing the discussion to this single aspect and attributing a degree of retrospective certainty to what "might have been" are a simplification of larger and more complex phenomena that need to be considered together as making up the conflict and the reasons why it is not yet resolved.

As a form of counterfactual analysis, the missed opportunities approach relies heavily on speculative second-guessing. *If only* A *had done (or not done)* B, *then* C *would/might have done (or not done)* D. An example of this sort of "if only ... then" history would be to explore a proposition like: *If only* Hitler and the Nazi Party had not come to power in Germany in 1933, *then* the Zionist movement *might not have* overwhelmed Mandatory Palestine with Jewish immigrants; and *then* the Palestinians *might have* been able to create an Arab state with a Jewish minority. This might appear a fascinating line of inquiry, but it is methodologically problematic. We can never really know how any of the parties *might have* reacted to hypothetical possibilities. *"If only ... then"* and *"what if ..."* propositions involve hypothetical actions and further hypothetical consequences which we have no way of establishing or confirming, even using the best 20/20 hindsight.[38]

As for negotiation attempts, there are a number of complex and interwoven reasons why some fail and others succeed.[39] Goodwill and an honest desire for "peace"—itself an elastic and imprecise word covering a range of terms and conditions—are not the only determining factors. Those who single these out for scrutiny often rush simplistically to judgment to condemn one party for missing a presumed opportunity to bring the conflict to an end. What makes matters worse is the frequent accompanying tendency to suggest a pattern which, according to the writer, proves that either Arab, Palestinian, Zionist, or Israeli decision-makers were simply not interested in peace, closing the indictment against one side or the other for perpetuating the conflict.[40] This is not always a useful or sound intellectual exercise, although it may satisfy the needs of those advocating on behalf of one of the parties in dispute.

The best-known examples of the missed opportunities approach are, as we noted, the new historians who found Israel's leaders guilty for missing multiple chances to end the conflict. This appears, for example, in Shlaim's early study of Syria's Husni Za'im, as well as in his later studies, *Collusion across the Jordan* and *The Iron Wall*.[41] In particular, Shlaim and other new historians criticize the Israeli leadership for not doing more to transform their limited armistice agreements, signed in 1949, into more extensive and stable peace treaties, and for not responding more generously to overtures from the Arab side (cf. above, pages 134–7). They cite archival evidence indicating that David Ben-Gurion, and even the dovish Moshe Shertok/Sharett and Abba Eban, took conscious decisions that clearly demonstrated their preference for maintaining an unstable status quo over a potential deal that would have involved negotiating over the price demanded by the (defeated) Arab states for a more durable peace: viz., withdrawal from the armistice lines to the proposed UN partition boundaries, and repatriation of the Palestinian refugees.[42]

The new historians were not, it should be pointed out, the first to second-guess the decisions of Zionist leaders for missing opportunities. Studies critical of Israel's early handling of the refugee question were published by scholars Don Peretz and Rony Gabbay in the 1950s, and broader critiques covering the pre-1948 period were authored by leftist activists Aharon Cohen and Simha Flapan in the 1960s and 1970s.[43] In the pre-1948 *yishuv* itself, a number of maverick Jewish personalities who were personally involved in talks with Arabs and Palestinians engaged in public criticism of the official Zionist leadership for not according due attention to the tasks of winning over the local population. These criticisms were sometimes formulated in terms of Zionists' focus on cultivating the support of outside powers and their failure, whether out of ignorance or arrogance, to obtain "an Arab Balfour Declaration" that might have (it was argued) better guaranteed their peaceful future as residents of Palestine/*Eretz-Israel*.[44]

On this score, mainstream Zionist/Israeli historiography argues in its defense that, largely because Zionist and Israeli leaders so desperately wanted and *needed* acceptance by and peace with the Arab world, they actually went to great lengths *not* to miss any conceivable opportunity for an agreement or entente. Chaim Weizmann's aborted 1919 agreement with Amir Faysal is often cited as the most prominent illustration of these efforts to win Arab acquiescence in the Zionist program for Palestine.[45] During the Mandate period Zionist officials explored a number of dubious initiatives from the other side and gave them more serious attention than they perhaps deserved, precisely to avoid criticism for losing a chance for a real breakthrough.[46] The problem, they claim, lay not with themselves, but rather with Arab unreasonableness and unwillingness.

A number of scholars have sought to make more judicious use of the missed opportunities approach. In 1991 Itamar Rabinovich of Tel Aviv University's Dayan Center published *The Road Not Taken: Early Arab–Israeli Negotiations*.[47] The book was an expansion of research that had been provoked by new historian Avi Shlaim's 1986 article on a negotiation episode involving Husni Za'im, in the course of which Shlaim blamed Israel for "fritter[ing] away" a "historic opportunity" for peace with the Syrian leader (who was soon deposed and murdered).[48] While disclaiming any intention to defend any of the actors, allocate blame, or to focus on what he called "the ever-intriguing issue of 'missed opportunities'," Rabinovich's book was indeed a corrective to the missed opportunities approach as sometimes misused by the new historians.

Without directly contradicting the newly revealed evidence of short-sightedness on the part of Israeli decision-makers of the late 1940s and early 1950s, Rabinovich spread the responsibility for the failure to achieve peace more evenly among the conflicting parties. Drawing on his expertise in Arab regional politics and on a wider selection of primary and secondary sources, he took a hard-nosed look at whether anyone on the Arab side of a potential deal was really prepared to accept and make peace with Israel, *if only* the Israelis had shown more willingness to make concessions. In his careful review of three post-1948 case studies, Rabinovich provided evidence showing that none of Israel's potential peace partners in Syria, Egypt, or Jordan was in any realistic position to follow through on a potential agreement and "deliver the goods" against domestic opposition—even had the Israelis been more forthcoming or generous in their bargaining stances. Going beyond simplistic and accusatory treatments of missed opportunities, Rabinovich offers a model of careful analysis that can be tested, refined, or contradicted by further research and the integration of additional source materials as they become available.[49]

As with the second-guessing of Zionist and Israeli decision-makers, there are also many writers who manipulate the missed opportunities approach for the purpose of criticizing the Arabs and Palestinians for the absence of peace. The late Israeli diplomat Abba Eban once quipped that the Arabs "never miss an opportunity to miss an opportunity," which became a stock-phrase used by Israelis to blame the other side on many occasions when a window of opportunity was opened and slammed shut again. Most of those who quote this witty phrase do so in the context of the "blame game." In so doing, they promote the self-serving view that, while Israel is always ready to make sacrifices for peace, the Arabs and Palestinians are somehow congenitally unable to seize those opportunities—whether out of implacable enmity, a lack of political savvy, inability to understand their own best interests, the curse of permanently incompetent leadership, or some evil anti-Israel impulse that turns out to be equally, if not more, harmful to themselves than to their enemies.[50]

Those who choose to blame Palestinian "extremism" and "rejectionism" in the missing of opportunities often point to Palestinian rejection of the 1937 Peel *Report* and the 1947 UNSCOP Report and their proposed maps. To quote one recent highly polemical use of the missed opportunities approach:

> The useless suffering that the Palestinian leadership and elites inflicted on their own people and on all they encountered (Jews, Jordanians, Lebanese, and victims of terrorism worldwide) is a direct product of their obsession with justice. Had they been willing to accept the inevitable historic compromise, they could have had a Palestinian state in 1947 in much more than today's West Bank and Gaza Strip. Thirty years ago, before most of the settlements were even established, they could have developed PM Menachem Begin's autonomy into a sovereign state of their own (Arafat himself said as much). Seven years ago [at Camp David, July 2000], they were offered a state over 97 percent of the territories, with Jerusalem as a capital, control over the Temple Mount and $40 billion for refugee resettlement. Had they substituted the unrealistic quest for ultimate justice with a viable compromise, they could have offered three generations of their children a promising future.[51]

This outlook is flawed in its accusatory selection and slanting of facts, as well as its omission of essential elements that may help to explain why Palestinians could not have—or, in their own best interests, perhaps even *should* not have—accepted those proposals. A more nuanced examination of those missed opportunities must also inquire into whether the proposals themselves were workable, truly accepted by the other side, flawed, or for some reason doomed to failure—even if they had been accepted by the Palestinians as a basis for discussion.[52]

It goes beyond the scope of the present chapter to attempt a full counterfactual analysis of these seminal decisions. Yet one can raise the following questions requiring careful investigation before being able to reach credible conclusions about what *might have been* the result *if only* the Palestinian leadership had accepted to work with the Peel or the UNSCOP proposals. For example,

1   Would the proposed Peel boundaries, restricting the proposed Jewish state to an enclave or mini-state in only 20 percent of western Palestine (Galilee and the Mediterranean coast north of Tel Aviv), have remained on the table, given the Zionist leadership's energetic rejection of those boundaries, even while announcing its acceptance in principle of the Peel *Report*? Over the course of the coming year the Jewish Agency marshaled and submitted extensive research reports to the Woodhead "Technical" Commission making the case for a substantially larger area.

2 Would the Arab state proposed by Peel have been a viable one? The British plan called not for an independent Palestinian state (which would likely have been led by the Mufti and his followers), but rather for the Arab areas of partitioned Palestine to be placed under Britain's loyal ally, the Amir Abdullah, in effect creating an expanded Transjordanian state. The Amir's rule was definitely perceived as "foreign" by most Palestinians, and would have been overwhelmingly rejected by Palestinian political factions. Indeed, recognizing this hostility, Abdullah almost immediately curbed his initial enthusiasm for the Peel proposals.

3 Could the necessary population transfers have been implemented? Imbalances in the demographic distribution of Jews and Arabs in the two proposed states by Peel would have necessitated border adjustments and—more problematic and perhaps unworkable— transfers of population. Some 225,000 Arabs would have found themselves within the boundaries of the proposed Jewish state (incorporating a Jewish population of 396,000), with 1250 Jews in the proposed Arab state.[53] Ten years later, the UNSCOP map (a patchwork of triangles) and mixtures of population were even more complicated: the proposed Jewish state would have had a Jewish population of 500,000 with a huge Arab minority numbering around 416,000. The proposed Arab state would have had an Arab population of 715,000, with 6,000 Jews within its boundaries.

In contrast to the frequent use of the missed opportunities approach as part of the "blame game," more serious and impartial historical analysis is now being produced that tackles questions about whether the Palestinians might not have lost their homeland to the Zionists, or might have worked out a tolerable arrangement with them, *if only* they had behaved differently at crucial moments in their history. Although equally susceptible, along with Israeli new historians, to the pitfalls of counterfactual analysis, a few scholars have done important probing of some of those possible turning-points in the history of the conflict.

In Chapter 4, for example, we recounted how the Palestinians in 1922– 1923 rejected British proposals for limited self-government. In one chapter of his valuable study of missed opportunities,[54] Philip Mattar undertakes a detailed look at this episode and the context in which Palestinian leaders decided to reject three successive British proposals: an elected legislative council, an appointed advisory council, and an "Arab Agency" modeled on the Jewish Agency. In choosing to boycott these British initiatives for limited self-governing institutions, Mattar asks, did the Palestinian leaders deprive their people of a tool that might have slowed down the advance of Zionism and enhanced their own chances for statehood?

After a careful examination of a broad range of primary sources, Mattar clearly views the rejection of the 1922 legislative council proposals as having been a crucial mistake. This decision, he argues, meant that Palestinians denied themselves a forum for regular access to British officials, while the Jewish Agency continued to advise the Palestine government in Jerusalem and the Zionist Organization influenced the British government in London and the League of Nations in Geneva.[55] By rejecting the 1922–1923 proposals, they further missed out on a regular mechanism to press for British commitment to the second part of their "dual obligation" (above, Chapter 4) under the Balfour Declaration and the Mandate.

Regular council meetings, although likely to be the scene of much political bickering and grandstanding, would have been chaired by the liberal High Commissioner, Sir Herbert Samuel. As a venue, the council might have allowed both Palestinians and Zionists to work together on *ad hoc* economic, social, and cultural issues of mutual benefit, creating personal encounters that could have led some individuals, at least, to moderate their political positions and search for common ground. Even allowing for predictable deadlocks over "hot" issues like immigration quotas, a legislative council that had powers to enact laws and regulations and ratify budgets would, Mattar argues, have provided the Palestinians with some tools for protecting and modernizing their community, enabling it to better compete with the Europeanized Jewish *yishuv*.

All in all, Mattar believes that "the Palestinians would have been in a more advantageous position than what transpired" if only they had accepted to participate in the proposed legislative council:

> With no discernable strategy of either confrontation or cooperation [vis-à-vis the British rulers of the country], they allowed the Yishuv to grow, to establish military and governmental institutions. Their leaders often met British officials but only to protest, demand, threaten, or plead, which led to little if any policy change.

Despite moral qualms about their participation requiring tacit acquiescence in the Jewish national home and the Mandate, "they stood to gain more from working within the Government, than outside of it." Not, Mattar concedes, that their participation would, by itself, have been enough to halt the flow of Jewish immigration and land purchase, given the overall imbalance between Zionist strengths and Palestinians weaknesses.

Yet it is hard to imagine how acceptance of the Council could have done anything but improve their political position and socioeconomic conditions. They could have helped in drafting legislation. They could have had official input into expenditures and quotas for Jewish immigration. They could have used their official positions to criticize British policy and appeal for British and world support. Most of all, they would have put themselves in a position to ask for more.

Unlike the polemical use of evidence shown earlier, and unlike apologetics arguing that Palestine's fate would have been different *if only* Palestinians had followed Ragheb Nashashibi's advice to accept these British proposals,[56] Mattar's method is to draw upon painstaking research into episodes such at this one. His conclusions are no less harsh than those quoted above, but the tone is altogether different: "By seeking total justice, instead of attainable justice, they attained nothing, and eventually lost their homes, lands, and homeland. That is, by ignoring practical politics and by allowing only ideology and emotions to drive their policies and actions, they insured failure."

Auguring well for scholarship about this conflict, Mattar's judicious application of a missed opportunities approach to Palestinian decision-making is being repeated for other Palestinian and Zionist/Israeli moments of decision. In *The Iron Cage*, for example, Columbia University professor Rashid Khalidi engages in a similar counterfactual exercise, raising many critical questions about what the Palestinians might have done differently, such as

- Could they have compromised and accepted some form of Jewish national home within the context of an Arab state in Palestine before 1939?
- Had they done so, would this have had any effect on the powerful drive of the Zionist movement for an independent Jewish state in Palestine?
- Would the Palestinians have been better off had they been more militant in dealing with the British much earlier?
- Would they have benefited had they been able to rein in the revolt of 1936–1939 and win some political gains from it?

Reviewing options and possible outcomes of these *"what-if?"* propositions in the circumstances of the 1930s and 1940s, Khalidi concludes that it would be "difficult or impossible" to imagine a successful trajectory either to Palestinian statehood or to a reconciliation between Zionist and Palestinian national aspirations.[57] Similar careful counterfactual analysis could be used to examine whether the Palestinians should be blamed, or blame themselves, for missing another opportunity to contain or block the expansion of the Jewish national home when they decided in May 1939 to reject the MacDonald White Paper, rather than exploit its favorable clauses (see above, Chapter 5).

Whether one chooses to agree or disagree with a particular set of conclusions, appropriate usage of the missed opportunities approach holds much promise for sound historical analysis on both sides. But, as noted, careful counterfactual analysis means avoiding simplistic certainties where only probabilities are warranted. Continuing research and the recovery of new evidence can serve to refine and improve upon conclusions reached.

Trends in Palestinian and Israeli Historiography

Why did critical, revisionist history of the conflict begin and prosper among Israeli rather than Palestinian scholars? And why is there, until today, no Palestinian equivalent to the Israeli "new historians"?

Part of the explanation is technical, but quickly becomes connected to the ongoing dynamics of the conflict itself. For a variety of reasons, primary sources in the form of diplomatic correspondence and memoranda are more plentiful and more easily accessible on the Israeli side. The Western tradition of open public archives is not generally replicated in the Arab world. The Palestinian community, stateless and dispersed, lacked the structures and resources needed to facilitate and promote the accumulation of authoritative documentation on Palestinian history on the same scale as the rival Central Zionist Archives and Israel State Archives. For years, exiled Palestinians relied on the Beirut-based PLO Research Center and the Institute for Palestine Studies to collect and preserve these parts of their national heritage; but much of the task of preservation of documents was left to individuals and families. The limitations of written testimony are being partially counteracted by a new generation of collectors of oral history.[58]

The asymmetrical power relationship between the two parties has further implications for the writing of the history of the dispute. Ilan Pappé has claimed that Israel not only colonized the Palestinians' land, but has for many years also colonized the writing of their history.

[B]y and large, Israeli historians conveyed the message that Israelis were the victims of the conflict, and constituted the rational party in the struggle over Palestine, while the Palestinians were irrational if not fanatic, intransigent and immoral .... The stronger party ... has the power to write the history in a more effective way. In our particular case, [Israel] had formed a state and employed the state's apparatus for successfully propagating its narrative in front of domestic as well as external publics. The weaker party [Palestinians] ... was engaged in a national liberation struggle, unable to lend its historians a hand in opposing the propaganda of the other side.[59]

One result of this asymmetry is that early Palestinian historical writing was characterized as "a form of resistance by means of formulating a national Palestinian narrative" which resembles "emotional speeches and direct national[ist] propaganda rather than a search for the truth."[60] In this sense, Palestinian historiography may also suffer as part of a wider Arab intellectual malaise in which the writing of history "has been functioning ... less as a genuine inquiry than as a psychological defense."[61]

Rejecting or ignoring claims of an imbalance of power, some Israelis involved in dialogues with Palestinians have nonetheless argued that, now that they have subjected themselves to the painful process of myth-busting by their new historians, it is time for the Palestinian side to follow suit with an equally energetic campaign to rewrite Palestinian history and subject its myths and narratives to rigorous scrutiny.

There are several responses that Palestinians and others offer to this challenge by their Israeli colleagues. While the conflict persists in its present form, they point out, Israeli historians enjoy the luxury of criticizing their own side's victor's history with relative ease and impunity, risking only minor damage to the national self-image or (possibly, but not necessarily) their career advancement. Palestinian academics cannot, they argue, be considered a symmetrical or parallel case. Being members of the weaker, defeated party and living largely under occupation and as guests in undemocratic states, their historians are under siege and cannot openly attack leaders or régimes, or engage in the slaughter of sacred national cows. They are loath (not unlike many Israelis) to engage in acts of self-criticism which may provide ammunition to the enemy and be deemed detrimental to their ongoing national struggle.

There is another reason why Palestinians who, while willing to re-examine critically their own narrative, do not find themselves replicating the crusading zeal of Israel's new historians. As Rashid Khalidi points out, the latter's research findings have largely borne out the factual accuracy of "many elements of the standard Palestinian narrative"[62]—thus leaving less to deconstruct and debunk on their side. Some Palestinians take this point even further, viewing the emergence of Israel's new historians simply as a belated recognition of the non-tenability of the "old and distorted official history" of Zionism and Israel, and proof of the correct-ness and validity of their own narrative of victimization at the hands of Zionist colonialism. "The need for new Israeli historians," wrote Palestin-ian poet Zakaria Mohammed,

> derived from the existence of a history that cannot [with]stand serious criticism. After all, ... what serious historian can describe the Zionist

movement as a movement of national liberation? ... The Palestinian views the new Israeli historian as a penitent rather than a "new historian." His history is no more than "a confession" before the "priest of history." This is an admission of sin and no more. The Palestinian historian [on the other hand] cannot be repentant because he has nothing to confess to the "priest of history."[63]

Such sharply defined differences between the approaches of Israeli and Palestinian historians, and even among Israelis and Palestinians themselves, are a telling indication of how far apart the writers of the contested histories of Israel and Palestine remain. Similar dilemmas and disputes have occurred regarding the writing and revising of Israeli and Palestinian school textbooks since 1993.[64] Despite some interesting and original classroom experiments—notably the PRIME project's presentation of parallel Israeli and Palestinian narratives to children on both sides—the immediate results have been disappointing, largely owing to the effects of the conflict still being experienced on the street.[65]

Even when academics meet to talk openly on pleasant neutral territory, the interaction is not always encouraging. An irreconcilable clash could be seen in the tension, anger, and frustration shown at a 2003 closed-door international conference of experts on the two parties' narratives hosted by the World Peace Foundation and the Belfer Center for Science and International Affairs at the Kennedy School of Government at Harvard University.[66] While Israeli academics, ranging from center-right to leftist to extreme left, exhibited varying degrees of criticism of the Israeli national narrative in the presence of their Palestinian colleagues, Palestinian participants refused to be drawn into the same exercise. Nadim Rouhana, an Israeli-based Palestinian social psychologist, used his opportunity to discuss the Palestinian narrative to launch into a scathing attack on the inherent violence, exclusion, and oppression ("Zionism's culture of force") that Israel still inflicts on the Palestinians, who should not be blamed for resisting.[67] An Israeli historian and peace activist, while acknowledging the reality of Palestinian grievances, took offense at his colleague's aggressive presentation, which implied a delegitimization of his own existence as a native-born peaceloving Israeli. He suggested that his Palestinian colleague's exposition exhibited all the objectionable characteristics of an "exclusionist" narrative, suggesting instead that "self-critical revision" had to be applied by both Palestinians and Israelis, and should involve three strategies:

1. To uncover and peel off the prevailing narrative's exclusionist nationalist and self-congratulatory ideologies that tend to distort it.
2. To transcend simplistic generalizations and labeling, and discover the full complexity of the disputed events, both their motives and causations.

3. To try to understand the motives and the rationale of the "enemy's" behavior, and to present the narrative with maximum sensitivity to the sensibilities of the opposite side, with human compassion and a deeper understanding of the tragic nature of the conflict.[68]

It is unclear whether Bar-On's proposed guidelines made any impression on his Palestinian co-participants at this closed-door seminar, or altered their approach to their contested histories.

Many scholars on both sides would accept the late Edward Said's general exhortation to view the appearance of Israel's new historians as an opportunity to engage in dialogue while scrutinizing their own history with a new critical outlook.[69] Many would also accept Rashid Khalidi's remark that the Palestinian nationalist narrative "includes its share of myth." But few Palestinians would go as far as Khalidi (based at New York's Columbia University) does in itemizing key myths specifically about the Zionist-other that deserve debunking. Many would find it especially difficult to agree with his critique of the Palestinians'

reductionist view of Zionism as no more than a colonial enterprise. This enterprise was and is colonial in terms of its relationship to the indigenous Arab population of Palestine; Palestinians fail to understand, or refuse to recognize, however, that Zionism *also* [emphasis orig.] served as the national movement of the nascent Israeli polity being constructed at their expense. There is no reason why both positions cannot be true.[70]

What is amply clear from the Harvard and other attempts[71] to bring academics together is the extreme difficulty in devising a common Palestinian–Israeli project for revising history, challenging myths, and criticizing national narratives.[72] Yet, whatever can be accomplished separately or jointly among historians of different backgrounds, "[d]econstructing these ideas will be crucially important to an eventual reconciliation of the two peoples."[73]

Notes

1   Some examples are: The Peace Research Institute in the Middle East (PRIME) website at http://vispo.com/PRIME; Seeds of Peace website at http://www.seedsofpeace.org; Compassionate Listening website at http://www.compassionatelistening.org; Search for Common Ground website at http://www.sfcg.org.

2   J. M. N. Jeffries, *Palestine: The Reality*, London, Longmans Green, 1939; M. F. Abcarius, *Palestine through the Fog of Propaganda*, introduction by Major-General Sir E. L. Spears, London, New York, etc.: Hutchinson,

1946. [Westport, CT: Hyperion Press reprint 1976]; *Myths and Facts: A Concise Record of the Arab–Israeli Conflict*, Washington, DC: Near East Report (Washington Letter on American Policy in the Middle East), 1964; rev. and updated 1976, 1985, 1989; *Myths and Facts: A Guide to the Arab–Israeli Conflict*, edited by Mitchell G. Bard; foreword by Eli E. Hertz: Chevy Chase, MD: American–Israeli Cooperative Enterprise, 2001; revised and updated 2002. Available online as on the website of the Jewish Virtual Library, accessed 16 August 2008 at http://www.jewishvirtuallibrary.org/jsource/myths/mftoc.html; Frank Gervasi, *The Case for Israel*, foreword by Abba Eban, New York: Viking Press, 1967; Jacob A. Rubin, *True and False about Israel*, New York: Herzl Press, for the American Zionist Federation, 1972; Samuel Katz, *Battleground: Fact and Fantasy in Palestine*, updated and expanded ed., New York / Jerusalem: Steimatzky, 1985; "Zionist Mythinformation: The PLO Replies," Ottawa, Canada: Palestine Information Office, n.d. [c. 1980]; Tom Naylor, "Palestine & Zionism: Ten Myths," *This Magazine*, December 1981– January 1982; *Know the Facts: A Historical Guide to the Arab–Israeli Conflict*, ed. David Niv, Jerusalem: Department of Education and Culture, World Zionist Organization, 1985; John Quigley, *The Case for Palestine: An International Law Perspective*, rev. and updated ed., Durham, NC / London: Duke University Press, 2005; Alan Dershowitz, *The Case for Israel*, New York: John Wiley, 2003.

3 For examples of the latter, see procon.org's page on this conflict at http://israelipalestinian.procon.org/ and "bitterlemons.org Palestinian–Israeli Crossfire" at http://www.bitterlemons.org/.

4 A mainstream pro-Israeli website is Myths & Facts, available online at the "Jewish Virtual Library" at http://www.jewishvirtuallibrary.org/jsource/myths/mftoc.html. Extremely militant is the Kahanist "Masada 2000," online at http://www.masada2000.org. Leading pro-Palestinian websites include Electronic Intifada available online at http://electronicintifada.net/ and Palestine Remembered available online at http://www.palestineremembered.com.

5 David Matz, "Reconstructing Camp David," *Negotiation Journal* 22:1 (Jan 2006), 89–103.

6 Compare, for example, the pro-Palestinian "Faculty for Israeli–Palestinian Peace" online at http://www.ffipp.org with the pro-Israeli "Scholars for Peace in the Middle East" online at http://www.spme.net. Other pro-Israeli websites drawing on academics are the Canadian Institute for Jewish Research, online at http://www.isranet.org, and Professors for a Strong Israel, at http://www.professors.org.il.

7 Sylvia G. Haim, " 'The Arab Awakening': A Source for the Historian?" *Die Welt des Islams*, n.s. vol. II (1953), 248–9.

8 *Encyclopedia of the Palestinians*, rev. ed., ed. Philip Mattar, New York: Facts on File, 2005, xv.

9   Yehuda Lukacs and Abdalla M. Battah, eds., *The Arab–Israeli Conflict: Two Decades of Change*, Boulder, CO / London: Westview Press, 1988, 3.

10 For a more sanguine view, see Bernard Wasserstein, *Israelis and Palestinians: Why Do They Fight? Can They Stop?* 3rd ed., New Haven, CT / London: Yale University Press / London: Profile Books, 2008, 3.

11 Accessed online 16 August 2008 at http://www.campus-watch.org. This website is modeled on mostly pro-Israel "media-watch" operations dedicated to exposing what they consider to be biased media coverage of the conflict. See also the mainstream CAMERA (Committee for Accurate Middle East Reporting in America), online at http://www.camera.org, and the "SHIT List" of "Self-Hating and/or Israel Threatening" Jews individuals posted at the fringe website http://www.masada2000.org/shit-list.html. For a critique of Campus-Watch, see http://electronicintifada.net/v2/article732.shtml accessed online 16 August 2008.

12 Interested readers can attempt to follow the intricacies of three such cases by visiting the personal websites of Norman Finkelstein, on denial of tenure (Summer 2007), accessed online 16 August 2008 at http://www.norman-finkelstein.com/article.php?pg=11&ar=1070; on Joseph Massad, see "Special Document" dossier in *Journal of Palestine Studies* 34:2 (Winter 2005), 70–84, and 34:4 (Summer 2005), 75–107; undated petition at http://www.petitiononline.com/jmassad/petition.html and critique at http://camera.org/index.asp?x_context=2&x_outlet=118&x_article=874, both accessed online 16 August 2008; See Nadia El-Haj and Jane Kramer, "The Petition: Israel, Palestine, and a Tenure Battle at Barnard," *The New Yorker*, 14 April 2008, 50–9 (abstract online at http://www.newyorker.com/reporting/2008/04/14/080414fa_fact_kramer); see also http://www.muzzlewatch.com/?p=227, and http://www.zionism-israel.com/log/archives/00000443.html.

13 On the problems and limits of objectivity, see, e.g., Joyce Appleby, Lynn Hunt, and Margaret Jacob, *Telling the Truth about History*, New York / London: W. W. Norton, 1994, ch. 7; Richard J. Evans, *In Defense of History*, London / New York: W. W. Norton, 1999, ch. 8.

14 David Shulman, *Dark Hope: Working for Peace in Israel and Palestine*, Chicago: University of Chicago Press, 2007, 12.

15 Avi Shlaim, "The Debate about 1948," in *The Israel/Palestine Question*, ed. Ilan Pappé, London / New York: Routledge, 1999, 177.

16 Benny Morris, "Politics by Other Means," *The New Republic*, 22 March 2004.

17 Benny Morris, "Peace? No Chance," *The Guardian*, 21 February 2002; Benny Morris, An Interview with Ehud Barak, "Camp David and After: An Exchange," *New York Review of Books* 49:10 (13 June 2002); Benny Morris and Ehud Barak, "Camp David and After—Continued," *New York Review of Books* 49:11 (27 June 2002), accessed 15 September 2008 at http://www.nybooks.com/articles/15501 and http://www.nybooks.com/articles/15540.

18 Avi Shlaim, "A Betrayal of History," *The Guardian*, 22 February 2002. For Arab responses to Morris's so-called about-face, see Mustafa Kabha,

"A Palestinian Look at the New Historians and Post-Zionism in Israel," in *Making Israel*, ed. Benny Morris, Ann Arbor: University of Michigan Press, 2007, 310–12.

19 Ari Shavit, "Survival of the Fittest" (interview with Benny Morris), *Ha-Aretz*, 9 January 2004.

20 Christopher Farah, "The Arabs Are After Our Blood" (interview with Benny Morris), www.salon.com, 23 January 2004.

21 E.g., "immensely well informed, thorough, careful in the use of evidence, thoughtful and thought-provoking," Avi Shlaim, "No Sentiments in War," *The Guardian*, 31 May 2008, accessed online 17 August 2008 at http://www.theguardian.co.uk; Roane Carey, "Dr. Benny and Mr. Morris: The Historian and the Twisted Politics of Expulsion," *CounterPunch* 19–20 July 2008, accessed 23 July 2008 at http://www.counterpunch.org/carey07192008.html. Cf. Benny Morris, *1948: A History of the First Arab–Israeli War*, New Haven, CT: Yale University Press, 2008.

22 Ilan Pappé, *Britain and the Arab–Israeli Conflict, 1948–51*, London: Macmillan Press / St. Antony's College, 1988.

23 Ilan Pappé, *A History of Modern Palestine: One Land, Two Peoples*, 2nd ed., Cambridge: Cambridge University Press, 2006, 11–12. For an earlier (1993) declaration of Pappé's support of the Palestinian cause in the prestigious Hebrew periodical *Teoria u-Vikoret*, see Mordechai Bar-On, "Historiography as an Educational Project: The Historians' Debate in Israel and the Middle East Peace Process," in *The Middle East Peace Process: Interdisciplinary Perspectives*, ed. Ilan Peleg, Albany: State University of New York Press, 1998, 31.

24 See also Ted Swedenburg's similar profession of solidarity with the Palestinians and their resistance, and his confession that his study of the 1936–1939 revolt "required an effort to unlearn an academic training in anthropology and history that enjoins one to uncover the objective truth." Ted Swedenburg, *Memories of Revolt: The 1936–1939 Rebellion and the Palestinian National Past*, Fayetteville: University of Arkansas Press, 2003, xxviii.

25 Ilan Pappé, *The Ethnic Cleansing of Palestine*, Oxford: Oneworld Publications, 2006.

26 Jimmy Carter, *Palestine: Peace not Apartheid*, New York: Simon and Schuster, 2007.

27 Lisa Taraki, "The Excessive Charms of the Internet," *International Journal of Middle East Studies* 39:4 (November 2007), 528.

28 Northrop Frye, "The Knowledge of Good and Evil," in N. Frye, Stuart Hampshire, and Conor Cruise O'Brien, *The Morality of Scholarship*, ed. Max Black, Ithaca, NY: Cornell University Press, 1967, 22.

29 Sara Roy, "Humanism, Scholarship, and Politics: Writing on the Palestinian–Israeli Conflict," *Journal of Palestine Studies* XXXVI:2 (Winter 2007), 54–65.

30 For a defense of "positivist" history and an effective critique of the postmodern, relativist approach, see, e.g., Appleby, Hunt, and Jacob, *Telling the Truth about History*, and Evans, *In Defense of History*.

31 Northrop Frye, "The Knowledge of Good and Evil," in Frye et al., *The Morality of Scholarship*, 28.

32 Derek Penslar, *Israel in History. The Jewish State in Comparative Perspective*, London / New York: Routledge, 2007, 23.

33 Bar-On, "Historiography as an Educational Project," 23.

34 These scholars continue to be vilified by right-wing and centrist Israelis and Jews. See, e.g., Martin Sherman, "Post-Zionism's Fatal Flaw," *YNet News*, 11 August 2008, accessed online 28 August 2008 at http://www.ynetnews. com/articles/0,7340,L-3580743,00.html.

35 For a broad discussion of the Israeli cultural and political treatment of heroes and heroism in the early 1990s, see Calev Ben-David, "Heroes under Attack," *The Jerusalem Report*, 29 December 1994, 12–17.

36 On the new historians and the academic and public debates they aroused, see Aharon Megged, "The Israeli Suicide Drive," *Ha-Aretz* (Supplement), 10 June 1994, 27f.; *History and Memory: Studies in Representation of the Past* 7:1 (Spring/Summer 1995), *Israeli Historiography Revisited*, ed. Gulie Ne'eman Arad; Avi Shlaim, "The Debate about 1948," *International Journal of Middle East Studies* 27 (August 1995), 287–304; Penslar, *Israel in History*, chs. 1–2; Bar-On, "Historiography as an Educational Project," 21–38; Joseph Heller, *The Birth of Israel, 1945–1949: Ben-Gurion and His Critics*, Gainesville, etc.: University Press of Florida, 2000, 295–307; *Making Israel*, ed. Benny Morris, Ann Arbor: University of Michigan Press, 2007. A particularly hostile attack is Efraim Karsh, *Fabricating Israeli History: The 'New Historians'*, 2nd rev. ed., London: Frank Cass, 2000.

37 For a survey of Palestinian and Arab responses to Israel's new historians, see Kabha, "A Palestinian Look," 299–318.

38 For thoughtful considerations of some of the difficulties of counterfactual analysis, see I. William Zartman, *Cowardly Lions: Missed Opportunities to Prevent Deadly Conflict and State Collapse*, Boulder, CO / London: Lynne Rienner, 2005, 3–5; Mordechai Bar-On, "Conflicting Narratives or Narratives of a Conflict: Can the Zionist and Palestinian Narrative of the 1948 War Be Bridged?" in *Israeli and Palestinian Narratives of Conflict: History's Double Helix*, ed. Robert I. Rotberg, Bloomington / Indianapolis: Indiana University Press, 2006, 157–8; Zeev Maoz, *Defending the Holy Land: A Critical Analysis of Israel's Security and Foreign Policy*, Ann Arbor: University of Michigan Press, 2006, 387–8.

39 For an example of a study that explores seven interrelated factors affecting success and failure, see Laura Zittrain Eisenberg and Neil Caplan, *Negotiating Arab–Israeli Peace: Patterns, Problems, Possibilities*, Bloomington / Indianapolis: Indiana University Press, 1998. For a political scientist's sharp critique of Israeli decision-making using a multifactor analysis over a range of missed opportunities, see Maoz, *Defending the Holy Land*, ch. 10.

40 For examples of this approach, see Jerome Slater, "What Went Wrong? The Collapse of the Palestinian–Israeli Peace Process," *Political Science Quarterly* 116:2 (Summer 2001), 171–99, and "Lost Opportunities for Peace in the

Arab–Israeli Conflict: Israel and Syria, 1948–2001," *International Security* 27:1 (Summer 2002), 79–106.

41 Avi Shlaim, *Collusion across the Jordan: King Abdullah, the Zionist Movement, and the Partition of Palestine*, Oxford: Clarendon Press, 1988; Avi Shlaim, *The Iron Wall: Israel and the Arab World*, London: Allen Lane / Penguin Press, 2000, 47–53. For a critique see Neil Caplan, "Zionism and the Arabs: Another Look at the 'New' Historiography" (review essay), *Journal of Contemporary History* 36:2 (April 2001), 356–60.

42 Shlaim, *Iron Wall*; Flapan, *Birth of Israel*, 201–32; Tom Segev, *1949: The First Israelis*, New York / London: Free Press / Collier Macmillan, 1986, 34–40; Pappé, *Making*, chs. 7–9; Bar-On, "Historiography as an Educational Project," 30.

43 Don Peretz, *Israel and the Palestine Arabs*, Washington, DC: Middle East Institute, 1958; Rony E. Gabbay, *A Political Study of the Arab-Jewish Conflict: The Arab Refugee Problem (A Case Study)*, Genève: Librairie E. Droz [Paris: Librairie Minard], 1959; Aharon Cohen, *Israel and the Arab World*, New York: Funk and Wagnalls, 1970 [translation of Hebrew work published in 1964]; Simha Flapan, *Zionism and the Palestinians*, New York: Barnes and Noble / London: Croom Helm, 1979.

44 See, e.g., Neil Caplan, *Futile Diplomacy*, vol. I: *Early Arab–Zionist Negotiation Attempts, 1913–1931*, London: Frank Cass, 1983, 113–14, 192, 201; Cohen, *Israel and the Arab World*; Flapan, *Zionism and the Palestinians*; *Dissenter in Zion: From the Writings of Judah L. Magnes*, ed. Arthur A. Goren, Cambridge, MA / London: Harvard University Press, 1982.

45 E.g., Benjamin Netanyahu, *A Durable Peace: Israel and Its Place among the Nations*, rev. ed., New York: Warner Books, 2000, 48–9 and Appendix A (405–7), B (409–10). For a skeptical view, see A. L. Tibawi, "T. E. Lawrence, Faisal and Weizmann: The 1919 Attempt to Secure an Arab Balfour Declaration," *Royal Central Asian Journal* 56:2 (June 1969), 156–63. For an overview, see Neil Caplan, "Faisal Ibn Husain and the Zionists: A Re-examination with Documents," *International History Review* V:4 (November 1983), 561–614.

46 Caplan, *Futile Diplomacy*, vols. I–II, *passim*.

47 Itamar Rabinovich, *The Road Not Taken: Early Arab–Israeli Negotiations*, New York / Oxford: Oxford University Press, 1991. The Hebrew version, *ha-Shalom she-Hamak (The Peace that Slipped Away)*, had been published earlier that year.

48 Avi Shlaim, "Husni Za'im and the Plan to Resettle Palestinian Refugees," *Journal of Palestine Studies* 15:4 (Summer 1986), 68–80.

49 For another example of a careful case study, see Mordechai Gazit, "Egypt and Israel—Was There a Peace Opportunity Missed in 1971?" *Journal of Contemporary History* 32:1 (January 1997), 97–115.

50 For a critical discussion, see Maoz, *Defending the Holy Land*, 2006, ch. 10 ("Never Missing an Opportunity to Miss an Opportunity: The Israeli Non-policy of Peace in the Middle East"). See also Khalidi, *Iron Cage*, 291 (n. 2).

51 Dan Schueftan, "Historic Compromise and Historic Justice," in "The 1937 Peel Report revisited," 14 January 2008, edition 2, bitterlemons.org

Palestinian–Israeli Crossfire, accessed online on 25 August 2008 at http://www.bitterlemons.org/previous/bl140108ed02.html.

52 For a recent debate among Palestinian and Israeli academics, see *Shared Histories: A Palestinian–Israeli Dialogue*, eds. Paul Scham, Walid Salem, and Benjamin Pogrund, Walnut Creek, CA: Left Coast Press, 2005, 177–204.

53 For a recent re-examination of the unworkability of the Peel recommendations, see Wasserstein, *Israelis and Palestinians*, 109–14.

54 Philip Mattar, unpublished ms., ch. 2. I am deeply grateful to Dr. Mattar for sharing his unpublished draft with me. Material and quotations in the following paragraphs are taken from this source. Khalidi raises similar counterfactual questions. See Khalidi, *Iron Cage*, 33–4, 44–6, 64, 118.

55 By refusing to seriously engage the British a year earlier, Palestinian leaders had also missed an important opportunity to influence the wording of the June 1922 Churchill White Paper, the most important British policy paper on Palestine between 1917 and 1937. See also Yehoshua Porath, *The Emergence of the Palestinian Arab National Movement, 1918–1929*, London: Frank Cass, 1974, 144–6.

56 Nasser Eddine Nashashibi, *Jerusalem's Other Voice: Ragheb Nashashibi and Moderation in Palestinian Politics, 1920–1948*, Exeter: Ithaca Press, 1990, esp. ch. 9.

57 Khalidi, *Iron Cage*, 118–20.

58 On the problems of Palestinian primary written and oral sources, see, e.g., Saleh Abdel-Jawad, "The Arab and Palestinian Narratives of the 1948 War," in Rotberg, *Israeli and Palestinian Narratives of Conflict*, 72–114, esp. 95–103; Khalidi, *Iron Cage*, xxxv–xxxviii; Adel Yahya, Aziz Haider, and Bernard Sabella, in Scham et al., *Shared Histories*, 232–41, 265; Mattar, *Encyclopedia of the Palestinians*, xiv–xv.

59 Ilan Pappé, "Introduction: New Historical Orientations in the Research on the Palestine Question," in *The Israel/Palestine Question*, ed. Ilan Pappé, London / New York: Routledge, 1999, 2–3.

60 Adel Yahya, in Scham et al., *Shared Histories*, 232.

61 W. Cantwell Smith, *Islam in Modern History*, Princeton, NJ: Princeton University Press, 1957, quoted in *Arab Nationalism: An Anthology*, ed. with an introduction by Sylvia G. Haim, Berkeley / Los Angeles: University of California Press, 1962, 38 n. 83. See also Avraham Sela, "Arab Historiography of the 1948 War: The Quest for Legitimacy," in *New Perspectives on Israeli History: The Early Years of the State*, ed. Laurence J. Silberstein, New York: New York University Press, 1991, 124–54.

62 Khalidi, *Iron Cage*, XXXIV. See also Kabha, "A Palestinian Look," 301, 313–14.

63 Zakaria Mohammed, "New Palestinian Historians?" *al-Ayyam*, 4 November 1999, quoted in Yaacov Lozowick, *Right to Exist: A Moral Defense of Israel's Wars*, New York, etc.: Doubleday, 2003, 82–3. See also the views of Wageh Kawthrani and Imad Abed al-Ghani, discussed in Kabha, "A Palestinian Look," 307, 313.

64 Critiques of Palestinian textbooks were undertaken by Palestinian Media Watch, accessed online 21 August 2008 at http://www.pmw.org.il/, and the Center for Monitoring the Impact of Peace (CMIP), now known as the Institute for Monitoring Peace and Cultural Tolerance in School Education (IMPACT-SE), accessed online 16 August 2008 at http://www.impact-se.org/. For some of the interesting literature on the textbooks controversies, see Elie Podeh, "History and Memory in the Israeli Educational System: The Portrayal of the Arab–Israeli Conflict in History Textbooks (1948–2000)," *History and Memory* 12 (2000), 65–100, esp. 89–91; Nathan J. Brown, *Palestinian Politics after the Oslo Accords: Resuming Arab Palestine*, Berkeley: University of California Press, 2003, ch. 6; Nathan J. Brown, "Contesting National Identity in Palestinian Education," in Rotberg, *Israeli and Palestinian Narratives of Conflict*, 225–43; Eyal Naveh, "The Dynamics of Identity Construction in Israel through Education in History," in Rotberg, *Israeli and Palestinian Narratives of Conflict*, 244–70; Jennifer Miller, *Inheriting the Holy Land: An American's Search for Hope in the Middle East*, New York: Ballantine Books, 2005, 45–68.

65 See Dan Bar-On and Sami Adwan, "The Psychology of Better Dialogue between Two Separate but Interdependent Narratives," in Rotberg, *Israeli and Palestinian Narratives of Conflict*, 205–24. The Peace Research Institute in the Middle East (PRIME) website is at http://vispo.com/PRIME/.

66 The present author attended these seminars. A preliminary report was authored by Deborah L. West, *Myth and Narrative in the Israeli–Palestinian Conflict*, Cambridge, MA: World Peace Foundation [WPF Report #34], 2003. A collection of papers from these conferences was edited and introduced by Robert I. Rotberg as *Israeli and Palestinian Narratives of Conflict*.

67 Nadim N. Rouhana, "Zionism's Encounter with the Palestinians: The Dynamics of Force, Fear, and Extremism," in Rotberg, *Israeli and Palestinian Narratives of Conflict*, 115–41.

68 Bar-On, "Conflicting Narratives," 153. His response to Rouhana is given on pages 143–50.

69 Said's views are briefly discussed in Kabha, "A Palestinian Look," 314–15.

70 Khalidi, *Iron Cage*, xxxiii–xxxiv.

71 E.g., Scham et al., *Shared Histories*. See the excellent review essay by Ned Lazarus, "Making Peace with the Duel of Narratives: Dual-Narrative Texts for Teaching the Israeli–Palestinian Conflict," *Israel Studies Forum* 23:1 (Summer 2008), 107–24.

72 Not every observer shares my pessimistic assessment. See, e.g., Wasserstein, *Israelis and Palestinians*, 3.

73 Khalidi, *Iron Cage*, xxxiv.

12

Confronting the Obstacles

As we enter the second decade of the 21st century, the latest incarnations of the original Zionist–Palestinian–Arab conflict and successor Israeli–Arab dispute continue to withstand efforts to resolve them. The protracted[1] and intractable nature of these intertwined struggles suggests that they may never be definitively resolved through compromise arrangements, splitting of differences, and removal of perceived injustices. There may be, as I suggested in Chapter 1, only ways to manage the conflict by containing the festering grievances at a low and tolerable level. Even those working for such a limited aim cannot guarantee that the conflict will not explode into new local, regional, or international crises, making crisis-prevention strategies relevant and necessary to avert future explosions into overt violence.[2]

How can we best confront the longstanding obstacles to reconciliation and peace between the parties? And how can we best deal with the related obstacles to our own ability—as students, observers, or activists—to present and understand the contested histories of Israelis and Palestinians in a useful way?

Issues in Dispute: Drawing upon the Past, Imagining the Future

At any given moment, a summary of the issues separating Israelis and Palestinians can take on different forms. At the time of writing (2009), a list can be handily created by drawing on the unresolved permanent status issues as outlined in the unconsummated 1993 Oslo Accords:

- achieving and maintaining a real and solid commitment from all parties to both Palestinian and Israeli statehood, through mutual recognition;
- determination of the borders between the state of Israel and the future independent state of Palestine in (what percent of?) the West Bank and Gaza, and completing a schedule of withdrawal of Israeli forces from areas to be assigned to Palestine;
- the future of Jewish settlements built in the West Bank since 1967: which will stay, in exchange for what land swaps, and which will be evacuated?
- security arrangements for the two future neighboring states;
- the return and/or compensation of Palestinian refugees who were expelled or fled in the wars of 1948 and 1967. How many will return to Palestine, how many to Israel?—And what of Israel's claim, not recognized by the Palestinians, to factor in reciprocal consideration of Jews who were forced to leave Arab countries in periods of war?
- the future of Jerusalem, claimed as national capital by both Israel and the Palestinians and regarded as a holy city to hundreds of millions of Muslims, Christians, and Jews. Can it be a shared, or a divided, city? Under whose sovereignty?

When one reviews the essential minimum demands ("red lines") and interests of the main parties, along with their often surprising ability to withstand pressure to alter these minimum demands, the conflict may appear intractable. Yet the testimony of the negotiators at Taba in January 2001 and the participants in the October 2003 Geneva Initiative suggests that, through clever formulations and a true spirit of compromise, a bridging of almost all the gaps may yet be within reach.[3]

Meanwhile, on a daily basis, the unresolved conflict manifests itself not only in sporadic speculations about possible diplomatic manoeuvres but, on a more regular basis, in violent or oppressive forms. Israeli civilians are killed or wounded by rocket fire and terrorist attacks by Palestinians, and Palestinian civilians are killed and wounded in operations by Israeli forces. West Bank residents are also increasingly subject to violence committed by settler thugs.[4] Palestinians living under Israeli occupation suffer human rights abuses and endure hardships and humiliations, most visibly at checkpoints. Protest rallies and court action periodically challenge the legitimacy of the separation barrier or security wall erected by Israelis between the two populations and the legality of expropriations of Palestinian land for the purpose. Likewise, Palestinian leaders issue diplomatic protests over the continued building of new Jewish settlements and expansion of existing ones in areas that are ostensibly to be the subject of negotiation between the parties whenever stalled talks do resume.

Drawing on the past and retracing the evolution of earlier forms of the same issues (Chapters 3–10) does not, unfortunately, provide us with easy lessons for how to move Palestinians and Israelis closer towards peace or reconciliation. Drawing upon the contested histories of the parties can, however, enable contemporary observers to appreciate the complexity of these disputed issues, along with the depth of feelings and insecurities felt by all the protagonists. For pragmatic solution-seekers, such appreciation of past difficulties may translate into a rough guide to "What *Won't* Work" rather than "What *Will* Work." Solution-oriented analysts who draw on the past wisely will also realize the limits of making "*if-only*" recommendations calling for the better behavior of one or more of the protagonists. All in all, drawing on the past can be most helpful in terms of preventing us from underestimating the powerful obstacles that need to be confronted if real progress towards a solution is to be made.

Thinking ahead to "the shape of the future,"[5] we should not imagine that there is much room for inventing anything radically new, although many will continue to invoke the cliché, "Let's think outside the box." People engaging in such discussions today will be drawing, knowingly or unknowingly, on a wealth of previously proposed plans and ideas. Our record of the contested histories (Chapters 3–10) includes an abundance of not only violent encounters but also peace efforts, mostly failed but some partially successful.

At the time of writing (2009), a number of political and intellectual figures are engaging in philosophical, political, and demographic discussions about whether the futures for Israelis and Palestinians would be best served by a *two-state* solution (separation, partition) or by living under an appropriate constitutional régime within a *single* (binational or other) state.[6] Apart from the doomsday scenario wherein one party completely wipes out the other, these are essentially the only choices available to the protagonists. Given recent negotiating experiences (the near-miss at Taba; the Roadmap; the Saudi initiative; the Geneva Initiative), two states for two nations, however imperfect, seems to promise a glimmer of hope, despite a resurgence in predictions of the demise of this option. Whatever their personal preferences, those engaged in imagining the shape of the future will be better informed—and ultimately more effective in promoting their preferred solution—by appropriately drawing on the plans and positions already considered in the past, especially the partition and binationalist plans mooted during the 1930s and 1940s.[7]

Righteous Victimhood

The list of issues given above offers only a partial sense of what obstacles need to be confronted before expecting movement from the lingering stalemate towards some kind of eventual solution. As resistant as they have been to resolution, these are essentially *tangible* issues capable of being negotiated. Yet above and beyond these tangible issues lie a number of *existential* and *intangible* obstacles that may be more difficult to overcome.

The interlacing of both tangible and intangible obstacles can be seen in a review of the eleven *core arguments* that we have highlighted over the course of the conflict's history. These are still essentially unresolved, both among the parties themselves and among those who write and comment on the conflict:

1   Who was there first, and whose land was it to begin with?

2   Was the Zionist solution to the Jewish question a Jewish variant of national revivals and struggles for liberation? Or was Zionism part of an aggressive colonialist expansion into the Middle East, whose raison d'être was to exploit, dispossess, or overpower the indigenous population?

3   Did the British create or aggravate the conflict between Palestinian Arabs and Zionist Jews by unduly favoring one party over the other?

4   Were the protests and demands of Palestinian leaders legitimate expressions of an authentic Palestinian national feeling?

5   Did Zionism bring harm or benefit to the indigenous population of Palestine and the region?

6   Is the [Palestinians'] [Arabs'] [Zionists'] [Israelis'] resort to violence justified, or is it to be condemned?

7   What linkage, if any, should be made between the destruction of European Jewry during the Holocaust and the question of who should rule Palestine/Israel?

8   Was UNGA Resolution 181 (Partition) a legitimate exercise of the authority of the United Nations in international law, and were the Arab states and the Palestinians wise to reject it?

9   How did Palestinians become refugees in 1948–1949? And why did they remain refugees for so long?

10 Is the land conquered by Israel in June 1967 on the West Bank of the Jordan to be considered "occupied territory," and does Israel have the right to build Jewish settlements there?

11 What are the true intentions of the Palestinians and the PLO: To eliminate the Jewish state of Israel and replace it with an Arab state of Palestine? Or to create a Palestinian Arab state in part of historic Palestine, to coexist alongside an Israeli Jewish state?

By conceptualizing the contested histories of Israelis and Palestinians in terms of this series of interlocking questions, we get a sharper sense of the obstacles that must be confronted if ever there is to be a resolution to this dispute. The cumulative result of these eleven "dead-ends" is what makes the Arab–Israeli conflict such a protracted and perhaps insoluble dispute.

A major attitudinal obstacle underpinning all the arguments on the above list is the tendency of both parties to deflect responsibility onto the other as the root cause of their misfortunes. Israelis and Palestinians are locked into viewing themselves as the victims of the other—not just victims, but (in Benny Morris' apt phrase) *righteous* victims. This mindset I consider as the main obstacle to peace and reconciliation; disarming it or reducing its impact is an essential prerequisite to unblocking deadlocks on a whole range of specific issues.

It may not be possible to break out completely of the impasse caused by the parties' interlinked perceptions of being each other's victims. As Israeli peace activist and novelist Amos Oz admits, "even when this conflict is history, there will still be bitter disagreement ... [a]nd neither of the parties will ever give up its claim to victimhood." This, he believes, is something that the parties will simply have to live with and work around.[8] In his writings and speeches Oz suggests that it might be helpful to view both protagonists as fellow-victims of a third-party victimizer, namely, Christian Europe:

> the Arabs [were victimized] through colonialism, imperialism, oppression and exploitation, while the Jews have been the victims of discrimination, pogroms, expulsions and, ultimately, mass murder .... [S]ome of the worst conflicts develop between victims of the same oppressors: two children of the same cruel parent do not necessarily love each other. They often see in each other the image of their past oppressor. So it is, to some extent, between Israelis and Arabs: the Arabs fail to see us as a bunch of survivors. They see in us a nightmarish extension of the oppressing colonising Europeans. We Israelis often look at Arabs not as fellow victims but as an incarnation of our past oppressors: Cossacks, pogrom-makers, Nazis who have grown moustaches and wrapped themselves in kaffiyehs, but who are still in the usual business of cutting Jewish throats.[9]

An important component of each party's sense of victimization is its profound sense of insecurity. Those involved in dialogue attempts realize the essential need to discover how to transcend one's *own* fears and insecurities in order to be able to empathize with the *other*'s equally authentic feelings of vulnerability. We saw this vividly in Chapter 6 when we juxtaposed the impacts of the *shoah* and the *nakba* on Israeli Jews and Palestinian Arabs.

One of the first things that struck Marwan Muasher, Jordan's first Ambassador to Israel, when he took up his post in the mid-1990s was

> the deep sense of insecurity that the average Israeli felt. I had grown up in an Arab society that believed its security to be under constant threat from a regional power, a huge military machine that had resulted in the loss of Palestine, a lingering refugee problem, and the occupation of land belonging to three Arab states. Not until I went to Israel did I discover that the feeling was mutual. Israelis, too, felt a deep sense of insecurity from being in the middle of a "hostile" neighborhood. Each side shares a genuine fear about the other and harbors a profound sense that its personal and existential security is threatened by the other. Both sides also share another thing: an almost total lack of understanding of the depth of the insecurity they feel about each other.[10]

Equally striking revelations greet Israelis who have the opportunity to live with Palestinians and Arabs.

In some ways, the feelings of being victims may not be perfectly symmetrical. Palestinians may feel victimized and aggrieved by what they consider to be injustices perpetrated on them while third-parties continue to sympathize more with their enemies and oppressors. The Israeli sense of victimhood may be more connected to a deep Jewish and existential angst—a fear of annihilation, feeling at times that "the whole world is against us." Such pervasive, almost paranoiac, fears effectively prevent Israelis from perceiving Palestinian anger and violence as legitimate expressions of their resistance to living under occupation, or their struggle for their own state. Winning a series of wars without winning true peace has fostered among many Israelis a sense of despair and cynicism. Often aided by mantras developed by self-serving political leaders, people convince themselves that the problem exists because there is no one to talk to on the other side,[11] and that, for the Israelis, *"ein breira"*—there is "no choice" but to fight the Arabs because they won't rest until they destroy Israel.

Many Palestinians, overwhelmed by their defeats, dispersion, and dispossession at the hands of powerful Israelis, are understandably unable to empathize with their enemy's claims to feelings of vulnerability. Many Palestinians feel justified in their resort to force and violence in their attempts to regain their lost homeland or resist occupation. They also labor under a sense of abandonment, reinforced by seeing their claims and complaints endorsed rhetorically by the international community while being ignored in practice by a strong Israel, backed by Western powers and world Jewry. As preposterous as their belief may appear to Israelis, many Palestinians and Arabs genuinely believe that recent history proves that Israeli leaders are really intent on ethnically cleansing the land of its original Palestinian-Arab inhabitants and expanding borders to make room for more Jews, and that all Israeli expressions of a desire for peace are deception.

It is hard to break out of these reciprocal images of and attitudes towards the other. Deadlocked Israelis and Palestinians, as righteous victims, present their claims and dismiss the other party's counterclaims in a kind of vicious circle of closed logic that would need to be broken across a whole range of issues. In extreme form, each side seems to be saying: "The other party does not have a case; our party's position is irrefutable. The other party's narrative is totally propaganda. There is nothing to discuss. Ergo, let the conflict continue until our side ultimately wins—however long that takes."[12]

Partial breakthroughs may become possible only when this closed-ended mentality shows some opening, as when at least one party says, however tentatively: "OK, I accept that the other party *may* have a case on some selected grievances. The other party's narrative does contain some valid points. But it is still warped by self-serving propaganda and does not nullify the truth of our inherently more authentic narrative. There may be room to discuss some aspects of the conflict, however cautiously, if the other side shows an openness to change its views."

Finally, people who are most ready for reconciliation might have evolved their thinking a bit further, to be able to say: "The other party's narrative is legitimate, but it is different from ours. We each need to learn more about the other's narrative with an open mind, however uncomfortable that makes us feel. Both narratives may contain errors and misunderstandings, but these can be reduced or eliminated. We need to undertake this together by engaging in respectful and empathetic dialogue about our two conflicting narratives." Any movement towards achieving a measure of reconciliation would require negotiators, opinion leaders, and political leaders on both sides to move towards the latter mode of thinking, which has become popular in dialogue groups.

But such attitudinal transformations are not easily arrived at, and require extremely difficult (to some, unthinkable) revisions to their people's basic beliefs. Accepting the legitimacy of major parts of the other party's narrative would involve the extremely unsettling possibility that the existence, rights, and entitlements of one's own side may not be as valid as once believed. It would involve accepting blame and responsibility for causing harm or injustice to the other party, reversing generations of firm belief that one's side had been blameless.

Any effort directed towards clarifying and redefining the causes of each party's sense of being the victim of the other side is always a worthwhile step towards preparing the parties for eventual reconciliation. Unfortunately, it seems difficult to conclude, on the basis of the historical record and current sentiment, that the two sides will easily overcome their obsession with their respective exclusive claims to victimhood, or that the parties are coming close to acknowledging their share of responsibility for past errors committed or traumas inflicted on the other.

In any case, the conflict on the ground would need to subside and remain quiescent for an extended period—an effective truce, whether planned or accidental—before people are able to even consider making the difficult mental leaps described above. Unfortunately, the history of underlying tensions has shown that violence can and does erupt at any time, often breaking fragile periods of quiet and spoiling ongoing grass-roots or other efforts at lowering mistrust and encouraging mutual understanding.

Obstacles to Understanding the Conflict

Our understanding of the issues in dispute and the parties' competing narratives is only one dimension of the challenge we face in trying to understand the conflict. Our efforts can be enhanced—or hindered—by the ways we choose to study or present the issues. As we have seen in Chapter 11, there are a number of layers that academics and other observers sometimes superimpose, unhelpfully, onto the contested histories in the ways they choose to present the conflict. Rather than clarifying the issues, they can introduce distortions and confusion, adding further obstacles to our ability to understand the conflict.

The following is a short checklist of things to avoid if one is to focus one's attention most usefully on the contested histories of Arabs, Israelis, and Palestinians with a view to better understanding the current unresolved conflict.

1 Avoid investing in trying to win "no-win" arguments

Respecting and reflecting the parties' own parallel expressions of realism and pessimism, the treatment of the origins and evolution of today's Arab–Israel conflict in Chapters 3–10 has highlighted a series of eleven unresolved, and sometimes interlocking, deadlocks (core arguments). While readers are free to speculate on how past deadlocks might have been broken by seizing upon, rather than missing, opportunities (point 2 below), I believe that most of these eleven designated core arguments are essentially irresolvable—whether on the ground or at the level of debate and argument.

Given the closed mindsets of the parties as righteous victims, one side's claims are almost impossible for the other to accept. Even with the benefit of the most skilful, eloquent, and passionate argument, there is virtually no chance that one party will convince the other to change its position. These are essentially "no-win" arguments also because supplying correct facts or different interpretations for those presumed erroneous, missing, or misguided will usually prove a thankless task; the argument will remain deadlocked between the contesting parties.

I am not suggesting that the parties themselves should, or could, abandon these arguments simply because they are futile. Rather, I am recommending that anyone wishing to truly understand the conflict should not, beyond learning about the details and depth of each side's passionately held positions on these core arguments, invest inordinate amounts of time and energy in trying to prove definitively which side's claim is correct or incorrect. While research into all aspects of these core arguments is useful and in some cases essential, research aimed specifically at trying *to win* or *resolve* those arguments may be superficially exciting and adversarially useful, but ultimately not very helpful.

2   Avoid using the missed opportunities approach for blaming the actors

As we saw in the previous chapter, there is much to be learned about the protagonists and the evolution of the conflict from careful counterfactual analysis. What should be avoided, however, is the temptation to resort to simplistic explanations of why peace or victory was not achieved. There is not much to be gained, outside of polemical or partisan advantage, from investing precious research time and energy in attempting to prove that Palestinians, Arabs, Israelis, or a particular leader should be blamed for missing opportunities for peace.

A realistic review and a nuanced understanding of possible missed opportunities can, however, be a useful tool in developing arguments over what went wrong in the past. For best results, research should not be agenda-driven. Each case should be studied using a full range of available sources and following rigorous scholarly methodology. Such historical analyses can, in turn, lead to useful discussions of whether to accept or reject contemporary proposals for peace, or serve as background for today's decision-makers facing other strategic choices.

3   Avoid overloading the circuits by superimposing issues of justice, truth, and recognition

It is difficult to exclude considerations of justice—redress of wrongs inflicted; the struggle against oppression, occupation, or denial of rights;

the longing for homeland; the search for security and against violence and terror—from discussions of the history of this conflict. There is no doubt that the quest for justice and recognition motivates the protagonists. Likewise, a quest for justice and truth also inspires many professionals involved in writing and commenting about the contested histories of Palestinians and Israelis.

We empower politicians and advocates, along with spiritual and community leaders, to guide us and act on our behalf in pursuing what we believe to be truth and justice. But it is not clear to me to what extent we should be looking to scholars and historians to do the same. When they do, academics invariably become involved in the machinery of advocacy on behalf of one of the parties they are studying. When historians include, or prioritize, such pursuits among their tasks in producing scholarship on the subject of the conflict, they run the risk of being obstructed, or diverted, from achieving other more professionally appropriate and achievable tasks (see above, page 226).

If scholars and academics espouse the narrative of one side or its quest for recognition or justice as being uniquely correct and worthy, their teaching and publications in the service of this cause will be doing a disservice to their students and readers who seek and deserve an impartial understanding of the parties' conflicting demands, attitudes, and self-views. Scholars, even while being empathetic, can do more for their students' and readers' understanding of the conflict by distancing themselves from—rather than adopting—the "us (good) versus them (evil)" mentality exhibited by the parties themselves.

The notion that academics should avoid promoting in their scholarly writing the narrative, quest for recognition, or grievances of one party against the other seems to me a laudable one—involving self-restraint which has unfortunately been in short supply in academia in recent years. There is ample room in public-political forums and in the media for advocacy on behalf of each party's quest for justice, recognition, or redress of grievances without also importing and embracing them as part of the scholar's mandate.

4   Avoid the perils of wishful thinking

Solution-oriented and humanitarian-minded people believe that this conflict must, one day, be resolved. Because it exacts such a human toll on its participants, they argue, it *simply cannot* go on. For many people, the purpose of writing, teaching, and learning about the conflict is a mightily practical one: to learn how best to bring it to an end. And people do need to believe that, somehow, there is a "light at the end of the tunnel."

These natural and noble instincts carry with them several pitfalls. One is the focus on what the observer believes *ought* to have been or *ought* to be, often misleadingly realized at the cost of accurately presenting what actually *was* and *is*. Humanitarian and peacemaking impulses are (happily) irrepressible, but they should not be pursued at the cost of an accurate reading of the contested histories of the parties—what *really* happened and how the parties *really* felt, acted, and reacted, however unpleasant that history and those realities may at times be.

Grass-roots activity for Israeli–Arab peace has always existed at modest levels, but has mushroomed in recent years. Especially during the optimistic period following the signing of the Oslo Accords in 1993, many new peacebuilding initiatives were undertaken by NGOs in Israel, Palestine, and abroad, aimed at overcoming fears and fostering people-to-people understanding and reconciliation.[13] To the extent that such efforts are well-grounded in an appreciation of the contested histories of Israelis and Palestinians, they will persist and spread, with the result of making a wider public more sensitive to positions and feelings of the other, and giving them an intelligent grasp of the gaps that need to be bridged.

With the collapse of the Camp David summit and the eruption of the al-Aqsa *intifada* in 2000, broad segments of the Palestinian and Israeli public, including some of the most dedicated fighters for peace and reconciliation, experienced shock and disillusionment. Yet the determination of peace activists to continue working for mutual understanding was expressed, as we saw in Chapter 10, in the Geneva Initiative launched in late 2003. The latter effort may be cited as a sound example of realistic idealism that successfully avoids the naïveté of wishful thinking, largely because it was the product of Israelis and Palestinians with recent hands-on negotiating experience.[14] In the broader sweep of the contested histories of Palestinians and Israelis, we can see that there has indeed been progress from the mutual boycott that prevailed until the 1980s towards mutual recognition and de-escalation of the conflict since 1991. Yet large gaps remain to be bridged.

Six Explanations

In my own efforts to understand and navigate the perplexities of the Arab–Israeli and Israel–Palestinian conflicts, I have attempted to catalogue the range of possible explanations that have been offered to account for how the Arab–Israel conflict started, and why it is so hard to resolve. The following six explanations are offered as a tool for summarizing and understanding the multiple ways in which the conflict has been presented by the protagonists, their supporters, historians, and interested students.[15]

1 Since ancient times, Jews and Arabs have been enemies and rivals, each party representing a different civilization, worldview, and religion that are (and always will be) at war with the other.
2 Since the late 1800s, Jews and Zionists pursued their goals of immigration into and settlement in Palestine aggressively, taking over the country without respecting the rights of the longstanding Arab residents of the area.
3 Palestinians/Arabs have been selfish and unreasonable in refusing to accept and make peace with the Jews and Zionists, refusing to recognize the historic right of the Jews to return to their ancient homeland.
4 Outside powers (imperialism—Britain, France, US, USSR)—wanting to control the Middle East region—have manipulated Jews and Arabs into mutual suspicion, hatred, and conflict for their own selfish ends.
5 Jews and Arabs hardly communicate with one another, and their conflict is based on misunderstandings, fears, and brainwashing (propaganda).
6 Jews and Arabs are locked into an unavoidable clash of two national groups competing for mastery over the same territory.

Each of the six explanations has its supporters, advocates, and believers. Each contains some factual truth, can be supported by a selective reading of the historical evidence, and each offers its believers some symbolic or ideological resonance.

Each of the six is also based on assumptions that apportion responsibility and blame differently. The first explanation, for example, reflects a cosmic perspective in which ordinary human beings (from whatever camp) are not really accountable, except perhaps to the extent that they do or do not fulfill the divine will as understood by the followers. Explanation #2 is a classic formulation of the Arab view of Zionism and Israel as colonial usurpers of Palestinian and Arab rights, while #3 reflects the Zionist/Israeli view that the Palestinians and Arabs bear most of the blame for the conflict. Explanation #4 shifts the blame away from both Arabs and Israelis onto outsiders, while #5 implies that only a few cynical leaders who engage in deliberate brainwashing are responsible.

In terms of solutions, each of the six can also be associated with recommending a type of proposed remedy to undo or diminish the damage caused by those who are to blame. People who subscribe to the first explanation will propose that the interlopers, however defined, simply be removed so that the divine promise of redemption can be executed for the creation of either a Jewish or an Islamic state in the disputed area. Those who hold to Explanation #2 would resolve the conflict by eliminating the offending intrusion of Zionism and restoring the disputed land to its Palestinian-Arab owners. Those who espouse Explanation #3 would expect Palestinian and Arab leaders to accept the reasonableness of sharing the disputed land by making room for Jews to exercise the right of return to their ancient homeland. Believers in Explanation #4 will argue that the conflict should be insulated from negative outside influences so as to allow the benefits of peace to be shared by peaceloving Israelis, Palestinians, and Arabs. Explanation #5 appeals to grass-roots activists who would rely on an alert and sensitive civil society to insist on enlightened policies from their designated leaders.

Despite the popularity of Explanation #4 in some circles (including conspiracy theorists), I believe that its contrary reformulation—viz., the *positive* role of outside powers—is merited by the historical record.[16] US and international intervention was what brought about the limited gains of Egyptian–Israeli peace (1977–1979) and the Israel–Palestine and Israel–Jordan breakthroughs following the Madrid Peace Conference and negotiations in the secret Oslo back-channel (1991–1993). As much as self-interested outside interference can be blamed for missing some opportunities, third-party intervention has equally (if not more) often helped to move the conflicting parties away from confrontation and towards consideration of a settlement. Given the existential nature of the core Israeli–Palestinian impasse and the deep-rootedness of their mutual enmity and mistrust, progress in the current decade towards near-breakthroughs would seem to have much expect from third-parties, whether international or regional: American, Jordanian, Egyptian, and the Arab League.

The premise on which this book has been built is, of course, that explanation #6 is the most credible of the six. The historical record over more than a century indicates an almost unbridgeable gap between the declared nationalist aspirations of Palestinian Arabs and Zionists/Israelis. The past 130 years are also full of examples illustrating the determination and ability of the both parties to stick to these irreconcilable national aims despite recurring suffering, losses, and setbacks.

To conclude, let us recall David Ben-Gurion's and Awni Abd al-Hadi's parallel hard-nosed recognition in 1919 and 1932 respectively of this clash of nationalisms (Chapter 1) as we reproduce the more recent views of Mordechai Bar-On, a soldier who fought in the 1948 war, subsequently served as Moshe Dayan's *chef de bureau* in the 1950s, and later became an academic and peace activist:

> The century-old conflict between the Zionist movement and the Arab national movement is neither the result of an error committed by either side

nor the result of a misunderstanding by either side of the true motivations of the other. The bitter confrontation was unavoidable from the moment that Jews decided, at the end of the nineteenth century, to regain their national sovereignty in Palestine, a piece of territory they always referred to as the Land of Israel (Eretz-Israel) but which was occupied by another people. The root of the conflict lies in a tragic clash between two sets of motivations and processes, which, to begin with, were essentially independent of one another but in time became inextricably entangled and collided head-on. It was a clash of deep-set aspirations and motivations, each born under totally different circumstances at a different place and time, that eventually drew both protagonists into continuous violent hostilities.[17]

This explanation of the conflict may not be accepted by all, but it is an honest starting point, from the perspective of one of the protagonists, for understanding what this conflict is really about, why it is not yet resolved, and why it may never be fully resolved.

Notes

1 For thoughtful discussions on the resolution of protracted conflicts, see Michael Brecher and Jonathan Wilkenfeld, *A Study of Crisis*, Ann Arbor: The University of Michigan Press, 2000; Fred Charles Iklé, *Every War Must End*, 2nd rev. ed., New York: Columbia University Press, 2005.

2 For a less pessimistic assessment, see Bernard Wasserstein, *Israelis and Palestinians: Why Do They Fight? Can They Stop?* 3rd ed., New Haven, CT / London: Yale University Press / London: Profile Books, 2008. Israelis and Palestinians, he writes (p. 2) are not "animated by crazed psychopathy. They fight over definable interests, motivated by comprehensible value-systems, in pursuit of identifiable goals." His thoughtful and provocative book examines the demographic, socioeconomic, environmental and territorial aspects of the conflict with an optimistic view towards future possibilities for ending the conflict.

3 Gilead Sher, *The Israeli–Palestinian Peace Negotiations, 1999–2001: Within Reach*, New York: Routledge, 2006; Menachem Klein, *A Possible Peace between Israel and Palestine: An Insider's Account of the Geneva Initiative*, transl. Haim Watzman, New York: Columbia University Press, 2007; David Matz, "Trying to Understand the Taba Talks (Part I)," *Palestine–Israel Journal of Politics, Economics and Culture* 10:3 (2003), 96–105, and "Why Did Taba End?" Part II, *Palestine–Israel Journal of Politics, Economics and Culture* 10:4 (2003), 92–8.

4 See, e.g., the disturbing journal published by David Shulman, *Dark Hope: Working for Peace in Israel and Palestine*, Chicago: University of Chicago Press, 2007.

5 Middle East project of the Search for Common Ground, website accessed 26 August 2008 at http://www.sfcg.org/programmes/cgp/cgp_tsotf2.html.

6   See, e.g., Naomi Shepherd, "One State: A Solution for Israel/Palestine or a Threat?" *The Guardian*, 22 August 2008, accessed online 25 August 2008 at guardian.co.uk.

7   For a recent attempt to consider present options through the past, see "The 1937 Peel Report revisited," commentary by Yossi Alpher, Ghassan Khatib, Dan Schueftan and Musa Budeiri, 14 January 2008, edition 2, bitterlemons. org Palestinian–Israeli Crossfire, accessed online on 25 August 2008 at http://www.bitterlemons.org/previous/bl140108ed02.html.

8   Amos Oz, *How to Cure a Fanatic*, Princeton, NJ: Princeton University Press, 2006, 89.

9   Amos Oz, *Under this Blazing Light: Essays*, transl. Nicholas de Lange, New York: Cambridge University Press, 1995, 8–9.

10 Marwan Muasher, *The Arab Center: The Promise of Moderation*, New Haven, CT: Yale University Press, 2008, 60. For an award-winning journalist's attempt to portray the fears and vulnerabilities of Israelis and Palestinians, see David K. Shipler, *Arab and Jew: Wounded Spirits in a Promised Land*, rev. ed., New York: Penguin, 2002.

11 See the interesting survey research on former Israeli prime minister Ehud Barak by Daniel Bar-Tal and Eran Halperin in the Hebrew periodical *Megamot* in Summer 2008, discussed in Akiva Eldar, "Face the Nation," *Ha-Aretz*, 19 August 2008.

12 Some Arabs draw hope from the historical precedent of the invading Roman Catholic crusaders who sacked Jerusalem in 1099 but were finally driven out of the Holy Land in 1291 CE.

13 For an overview of many grass-roots activities, see "JustVision: Supporting Israeli and Palestinian Non-Violent Civic Peace Builders Through media and Education," website accessed 22 August 2008 at http://www.justvision.org/; *Bridging the Divide: Peacebuilding in the Israeli–Palestinian Conflict*, eds. Edy Kaufman, Walid Salem, and Juliette Verhoeven, foreword by N. Chazan and H. Siniora, Boulder, CO: Lynne Rienner, 2006.

14 See, e.g., Menachem Klein, *A Possible Peace between Israel and Palestine: An Insider's Account of the Geneva Initiative*, transl. Haim Watzman, New York: Columbia University Press, 2007. "The Geneva Initiative: Ending the Israeli Palestinian Conflict" website accessed 22 August 2008 at http://www.geneva-accord.org/.

15 This typology was inspired by Y. Harkabi, "Who is to Blame for the Persistence of the Arab–Israel Conflict? Lessons from Five Explanations," in Harkabi, *Palestinians and Israel*, New York: John Wiley (Halsted Press), 1974, 220–41, and has been applied in several studies of Arab–Zionist and Israeli–Arab negotiations. See, e.g., Neil Caplan, "Negotiation and the Arab–Israeli Conflict," *Jerusalem Quarterly* 6 (Winter 1978), 3–19; Laura Zittrain Eisenberg and Neil Caplan, *Negotiating Arab–Israeli Peace: Patterns, Problems, Possibilities*, Bloomington / Indianapolis: Indiana University Press, 1998, 17–18.

16 Shilbey Telhami also regards effective third-party mediation as one of three factors that can lead to a breakthrough of an otherwise intractable conflict.

Shibley Telhami, "Beyond Resolution? The Palestinian–Israeli Conflict," in *Grasping the Nettle: Analyzing Cases of Intractable Conflict*, eds. Chester A. Crocker, Fen Osler Hampson, and Pamela Aall, Washington, DC: United States Institute of Peace Press, 2005, 369–72.

17 Mordechai Bar-On, "Remembering 1948: Personal Recollections, Collective Memory, and the Search for 'What Really Happened'," in *Making Israel*, ed. Benny Morris, Ann Arbor: University of Michigan Press, 2007, 32–3.

Chronology

1882		First group of Zionists emigrates from Tsarist Russia to Ottoman Palestine, beginning of the first *aliya* (wave of Zionist immigration)
1891		First petition to Ottoman authorities by Palestinian Arabs protesting Jewish immigration and land sales
1896		Theodor Herzl publishes *Der Judenstaat (The Jewish State)*
1897		First World Zionist Congress convenes in Basle, Switzerland
1903		Pogroms in Kishinev; start of the second *aliya*
1908		Young Turk Revolution; Ottoman parliament reinstated
1913		First Arab Nationalist Congress meets in Paris
1914		World War; Turkey aligns with Germany against Britain and France
1915		Sir Henry McMahon correspondence with King Husayn of the Hejaz
1916		Sykes–Picot agreement on Anglo–French division of Fertile Crescent into spheres of influence after the War
1917	November/ December	British issue Balfour Declaration; British troops enter Jerusalem
1918	October	British forces move through Northern Palestine; Turks surrender and sign armistice; Amir Faysal, son of King

		Husayn, installed in Damascus (until July 1920)
1919	January	Chaim Weizmann and Faysal sign a treaty in London, in preparation for Paris Peace Conference
	July/August	King–Crane Commission visits Middle East and issues report
1920	April	Riots and attacks on Jews in Jerusalem; League of Nations Council meeting in San Remo awards mandates to Britain (over Palestine, Iraq) and France (over Syria)
	July	Sir Herbert Samuel arrives as first British High Commissioner [HC] for Palestine; military administration ends
	December	Palestine Arab Congress meets in Haifa, elects Arab Executive to represent Palestinian interests; founding convention of the *Histadrut* (General Federation of Jewish Labor), with responsibilities for the *Hagana* (underground militia)
1921	March	Colonial Secretary Winston Churchill visits Palestine; endorses Amir Abdullah's rule over Transjordan as part of the Palestine Mandate
	May	Arab riots and attacks on Jews in Jaffa and nearby settlements; Hajj Amin al-Husayni named "Grand Mufti" of Palestine
	October	Haycraft Commission reports on Jaffa "disturbances"
1922	March	Amin al-Husayni elected president of newly created Supreme Muslim Council
	June	British issue Statement of Policy, "Churchill White Paper"
	July	League of Nations sanctions Mandate for Palestine
	September 1922 to November 1923	British attempt without success to set up an elected legislative council, an appointed advisory council, and an Arab Agency

1926–1927		Hard times in Palestine; more Jews emigrate than immigrate; unemployment is high; continuing calm leads British to reduce military garrison
1928	September	Incident at the Western ("Wailing") Wall in Jerusalem triggers Jewish outrage and protests; Muslims, in turn, express fears of Jewish encroachments on Islamic holy places
1929	August	Tensions and incidents regarding "Wailing" Wall spark Arabs attack on Jews in the old city of Jerusalem; attacks spread to Hebron and Safed
1930	April	Shaw Commission Report on August 1929 "disturbances" is published
	October	Hope Simpson Report on land settlement, immigration, and development is published, along with new British Statement of Policy, "Passfield White Paper"
1931	February	British PM Ramsay MacDonald publishes letter to Dr. Weizmann, reassuring him of continued support of Zionism; Arabs denounce MacDonald's "Black Letter"
	December	General Islamic Congress convened by Hajj Amin al-Husayni in Jerusalem; parallel meetings of pan-Arab nationalists
1932	August	Awni Abd al-Hadi and others found the Istiqlal (Independence) Party
	October	Iraq becomes independent and joins the League of Nations
	November	HC Sir Arthur Wauchope announces intention to set up representative institutions for Palestine, beginning with municipal elections
1933	January	Adolf Hitler appointed Chancellor of Germany
	March	Arab Executive adopts non-cooperation and boycott resolutions against British and Zionist goods, land sales
	August	Palestine police eviction of Arab tenant farmers from Wadi al-Hawarith
	October	Palestinian Arabs' illegal demonstrations in Jaffa, Haifa, Nablus, and Jerusalem turn

		violent; protests are deliberately directed against British only
1934	December	National Defense Party is formed, with Ragheb al-Nashashibi as president
1935	March	Palestine Arab Party is formed, with Jamal al-Husayni as president
	June	Reform Party is founded, led by Jerusalem mayor Dr. Husayn Fakhri al-Khalidi
	September	XIXth Zionist Congress ends; David Ben-Gurion becomes chairman of the Jewish Agency Executive
	October	British inspectors at Jaffa port uncover weapons ostensibly bound for the *Hagana* smuggled into Palestine
	November	Rebel Shaykh Izz ad-Din al-Qassam and several followers die in a gunfight with British troops; his funeral in Haifa draws large crowds who revere Qassam as a national hero and martyr
	November	Coalition of five Palestinian political parties is formed and submits three demands to British: (a) immediate stoppage of Jewish immigration, (b) prohibition of transfer of lands from Arabs to Jews, and (c) establishment of democratic government
	December	HC unveils proposals for a legislative council
1936	February to April	British Cabinet publishes proposals for a legislative council for Palestine; Parliamentary debates; Palestine Arabs invited to send delegation to London for discussions
	April	Arab rebels' attack on convoy, killing two Jewish travelers, provokes counterattacks, tensions, and rioting near Jaffa and Tel Aviv; British declare state of emergency; Arab Higher Committee [AHC] formed to coordinate general strike until the Palestinian Arabs' three main demands are met
	April to October	Country paralyzed by an Arab general strike and terrorized by rebels
	October	AHC announces an end to the general strike

	November	Royal Commission, headed by Lord Peel, arrives in Palestine to hear testimony about the "underlying causes of the disturbances" and other matters
1937	July	(Peel) Royal Commission publishes Report proposing partition of Palestine; AHC rejects proposals; Arab rebellion resumes
	July/August	XXth Zionist Congress votes conditional acceptance of Peel partition
	September	Pan-Arab conference meets in Bludan, Syria, rejects partition; Palestinian terrorists assassinate senior British official in Nazareth
	October	AHC outlawed, Mufti flees to Beirut, later to Iraq and to Germany
1938	July	Conference at Evian discusses but does nothing to resolve problem of European Jewish refugees
	October	Cairo Inter-parliamentary Conference for the Defense of Palestine
1939	February/ March	Arab–British and British–Zionist "round table" conferences at St. James' Palace reach no agreement
	May	British Statement of Policy, "MacDonald White Paper," restricting Jewish immigration, land purchases; Arabs and Zionists reject new policy
	September	Outbreak of World War II
1942	January	Nazi officials meet at Wannsee Conference (Berlin) to coordinate plans for "final solution," i.e., total annihilation of Europe's Jewish population
	May	Emergency Zionist Conference at Biltmore Hotel, New York, adopts resolutions demanding "Jewish commonwealth" in and free immigration to Palestine
1943	April	Bermuda Conference discusses but does nothing to resolve problem of European Jewish refugees
1944	November	Zionist (Stern, LEHI) terrorists assassinate Lord Moyne in Cairo

1945	March	Alexandria Foundation of the League of Arab States, demand for independent Arab Palestine
	May	End of World War II
	November	Anglo–American Committee of Inquiry appointed
1946	May	Anglo–American Committee of Inquiry issues report, recommending immediate admission of 100,000 Jewish refugees from Europe
	July	Zionist (Irgun) terrorists blow up wing of King David Hotel in Jerusalem housing British military HQ
	September	London Conference of Arab leaders and British meetings with Zionist officials; no agreement reached
1947	February	Britain announces intention to return the Palestine mandate to the United Nations
	May	UN General Assembly appoints Special Committee on Palestine [UNSCOP] to investigate and make recommendations
	August/ September	UNSCOP recommends partition of Palestine; British announce decision to terminate the Mandate and withdraw from Palestine
	November	UN General Assembly passes Resolution 181 adopting UNSCOP report; AHC rejects; armed struggle intensifies for control of Arab and Jewish areas of Palestine; Arab League begins plans to prevent implementation of UN resolution
1948	May	British leave Palestine; Ben-Gurion proclaims state of Israel; Arab armies attack Jewish state; UN appoints Count Folke Bernadotte as mediator
	May 1948 to January 1949	First Arab–Israeli war involving forces of Israel, Egypt, Jordan, Syria, Lebanon, Iraq, and Palestinians, alternating with several truces
	September	LEHI (Stern) terrorists assassinate UN Mediator Bernadotte
	December	UN General Assembly adopts Resolution 194 establishing Conciliation Commission

		[UNCCP], urging the return of or compensation to Palestinian refugees, and calling for internationalization of Jerusalem
1949	February	Egypt and Israel sign General Armistice Agreement [GAA] at Rhodes under auspices of UN Acting Mediator, Ralph Bunche
	March	Israeli–Lebanon GAA and Israel–Jordan GAA signed
	April to September	UNCCP hosts peace conference in Lausanne (no result)
	May	Israel admitted to membership in the UN
	July	Syria–Israel GAA signed
1950	January to July	UNCCP hosts peace conference in Geneva (no result)
	December	Jordan annexes West Bank
1951	July	Jordan's King Abdullah assassinated while visiting Jerusalem
	September to November	UNCCP hosts peace conference in Paris (no result)
1952	July	Egyptian army officers, including future president Gamal Abdul Nasser, overthrow King Farouk
1953	May	Hussein becomes King of Jordan (until 1999)
	October	Israeli reprisal raid on Qibya, led by Ariel Sharon
1955	February	Israeli attack on Gaza
	September	Public announcement of extensive Soviet military aid to Egypt
1956	July	Nasser nationalizes Suez Canal Company
	October	Israel invades Gaza and Egypt's Sinai, followed by British and French occupation of Suez Canal zone; US, USSR, and UN press parties to retreat
	November	UN creates UNEF, its first peacekeeping mission, to be positioned along Egypt–Israel frontier
1957	January/ March	Israeli forces complete withdrawal from Gaza, Sinai, and Sharm al-Shaykh
1959	January	Yasir Arafat and others form Fatah liberation movement

1964	January	Arab League meeting in Cairo creates Palestine Liberation Organization [PLO]
	May	PLO's Palestine National Council [PNC] holds first meeting in East Jerusalem, adopts a Palestinian National Charter
1965	January	Fatah's first raid into Israel, from Jordanian territory
1966	November	Large-scale Israeli reprisal raid on as-Samu in West Bank, Jordan
1967	April/ May	Escalating tensions and attacks along and across Israeli–Syria frontier
	May	Nasser mobilizes troops, orders UNEF troops out of Sinai, blockades Straits of Tiran to shipping to/from Israel
	June	Decisive Israeli victory in war against Egypt, Jordan, Syria; captures Sinai, West Bank, and Golan Heights
	September	Arab League summit at Khartoum adopts resolutions on no negotiations with, recognition of, or peace with Israel
	November	UN Security Council passes Resolution 242 calling for Israeli withdrawal to secure and recognized borders; Gunnar Jarring appointed UN Special Representative
	December	Formation of the Popular Front for the Liberation of Palestine [PFLP] under George Habash
1968	March	Invading Israeli forces battle Palestinians and Jordanians at Karameh, Jordan
	July	Fourth PNC Meeting, Cairo, revises Palestinian National Charter; hijacking of Israeli airliner by PFLP to Algiers
1969	February	Fatah's Arafat elected chairman of the PLO
	March 1969 to August 1970	Egyptian–Israeli War of Attrition
1970	September	Death of Egyptian president Nasser, succeeded by Anwar Sadat; multiple PFLP hijackings bring aircraft to Jordan; Jordanian Army battles and expels Palestinian guerilla groups; PLO headquarters move to Beirut
1972	May	Terrorist attack at Tel Aviv Airport

	September	Palestinian "Black September" terrorists attack Israeli athletes at Munich Olympics
1973	October	Egypt and Syria attack Israel; UN Security Council Resolution 338 reiterates 242 and calls for negotiations
	December	Opening session of inconclusive Geneva Conference
1974	June	12th PNC meeting in Cairo adopts new political program, accepting to create a national authority on any part of liberated Palestine
	October	UN General Assembly and Arab League summit meeting at Rabat recognize PLO as sole legitimate representative of the Palestinian people
	November	Yasir Arafat addresses the UN General Assembly
1975	September	Signing of final Israeli–Egyptian disengagement agreement in Sinai; US and Israel agree on conditions for negotiating with the PLO
	November	UN General Assembly passes Resolution 3379 declaring "zionism" to be a form of racism
1977	May	Israel elects Menachem Begin prime minister, first Likud victory over Labor Party
	November	Egyptian president Sadat becomes first Arab leader to visit Israel, launching peace negotiations
1978	September	Israel and Egypt sign Camp David Accords mediated by US president Jimmy Carter
1979	March	Israel and Egypt sign peace treaty
1981	June	Israeli jets destroy Iraqi nuclear reactor near Baghdad
	October	Sadat assassinated; succeeded by Hosni Mubarak
1982	April	Israel completes withdrawal from Sinai
	June	Israeli invasion of Lebanon
	September	Reagan Plan; Fez Arab Summit adopts Saudi (Fahd) Plan (1981); Phalangists massacre Palestinians in Sabra and Shatila refugee

		camps outside Beirut; PLO evacuates and moves headquarters to Tunis
1985	October	Israeli Air Force bombs PLO headquarters in Tunis
1986	October	Members of Palestine Liberation Front hijack Italian cruise liner *Achille Lauro*
1987	December	Outbreak of first Palestinian uprising, *intifada*
1988	February	First appearance of Hamas movement
	July	King Hussein ends Jordan's administrative responsibilities for and legal ties with West Bank
	November	PNC Meeting in Algiers declares Palestinian statehood, implied recognition of Israel
	December	Arafat addresses UN General Assembly, announcing PLO acceptance of UN Security Council Resolutions 242 and 338
1990	August	Iraq invades Kuwait
1991	January	US begins war against Iraq ("Gulf War")
	October	Madrid Peace Conference convened by US president George H. W. Bush, followed in December by talks in Washington DC
1992	June	Labor Party's Yitzhak Rabin elected prime minister of Israel
1993	September	Rabin and Arafat sign letters of mutual recognition and Oslo Accord (Declaration of Principles) for Palestinian self-government and Israeli withdrawal
1994	July	Arafat returns to head Palestinian Authority [PA] following the start of Israeli withdrawal from Palestinian lands
	October	Israel and Jordan sign peace treaty
1995	September	"Oslo II" agreement between Israel and PA for further Israeli withdrawals
	November	Rabin assassinated
1996	January	Arafat elected president of the PA
	May	Likud's Benjamin Netanyahu defeats Labor's Shimon Peres to become prime minister
1997	January	Netanyahu and Arafat sign protocol regarding Hebron evacuation under US mediation

1998	October	Netanyahu and Arafat negotiate Wye River Accord for further Israeli withdrawals, mediated by US president Bill Clinton
1999	February	King Hussein of Jordan dies; succeeded by Abdullah II
	May	Labor's Ehud Barak defeats Likud's Netanyahu to become prime minister
	September	Israel–Palestinian accord signed at Sharm el-Sheikh
2000	May	Israel unilaterally withdraws remaining forces from Southern Lebanon
	July	Clinton invites Arafat and Barak to Camp David; no agreement reached
	September	Ariel Sharon visits Temple Mount; subsequent demonstrations and police repression spark second Palestinian *intifada*
	December	US president Clinton outlines "Parameters" for an Israeli–Palestinian agreement
2001	January	Israeli–Palestinian talks at Taba, Egypt; no agreement reached
	February	Likud's Ariel Sharon defeats Labor's Barak to become prime minister
	September	al-Qaeda terrorist attacks on New York, Washington
2002	March	Saudi peace proposals endorsed by Arab League meeting in Beirut; UN Security Council adopts Resolution 1397 endorsing two-state solution; after upsurge in terror, Israel reoccupies parts of West Bank
2003	April	Mahmoud Abbas [Abu Mazen] becomes first Palestinian prime minister; Quartet (US–Russia–UN–EU) publish text of "Roadmap" peace plan for Israel–Palestine
	June	Sharon and Abbas attend summit meeting at Aqaba, Jordan, convened by US president George W. Bush; Israel begins construction on "security fence"
	October	UN Security Council Resolution 1515 endorses Quartet Roadmap and two-state solution; non-governmental Israeli and Palestinian negotiators unveil Geneva Accord

2004	April	Sharon announces plans for Israel's unilateral disengagement from Palestinian territories
	November	Arafat dies in Paris
2005	January	Mahmoud Abbas elected president of the PA
	August	Israel removes troops and between 8000 and 9000 settlers from Gaza Strip
2006	January	Israeli PM Sharon incapacitated by cerebral stroke, replaced by Ehud Olmert; Hamas wins large majority in Palestinian Legislative Council elections
	July	Israeli–Hizbullah war along Israeli–Lebanon frontier
2007	March	Arab League peace plan endorsed during Saudi summit
	June	Hamas militias overpower Fatah forces in civil war in Gaza
	July	Arab League representatives visit Jerusalem to promote peace plan
	November	Olmert and Abbas attend Annapolis Peace Conference, convened by US president Bush

Bibliography

1948: Sixty Years After, special issue of *Palestine–Israel Journal of Politics, Economics and Culture* 15:1–2 (2008).

Abbas, Mahmoud [Abu Mazen], *Through Secret Channels: The Road to Oslo: Senior PLO Leader Abu Mazen's Revealing Story of the Negotiations with Israel*, Concord, MA: Paul [Reading: Garnet], 1995.

Abbasi, Mustafa, "The End of Arab Tiberias: The 1948 Battle for the City," *Journal of Palestine Studies* 37:3 (Spring 2008), 6–29.

Abboushi, W. F., *The Unmaking of Palestine*, Wisbech, UK: Middle East and North African Studies Press / Boulder, CO: Lynne Rienner, 1985.

Abcarius, M[ichel] F[red], *Palestine through the Fog of Propaganda*, introduction by Major-General Sir E. L. Spears, London /New York [etc.]: Hutchinson, 1946. [Westport, CT: Hyperion Press reprint 1976].

Abdel-Jawad, Saleh, "The Arab and Palestinian Narratives of the 1948 War," in *Israeli and Palestinian Narratives of Conflict: History's Double Helix*, ed. Robert I. Rotberg, Bloomington / Indianapolis: Indiana University Press, 2006, 72–114.

Abu El-Haj, Nadia, *Facts on the Ground: Archeological Practice and Territorial Self-Fashioning in Israeli Society*, Chicago: University of Chicago Press, 2001.

Abu-Amr, Ziad, "Hamas: A Historical and Political Background," *Journal of Palestine Studies* 22:4 (Summer 1993), 5–19.

Abu-Odeh, Adnan, *Jordanians, Palestinians and the Hashemite Kingdom in the Middle East Peace Process*, Washington, DC: United States Institute of Peace Press, 1999.

Abu-Sharif, Bassam, and Uzi Mahnaimi, *Best of Enemies: The Memoirs of Bassam Abu-Sharif and Uzi Mahnaimi*, Boston, MA: Little, Brown, 1995.

Abunimah, Ali, "Israel's 'Auschwitz Borders' Revisited," *Desertpeace*, 8 December 2008, accessed online 14 February 2009 at http://desertpeace.wordpress.com/2008/12/08/israels-auschwitz-borders-revisited/

Adam, Heribert, and Kogila Moodley, *Seeking Mandela: Peacemaking between Israelis and Palestinians*, Philadelphia, PA: Temple University Press, 2005.

Agha, Hussein, Shai Feldman, Ahmad Khalidi, and Zeev Schiff, *Track-II Diplomacy: Lessons from the Middle East*, Cambridge, MA: MIT Press, 2003.

Alami, Musa, "The Lesson of Palestine," *Middle East Journal* 3:4 (October 1949), 373–405.

Antonius, George, *The Arab Awakening: The Story of the Arab National Movement*, New York: G. P. Putnam's Sons, 1946 [orig. London: Hamish Hamilton, 1938; reprinted New York: Capricorn, 1965].

Appleby, Joyce, Lynn Hunt, and Margaret Jacob, *Telling the Truth about History*, New York / London: W. W. Norton, 1994.

Arab Executive Committee, Memorandum on the White Paper of October 1930, prepared by Aouni Abdul-Hadi, Jerusalem, December 1930, reproduced in *Documents of the Palestinian National Movement, 1918–1939: From the Papers of Akram Zuaytir*, ed. Bayan Nuwayhid al-Hout, Beirut: Institute for Palestine Studies, 1979, doc. 167 [pp. 333–53].

Arab Higher Committee, *Memorandum Submitted by the Arab Higher Committee to the Permanent Mandates Commission and the Secretary of State for the Colonies*, [Jerusalem] dated 23 July 1937, reprinted in *The Rise of Israel* v. 17, *Arab–Jewish Relations, 1921–1937*, ed. and introduced by Aaron S. Klieman, New York / London: Garland Publishing, 1987, 216–30.

The Arab–Israeli Conflict, ed. John Norton Moore, 3 vols., Princeton, NJ: Princeton University Press, 1974.

The Arab–Israeli Conflict: Perspectives, 2nd ed., ed. Alvin Z. Rubinstein, New York: HarperCollins, 1991.

The Arab–Israeli Conflict: Two Decades of Change, eds. Yehuda Lukacs and Abdalla M. Battah, Boulder, CO / London: Westview Press, 1988.

Arab–Jewish Relations: From Conflict to Resolution? Essays in Honour of Prof. Moshe Ma'oz, eds. Elie Podeh and Asher Kaufman, Brighton: Sussex Academic Press, 2005.

Arab Nationalism: An Anthology, ed. with an introduction by Sylvia G. Haim, Berkeley / Los Angeles: University of California Press, 1962.

Aronson, Geoffrey, *Creating Facts: Israel, Palestinian and the West Bank*, Washington, DC: Institute for Palestine Studies, 1987.

The Assassination of Yitzhak Rabin, ed. Yoram Peri, Stanford, CA: Stanford University Press, 2000.

Avineri, Shlomo, *The Making of Modern Zionism: Intellectual Origins of the Jewish State*, New York: 1981.

Avineri, Shlomo, "The Socialist Zionism of Chaim Arlosoroff," *Jerusalem Quarterly* 34 (Winter 1985), 68–87.

Avneri, Arieh L., *The Claim of Dispossession: Jewish Land-Settlement and the Arabs, 1878–1948*, New Brunswick, NJ: Transaction Books, 1984 (transl. from the Hebrew [1980] by the Kfar-Blum Translation Group).

Avnery, Uri, *My Friend, the Enemy*, Westport, CT: Lawrence Hill, 1986.

Baihum, Muhammad Jamil, "Arabism and Jewry in Syria," (1957), transl. in *Arab Nationalism: An Anthology*, ed. with an introduction by Sylvia G. Haim, Berkeley / Los Angeles: University of California Press, 1962, 128–46.

Barak, Ehud, "The Myths Spread about Camp David Are Baseless," in *The Camp David Summit—What Went Wrong? Americans, Israelis, and Palestinians Analyze the Failure of the Boldest Attempt Ever to Resolve the Palestinian–Israeli Conflict*, eds. Shimon Shamir and Bruce Maddy-Weitzman, Brighton, UK / Portland, OR: Sussex Academic Press, 2005, 117–47.

Bar-On, Dan, and Saliba Sarsar, "Bridging the Unbridgeable: The Holocaust and al-Nakba," *Palestine–Israel Journal* 11:1 (2004), 63–70.

Bar-On, Dan, and Sami Adwan, "The Psychology of Better Dialogue between Two Separate but Interdependent Narratives," in *Israeli and Palestinian Narratives of Conflict: History's Double Helix*, ed. Robert I. Rotberg, Bloomington / Indianapolis: Indiana University Press, 2006, 205–24.

Bar-On, Mordechai, *The Gates of Gaza: Israel's Road to Suez and Back, 1955–1957*, transl. Ruth Rossing, New York: St. Martin's Press, 1994.

Bar-On, Mordechai, "Historiography as an Educational Project: The Historians' Debate in Israel and the Middle East Peace Process," in *The Middle East Peace Process: Interdisciplinary Perspectives*, ed. Ilan Peleg, Albany: State University of New York Press, 1998, 21–38.

Bar-On, Mordechai, "Remembering 1948: Personal Recollections, Collective Memory, and the Search for 'What Really Happened'," in *Making Israel*, ed. Benny Morris, Ann Arbor: University of Michigan Press, 2007, 29–46.

Bar-On, Mordechai, "Three Days in Sèvres, October 1956," *History Workshop Journal* 62 (2006), 172–86.

Bar-On, Mordechai, Benny Morris, and Motti Golani, "Reassessing Israel's Road to Sinai/Suez, 1956: A Trialogue," in *Traditions and Transitions in Israel Studies: Books on Israel volume 6*, eds. Laura Zittrain Eisenberg, Neil Caplan, Naomi B. Sokoloff, and Mohammed Abu-Nimer, Albany: State University of New York Press, 2002, 3–41.

Bar-Siman-Tov, Yaacov, *The Israeli–Egyptian War of Attrition, 1969–1970*, New York: Columbia University Press, 1980.

Bar-Yaacov, N., *The Israeli–Syrian Armistice: Problems of Implementation, 1949–1966*, Jerusalem: Magnes Press (Hebrew University), 1967.

Bauer, Yehuda, "From Cooperation to Resistance: The Haganah 1938–1946," *Middle Eastern Studies* II (1965–1966), 182–210.

Bauer, Yehuda, *From Diplomacy to Resistance: A History of Jewish Palestine, 1939–1945*, transl. Alton M. Winters, Philadelphia, PA: Jewish Publication Society, 1970.

Bauer, Yehuda, *A History of the Holocaust*, Danbury, CT: Franklin Watts, 1982.

Bauer, Yehuda, *Rethinking the Holocaust*, New Haven, CT / London: Yale University Press, 2001.

Begin, Menachem, *The Revolt [Story of the Irgun]*, foreword by Rabbi Meir Kahane, Los Angeles: Nash Publishing, 1972 [orig. New York: Schuman / London: W. H. Allen, 1948/1951].

Beilin, Yossi, *Touching Peace: From the Oslo Accord to a Final Agreement*, transl. from the Hebrew by Philip Simpson, London: Weidenfeld and Nicolson, 1999.

Bell, J. Bowyer, *Terror out of Zion: Irgun Zvai Leumi, LEHI, and the Palestine Underground, 1929–1949*, New York: St. Martin's Press, 1977 [reissued as *Terror out of Zion: The Fight for Israeli Independence*, with a new introduction by the author and a foreword by Moshe Arens, New Brunswick, NJ: Transaction, 1996].

Ben-David, Calev, "Heroes under Attack," *The Jerusalem Report*, 29 December 1994, 12–17.

Ben-Gurion, David, *My Talks with Arab Leaders*, transl. Aryeh Rubinstein and Misha Louvish, ed. Misha Louvish, Jerusalem: Keter, 1972.

Ben-Gurion, David, "Our Friend: What Wingate Did for Us," *Jewish Observer and Middle East Review*, 27 September 1963, 15–16, reproduced in *From Haven to Conquest: Readings in Zionism and the Palestine Problem until 1948*, ed. and introduced by Walid Khalidi, Beirut: 1971; 2nd printing, Washington, DC: Institute for Palestine Studies, 1987, 382–7.

Benvenisti, Meron, *Conflicts and Contradictions*, New York: Villard Books, 1986.

Benvenisti, Meron, *Sacred Landscape: The Buried History of the Holy Land since 1948*, transl. Maxine Kaufman-Lacusta, Berkeley / London: University of California Press, 2000.

Ben-Yehuda, Hemda, "Policy Transformation in the Middle East: Arms Control Regimes and National Security Reconciled," in *Review Essays in Israel Studies: Books on Israel, vol. V*, eds. Laura Zittrain Eisenberg and Neil Caplan, Albany: State University of New York Press, 2000, 173–91.

Ben-Yehuda, Nachman, *The Masada Myth: Collective Memory and Mythmaking in Israel*, Madison: The University of Wisconsin Press, 1995.

Berger, Earl, *The Covenant and the Sword: Arab–Israeli Relations, 1948–56*, Toronto: University of Toronto Press [London: Routledge and Kegan Paul], 1965.

Bickerton, Ian J., and Carla L. Klausner, *A History of the Arab–Israeli Conflict*, 5th ed., Upper Saddle River, NJ: Pearson / Prentice Hall, 2007.

Biger, Gideon, "The Boundaries of Israel–Palestine, Past, Present and Future: A Critical Geographical View," *Israel Studies* 13:1 (Spring 2008), 68–93.

Bishara, Marwan, *Palestine/Israel: Peace or Apartheid: Prospects for Resolving the Conflict*, London: Zed Books / Halifax, NS: Fernwood, 2001.

Blaming the Victims: Spurious Scholarship and the Palestinian Question, eds. Edward W. Said and Christopher Hitchens, London / New York: Verso: 1988.

Blechman, Barry M., "The Impact of Israel's Reprisals on Behavior of the Bordering Arab Nations Directed at Israel," *Journal of Conflict Resolution* 16:2 (June 1972), 155–81.

Boutros-Ghali, Boutros, *Egypt's Road to Jerusalem*, New York: Random House, 1997.

Bowden, Tom, "The Politics of the Arab Rebellion in Palestine, 1936–39," *Middle Eastern Studies* XI:2 (May 1975), 148–74.

Bowersock, G. W., "Palestine: Ancient History and Modern Politics," *Journal of Palestine Studies* 56 (Summer 1985), 49–57, reproduced in *Blaming the Victims: Spurious Scholarship and the Palestinian Question*, eds. Edward W. Said and Christopher Hitchens, London: Verso, 2001, 181–91.

Brecher, Michael, *Decisions in Israel's Foreign Policy*, New Haven, CT: Yale University Press, 1975.

Brecher, Michael, *The Foreign Policy System of Israel: Setting, Images, Process*, London / Toronto / Melbourne: Oxford University Press, 1972.

Brecher, Michael, and Jonathan Wilkenfeld, *A Study of Crisis*, Ann Arbor: The University of Michigan Press, 2000.

Bridging the Divide: Peacebuilding in the Israeli–Palestinian Conflict, eds. Edy Kaufman, Walid Salem, and Juliette Verhoeven, foreword by N. Chazan and H. Siniora, Boulder, CO: Lynne Rienner, 2006.

Bronstein, Eitan, "The Nakba in Hebrew: Israeli–Jewish Awareness of the Palestinian Catastrophe and Internal Refugees," in *Catastrophe Remembered: Palestine, Israel and the Internal Refugees: Essays in Memory of Edward W. Said*, ed. Nur Masalha, London / New York: Zed Books, 2005, 214–41.

Bruno, Michael, "Israeli Policy in the 'Administered Territories'," in *Israel, the Arabs and the Middle East*, eds. Irving Howe and Carl Gershman, New York: Bantam, 1972, 249–65.

Brzezinski, Zbigniew, *Power and Principle: Memoirs of the National Security Advisor, 1977–1981*, New York: Farrar, Straus, Giroux, 1983.

Buehrig, Edward H., *The UN and the Palestinian Refugees: A Study in Nonterritorial Administration*, Bloomington: Indiana University Press, 1971.

Burg, Avraham, *The Holocaust is Over: We Must Rise from Its Ashes*, London: Palgrave-Macmillan, 2008.

Burns, E. L. M., *Between Arab and Israeli*, New York: Ivan Obolensky, 1963.

The Camp David Summit—What Went Wrong? Americans, Israelis, and Palestinians Analyze the Failure of the Boldest Attempt Ever to Resolve the Palestinian–Israeli Conflict, eds. Shimon Shamir and Bruce Maddy-Weitzman, Brighton, UK /Portland, OR: Sussex Academic Press, 2005.

Caplan, Neil, "Arab–Jewish Contacts in Palestine after the First World War," *Journal of Contemporary History* XII:4 (October 1977), 635–68.

Caplan, Neil, "Faisal Ibn Husain and the Zionists: A Re-examination with Documents," *International History Review* V:4 (November 1983), 561–614.

Caplan, Neil, *Futile Diplomacy*, vol. I: *Early Arab–Zionist Negotiation Attempts, 1913–1931*, London: Frank Cass, 1983.

Caplan, Neil, *Futile Diplomacy*, vol. II: *Arab–Zionist Negotiations and the End of the Mandate*, London: Frank Cass, 1986.

Caplan, Neil, *Futile Diplomacy*, vol. III: *The United Nations, the Great Powers and Middle East Peacemaking, 1948–1954*, London: Frank Cass, 1997.

Caplan, Neil, *Futile Diplomacy*, vol. IV: *Operation Alpha and the Failure of Anglo–American Coercive Diplomacy in the Arab–Israeli Conflict, 1954–1956*, London: Frank Cass, 1997.

Caplan, Neil, "The Holocaust and the Arab–Israeli Conflict," in *So Others Will Remember: Holocaust History and Survivor Testimony*, ed. Ronald Headland, Montreal: Vehicule Press, 1999, 82–97.

Caplan, Neil, "Negotiation and the Arab–Israeli Conflict," *Jerusalem Quarterly* 6 (Winter 1978), 3–19.

Caplan, Neil, *Palestine Jewry and the Arab Question, 1917–1925*, London: Frank Cass, 1978.

Caplan, Neil, "The 'Sharettist Option' Revisited," in *Arab–Jewish Relations: From Conflict to Resolution? Essays in Honour of Prof. Moshe Ma'oz*, eds. Elie Podeh and Asher Kaufman, Brighton: Sussex Academic Press, 2005, 64–73.

Caplan, Neil, "Zionist Visions of Palestine, 1917–1936," *The Muslim World* LXXXIV: 1–2 (January–April 1994), 19–35.

Carter, Jimmy, *Keeping Faith: Memoirs of a President*, New York: Bantam, 1982.

Carter, Jimmy, *Palestine: Peace not Apartheid*, New York: Simon and Schuster, 2007.

Cattan, Henry, *Palestine and International Law: The Legal Aspects of the Arab–Israel Conflict*, 2nd ed., foreword by W. T. Mallison, Jr., London: Longman, 1976.

Chapman, Colin, *Whose Promised Land?* updated ed., Oxford: Lion Publishing, 1992.

Childers, Erskine B., "The Other Exodus," *The Spectator* (London), 12 May 1961, reproduced in *From Haven to Conquest: Readings in Zionism and the Palestine Problem until 1948*, ed. and introduced by Walid Khalidi, Beirut: 1971; 2nd printing, Washington, DC: Institute for Palestine Studies, 1987, 795–806.

Childers, Erskine B., "The Wordless Wish: From Citizens to Refugees," in *The Transformation of Palestine*, ed. Ibrahim Abu Lughod, 2nd ed., Evanston, IL: Northwestern University Press, 1987, 165–202.

Chill, Dan S., *The Arab Boycott of Israel: Economic Aggression and World Reaction*, New York: Praeger, 1976.

Chomsky, Noam, *Peace in the Middle East? Reflections on Justice and Nationhood*, New York, 1974.

Christison, Kathleen, "The Arab–Israeli Policy of George Shultz," *Journal of Palestine Studies* 18:2 (Winter 1989), 29–47.

Cleveland, William, *A History of the Modern Middle East*, Boulder, CO: Westview Press, 2005.

Cohen, Aharon, *Israel and the Arab World*, New York: Funk and Wagnalls, 1970.

Cohen, Avner, *Israel and the Bomb*, New York: Columbia University Press, 1998.

Cohen, Geula, *Woman of Violence: Memoirs of a Young Terrorist, 1943–1948*, transl. Hillel Halkin, New York: Holt, Rinehart and Winston, 1966.

Cohen, Hillel, "Why Do Collaborators Collaborate? The Case of Palestinians and Zionist Institutions, 1917–1936," in *Arab–Jewish Relations: From Conflict to Resolution? Essays in Honour of Prof. Moshe Ma'oz*, eds. Elie Podeh and Asher Kaufman, Brighton: Sussex Academic Press, 2005, 43–63.

Cohen, Israel, *The Zionist Movement*, London: Frederick Muller, 1945.

Cohen, Michael J., "Churchill and the Balfour Declaration: The Interpretation, 1920–1922," in *The Great Powers in the Middle East, 1919–1939*, ed. Uriel Dann, New York / London: Holmes and Meier, 1988, 91–108.

Cohen, Michael J., "Sir Arthur Wauchope, the Army, and the Rebellion in Palestine, 1936," *Middle Eastern Studies* IX (1973), 19–34.

Cohen, Michael J., *Palestine and the Great Powers, 1945–1948*, Princeton, NJ: Princeton University Press, 1982.

Cohen, Stanley, *States of Denial, Knowing about Atrocities and Suffering*, Cambridge, UK / Malden, MA: Polity/Blackwell, 2001.

Cohen, Stephen, "Intractability and the Israeli–Palestinian Conflict," in *Grasping the Nettle: Analyzing Cases of Intractable Conflict*, Washington, DC: United States Institute of Peace Press, 2005, 343–55.

Collins-Kreiner, N., Y. Mansfeld, and N. Kliot, "The Reflection of a Political Conflict in Mapping: The Case of Israel's Borders and Frontiers," *Middle Eastern Studies* 42:3 (2006), 381–408.

Corbin, Jane, *Gaza First: The Secret Norway Channel to Peace between Israel and the PLO*, London: Bloomsbury, 1994.

Crocker, Chester A., Fen Osler Hampson, and Pamela Aall, "From Intractable to Tractable: The Outlook and Implications for Third Parties," in *Grasping the Nettle: Analyzing Cases of Intractable Conflict*, Washington, DC: United States Institute of Peace Press, 2005, 375–86.

Crossman, Richard, *Palestine Mission: A Personal Record*, New York: Harper and Bros., 1947.

Crum, Bartley, *Behind the Silken Curtain: A Personal Account of Anglo–American Diplomacy in Palestine and the Middle East*, New York: Simon and Schuster, 1947.

Dann, Uriel, "Glubb's Ouster and its Aftermath," in U. Dann, *King Hussein and the Challenge of Arab Radicalism: Jordan, 1955–1967*, New York / Oxford: Oxford University Press, 1989, 31–8.

Davis, Uri, *Apartheid Israel: Possibilities for the Struggle Within*, London: Zed Books, 2003.

Davis, Uri, *Israel: An Apartheid State*, London: Zed Books, London 1987 and 1990.

Dawidowicz, Lucy S., *The War against the Jews, 1933–1945*, New York, etc.: Bantam Books, 1986.

Dayan, Moshe, *Breakthrough: A Personal Account of the Egypt–Israel Peace Negotiations*, London: Weidenfeld and Nicolson, 1981.

Dayan, Moshe, *Diary of the Sinai Campaign*, New York: Harper and Row, 1966.

Dayan, Moshe, "Israel's Border and Security Problems," *Foreign Affairs* 33:2 (January 1955), 250–67.

Dayan, Moshe, *Living with the Bible*, London: Weidenfeld and Nicolson, 1978.

Dekel, Ephraim, *Briha: Flight to the Homeland*, transl. from the Hebrew by Dina Ettinger, ed. Gertrude Hirschler, New York, Herzl Press, 1973.

Dershowitz, Alan, *The Case for Israel*, New York: John Wiley, 2003.

Dershowitz, Alan, "Civil Liberties in Israel: The Problem of Preventive Detention," in *Israel, the Arabs and the Middle East*, eds. Irving Howe and Carl Gershman, New York: Bantam, 1972, 266–99.

Dessouki, Ali E. Hillal, "Arab Intellectuals and al-Nakba: The Search for Fundamentalism," *Middle Eastern Studies* IX (1973), 187–95.

Diamant, Etty, "Return to Haifa Confronts Holocaust Victims with Palestinian Refugees," *Palestine–Israel Journal of Politics, Economics and Culture* 15:1–2 (2008), 210–12.

Dissenter in Zion: From the Writings of Judah L. Magnes, ed. Arthur A. Goren, Cambridge, MA / London: Harvard University Press, 1982.

A Documentary History of the Arab–Israeli Conflict, ed. and with historical introductions by Charles L. Geddes, New York, etc.: Praeger, 1991.

Doumani, Beshara, "Rediscovering Ottoman Palestine: Rewriting Palestinians into History," in *The Israel/Palestine Question*, ed. Ilan Pappé, London / New York: Routledge, 1999, 11–40.

Dowek, Ephraim, *Israeli–Egyptian Relations, 1980–2000*, foreword by Yitshak Shamir, London: Frank Cass, 2001.

Dowty, Alan, *Israel/Palestine*, 2nd ed., Malden, MA / Cambridge, UK: Polity Press, 2008.

Dowty, Alan, *The Jewish State: A Century Later*, Berkeley / Los Angeles / London: University of California Press, 1998.

Dumper, Michael, *The Politics of Sacred Space: The Old City of Jerusalem in the Middle East Conflict*, Boulder, CO: Lynne Rienner, 2002.

Dynamics of a Conflict: A Re-examination of the Arab–Israeli Conflict, ed. Gabriel Sheffer, Atlantic Highlands, NJ: Humanities Press, 1975.

Eban, Abba, *An Autobiography*, New York: Random House, 1977.

Eban, Abba, *Personal Witness: Israel through My Eyes*, New York: G. P. Putnam's Sons, 1992.

Eban, Abba, "Some Unsystematic Thinking about the Arab–Israeli Conflict," in *Dynamics of a Conflict: A Re-examination of the Arab–Israeli Conflict*, ed. Gabriel Sheffer, Atlantic Highlands, NJ: Humanities Press, 1975, 349–66.

Efrat, Elisha, "Jerusalem: Partition Plans for a Holy City," in *Israel: The First Hundred Years*, vol. 2, *From War to Peace?* ed. Efraim Karsh, London: Frank Cass, 2000, 238–57.

Eisenberg, Laura Zittrain, and Neil Caplan, *Negotiating Arab–Israeli Peace: Patterns, Problems, Possibilities*, Bloomington / Indianapolis: Indiana University Press, 1998.

Elam, Yigal, "*Haganah, Irgun* and 'Stern': Who Did What?" *Jerusalem Quarterly* 23 (Spring 1982), 70–8.

Eldar, Akiva, "The Refugee Problem at Taba: Akiva Eldar interviews Yossi Beilin and Nabil Sha'ath," *Palestine–Israel Journal of Politics, Economics and Culture* 9:2 (2002), 12–23.

Elon, Amos, *The Israelis: Founders and Sons*, New York: Holt, Rinehart and Winston, 1971.

Elpeleg, Zvi, *The Grand Mufti: Haj Amin al-Hussaini, Founder of the Palestinian National Movement*, transl. David Harvey, ed. Shmuel Himelstein, London: Frank Cass, 1993.

Encyclopedia of the Palestinians, rev. ed., ed. Philip Mattar, New York: Facts on File, 2005.

ESCO Foundation for Palestine, Inc., *Palestine: A Study of Jewish, Arab, and British Policies*, 2 vols., New Haven, CT: Yale University Press, 1947.

Evans, Richard J., *In Defense of History*, London / New York: W. W. Norton, 1999.

Evron, Boaz, "The Holocaust: Learning the Wrong Lessons," *Journal of Palestine Studies* 10:3 (Spring 1981), 16–25.

Exile and Return: Predicaments of Palestinians and Jews, eds. Ann M. Lesch and Ian S. Lustick, Philadelphia: University of Pennsylvania Press, 2005.

Feinberg, Nathan, "The Question of Sovereignty over Palestine," *On an Arab Jurist's Approach to Zionism and the State of Israel*, reproduced in *The Arab–Israeli*

Conflict: Readings and Documents, abridged and rev. ed., ed. John Norton Moore, Princeton, NJ: Princeton University Press, 1977, 63–5.

Feinberg, Nathan, *Studies in International Law: With Special Reference to the Arab–Israel Conflict*, Jerusalem: Magnes Press, Hebrew University, 1979.

Finkelstein, Israel, and Neil Asher Silberman, *The Bible Unearthed: Archaeology's New Vision of Ancient Israel and the Origin of Its Sacred Texts*. New York: Free Press, 2001.

Finkelstein, Norman G., "Disinformation and the Palestine Question: The Not-So-Strange Case of Joan Peters's *From Time Immemorial*," in *Blaming the Victims: Spurious Scholarship and the Palestinian Question*, eds. Edward W. Said and Christopher Hitchens, London: Verso, 2001, 33–69.

Finkelstein, Norman G., *Image and Reality of the Israel–Palestine Conflict*, new and rev. ed., New York: W. W. Norton [2nd ed., London: Verso], 2003.

Firestone, Reuven, *Children of Abraham: An Introduction to Judaism for Muslims*, Hoboken, NJ: Ktav, 2001.

Fischbach, Michael R., "Palestinian and Mizrahi Jewish Property Claims in Discourse and Diplomacy," in *Exile and Return: Predicaments of Palestinians and Jews*, eds. Ann M. Lesch and Ian S. Lustick, Philadelphia: University of Pennsylvania Press, 2005, 207–24.

Fischbach, Michael R., "Palestinian Refugee Compensation and Israeli Counter-claims for Jewish Property in Arab Countries," *Journal of Palestine Studies* 38:1 (Autumn 2008), 6–24.

Flapan, Simha, *The Birth of Israel: Myths and Realities*, New York: Pantheon, 1987.

Flapan, Simha, *Zionism and the Palestinians*, New York: Barnes and Noble / London: Croom Helm, 1979.

Forsythe, David P., *United Nations Peacemaking: The Conciliation Commission for Palestine*, Baltimore, MD / London: Johns Hopkins University Press, 1972.

Freiberg, Dov, *To Survive Sobibor*, transl. Barbara Doron, Jerusalem / New York: Gefen, 2007.

Friedman, Isaiah, *Palestine, A Twice-Promised Land?* New Brunswick, NJ: Transaction Publishers, 2000.

Friedman, Isaiah, *The Question of Palestine, 1914–1918: British–Jewish–Arab Relations*, London: Routledge and Kegan Paul, 1973.

Friedman, Robert I., *Zealots for Zion: Inside Israel's West Bank Settlement Movement*, New York: Random House, 1992.

From Haven to Conquest: Readings in Zionism and the Palestine Problem until 1948, ed. and introduced by Walid Khalidi, Beirut: 1971; 2nd printing, Washington, DC: Institute for Palestine Studies, 1987.

Frye, Northrop, "The Knowledge of Good and Evil," in N. Frye, Stuart Hampshire, and Conor Cruise O'Brien, *The Morality of Scholarship*, ed. Max Black, Ithaca, NY: Cornell University Press, 1967, 3–28.

Frye, Northrop, Stuart Hampshire, and Conor Cruise O'Brien, *The Morality of Scholarship*, ed. Max Black, Ithaca, NY: Cornell University Press, 1967.

The Future of Palestine and Israel: From Colonial Roots to Postcolonial Realities, ed. Aslam Farouk-Alli, Midrand, South Africa: Institute for Global Dialogue, 2007.

Gabbay, Rony E., *A Political Study of the Arab–Jewish Conflict: The Arab Refugee Problem (A Case Study)*, Geneva: Librairie E. Droz [Paris: Librairie Minard], 1959.

Galnoor, Yitzhak, *The Partition of Palestine: Decision Crossroads in the Zionist Movement*, Albany: State University of New York Press, 1995.

Garcia-Granados, Jorge, *The Birth of Israel: The Drama as I Saw It*, New York: Knopf, 1948.

Garfinkle, Adam M., "Genesis," in *The Arab–Israeli Conflict: Perspectives*, 2nd ed., ed. Alvin Z. Rubinstein, New York: HarperCollins, 1991, ch. 1.

Gazit, Mordechai, "Egypt and Israel—Was there a Peace Opportunity Missed in 1971?" *Journal of Contemporary History* 32:1 (January 1997), 97–115.

Gazit, Shlomo, *Trapped Fools: Thirty Years of Israeli Policy in the Territories*, introduction by Shimon Peres, London: Frank Cass, 2003.

Gelber, Yoav, "The History of Zionist Historiography: From Apologetics to Denial," in *Making Israel*, ed. Benny Morris, Ann Arbor: University of Michigan Press, 2007, 47–80.

Gershoni, Israel, "Rejecting the West: The Image of the West in the Teachings of the Muslim Brotherhood, 1928–1939," in *The Great Powers in the Middle East, 1919–1939*, ed. Uriel Dann, New York / London: Holmes and Meier, 1988, 370–90.

Gerson, Allan, *Israel, the West Bank and International Law*, London / Totowa, NJ: Frank Cass, 1978.

Gervasi, Frank, *The Case for Israel*, foreword by Abba Eban, New York: Viking Press, 1967.

Gilbert, Martin, *The Routledge Atlas of the Arab–Israeli Conflict*, 7th ed., London / New York: Routledge, 2002.

Ginor, Isabella, "The Cold War's Longest Cover-up: How and Why the USSR Instigated the 1967 War," *MERIA* 7:3 (September 2003).

Ginor, Isabella, "The Russians Were Coming: The Soviet Military Threat in the 1967 Six-Day War," *MERIA* 4:4 (December 2000).

Ginor, Isabella, "Under the Yellow Arab Helmet Gleamed Blue Russian Eyes: Operation *Kavkaz* and the War of Attrition," *Cold War History* 3:1 (October 2002), 129–56.

Ginor, Isabella, and Gideon Remez "The Six-Day War as a Soviet Initiative: New Evidence and Methodological Issues," *MERIA* 12:3 (September 2008).

Ginor, Isabella, and Gideon Remez, "The Spymaster, the Communist, and Foxbats over Dimona: The USSR's Motive for Instigating the Six-Day War," *Israel Studies* 11:2 (Summer 2006), 88–130.

Glock, Albert, "Archaeology as Cultural Survival: The Future of the Palestinian Past," *Journal of Palestine Studies* 23:3 (1994), 70–84.

Glock, Albert, "Cultural Bias in the Archaeology of Palestine," *Journal of Palestine Studies* 24:4 (1995), 48–59.

Glubb, J. B., "Violence on the Jordan–Israel Border: A Jordanian View," *Foreign Affairs* 32:4 (July 1954), 552–62.

Gluska, Ami, "'The War over the Water' during the 1960s," in *A Never-Ending Conflict: A Guide to Israeli Military History*, ed. Mordechai Bar-On, Westport, CT / London: Praeger, 2004, 109–31.

Goitein, S. D., *Jews and Arabs: Their Contacts through the Ages*, 3rd ed., New York: Schocken, 1974.

Golan, Galia, *Israel and Palestine: Peace Plans and Proposals from Oslo to Disengagement*, Princeton, NJ: Markus Wiener, 2007.

Golani, Motti, *Israel in Search of War: The Sinai Campaign, 1955–1956*, Brighton: Sussex Academic Press, 1998.

Gonen, Jay Y., *A Psychohistory of Zionism*, New York: Mason-Charter, 1975.

Gorenberg, Gershom, *The Accidental Empire: Israel and the Birth of the Settlements, 1967–1977*, New York: Times Books, 2006.

Gottheil, Fred M., "Arab Immigration into Pre-State Israel: 1922–1931," in *Palestine and Israel in the 19th and 20th Centuries*, eds. Elie Kedourie and Sylvia G. Haim, London: Frank Cass, 1982, 143–52.

Grasping the Nettle: Analyzing Cases of Intractable Conflict, eds. Chester A. Crocker, Fen Osler Hampson, and Pamela Aall, Washington, DC: United States Institute of Peace Press, 2005.

Great Britain, The Anglo–American Committee of Enquiry Regarding the Problems of European Jewry and Palestine, *Report, 1946* (Lausanne 20 April 1946), Cmd. 6808, London: HMSO, 1946.

Great Britain, Colonial Office, *Palestine: Report on Immigration, Land Settlement and Development by Sir John Hope Simpson*, Cmd. 3686, October 1930.

Great Britain, Colonial Office, *Palestine: Statement of Policy*, Cmd. 3692, October 1930 ("Passfield White Paper," reproduced in *A Documentary History of the Arab–Israeli Conflict*, ed. and with historical introductions by Charles L. Geddes, New York, etc.: Praeger, 1991, 113–40).

Great Britain, Colonial Office, *Palestine: Statement of Information Relating to Acts of Violence*, July 1946, Cmd. 6873, London: HMSO, 1946.

Great Britain, Palestine Royal Commission, *Minutes of Evidence Heard at Public Sessions (with Index)*, Colonial No. 134, London: HMSO, 1937. Reproduced in *The Rise of Israel*, vol. 22: *The Palestine Royal Commission*, ed. and with an introduction by Aaron S. Klieman, New York / London: Garland, 1987.

Great Britain, Palestine Royal Commission, *Report Presented by the Secretary of State for the Colonies to Parliament by Command of His Majesty, July 1937*, Cmd. 5479, London: HMSO, 1937.

Great Britain [United Kingdom], *A Survey of Palestine, Prepared in December 1945 and January 1946 for the Information of the Anglo–American Committee of Inquiry*, HMSO: 1946, reprinted 1991 by the Institute for Palestine Studies, Washington, DC.

The Great Powers in the Middle East, 1919–1939, ed. Uriel Dann, New York / London: Holmes and Meier, 1988.

Grob, Leonard, and John K. Roth, eds., *Anguished Hope: Holocaust Scholars Confront the Palestinian–Israeli Conflict*, Grand Rapids, MI: Eerdmans, 2008.

Gross, Netty C., "Demolishing David," *Jerusalem Report*, 11 September 2000, 40–6.

Gunning, Jeroen, *Hamas in Politics: Democracy, Religion and Violence*, New York: Columbia University Press, 2008.

Habibi, Emil, "Your Holocaust, Our Catastrophe," *The Tel Aviv Review* I:1 (January 1988), 332–6.

Hadawi, Sami, *Arab Boycott of Israel: Peaceful, Defensive and Constructive*, Ottawa: Arab League Information Center, 1977.

Hanieh, Akram, *The Camp David Papers*, Ramallah: Al-Ayyam Newspaper, 2000; an abbreviated version appears in the *Journal of Palestine Studies* 30:2 (Winter 2001), 75–97.

Hareven, Shulamith, *The Vocabulary of Peace: Life, Culture and Politics in the Middle East*, San Francisco: Mercury House, 1995.

Harkabi, Yehoshafat, "The Debate at the Twelfth Palestinian National Council" (July 1974), in Harkabi, *Palestinians and Israel*, New York: John Wiley (Halsted Press), 1974, 269–83.

Harkabi, Yehoshafat, "The Last Reminiscence, January 14, 1994" an interview with Pinhas Ginossar and Zaki Shalom, *Israel Studies* I:1 (Spring 1996), 171–95.

Harkabi, Yehoshafat, "The Meaning of 'a Democratic Palestinians State'" (April 1970), in Harkabi, *Palestinians and Israel*, New York: John Wiley (Halsted Press), 1974, 70–106.

Harkabi, Yehoshafat, *The Palestinian Covenant and Its Meaning*, London: Valentine Mitchell, 1979.

Harkabi, Yehoshafat, *Palestinians and Israel*, New York: John Wiley (Halsted Press), 1974.

Harkabi, Yehoshafat, "Who is to Blame for the Persistence of the Arab–Israel Conflict?: Lessons from Five Explanations," in Harkabi, *Palestinians and Israel*, New York: John Wiley (Halsted Press), 1974, 220–41.

Heikal, Mohamed, *The Road to Ramadan*, New York: Quadrangle, 1975.

Heikal, Mohamed, *Secret Channels: The Inside Story of Arab–Israeli Peace Negotiations*, London: HarperCollins, 1996.

Heller, Joseph, *The Birth of Israel, 1945–1949: Ben-Gurion and His Critics*, Gainesville, etc.: University Press of Florida, 2000.

Heller, Joseph, *The Stern Gang: Ideology, Politics, and Terror, 1940–1949*, London / Portland, OR: Frank Cass, 1995.

Heller, Mark A., *A Palestinian State: The Implications for Israel*, Cambridge, MA: Harvard University Press, 1983.

Heller, Mark A., and Sari Nusseibeh, *No Trumpets, No Drums: A Two-State Settlement of the Israeli–Palestinian Conflict*, New York: Hill and Wang, 1991.

Herman, Simon N., "In the Shadow of the Holocaust," *Jerusalem Quarterly* 3 (Spring 1977), 85–102.

Herman, Simon N., *Israelis and Jews: The Continuity of an Identity*, Philadelphia, PA: Jewish Publication Society, 1971.

Herzog, Chaim, *The Arab–Israeli Wars*, New York: Random House, 1982.

Herzog, Chaim, *The War of Atonement: The Inside Story of the Yom Kippur War*, London: Greenhill Books, 2003.

Hitchens, Christopher, "Broadcasts," in *Blaming the Victims: Spurious Scholarship and the Palestinian Question*, eds. Edward W. Said and Christopher Hitchens, London: Verso, 2001, 73–83.

Horowitz, David, *State in the Making*, transl. Julian Meltzer, New York: Alfred A. Knopf, 1953.

Hourani, Albert, "The Case against a Jewish State in Palestine: Albert Hourani's Statement to the Anglo–American Committee of Enquiry of 1946," *Journal of Palestine Studies* 35:1 (Autumn 2005), 80–90.

Hourani, Cecil A., "The Moment of Truth: Towards a Middle East Dialogue," *Encounter* 29:5 (1967), 3–14, reproduced in *A Middle East Reader*, ed. Irene L. Gendzier. Indianapolis / New York: Pegasus, 1969, 384–405.

Hurewitz, J. C., *The Struggle for Palestine*, New York: Norton, 1950 [Greenwood Reprint 1968].

Hurewitz, J. C., ed., *Diplomacy in the Near and Middle East: A Documentary Record 1535–1956*, Cambridge: Cambridge University Press, 1987.

Hutchison, E. H., *Violent Truce: A Military Observer Looks at the Arab–Israeli Conflict, 1951–1955*, New York: Devin-Adair, 1956.

Iklé, Fred Charles, *Every War Must End*, 2nd rev. ed., New York: Columbia University Press, 2005.

Ilan, Amitzur, *Bernadotte in Palestine: A Study in Contemporary Humanitarian Knight-Errantry*, New York: St. Martin's Press, 1989.

Intifada: the Palestinian Uprising against Israeli Occupation, eds. Zachary Lockman and Joel Beinin, Boston, MA: South End Press, 1989.

Israel in the Middle East: Documents and Readings on Society, Politics, and Foreign Relations, Pre-1948 to the Present, 2nd Edition, eds. Itamar Rabinovich and Jehuda Reinharz, Lebanon, NH: Brandeis University Press / University Press of New England, 2008.

Israel State Archives, *Documents on the Foreign Policy of Israel*, vol. 6 (1951), ed. Yemima Rosenthal, Jerusalem: 1991.

Israel State Archives, *Documents on the Foreign Policy of Israel*, vol. 8 (1953), ed. Yemima Rosenthal, Jerusalem: 1995.

The Israel–Arab Reader: A Documentary History of the Middle East Conflict, 7th rev. ed., eds. Walter Laqueur and Barry Rubin, New York: Penguin, 2008.

The Israel/Palestine Question, ed. Ilan Pappé, London / New York: Routledge, 1999.

Israeli, Raphael, "Is Jordan Palestine?," in *Israel, the Hashemites and the Palestinians: The Fateful Triangle*, eds. Efraim Karsh and P. R. Kumaraswamy, London: Frank Cass, 2003, 49–66.

Israeli Historical Revisionism: From Left to Right, eds. Anita Shapira and Derek J. Penslar, London: Frank Cass, 2003.

Israeli Historiography Revisited, Special issue of *History & Memory* 7:1 (Spring/Summer 1995), ed. Gulie Ne'eman Arad.

Israeli and Palestinian Narratives of Conflict: History's Double Helix, ed. Robert I. Rotberg, Bloomington / Indianapolis: Indiana University Press, 2006.

The Israeli–Palestinian Conflict: A Documentary Record, 1967–1990, ed. Yehuda Lukacs, Cambridge: Cambridge University Press, 1992.

Jeffay, Nathan, "The Other Middle East Refugees," *Jerusalem Report*, 4 August 2008, 33–4.

Jeffries, J. M. N., *Palestine: The Reality*, London, Longmans Green, 1939.

John, Robert, and Sami Hadawi, *The Palestine Diary*, 2 vols., foreword by Arnold J. Toynbee, Beirut: Palestine Research Center, 1970.

Kabha, Mustafa, "A Palestinian Look at the New Historians and Post-Zionism in Israel," in *Making Israel*, ed. Benny Morris, Ann Arbor: University of Michigan Press, 2007, 299–318.

Kahan, Yitzhak, Aharon Barak, and Yona Efrat, *Report of the Commission of Inquiry into the facts and factors connected with the atrocity carried out by a unit of the Lebanese Forces against the civilian population in the Shatilla and Sabra camps.* Jerusalem, 7 February 1983, accessed online 22 July 2008 at http://www.mideastweb.org/Kahan_report.htm

Kamel, Mohamed Ibrahim, *The Camp David Accords: A Testimony*, New York: KPI, 1986.

Kanafani, Ghassan, *Palestine's Children: Returning to Haifa and Other Stories*, transl. Barbara Harlow and Karen E. Riley, Boulder, CO: Lynne Rienner, 2000.

Kaniuk, Yoram, *Commander of the Exodus*, transl. Seymour Simckes, New York: Grove Press, 1999.

Karsh, Efraim, "1948, Israel, and the Palestinians: Annotated Text," *Commentary* [April?] 2008, accessed June 2008 online at http://www.commentarymagazine.com/viewarticle.cfm/1948–israel–and–the–palestinians–annotated–text–11373.

Karsh, Efraim, *Fabricating Israeli History: The "New Historians,"* 2nd rev. ed., London: Frank Cass, 2000.

Karsh, Efraim, "*Nakbat Haifa*: The Collapse and Dispersion of a Major Palestinian Community," *Middle Eastern Studies* 37:4 (October 2001), 25–70.

Katz, Samuel [Shmuel], *Battleground: Fact and Fantasy in Palestine*, updated and expanded ed., New York / Jerusalem: Steimatsky, 1985.

Katz, Samuel [Shmuel], *Days of Fire: The Secret Story of the Making of Israel*, Jerusalem: Steimatsky [London: W. H. Allen], 1968.

Katz, Sheila H., *Women and Gender in Early Jewish and Palestinian Nationalism*, Gainesville, etc.: University Press of Florida, 2003.

Katz, Yossi, *Partner to Partition: The Jewish Agency's Partition Plan in the Mandate Era*, London / Portland, OR: Frank Cass, 1998.

Kaufman, Edward [Edy], and Manuel Hassassian, "Understanding Our Israeli/ Palestinian Conflict and Searching for Its Resolution," in *Regional and Ethnic Conflicts: Perspectives from the Front Lines*, eds. Judy Carter, George E. Irani, and Vamik D. Volkan, Upper Saddle River, NJ: Prentice Hall, 2008, 87–129.

Kayyali, A. W., *Palestine: A Modern History*, London: Croom Helm, [1978].

Kedar, Benjamin Z., "Masada: The Myth and the Complex," *Jerusalem Quarterly* 24 (Summer 1982), 57–63.

Kedourie, Elie, "Great Britain and Palestine: The Turning Point," in *Islam in the Modern World and Other Studies*, New York: Holt, Rinehart and Winston, 1980, 93–170.

Kedourie, Elie, *In the Anglo–Arab Labyrinth: The McMahon–Husayn Correspondence and Its Interpretations, 1914–1939*, Cambridge: Cambridge University Press, 1976, reprinted London: Frank Cass, 2000.

Kedourie, Elie, "Religion and Politics," in *The Chatham House Version and Other Middle Eastern Studies*, London: Weidenfeld and Nicolson, 1970, 317–50.

BIBLIOGRAPHY

Kelman, Herbert C., "Creating the Conditions for Israeli–Palestinian Negotiations," *The Journal of Conflict Resolution* 26:1 (March 1982), 39–75.

Kelman, Herbert C., "Overcoming the Barriers to Negotiation of the Israeli–Palestinian Conflict," *Journal of Palestine Studies* 16:1 (Autumn 1986), 13–28.

Kerr, Malcolm H., *The Arab Cold: Gamal Abd al-Nasir and His Rivals, 1958–1970*, 3rd ed., London / New York: [for the Royal Institute of International Affairs] Oxford University Press, 1971.

Khalidi, Rashid, *The Iron Cage: The Story of the Palestinian Struggle for Statehood*, Boston, MA: Beacon, 2006.

Khalidi, Rashid, *Palestinian Identity: The Construction of Modern National Consciousness*, New York: Columbia University Press, 1997.

Khalidi, Rashid, *Under Siege: P.L.O. Decisionmaking during the 1982 War*, New York: Columbia University Press, 1986.

Khalidi, Walid, *All That Remains: The Palestinian Villages Occupied and Depopulated by Israel in 1948*, Washington, DC: Institute for Palestine Studies, 1992.

Khalidi, Walid, *Before Their Diaspora: A Photographic History of the Palestinians, 1876–1948*, Washington, DC: Institute for Palestine Studies, 1984.

Khalidi, Walid, "The Fall of Haifa," *Middle East Forum* 35:10 (December 1959), 22–32, reproduced in "The Fall of Haifa Revisited," *Journal of Palestine Studies* 37:3 (Spring 2008), 30–58.

Khalidi, Walid, *Palestine Reborn*, London / New York: I. B. Tauris, 1992.

Khalidi, Walid, "Plan Dalet Revisited: Master Plan for the Conquest of Palestine," *Journal of Palestine Studies* 18:1 (Autumn 1988), 3–37.

Khalidi, Walid, "Revisiting the UNGA Partition Resolution," *Journal of Palestine Studies* 27:1 (Autumn 1997), 5–21.

Khalidi, Walid, "Selected Documents on the 1948 Palestine War," *Journal of Palestine Studies* 27:3 (Spring 1998), 60–105.

Khalidi, Walid, "Thinking the Unthinkable: A Sovereign Palestinian State," *Foreign Affairs* 56:4 (July 1978), 695–713, reproduced in Walid Khalidi, *Palestine Reborn*, London / New York: I. B. Tauris, 1992, 82–104.

Khalidi, Walid, "The United States and the Palestinian People," (Georgetown University, March 1989), reproduced in Walid Khalidi, *Palestine Reborn*, London / New York: I. B. Tauris, 1992, 141–71.

Khalidi, Walid, "Why Did the Palestinians Leave, Revisited," *Journal of Palestine Studies* 34:2 (Winter 2005), 42–54.

Khouri, Fred J., "Friction and Conflict on the Israeli–Syrian Front," *Middle East Journal* 17:1–2 (Winter–Spring 1963), 14–34.

Khouri, Fred J., "The Policy of Retaliation in Arab–Israeli Relations," *Middle East Journal* 20:4 (Autumn 1966), 435–55.

Kimmerling, Baruch, and Joel S. Migdal, *The Palestinian People: A History*, Cambridge, MA: Harvard University Press, 2003.

Klein, Menachem, *Jerusalem: The Contested City*, transl. Haim Watzman, New York: New York University Press, 2001.

Klein, Menachem, *The Jerusalem Problem: The Struggle for Permanent Status*, transl. Haim Watzman, Gainesville: University Press of Florida, 2003.

Klein, Menachem, *A Possible Peace between Israel and Palestine: An Insider's Account of the Geneva Initiative*, transl. Haim Watzman, New York: Columbia University Press, 2007.

Klieman, Aaron S., "Bureaucratic Politics at Whitehall in the Partitioning of Palestine, 1937," in *The Great Powers in the Middle East, 1919–1939*, ed. Uriel Dann, New York / London: Holmes and Meier, 1988, 128–53.

Klieman, Aaron S., *Israel and the World After 40 Years*, Washington, etc.: Pergamon-Brassey's, 1990.

Kolinsky, Martin, *Law, Order and Riots in Mandatory Palestine, 1928–35*, London: St. Martin's Press, 1993.

Korn, David A., *Stalemate: The War of Attrition and Great Power Diplomacy in the Middle East, 1967–1970*, Boulder, CO: Westview Press, 1992.

Kyle, Keith, *Suez: Britain's End of Empire in the Middle East*, New York: I. B. Tauris, 2003 [earlier edition 1991].

Laqueur, Walter Z., *A History of Zionism*, New York: Holt, Rinehart and Winston, 1972; reissued New York: Schocken Books, 1989 (with a new preface by the author).

Lassner, Jacob, and S. Ilan Troen, *Jews and Muslims in the Arab World: Haunted by Pasts, Real and Imagined*, Lanham / Boulder, etc.: Rowman and Littlefield, 2007.

Lazarus, Ned, "Making Peace with the Duel of Narratives: Dual-Narrative Texts for Teaching the Israeli–Palestinian Conflict," *Israel Studies Forum* 23:1 (Summer 2008), 107–24.

Lesch, Ann Mosely, *Arab Politics in Palestine, 1917–1939: The Frustration of a National Movement*, Ithaca, NY / London: Cornell University Press, 1979.

Lesch, David W., *The Arab–Israeli Conflict: A History*, New York / Oxford: Oxford University Press, 2008.

Litvak, Meir, and Esther Webman, "Perceptions of the Holocaust in Palestinian Public Discourse," *Israel Studies* 8:3 (Fall 2003), 123–40.

Lorch, Netanel, *One Long War: Arab Versus Jew since 1920*, New York: Herzl Press, 1976.

Louis, Wm. Roger, and Roger Owen, eds., *Suez 1956: The Crisis and Its Consequences*, Oxford: Clarendon Press, 1989.

Love, Kennett, *Suez: The Twice-Fought War*, New York / Toronto: McGraw-Hill, 1969.

Lowdermilk, Walter Clay, *Palestine, Land of Promise*, 2nd ed., New York and London: Harper and Bros., 1944.

Lowi, Miriam R., *Water and Power: The Politics of a Scarce Resource in the Jordan River Basin*, New York / Cambridge: Cambridge University Press, 1993.

Lozowick, Yaacov, *Right to Exist: A Moral Defense of Israel's Wars*, New York, etc.: Doubleday, 2003.

Lustick, Ian S., "Changing Rationales for Political Violence in the Arab–Israeli Conflict," *Journal of Palestine Studies* 20:1 (Autumn 1990), 54–79.

Lustick, Ian S., *For the Land and the Lord: Jewish Fundamentalism in Israel*, New York: Council on Foreign Relations, 1988.

Lustick, Ian S., "Terrorism in the Arab–Israeli Conflict: Targets and Audiences," in *Terrorism in Context*, ed. Martha Crenshaw, University Park, PA: Pennsylvania State University Press, 1995, 514–52.

Lustick, Ian S., *Unsettled States, Disputed Lands: Britain and Ireland, France and Algeria, Israel and West Bank-Gaza*, Ithaca, NY: Cornell University Press, 1993.

MacDonald, Robert W., *The League of Arab States: A Study in the Dynamics of Regional Organization*, Princeton, NJ: Princeton University Press, 1965.

Majali, Abdul Salam, Jawad A. Anani, and Munther J. Haddadin, *Peacemaking: The Inside Story of the 1994 Jordanian–Israeli Treaty*, foreword by HRH Prince El Hassan Bin Talal of Jordan, preface by David L. Boren, Norman: University of Oklahoma Press, 2006.

Making Israel, ed. Benny Morris, Ann Arbor: University of Michigan Press, 2007.

Malik, Charles, "The Near East: The Search for Truth," *Foreign Affairs* 30 (January 1952), reprinted in *Arab Nationalism: An Anthology*, ed. with an introduction by Sylvia G. Haim, Berkeley / Los Angeles: University of California Press, 1962, 189–224.

Mallison, Jr., W. T., "The Balfour Declaration: An Appraisal in International Law," in *The Transformation of Palestine*, ed. Ibrahim Abu Lughod, 2nd ed., Evanston, IL: Northwestern University Press, 1987, 61–111.

Mallison, W. Thomas, and Sally V. Mallison, *The Palestine Problem in International Law and World Order*, Harlow, UK: Longman, 1986.

Mandel, Daniel, *H. V. Evatt and the Establishment of Israel: The Undercover Zionist*, London: Frank Cass, 2004.

Mandel, Neville J., *The Arabs and Zionism before World War I*, Berkeley / Los Angeles: University of California Press, 1976.

Ma'oz, Moshe, *Palestinian Leadership on the West Bank: The Changing Role of the Mayors under Jordan and Israel*, with a contribution from Mordechai Nisan, London: Frank Cass, 1984.

Maoz, Zeev, *Defending the Holy Land: A Critical Analysis of Israel's Security and Foreign Policy*, Ann Arbor: University of Michigan Press, 2006.

Marblestone, Howard, "The Great Archaeological Debate," *Israel Studies Bulletin* 16:1 (Fall 2000), 23–9.

Marcus, Amy Dockser, *The View from Nebo: How Archaeology is Rewriting the Bible and Reshaping the Middle East*, Boston, MA: Little, Brown, 2000.

Marlowe, John, *Rebellion in Palestine*, London: Cresset Press, 1946.

Marmorstein, Emile, "European Jews in Muslim Palestine," in *Palestine and Israel in the 19th and 20th Centuries*, eds. Elie Kedourie and Sylvia G. Haim, London: Frank Cass, 1982, 1–14.

Masalha, Nur, *The Bible and Zionism: Invented Traditions, Archaeology and Post-Colonialism in Palestine–Israel*, London / New York: Zed Books, 2007.

Masalha, Nur, "A Critique of Benny Morris," *Journal of Palestine Studies* 21:1 (Autumn 1991), 90–7, reproduced in *The Israel/Palestine Question*, ed. Ilan Pappé, London / New York: Routledge, 1999, 211–20.

Masalha, Nur, *Expulsion of the Palestinians: The Concept of "Transfer" in Zionist Political Thought, 1882–1948*, Washington, DC: Institute for Palestine Studies, 1992.

Massad, Joseph, "Palestinians and Jewish History: Recognition or Submission?" *Journal of Palestine Studies* 30:1 (Autumn 2000), 52–67.

Massad, Joseph A., *The Persistence of the Palestinian Question: Essays on Zionism and the Palestinians*, London: Routledge, 2006.

Matthews, Weldon C., *Confronting an Empire, Constructing a Nation: Arab Nationalists and Popular Politics in Mandate Palestine*, London / New York: I. B. Tauris, 2006.

Mattar, Philip, "al-Aqsa Intifada," *Encyclopedia of the Palestinians*, rev. ed., ed. Philip Mattar, New York: Facts on File, 2005, 23–4.

Mattar, Philip, *The Mufti of Jerusalem: al-Hajj Amin al-Husayni and the Palestinian National Movement*, rev. ed., New York: Columbia University Press, 1992.

Matz, David, "Reconstructing Camp David," *Negotiation Journal* 22:1 (January 2006), 89–103.

Matz, David, "Trying to Understand the Taba Talks (Part I)," *Palestine–Israel Journal of Politics, Economics and Culture* 10:3 (2003), 96–105.

Matz, David, "Why Did Taba End?" Part II, *Palestine–Israel Journal of Politics, Economics and Culture* 10:4 (2003), 92–8.

Meital, Yoram, "Egyptian Perspectives on the Suez War," in *The 1956 War: Collusion and Rivalry in the Middle East*, ed. David Tal, London: Frank Cass [Cummings Center Series], 2001, 195–207.

Meital, Yoram, *Peace in Tatters: Israel, Palestine, and the Middle East*, Boulder, CO: Lynne Rienner, 2006.

Michelson, Benny, "Insurgency and Counterinsurgency in Israel, 1965–1985," in *A Never-Ending Conflict: A Guide to Israeli Military History*, ed. Mordechai Bar-On, Westport, CT / London: Praeger, 2004, 179–91.

The Middle East Peace Process: Interdisciplinary Perspectives, ed. Ilan Peleg, Albany: State University of New York Press, 1998.

A Middle East Reader, ed. Irene L. Gendzier, Indianapolis / New York: Pegasus, 1969.

The Middle East: Ten Years after Camp David, ed. William B. Quandt, Washington, DC: The Brookings Institution, 1988.

Miller, Aaron David, *The Much Too Promised Land: America's Elusive Search for Arab–Israeli Peace*, New York: Random House (Bantam Dell), 2008.

Miller, Aaron David, "The Palestinian Dimension," in *The Arab–Israeli Conflict: Perspectives*, 2nd ed., ed. Alvin Z. Rubinstein, New York: HarperCollins, 1991, ch. 5.

Mishal, Shaul, and Avraham Sela, *The Palestinian Hamas: Vision, Violence and Coexistence*, New York: Columbia University Press, 2000.

Mitchell, Thomas G., *Native vs. Settler: Ethnic Conflict in Israel/Palestine, Northern Ireland, and South Africa*, Westport, CT: Greenwood Press, 2000.

Moratinos Document (Taba, January 2001), as given in Akiva Eldar, "The Peace that Nearly Was at Taba," *Ha-Aretz*, 15 February 2002. Available online at www.mideastweb.org/moratinos.htm.

Morris, Benny, *1948: A History of the First Arab–Israeli War*, New Haven, CT: Yale University Press, 2008.

Morris, Benny, *The Birth of the Palestinian Refugee Problem, 1947–1949*, Cambridge: Cambridge University Press, 1987.

Morris, Benny, *The Birth of the Palestinian Refugee Problem Revisited*, Cambridge, UK / New York: Cambridge University Press, 2004.

Morris, Benny, "The Crystallization of Israeli Policy against a Return of the Arab Refugees: April–December, 1948," *Studies in Zionism* 6:1 (Spring 1985), 85–118.

Morris, Benny, An Interview with Ehud Barak, "Camp David and After: An Exchange," *New York Review of Books* 49:10 (13 June 2002); accessed 15 September 2008 at http://www.nybooks.com/articles/15501.

Morris, Benny, *Israel's Border Wars, 1949-1956: Arab Infiltration, Israeli Retaliation, and the Countdown to the Suez War*. Oxford: The Clarendon Press, 1993.

Morris, Benny, "A New Exodus for the Middle East?" *The Guardian*, 2 October 2002 accessed online at: www.guardian.co.uk

Morris, Benny, "Peace? No Chance," *The Guardian*, 21 February 2002.

Morris, Benny, "Politics by Other Means," *The New Republic*, 22 March 2004.

Morris, Benny, "Response to Finkelstein and Masalha," *Journal of Palestine Studies* 21:1 (Autumn 1991), 98–114.

Morris, Benny, *Righteous Victims: A History of the Zionist Arab Conflict, 1881–1999*, New York: Alfred A. Knopf, 1999 / London: John Murray, 2000.

Morris, Benny, and Ehud Barak, "Camp David and After—Continued," *New York Review of Books* 49:11 (27 June 2002), accessed 15 September 2008 at http://www.nybooks.com/articles/15540.

Mosley, Leonard, "Orde Wingate and Moshe Dayan," in *From Haven to Conquest: Readings in Zionism and the Palestine Problem until 1948*, ed. and introduced by Walid Khalidi, Beirut: 1971; 2nd printing, Washington, DC: Institute for Palestine Studies, 1987, 375–82.

Muasher, Marwan, *The Arab Center: The Promise of Moderation*, New Haven, CT: Yale University Press, 2008.

Muslih, Muhammad, "Towards Coexistence: An Analysis of the Resolutions of the Palestine National Council," *Journal of Palestine Studies* 19:4 (Summer 1990), 3–29; reprinted in *From War to Peace: Arab–Israeli Relations 1973–1993*, eds. Barry Rubin, Joseph Ginat, and Moshe Ma'oz, New York: New York University Press, 1995, 265–91.

Myths and Facts: A Guide to the Arab–Israeli Conflict, ed. Mitchell G. Bard; foreword by Eli E. Hertz, Chevy Chase, MD: American–Israeli Cooperative Enterprise, 2001; rev. and updated 2002.

Narratives of 1948, Special issue of *Palestine–Israel Journal of Politics, Economics and Culture* 9:4 (2002).

Nashashibi, Nasser Eddine, *Jerusalem's Other Voice: Ragheb Nashashibi and Moderation in Palestinian Politics, 1920–1948*, Exeter: Ithaca Press, 1990.

Naylor, Tom, "Palestine & Zionism: Ten Myths," *This Magazine*, December 1981–January 1982.

Neff, Donald, "Nixon's Middle East Policy: From Balance to Bias," in *US Policy on Palestine from Wilson to Clinton*, ed. Michael W. Suleiman, Normal, IL: AAUG Press, 1995, 133–62.

Nelson, Walter Henry, and Terence C. F. Prittie, *The Economic War against the Jews*, New York: Random House, 1977.

Netanyahu, Benjamin, *A Durable Peace: Israel and Its Place among the Nations*, rev. ed., New York: Warner Books, 2000.

A Never-Ending Conflict: A Guide to Israeli Military History, ed. Mordechai Bar-On, Westport, CT / London: Praeger, 2004.

Nevo, Joseph, *King Abdallah and Palestine: A Territorial Ambition*, London / New York: Macmillan [St. Antony's Series], 1996.

New Perspectives on Israeli History: The Early Years of the State, ed. Laurence J. Silberstein, New York: New York University Press, 1991.

Nisan, Mordechai, "Harkabi's Despair" *Midstream* XXV:5 (May 1979), 9–17.

Nusseibeh, Sari, with Anthony David, *Once upon a Country: A Palestinian Life*, New York: Farrar, Straus, and Giroux, 2007.

O'Brien, Conor Cruise, *The Siege: The Saga of Israel and Zionism*, New York: Simon and Schuster, 1986.

Oren, Michael B., *Origins of the Second Arab–Israel War: Egypt, Israel and the Great Powers: 1952–56*, London: Frank Cass, 1992.

Oren, Michael B., *Six Days of War: June 1967 and the Making of the Modern Middle East*, Oxford: Oxford University Press, 2002.

Oz, Amos, *How to Cure a Fanatic*, Princeton, NJ: Princeton University Press, 2006.

Oz, Amos, "The Tender among You, and Very Delicate," in *In the Land of Israel*, New York: Harcourt Brace Jovanovich, 1983, 87–100.

Oz, Amos, *Under This Blazing Light: Essays*, transl. Nicholas de Lange, New York: Cambridge University Press, 1995, 8–9.

Palestine and Israel in the 19th and 20th Centuries, eds. Elie Kedourie and Sylvia G. Haim, London: Frank Cass, 1982.

The Palestinian–Israeli Peace Agreement: A Documentary Record, rev. 2nd ed., Washington, DC: Institute for Palestine Studies, 1994.

The Palestinians: People, History, Politics, eds. Michael Curtis, Joseph Neyer, Chaim I. Waxman, and Allen Pollack, New Brunswick, NJ: Transaction Books [prepared under the auspices of the American Academic Association for Peace in the Middle East], 1975.

Pappé, Ilan, *Britain and the Arab–Israeli Conflict, 1948–51*, London: Macmillan Press / St. Antony's College, 1988.

Pappé, Ilan, *The Ethnic Cleansing of Palestine*, Oxford: Oneworld Publications, 2006.

Pappé, Ilan, *A History of Modern Palestine: One Land, Two Peoples*, 2nd ed., Cambridge: Cambridge University Press, 2006.

Pappé, Ilan, "Introduction: New Historical Orientations in the Research on the Palestine Question," in *The Israel/Palestine Question*, ed. Ilan Pappé, London / New York: Routledge, 1999, 1–7.

Pappé, Ilan, "Jordan between Hashemite and Palestinian Identity," in *Jordan in the Middle East: The Making of a Pivotal State*, eds. Joseph Nevo and Ilan Pappé, London: Frank Cass, 1994, 61–91.

Pappé, Ilan, *The Making of the Arab–Israeli Conflict, 1947–51*, London / New York: I. B. Tauris / St. Martin's Press, 1992.

Parker, Richard B., *The Politics of Miscalculation in the Middle East*, Bloomington: Indiana University Press, 1993.

Patai, Raphael, *The Arab Mind*, New York: Charles Scribner's Sons, 1973.

Patai, Raphael, *The Seed of Abraham: Jews and Arabs in Contact and Conflict*, Salt Lake City: University of Utah Press, 1986.

Pelcovits, Nathan A., *The Long Armistice: UN Peacekeeping and the Arab–Israeli Conflict, 1948–1960*, foreword by Samuel W. Lewis, Boulder / San Francisco / Oxford: Westview Press, 1993.

Peleg, Ilan, *Begin's Foreign Policy, 1977–1983: Israel's Turn to the Right*, Westport, CT: Greenwood, 1987.

Peleg, Ilan, *Human Rights in the West Bank and Gaza: Legacy and Politics*, Syracuse, NY: Syracuse University Press, 1995.

Penslar, Derek, *Israel in History: The Jewish State in Comparative Perspective*, London / New York: Routledge, 2007.

People and Politics in the Middle East, ed. Michael Curtis, New Brunswick, NJ: Transaction Books / E. P. Dutton [proceedings of the annual conference of the American Academic Association for Peace in the Middle East], 1971.

Peres, Shimon, *Battling for Peace: A Memoir*, New York: Random House, 1995.

Peretz, Don, *Israel and the Palestine Arabs*, Washington, DC: Middle East Institute, 1958.

Peters, Joan, *From Time Immemorial: The Origins of the Arab–Jewish Conflict over Palestine*, New York: Harper and Row, 1984.

Plascov, Avi, *The Palestinian Refugees in Jordan, 1948–1957*, London: Frank Cass, 1981.

Podeh, Elie, *From Fahd to Abdallah: The Origins of the Saudi Peace Initiatives and Their Impact on the Arab System and Israel*, Jerusalem: Hebrew University, Truman Institute, 2003.

Podeh, Elie, "History and Memory in the Israeli Educational System: The Portrayal of the Arab–Israeli Conflict in History Textbooks (1948–2000)," *History and Memory* 12 (2000), 65–100.

Podeh, Elie, "Regaining Lost Pride: The Impact of the Suez Affair on Egypt and the Arab World," in *The 1956 War: Collusion and Rivalry in the Middle East*, ed. David Tal, London: Frank Cass [Cummings Center Series], 2001, 209–24.

Popp, Roland, "Stumbling Decidedly into the Six-Day War," *Middle East Journal* 60:2 (Spring 2006), 281–309.

Porat, Dina, *The Blue and the Yellow Stars of David: The Zionist Leadership in Palestine and the Holocaust, 1939–1945*, Cambridge, MA: Harvard University Press, 1990.

Porath, Yehoshua, *The Emergence of the Palestinian Arab National Movement, 1918–1929*, London: Frank Cass, 1974.

Porath, Yehoshua, "Mrs. Peters's Palestine," *New York Review of Books*, 32:21–2, 16 January 1986, available at http://www.nybooks.com/articles/5249; "Mrs. Peters's Palestine: An Exchange" (Ronald Sanders, Daniel Pipes, Yehoshua Porath), *New York Review of Books*, 35:5, 27 March 1986, available at http://www.nybooks.com/articles/5172.

Porath, Yehoshua, *The Palestinian Arab National Movement, 1929–1939: From Riots to Rebellion*, London: Frank Cass, 1977.

Pressman, Jeremy, "Mediation, Domestic Politics, and the Israeli–Syrian Negotiations, 1991–2000," *Security Studies* 16:3 (July–September 2007), 350–81.

Pressman, Jeremy, "The Second Intifada: Background and Causes of Israeli–Palestinian Conflict," *Journal of Conflict Studies* 22:2 (Fall 2003), 114–41.

Pressman, Jeremy, "Visions in Collision: What Happened at Camp David and Taba?" *International Security* 28:2 (Fall 2003), 5–43.

Pundak, Ron, "From Oslo to Taba: What Went Wrong?" in *The Israeli–Palestinian Peace Process: Oslo and the Lessons of Failure: Perspectives, Predicaments and Prospects*, eds. Robert L. Rothstein, Moshe Ma'oz, and Khalil Shikaki, Brighton, UK / Portland, OR: Sussex Academic Press, 2002, 88–113.

Quandt, William B., *Camp David: Peacemaking and Politics*, Washington, DC: The Brookings Institution, 1986.

Quigley, John, *The Case for Palestine: An International Law Perspective*, rev. and updated ed., Durham / London: Duke University Press, 2005.

Qurie, Ahmed [Abu Ala], *From Oslo to Jerusalem: The Palestinian Story of the Secret Negotiations*, London: I. B. Tauris, 2006.

Rabie, Mohamed, *US–PLO Dialogue: Secret Diplomacy and Conflict Resolution*, Gainesville: University Press of Florida, 1995.

Rabinovich, Abraham, *The Yom Kippur War: The Epic Encounter that Transformed the Middle East*, New York: Schocken, 2005.

Rabinovich, Itamar, *The Road Not Taken: Early Arab–Israeli Negotiations*, New York / Oxford: Oxford University Press, 1991.

Rabinovich, Itamar, "Seven Wars and One Peace Treaty," in *The Arab–Israeli Conflict: Perspectives*, 2nd ed., ed. Alvin Z. Rubinstein, New York: HarperCollins, 1991, ch. 2.

Rabinovich, Itamar, *Waging Peace: Israel and the Arabs, 1948–2003*, rev. and updated ed., Princeton, NJ: Princeton University Press, 2004.

Rafael, Gideon, *Destination Peace: Three Decades of Israeli Foreign Policy: A Personal Memoir*, New York: Stein and Day, 1981.

Rejwan, Nissim, "Arab Advocate of Westernization," *New Outlook* 15 (October 1972), 27–34.

Review Essays in Israel Studies: Books on Israel, volume V, eds. Laura Zittrain Eisenberg and Neil Caplan, Albany: State University of New York Press, 2000.

Rodinson, Maxime, "Israël, fait colonial?" *Les Temps modernes* 22 (1967) 253bis, 17–88, later transl. as *Israel: A Colonial Settler-State?* intro. Peter Buch, transl. David Thorstad, New York, 1973.

Rodinson, Maxime, *Israel and the Arabs*, transl. Michael Perl, Harmondsworth: Penguin, 1968.

Ro'i, Yaacov, "The Zionist Attitude to the Arabs, 1908–1914," in *Palestine and Israel in the 19th and 20th Centuries*, eds. Elie Kedourie and Sylvia G. Haim, London: Frank Cass, 1982, 15–59.

Rokach, Livia, *Israel's Sacred Terrorism: A Study Based on Moshe Sharett's Personal Diary and Other Documents*, Belmont, MA: Association of Arab–American University Graduates, 1980.

Ross, Dennis, *The Missing Peace: The Inside Story of the Fight for Middle East Peace*, New York: Farrar, Straus, and Giroux, 2004.

Rouhana, Nadim N., "Zionism's Encounter with the Palestinians: The Dynamics of Force, Fear, and Extremism," in *Israeli and Palestinian Narratives of Conflict: History's Double Helix*, ed. Robert I. Rotberg, Bloomington / Indianapolis: Indiana University Press, 2006, 115–41.

Roy, Sara, "Humanism, Scholarship, and Politics: Writing on the Palestinian–Israeli Conflict," *Journal of Palestine Studies* XXXVI:2 (Winter 2007), 54–65.

Rubenberg, Cheryl A., "The Bush Administration and the Palestinians," in *U.S. Policy on Palestine from Wilson to Clinton*, ed. Michael W. Suleiman, Normal, IL: AAUG Press, 1995, 195–21.

Rubin, Barry, "America as Junior Partner: Anglo–American Relations in the Middle East, 1919–1939," in *The Great Powers in the Middle East, 1919–1939*, ed. Uriel Dann, New York / London: Holmes and Meier, 1988, 238–51.

Rubin, Jacob A., *True and False about Israel*, New York: Herzl Press, for the American Zionist Federation, 1972.

Rubinstein, Alvin Z., "Transformation: External Determinants," in *The Arab–Israeli Conflict: Perspectives*, 2nd ed., ed. Alvin Z. Rubinstein, New York: HarperCollins, 1991, ch. 3.

Rubinstein, Amnon, *From Herzl to Rabin: The Changing Image of Zionism*, New York: Holmes and Meier, 2000.

Rubinstein, Amnon, *The Zionist Dream Revisited: From Herzl to Gush Emunim and Back*, New York: 1984.

Sachar, Howard M., *A History of Israel: From the Rise of Zionism to Our Time*, New York: Alfred A. Knopf, 1976.

Sadat and His Legacy: Egypt and the World, 1977–1997, ed. and introduced by Jon B. Alterman, Washington, DC: Washington Institute for Near East Policy, 1998.

Said, Edward W., *The Question of Palestine*, New York: Vintage 1980.

Saliba, Samir N., *The Jordan River Dispute*, The Hague: Martinus Nijhoff, 1968.

Salibi, Kamal, *The Bible Came from Arabia*, London: J. Cape, 1985.

Samuel, Edwin, *A Lifetime in Jerusalem*, Jerusalem: Israel Universities Press, 1970.

Samuel, Maurice, *Harvest in the Desert*, Philadelphia, PA: Jewish Publication Society, 1944.

Sasson, Ted, and Shaul Kelner, "From Shrine to Forum: Masada and the Politics of Jewish Extremism," *Israel Studies* 13:2 (Summer 2008), 146–63.

Saunders, Harold H., *The Other Walls: The Arab–Israeli Peace Process in a Global Perspective*, rev. ed., Princeton, NJ: Princeton University Press, 1991.

Savir, Uri, *The Process: 1,100 Days that Changed the Middle East*, New York: Random House, 1998.

Sayigh, Yezid, "Arafat and the Anatomy of a Revolt," *Survival* 43:3 (Autumn 2001), 47–60.

Sayigh, Yezid, *Armed Struggle and the Search for State: The Palestinian National Movement, 1949–1993*, Oxford: Oxford University Press / Washington, DC: The Institute for Palestine Studies, 1997.

Sayigh, Yezid, "The Palestinian Strategic Impasse," *Survival* 44:4 (Winter 2002), 7–21.

Schiff, Ze'ev, and Ehud Ya'ari, *Intifada: The Palestinian Uprising—Israel's Third Front*, New York: Simon and Schuster, 1990.

Schueftan, Dan, "The Israeli–Egyptian 'War of Attrition,' 1969–1970," in *A Never-Ending Conflict: A Guide to Israeli Military History*, ed. Mordechai Bar-On, Westport, CT / London: Praeger, 2004, 147–59.

Segev, Samuel, "The Arab–Israeli Conflict under President Bush," in *From Cold War to New World Order: The Foreign Policy of George H. W. Bush*, eds. Meena Bose and Rosanna Perotti, Westport, CT: Greenwood, and Hofstra University, 2002, 113–36.

Segev, Tom, *1949: The First Israelis*, ed. Arlen Neal Weinstein, New York: Free Press / London: Collier Macmillan, 1986.

Segev, Tom, *The Seventh Million: The Israelis and the Holocaust*, New York: Hill and Wang, 1993.

Sela, Avraham, "Arab Historiography of the 1948 War: The Quest for Legitimacy," in *New Perspectives on Israeli History: The Early Years of the State*, ed. Laurence J. Silberstein, New York: New York University Press, 1991, 124–54.

Sela, Avraham, "Arab Nationalists and Nazi Germany, 1939–1945," in *So Others Will Remember: Holocaust History and Survivor Testimony*, ed. Ronald Headland, Montreal: Vehicule Press, 1999, 70–81.

Sela, Avraham, "The 'Wailing Wall' Riots (1929) as a Watershed in the Palestine Conflict," *The Muslim World* LXXXIV: 1–2 (January–April 1994), 60–94.

Shafir, Gershon, *Land, Labor, and the Origins of the Israeli–Palestinian Conflict, 1882–1914*, Cambridge, UK /New York: Cambridge University Press, 1989; updated ed., Berkeley / Los Angeles: University of California Press, 1996.

Shafir, Gershon, "Zionism and Colonialism: A Comparative Approach," in *The Israel/Palestine Question*, ed. Ilan Pappé, London / New York: Routledge, 1999, 81–96.

Shaked, Haim, "Continuity and Change: An Overview," in *The Arab–Israeli Conflict: Perspectives*, 2nd ed., ed. Alvin Z. Rubinstein, New York: HarperCollins, 1991, 191–214.

Shalev, Aryeh, *The Israeli–Syria Armistice Regime, 1949–1955*, Boulder, CO: Westview Press / Jerusalem: The Jerusalem Post [Jaffee Center for Strategic Studies, Study No. 21], 1993.

Shalev, Michael, *Labour and the Political Economy in Israel*, Oxford: Oxford University Press, 1992.

Shamir, Shimon, "The Collapse of Project Alpha," in *Suez 1956: The Crisis and Its Consequences*, eds. Wm. Roger Louis and Roger Owen, Oxford: Clarendon Press, 1989, 73–100.

Shamir, Yitzhak, "Israel's Role in a Changing Middle East," *Foreign Affairs* 60:4 (Spring 1982), 789–801.

Shanks, Hershel, "Archeology as Politics," *Commentary* (August 1986), 50–2.

Shapira, Anita, *Land and Power: The Zionist Resort to Force, 1881–1948*, transl. William Templer, Stanford, CA: Stanford University Press, 1999.

Shared Histories: A Palestinian–Israeli Dialogue, eds. Paul Scham, Walid Salem, and Benjamin Pogrund, Walnut Creek, CA: Left Coast Press, 2005.

Sharett, Moshe, "The 1953 Qibya Raid Revisited: Excerpts from Moshe Sharett's Diary," special document introduced by Walid Khalidi, annotated by Neil Caplan, *Journal of Palestine Studies* 31:4 (Summer 2002), 77–98.

Sharon, Ariel, with David Chanoff, *Warrior: The Autobiography of Ariel Sharon*, New York: Simon and Schuster, 1989.

Sheffer, Gabriel, "Principles of Pragmatism: A Reevaluation of British Policies toward Palestine in the 1930s," in *The Great Powers in the Middle East, 1919–1939*, ed. Uriel Dann, New York / London: Holmes and Meier, 1988, 109–27.

Shenhav, Yehouda, "Arab Jews, Population Exchange, and the Palestinian Right of Return," in *Exile and Return: Predicaments of Palestinians and Jews*, eds. Ann M. Lesch and Ian S. Lustick, Philadelphia: University of Pennsylvania Press, 2005, 225–45.

Sher, Gilead, *The Israeli–Palestinian Peace Negotiations, 1999–2001: Within Reach*, New York: Routledge, 2006

Shikaki, Khalil, "Ending the Conflict: Can the Parties Afford It?" in *The Israeli–Palestinian Peace Process: Oslo and the Lessons of Failure: Perspectives, Predicaments and Prospects*, eds. Robert L. Rothstein, Moshe Ma'oz, and Khalil Shikaki, Brighton, UK / Portland, OR: Sussex Academic Press, 2002, 37–46.

Shikaki, Khalil, "Refugees and the Legitimacy of Palestinian–Israeli Peace Making," in *Arab–Jewish Relations from Conflict to Resolution: Essays in Honour of Professor Moshe Ma'oz*, eds. Elie Podeh and Asher Kaufman, Brighton: Sussex Academic Press, 2006, 363–74.

Shimshoni, Jonathan, *Israel and Conventional Deterrence: Border Warfare from 1953 to 1970*, Ithaca, NY / London: Cornell University Press, 1988.

Shipler, David K., *Arab and Jew: Wounded Spirits in a Promised Land*, rev. ed., New York: Penguin, 2002.

Shlaim, Avi, *Collusion across the Jordan: King Abdullah, the Zionist Movement, and the Partition of Palestine*, Oxford: Clarendon Press, 1988.

Shlaim, Avi, "The Debate about 1948," in *The Israel/Palestine Question*, ed. Ilan Pappé, London / New York: Routledge, 1999, 171–92.

Shlaim, Avi, "Husni Za'im and the Plan to Resettle Palestinian Refugees," *Journal of Palestine Studies* 15:4 (Summer 1986), 68–80.

Shlaim, Avi, *The Iron Wall: Israel and the Arab World*, London: Allen Lane / Penguin Press, 2000.

Shlaim, Avi, *Lion of Jordan: King Hussein's Life in War and Peace*, London: Penguin, 2007.

Shlaim, Avi, "The Protocol of Sèvres: Anatomy of a War Plot," in *The 1956 War: Collusion and Rivalry in the Middle East*, ed. David Tal, London: Frank Cass [Cummings Center Series], 2001, 119–44.

Shlaim, Avi, "The Rise and Fall of the All-Palestine Government in Gaza," *Journal of Palestine Studies* 20:1 (Autumn 1990), 37–53.

Shulman, David, *Dark Hope: Working for Peace in Israel and Palestine*, Chicago: University of Chicago Press, 2007.

Siegman, Henry, "The Perils of Messianic Politics" (1988), in *Wrestling with Zion: Progressive Jewish–American Responses to the Israeli–Palestinian Conflict*, ed. and with an introduction by Tony Kushner and Alisa Solomon, New York: Grove Press, 2003, 113–15.

Simons, Chaim, *International Proposals to Transfer Arabs from Palestine, 1895–1947: A Historical Survey*, Hoboken, NJ: Ktav Publishing, 1988.

The Six Day War: A Retrospective, ed. Richard B. Parker, Gainesville: University Press of Florida, 1996.

Slater, Jerome "Lost Opportunities for Peace in the Arab–Israeli Conflict: Israel and Syria, 1948–2001," *International Security* 27:1 (Summer 2002), 79–106.

Slater, Jerome, "What Went Wrong? The Collapse of the Palestinian–Israeli Peace Process," *Political Science Quarterly* 116:2 (Summer 2001), 171–99.

Smith, Charles D., "The Invention of a Tradition: The Question of Arab Acceptance of the Zionist Right to Palestine during World War I," *Journal of Palestine Studies* XXII:2 (Winter 1993), 48–61.

Sofer, Arnon, *Rivers of Fire: The Conflict over Water in the Middle East*, transl. Murray Rosovsky and Nina Copaken, Lanham, MD: Rowman and Littlefield, 1999.

Spiegel, Steven L., *The Other Arab–Israeli Conflict: Making America's Middle East Policy from Truman to Reagan*, Chicago: University of Chicago Press, 1985.

Stein, Kenneth W., *Heroic Diplomacy: Sadat, Kissinger, Carter, Begin and the Quest for Arab–Israeli Peace*, New York: Routledge, 1999.

Stein, Kenneth W., "The Intifada and the 1936–39 Uprising: A Comparison," *Journal of Palestine Studies* 19:4 (Summer 1990), 64–85.

Stein, Kenneth W., *The Land Question in Palestine, 1917–1939*, Chapel Hill: University of North Carolina Press, 1984.

Stein, Leonard, *The Balfour Declaration*, London: Valentine Mitchell, 1961.

Stone, I. F., *Underground to Palestine, and Reflections Thirty Years Later* [reprint of the original 1946 edition], New York: Pantheon, 1978.

Stone, Julius, *Israel and Palestine: Assault on the Law of Nations*, Baltimore, MD: Johns Hopkins University Press, 1981.

The Suez–Sinai Crisis 1956: Retrospective and Reappraisal, eds. Selwyn Ilan Troen and Moshe Shemesh, London: Frank Cass, 1990.

Susser, Asher, "Jordan, the PLO and the Palestine Question," in *Jordan in the Middle East: The Making of a Pivotal State*, eds. Joseph Nevo and Ilan Pappé, London: Frank Cass, 1994, 211–28.

Swedenburg, Ted, *Memories of Revolt: The 1936–1939 Rebellion and the Palestinian National Past*, Fayetteville: University of Arkansas Press, 2003.

Swisher, Clayton E., *The Truth about Camp David: The Untold Story about the Collapse of the Middle East Peace Process*, New York: Nation Books, 2004.

Sykes, Christopher, *Crossroads to Israel, 1917–1948*, Bloomington: Indiana University Press, 1965 [Midland pb edition, 1973].

Syrkin, Marie, "The Palestinian Refugees: Resettlement, Repatriation or Restoration?" [from *Commentary* magazine 41:1 (1966)], in *Israel, the Arabs and the Middle East*, eds. Irving Howe and Carl Gershman, New York: Bantam, 1972, 157–85.

Syrkin, Marie, *The State of the Jews*, Washington, DC: New Republic Books / Herzl Press, 1980.

Syrkin, Marie, "Who Are the Palestinians?" in *People and Politics in the Middle East*, ed. Michael Curtis, New Brunswick, NJ: Transaction Books / E. P. Dutton [proceedings of the annual conference of the American Academic Association for Peace in the Middle East], 1971, 93–110.

Tal, Uriel, "Foundations of a Political Messianic Trend in Israel," *Jerusalem Quarterly* 35 (Spring 1985), 36–45.

Tamari, Salim, "In League with Zion: Israel's Search for a Native Pillar," *Journal of Palestine Studies* 12:4 (Summer 1983), 41–56.

Tawil, Raymonda Hawa, *My Home, My Prison*, New York: Holt, Rinehart and Winston, 1979.

Tekoah, Yosef, *In the Face of the Nations: Israel's Struggle for Peace*, ed. David Aphek, New York: Simon and Schuster, 1976.

Telhami, Shibley, "Beyond Resolution? The Palestinian–Israeli Conflict," in *Grasping the Nettle: Analyzing Cases of Intractable Conflict*, Washington, DC: United States Institute of Peace Press, 2005, 357–72.

Tessler, Mark, *A History of the Israeli–Palestinian Conflict*, Bloomington / Indianapolis: Indiana University Press, 1994; revised ed. 2009.

Tessler, Mark, "Intifada, 1987–1993," *Encyclopedia of the Palestinians*, rev. ed., ed. Philip Mattar, New York: Facts on File, 2005, 224–32.

Tessler, Mark, "Narratives and Myths about Arab Intransigence toward Israel," in *Israeli and Palestinian Narratives of Conflict: History's Double Helix*, ed. Robert I. Rotberg, Bloomington / Indianapolis: Indiana University Press, 2006, 174–93.

Teveth, Shabtai, *Ben-Gurion and the Holocaust*, New York: Harcourt Brace, 1996.

Teveth, Shabtai, *Ben-Gurion: The Burning Ground, 1886–1948*, Boston, MA: Houghton Mifflin, 1987.

Teveth, Shabtai, "The Palestinian Refugee Problem and Its Origins" (review article), *Middle Eastern Studies* 26:2 (April 1990), 214–49.

Tibawi, A. L., "T. E. Lawrence, Faisal and Weizmann: The 1919 Attempt to Secure an Arab Balfour Declaration," *Royal Central Asian Journal* 56:2 (June 1969), 156–63.

Tibawi, A. L., "Visions of the Return: The Palestine Arab Refugees in Arabic Poetry and Art," *Middle East Journal* 17:5 (Autumn, 1963), 507–26.

Touval, Saadia, *The Peace Brokers: Mediators in the Arab–Israeli Conflict, 1948–1979*, Princeton, NJ: Princeton University Press, 1982.

Toward Peace in the Middle East, report of the Brookings Institution Middle East Study Group, Washington, DC: December 1975.

Traditions and Transitions in Israel Studies: Books on Israel volume 6, eds. Laura Zittrain Eisenberg, Neil Caplan, Naomi B. Sokoloff, and Mohammed Abu-Nimer, Albany: State University of New York Press, 2002.

The Transformation of Palestine: Essays on the Origins and Development of the Arab–Israeli Conflict, 2nd ed., ed. Ibrahim Abu Lughod, foreword by Arnold J. Toynbee, Evanston, IL: Northwestern University Press, 1987.

Troen, S. Ilan, "De-Judaizing the Homeland: Academic Politics in Rewriting the History of Palestine," *Israel Affairs* 13:4 (2007), 872–84.

Troen, S. Ilan, "The Protocol of Sèvres: British/French/Israeli Collusion against Egypt, 1956," *Israel Studies* I:2 (Fall 1996), 122–39.

Turki, Fawaz, *The Disinherited: Journal of a Palestinian Exile*, 2nd ed., London / New York: Monthly Review Press, 1974.

United Nations Resolutions on Palestine and the Arab–Israeli Conflict, vol. I: 1947–1974, rev. ed., ed. George J. Tomeh, Washington, DC: Institute for Palestine Studies, 1988.

United Nations Special Committee on Palestine (UNSCOP), *Report* of the United Nations Special Committee on Palestine (USNCOP), 3 September 1947, accessed online 21 March 2008 at http://domino.un.org/UNISPAL.NSF/99818751a6a4 c9c6852560690077ef61/07175de9fa2de563852568d3006e10f3.

United Nations, Division for Palestinian Rights, "The Origins and Evolution of the Palestine Problem: 1917–1988—PART I, 1917–1947," posted 30 June 1990, accessed 13 April 2008 at http://domino.un.org/UNISPAL.NSF/561c6ee353d7 40fb8525607d00581829/aeac80e740c782e4852561150071fdb0.

United Nations, *The Question of Palestine*, New York: United Nations, 1979 [prepared for, and under the guidance of, the Committee on the Exercise of the Inalienable Rights of the Palestinian People].

Vance, Cyrus, *Hard Choices: Critical Years in America's Foreign Policy*, New York: Simon and Schuster, 1983.

Viorst, Milton, *Reaching for the Olive Branch: UNRWA and Peace in the Middle East*, Washington, DC: Middle East Institute, 1989.

Von Horn, Carl, *Soldiering for Peace*, London: Cassell, 1966.

The War for Palestine: Rewriting the History of 1948, eds. Eugene L. Rogan and Avi Shlaim, Cambridge: Cambridge University Press, 2001.

Wasserstein, Bernard, *Divided Jerusalem: The Struggle for the Holy City*, 3rd ed., New Haven, CT: Yale University Press, 2008.

Wasserstein, Bernard, *Israelis and Palestinians: Why Do They Fight? Can They Stop?* 3rd ed., New Haven, CT / London: Yale University Press / London: Profile Books, 2008.

Weinstock, Nathan, *Le Sionisme contre Israël*, Paris: François Maspéro, 1969.

Weizman, Ezer, *The Battle for Peace*, New York: Bantam, 1981.

Weizmann, Chaim, *The Letters and Papers of Chaim Weizmann*, series B: vol. II, December 1931–April 1952, ed. Barnet Litvinoff, Rutgers, NJ: Transaction Books / Jerusalem: Israel Universities Press, 1984.

Weizmann, Chaim, "Palestine's Role in the Solution of the Jewish Problem," *Foreign Affairs* 20:2 (1942), 324–38, reprinted in *A Middle East Reader*, ed. Irene L. Gendzier, Indianapolis / New York: Pegasus, 1969, 311–25.

Weizmann, Chaim, *Trial and Error: The Autobiography of Chaim Weizmann*, London: Hamish Hamilton, 1949.

West, Deborah L., *Myth and Narrative in the Israeli–Palestinian Conflict*, Cambridge, MA: World Peace Foundation [WPF Report #34], 2003.

When Enemies Dare to Talk: An Israeli–Palestinian Debate (5/6 September 1978), ed. Simha Flapan, London: Croom Helm, 1979.

Wilson, Evan M., *A Calculated Risk: The U.S. Decision to Recognize Israel*, foreword by William B. Quandt, Cincinnati, OH: Clerisy Press, 2008 [reprint of *Decision on Palestine: How the U.S. Came to Recognize Israel* (1979)].

Wilson, Mary, *King Abdullah, Britain and the Making of Jordan*, Cambridge, UK / New York / etc.: Cambridge University Press, 1987.

Yehoshua, A. B. "The Holocaust as Junction," in *Between Right and Right*, New York: Doubleday, 1981, 1–19.

Zartman, I. William, *Cowardly Lions: Missed Opportunities to Prevent Deadly Conflict and State Collapse*, Boulder, CO / London: Lynne Rienner, 2005.

Zertal, Idith, *From Catastrophe to Power: Holocaust Survivors and the Emergence of Israel*, Berkeley / Los Angeles: University of California Press, 1998.

Zertal, Idith, *Israel's Holocaust and the Politics of Nationhood*, Cambridge: Cambridge University Press, 2005.

Zertal, Idith, and Akiva Eldar, *Lords of the Land: The War over Israel's Settlements in the Occupied Territories, 1967–2007*, transl. from the Hebrew by Vivian Eden, New York: Nation Books, 2007.

Zerubavel, Yael, *Recovered Roots: Collective Memory and the Making of Israeli National Tradition*, Chicago / London: University of Chicago Press, 1995.

The Zionist Idea: A Historical Analysis and Reader, ed. and introduced by Arthur Hertzberg, Garden City, NJ: 1959, reprinted New York: Atheneum, 1969.

Zisser, Eyal, "The 1982 'Peace for Galilee' War: Looking Back in Anger—Between an Option of a War and a War of no Option," in *A Never-Ending Conflict: A Guide to Israeli Military History*, ed. Mordechai Bar-On, Westport, CT / London: Praeger, 2004, 193–210.

Zuraik, Constantine, "Today and Yesterday—Two Prominent Aspects of the New Meaning of the Disaster," *Middle East Forum* XLIII:2–3 (1967), 13–20.

Zurayk, Constantine K., *The Meaning of the Disaster*, transl. R. Bayly Winder, Beirut: Khayat's, 1956.

Index

UNGA, *see* United Nations General Assembly

Unit 101, 138

United Nations Division for Palestinian Rights, 168, 171

United Nations Emergency Force [UNEF], 143, 145

United Nations General Assembly [UNGA], 6, 27, 108, 110, 132, 139, 143, 168, 170, 199; Resolution 181 (1947 Partition), 110–11, 118, 255; Resolution 194 (1948), 27, 113–15, 117–19, 121, 126–7 n.42, 135; Resolution 3236 (1974), 168–9; Resolution 3379 (zionism = racism, 1975), 6, 168–9, 204

United Nations Relief and Works Agency for Palestine Refugees in the Near East [UNRWA], 27, 113, 117, 132, 175 n.29

United Nations Security Council [UNSC], 110, 137, 139, 148, 164, 196; Resolution 242 (1967), 148, 164, 166, 199; Resolution 338 (1973), 152, 162, 199; Resolution 619 (1951), 137; Resolution 1397 (2002), 209

United Nations Special Committee on Palestine [UNSCOP], 22, 107–10, 237–8

United Nations Truce Supervisory Organization [UNTSO], 135, 139

United States, 12–13, 48, 96, 105–6, 108, 113, 123 n.12, 132, 137, 140–3, 145–6, 149, 151–2, 165–6, 172, 178–80, 195–7, 199, 201, 204–5, 207, 209, 264

UNRWA, *see* United Nations Relief and Works Agency for Palestine Refugees in the Near East

UNSC, *see* United Nations Security Council

UNSCOP, *see* United Nations Special Committee on Palestine

UNTSO, *see* United Nations Truce Supervisory Organization

USSR, 113, 132, 141–2, 144–6, 148–9, 151–2, 162, 171, 178–9, 181, 196, 201, 263

V

Versailles Peace Conference, *see* Paris Peace Conference

victimhood, victims, 10, 29–30, 32–3, 49–51, 79, 93, 95–6, 119–21, 140, 161–2, 187–8, 208, 221–2, 226, 231–2, 237, 241–2, 255–9

Village Leagues, 185

violence, 89–96; *see also* terror

W

wars: (1947–1949), 7, 28, 31, 110–18; (1956), 7, 29, 31, 131, 137, 139, 141, 142; (1967), 7, 29, 31, 131, 144–7; (1973), 7, 29, 31, 131, 151, 162, 178; (1982), 186–7; War of Attrition, 148

water, 134, 137, 144, 151, 202

Weizmann, Chaim, 3, 24, 59, 70, 73, 80–1, 101, 235

West Bank, 8, 19, 24, 27–8, 113, 133, 138, 141, 146–8, 150, 163, 166, 168, 171, 174 n.21, 180–5, 195–8, 201, 203, 210, 237, 253, 255

White Papers, 61, 64, 84; *see also* Churchill White Paper (1922), Passfield White Paper (1930), MacDonald White Paper (1939)

Wilson, Woodrow, Fourteen Points, 63

Wingate, Orde Charles, 90

Woodhead Commission, 87, 237

World Zionist Organization, 3, 18–19, 22, 44, 239

Wye Plantation Agreement, 206